Thinking with Cases

THINKING WITH CASES

Specialist Knowledge in Chinese Cultural History

Charlotte Furth,

Judith T. Zeitlin, and

Ping-chen Hsiung,

editors

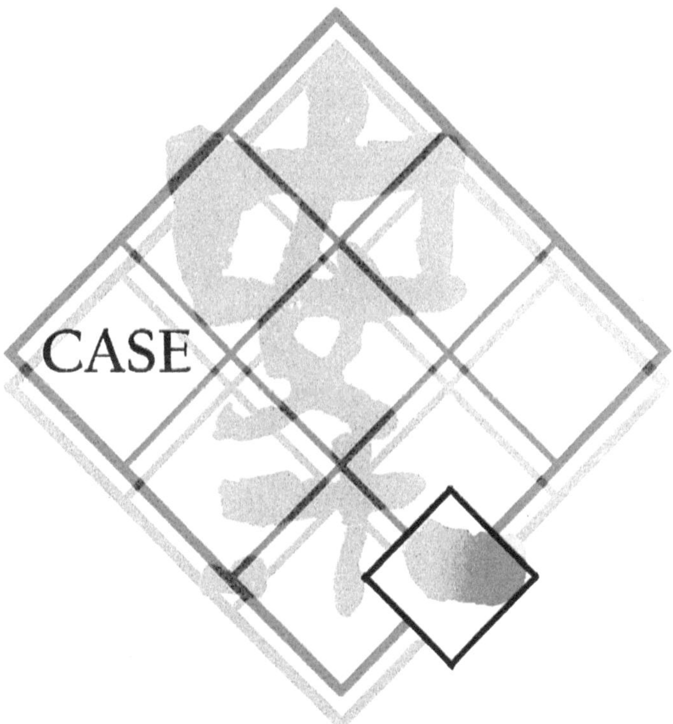

University of Hawai'i Press Honolulu

Printed in the United States of America
12 11 10 09 08 07 6 5 4 3 2 1

Library of Congress Cataloging-in-Publication Data
Thinking with cases : specialist knowledge in Chinese cultural history / Charlotte Furth, Judith T. Zeitlin, and Ping-chen Hsiung, editors.
p. cm.
Includes bibliographical references and index.
ISBN-13: 978-0-8248-3049-6 (hardcover : alk. paper)
ISBN-10: 0-8248-3049-0 (hardcover : alk. paper)
1. Social sciences—China—Case studies—Methodology. 2. Law—China—Cases. 3. Medicine—China—Case studies. I. Furth, Charlotte. II. Zeitlin, Judith T. III. Hsiung, Ping-chen.
H62.5.C5T45 2007
153.4′330951—dc22 2006024207

University of Hawai‘i Press books are printed on acid-free paper and meet the guidelines for permanence and durability of the Council on Library Resources.

Designed by Leslie Fitch
Printed by The Maple-Vail Book Manufacturing Group

Contents

Note on Citations and Abbreviations

JJFL Gao Ju 高舉, ed. *Da Ming lü jijie fuli* 大明律集解附例 (The Ming code with commentaries and attached regulations) [1610]. Reprint: 5 vols. Taipei: Chengwen chubanshe, 1969.

MQMY *Ming Qing mingyi quanshu dacheng* 明清名醫全書大成 (Complete works of famous physicians of the Ming and Qing dynasties). 30 vols., ed. Hu Guochen 胡國臣 et al. Beijing: Zhongguo Zhongyiyao chubanshe, 1990.

MS *Mingshi* 明史 (Ming history) [1739]. Modern punctuated ed. in 28 vols. Beijing: Zhonghua shuju, 1974.

RM Julia Ching, ed. *The Records of Ming Scholars*, by Huang Tsung-hsi [Zongxi]. Honolulu: University of Hawai'i Press, 1987.

SKCM *Siku quanshu cunmu congshu* 四庫全書存目叢書. Tainan (Taiwan): Zhuangyan Wenhua shiye, 1995–1997.

SKQS *Yingyin Wenyuange Siku quanshu* 景印文淵閣四庫全書. Taipei: Taiwan Shangwu yinshuguan, 1983–1986.

T Taishō shinshū daizōkyō 大正新修大藏經, ed. Takakusu Junjirō 高楠順次郎 and Watanabe Kaigyoku 渡邊海旭. Tokyo: Taishō issaikyō kankōkai, 1924–1932. References to T start with the text number, followed by the volume, page, register (a, b, or c), and, when appropriate, the line number(s).

XBDA/SC *Xingbu dang'an* 刑部檔案 (Board of Punishments archive), Sichuansi 四川司 (Sichuan Bureau) section. The Number One Historical Archives, Beijing.

XXSK Xuxiu siku quanshu 續修四庫全書. Shanghai: Shanghai guji chubanshe, 1995.

YJYL Mao Yilu 毛一鷺. *Yunjian yanlüe* 雲閒讞略 (Court opinions from Songjiang). 1610s?

ZJ *Zutang ji* 祖堂集, comp. Shi Jing 釋靜 and Shi Yun 釋筠 [952]. Reprint of Korean ed., in Yanagida, *Sodōshū sakuin.* References to *ZJ* are cited using the concordance format (section.folio.line).

ZZ *Dai Nihon zokuzōkyō* 大日本續藏經. Tokyo: Kokusho Kankōkai, 1975–1989. Reprint: Taipei: Xinwenfeng chuban gongsi, 1993–1994. References to ZZ start with the volume and page numbers, followed by the folio page, register (a or b on recto, c or d on verso), and, when appropriate, the line number(s).

Foreword

This project bears witness to the challenges and rewards of international collaborative research in Chinese studies. A group of us first became intrigued with the idea that Chinese case narratives across different domains of expertise were worth investigating in 1997 during a daylong colloquium on case histories in medicine at the UCLA Center for Chinese Studies in Los Angeles. Participants in that colloquium, including the editors of this volume, together with Francesca Bray, began with questions about medical records as sources for social history and historical anthropology but quickly branched out to ask questions about the epistemology and rhetoric of the case as a generic form and about its bearing on the status of premodern Chinese experts and their knowledge. The gestation of our thinking was a long one that moved across disciplines and continents and that involved many dozens of participants, only a minority of whom are included in this published volume. We are particularly indebted to these many scholars who joined with us to think about the issues in formal and informal settings over a half dozen years.

The project received a major boost in 1999 when Ping-chen Hsiung, based at the Academia Sinica in Taiwan, organized a Ming-Ch'ing Studies Group dedicated to bringing together experts who could think about the Chinese "case" from a variety of disciplinary perspectives, including law, religion, literature, linguistics, philosophy, and statecraft. This working group, which met regularly over three months, included, along with Hsiung and Furth, Academia Sinica scholars Chiu Peng-sheng in law, Li Yuzhen in religion, Ho Da-an in classical philology, Chang Chen-chia in medicine and divination, Hung-lam Chu in philosophy, and Wang Ayling in literature. Their discussions continued through 2000 and resulted in *Rang zhengju shuohua: Zhongguo pian* (Allow the evidence to speak: Case records in China; Taipei: Maitian, 2001), a volume edited by Professor Hsiung that serves as a prologue and companion to the present one. Among other contributions, the Taiwan group's researches laid out a historical genealogy of the Chinese *an* (case) as a genre and prompted us to explore its novel deployments in the fields of philosophy and religion.

The next stage of our conversation took place at the University of Chicago in October 2001, where the editors were joined by Thomas Buoye, Hung-lam Chu, Robert Hymes, Yasuhiko Karasawa, Robert Sharf, James St. André, Wang Ayling, and Pierre-Étienne Will as paper presenters. James Chandler from the University of Chicago and John Forrester of Cambridge University, England, served as superlative outside commentators, bringing in theoretical perspectives from literary studies and the history of science.

A final workshop, "Looking for Cases in Song and Ming Law," organized by Furth and held at the Center for Chinese Studies at UCLA in May 2003, was designed to address some of the many questions about case records in Chinese legal practice that those gathered in Chicago were unable to answer. Jiang Yonglin and Wu Yanhong joined the project at this point, while Bettine Birge, Brian McKnight, and Hugh Scogin served as in-house experts on China's legal history.

The present volume is deeply indebted to the intellectual contributions of all these scholars, who helped us raise far-ranging issues that could not be condensed into the pages of a single volume. We also wish to thank the two anonymous reviewers for the University of Hawai'i Press, and also our technical editor, Ling Hon Lam, whose quick intellect and command of classical language and texts greatly enhanced the clarity and consistency of the final manuscript.

Over the course of this venture we received support from a large number of institutions. We should thank the UCLA Center for Chinese Studies, the USC East Asian Studies Center, and the USC College of Letters, Arts and Sciences for subventions supporting our workshops in Los Angeles. The Franke Institute for the Humanities and the Center for East Asian Studies, both of the University of Chicago, and the China and Inner Asia Council Studies of the Association for Asian Studies provided grants that supported our conference at the University of Chicago. In Taipei the Ming-Ch'ing Studies Group of the Academia Sinica underwrote the working group and its various gatherings that led to the edited volume in Chinese.

We also wish to thank Patricia Crosby, editor at the University of Hawai'i Press, for her support of the project. In addition, we benefited from the able assistance of managing editor Cheri Dunn and copyeditor Susan Biggs Corrado. Lara Ruffolo provided assistance in the final stage of manuscript preparation, Catherine Stuer prepared the index, and Keyang Tang created the graphic design representing "the Chinese case" that adorns our cover.

Pinyin romanization and English translations of Chinese titles and terms have been standardized across all the chapters from our various authors and keyed to graphs in a common glossary and bibliography at the end of the volume. Following the conventions of Chinese medical historians, we capitalize the English translations of words for body systems, functions, and energies (Blood, Heart, Five Phases, etc.) to remind readers not to mistake these for biomedical organs or processes.

The editors
June 2006

Introduction

Thinking with Cases

CHARLOTTE FURTH

Evidence of keeping records about legal and medical cases in China is almost as old as Chinese writing itself. Consider the following story, pieced together from bamboo slips excavated around two decades ago from a tomb at Zhangjiashan, in modern Hubei Province. In 197 BCE, early in the reign of Gaozu, founding emperor of the Han dynasty, a police officer named Shi was ordered to apprehend a runaway slave named Wu. When Shi caught up with his suspect, the two fought with swords and both were wounded. Each man tried to justify his actions. Wu's story: I should not be considered a fugitive. Although I was slave in the state of Chu [before Han rule], when Chu fell to Han, I was registered as a Han commoner. I was resisting an unlawful attempt to arrest me. Shi's story: my instructions were to arrest a runaway slave, and when he violently resisted, I had to defend myself. Officials investigating the case argued that even if Wu was entitled to be considered a free commoner under Han rule, he should have surrendered and made his claims to the authorities. They looked into the record of Wu's registration and referred the case to higher authorities. Eventually the emperor himself signed off on the ruling that Wu should be tattooed and sentenced to hard labor and that Shi was to be set free. The record of this case was one of twenty-two, many similar in nature, bundled together in the grave under the title "Writings on Criminal Cases Subjected to Review [for a final decision]" (*Zou yan shu*).[1]

Or consider this narrative of an illness, one of twenty-five recorded by the emperor's official Grand Historian, Sima Qian, in his biography of Chunyu Yi, a 2nd century BCE physician who attracted imperial attention after he had been forced to defend himself against unspecified yet grave charges.

> Xiang Chu, an officer of Ban ward in Anling, was sick. I examined his pulses and said it was a case of "male blockage." When cut off below, blocked male [essence] ascends to the lung region. The disorder develops from within. I told him, "Take care not to expend your strength in physical exertion; if you do so you will

> certainly vomit blood and die." Chu later played kickball, took a violent chill, poured sweat and vomited blood. I again examined him and said, "by tomorrow evening you will be dead." The disorder developed from within. From examining his pulses, I knew Chu's disorder was one of yang reversal. Reversing direction, yang [qi] entered the vacancy of the interior, and the following day he died.[2]

Asked by the emperor to explain his medical arts, Chunyu Yi appears to have used his cases to claim that his skill at reading his patients' pulses was responsible for his remarkable ability to distinguish between fatal and curable disease and to prescribe effectively.

Though our glimpses of an early Han dynasty local courtroom come from an accident of archeological discovery, they show unsettled times but traces of an orderly process of legal decision making with reference both to imperial statutes and to higher judicial review in difficult cases. What is less clear is the role of writings like these as court records, since they were found as grave goods, bundled with other texts on medicine, military strategy, and mathematics in the tomb of a low-ranking official who may or may not have been a legal specialist. Our medical case narratives are much easier to connect to a physician who wrote them. The Han dynasty imperial historian Sima Qian tells us that the physician Chunyu Yi kept unspecified "consultation records" (*zhenji*) to assist in making his diagnoses, but he spoke of his cases in public only because he was forced to respond to an imperial inquiry. Texts like these attest to the antiquity of Chinese law and medicine, the two domains of specialist knowledge that have been perennially associated with the case as a form of documentation. While they point to the importance of written records in general and in the workings of government and law particularly, documents like these are too rare and fragmentary to supply more than a prologue to our story.

Instead, the essays in this volume trace the process whereby the project of thinking with cases in China came to self-consciousness over the succeeding millennium through the production of texts that gradually acquired a systematic and public character. Experts on medicine and law came to write case narratives to demonstrate efficacy or to claim validity for a judgment. They were joined by authors of religious and philosophical texts, the Buddhist *kōan* (*gong'an*), and later the neo-Confucian "cases of learning" (*xue'an*) in the sixteenth century. The rhetorical strategies and forms of argument used by these writers were closely allied with those found in collections of cases and historical examples composed as aids to statecraft. Such practices of thinking with cases reveal historically specific epistemologies that offer insight into how Chinese experts mediated between individual instances and more general patterns, how they dealt with tensions between classical canons and norms and practice-based judgment and between techno/

magical and literati/scholarly styles of constructing authority. As each of these different specialist domains fostered its own forms of case production, the case becomes a sign of the historical sociology of emerging professional spheres in China: those of the healer, the judge, the official, the priest. In all these ways, thinking about thinking with cases contributes to our understanding of the early evolution of the sciences and of society in China.

WHAT IS A CASE?

The broadest place to start is with the expansive notion, suggested by theorists of narrative form in literature, that any "instance" can in theory be carved out of the flow of events set in time and space and be set aside to be made particular. Rooted in the linguistic form of citing examples and instances in general, such phrases as "the case of" or "in the case that" are syntactical markers of the act of bracketing something as particular, worthy of separate consideration. Somewhere in the neighborhood of an example or an anecdote, a case, in the words of James Chandler, is the "genre that represents situations"—whose meaning must be probed within the form, evoking yet resisting generalizations around it. Chandler reminds us that etymologically the English word "case" shares a Latin derivation with "casuistry," the Jesuit science of moral situations. Such a theory of the case can serve literary analysis of all kinds and has been deployed by Chandler and others to call attention to the moral and didactic functions of storytelling, from fables to the novel.[3]

But the case as a form of specialist knowledge has a more specific function. It will have a literary dimension—employing a "style of reasoning" in the sense of artistic style, and be organized as narrative, tolerant of rhetorical flourishes, of plot, character, and drama—features that make some cases such an attractive inspiration for stories told to entertain. But when a detective case or medical case brackets particulars as facts, the forms of reasoning called for lead to claims to empirical knowledge and point to problem-solving interventions in the world. The significance of such a case is neither purely local, like an anecdote, nor does it point toward some general truth already known or assumed, as does an example or illustration.

Here the case is to be distinguished from a story, example, or instance by the kind of authority that authors claim for themselves—that of experts. Even though this authority may be moral and social, vested in learned, genteel, or virtuous persons rather than specialists defined by purely craft or technical qualifications, the expertise of the author is a vital element in establishing the credibility of the narrative. This factor affects the status of the particulars narrated: a story may be about real people and events, assumed to relate a factual history, but a case transforms facts into evidence. Here facts are not simply incidents of interest, illustrative or storytelling, but are marshaled in an argument in the service of claims. The appeal to evidence is itself a sign that something more than storytelling or illustration is probably at stake. This "something more" is what contributors to the present volume call "thinking with cases."

The historian of science John Forrester has stimulated recent interest in the epistemology of the "case" with a now classic article that argues that "thinking in cases" is in fact a broad method of producing valid knowledge that should be considered separately from either hypothetical-deductive methods of logic or the inductive methods of experimental science. Forrester's idea of a "style [or styles] of reasoning" followed A. C. Crombie, Ian Hacking, and Arnold Davidson, who had earlier posited a plurality of field-dependent "styles of reasoning."[4] Crombie and Hacking listed the following types: deduction from postulates, experimental exploration, modeling based on analogy, ordering of variety by comparison and taxonomy, statistical method, and historical derivation. To this list Forrester added cases. Cases are connected to one another by common patterns, while at the same time they never deny "the priority of individual cases over any possible generalizations invoking them."[5] Whatever the field, a case record sets out some truth claim that is specific to an individual situation, while the accumulation of individual narratives forms an archive available for consideration in common. In other words, cases come in groups or sets, and though they cannot yield any truly universal principals, the distribution of commonalities and differences in an ongoing set of cases forms patterns we can learn from.

Forrester's model of "thinking in cases" is about the styles of reasoning used to forge these relationships. His own examples from the history of case writing in early modern English/Northern European medicine and law point to a common historical epistemology of truth implicit in both, before the rise of experimental science undercut the claims of case-based reasoning in science. With experimental science, there emerged the powerful modern convention about a series of particulars that they should be aggregated by induction, leading to conclusions having a law-like generality. This ideal, applied statistically and informed by probability theory, shapes much contemporary thinking about producing knowledge from cases in the social sciences. However, Forrester's essay suggests that "thinking in cases" is not a rudimentary or flawed version of an inductive method. Unlike induction, it produces no law-like or probabilistic generalizations. Rather, cases are analyzed collectively in ways that place each one in a series in relationship to others, without, as Forrester says, denying the individual character of each. Forrester suggests to us that we look for three basically comparative "styles of reasoning" that can be in play when any collection of cases is considered as a set. First, one may order variation by classification into kinds, either by grouping like kinds into a species (this is taxonomy in the manner of classical botanical classification systems) or by considering the distribution of differences ranging from more to less similar (as does Darwinian classification challenging the concept of distinct, unchanging species). Second, one may compare cases by reference to a model or prototype, as when the labels "bird" or "saint" evoke some abstraction from any particular instance of these. When one imagines model cases accumulating over time to record evolutionary changes, one has a method of mapping that is called a model systems approach. Finally, there is the explicitly historical method of appealing to relationships of precedent/descent.

Looked at strictly as "styles of reasoning," all three of the types described above do not seem to be culture bound. Though they may appear in a variety of combinations, we seem to recognize them across the continents and the centuries. Are we claiming to find here universal rational components that are used in many varieties of local sciences? Broadly speaking, thinking with cases is analogical, and it seems designed to cope with certain perennial tensions between canon, norm, or code on the one hand and contingency and particularity on the other. But such generalizations may be too broad to be deep. So it is time to introduce context by looking at the case in Chinese history.

THE CASE IN CHINA: A HISTORICAL GENEALOGY

Philology suggests a very old and fundamental association of the Chinese word for "case" with the state. In the collection of legal case records found in the Zhangjiashan tomb, 247 dating from the beginning of the imperial era, the noun *an,* which today means "case," referred to an on-the-spot investigation into a crime. In the instances collected by Ho Da-an from early imperial texts and discussed in his essay in the Chinese companion volume to this one,[6] the term referred first to a table or tray and by extension to the document thereon. Han scribes sometimes substituted the ideograph *an* (which had the sense of "commentary") for the nominal *an;* gradually, the two ideographs came to represent a verb and its nominalized form (rather like the English word "report," which can refer to a document, its contents, or the act of making a report). Both evoked a class of documents that have been examined and dealt with by the appropriate bureaucratic authority. The early imperial noun *andu* (cabinet) even suggests the pigeonholes or compartments into which examined documents might be filed away. Originally a relatively trivial category defined by format rather than content, the scope of the word *an* expanded until, in the Tang era, it was used to refer to many different kinds of official documents or files, as well as to bureaucratic action involving them. One might "set up a document" (*li an*), "handle a document" (*zhang an*), or "read a document aloud" (*chang an*). Finally, there were phrases for deciding a "case" in the full legal sense: *pan an* (to issue judgment on a case).

The state, then, played a powerful role in the genesis of the historical epistemology of the case, which is confirmed by the fact that throughout imperial history people's paradigmatic concept of a case (*an*) was imagined as a matter of law. Still, the philological traces of the history of writing cases suggest that a rupture with officialdom was a precondition for the full development of compiling cases as a mode of specialist knowledge. In the Tang dynasty (618–905 CE), when the first comprehensive code of imperial laws was compiled, *gong'an,* later the standard classical term for the legal case, was not written to identify a specifically judicial record. Rather, the term appeared occasionally in Tang texts to refer generally to any bureaucratic document about a matter under official consideration. But the earliest specialist *gong'an* were created in the course of theological disputation by Tang and later Northern Song (960–1225 CE) Buddhist monks and were added to over several centuries via oral transmission from master to student long before they were ever written down. These became the Chan *gong'an* (familiar in the West in their Japanese form as the Zen *kōan*)—the earliest genre of "case" literature in China, which is analyzed by Robert Sharf in this volume (chap. 7). They were first recorded as part of the collected sayings (*yulu*) of various early Chan Buddhist masters and codified finally only in collections printed in the fourteenth century. Two things stand out here: first, the case is making a detour through oral culture; and second, the genre develops through private writing.

If philology is one path for tracing the history of the Chinese case, the tenth-century invention of printing, making it possible to compile cases as public documents, leads back to law. The earliest surviving printed law case collections turn out to be three interrelated texts that were a product of the enormous expansion of legal institutions in the Northern Song dynasty (960–1225 CE) and that were handed down thereafter, reprinted in the eighteenth-century imperial library's *Complete Collection of the Four Treasuries* (*Siku quanshu*) under the category of "the legalist school."[7] The earliest, the tenth-century *Collection of Doubtful Cases* (*Yiyu ji*), compiled by He Ning and He Meng, two minor judicial officers, contributed some of its cases to its successor, *The Magic Mirror for Deciding Cases* (*Zheyu guijian*), compiled by Zheng Ke (fl. ca. 1133). Both of these were drawn upon to complete the selection of seventy-two pairs of cases in the most famous of the three works, *Parallel Cases from under the Pear-tree* (*Tangyin bishi,* ca. 1211). This last is the case collection best known to us through the English translation by Robert Van Gulik. All three collections, made up entirely of third-person reports summarizing actual criminal investigations, make claims for validity in two ways: they rely in part on official histories for their techniques of narration and commentary, and they offer advice on criminal detection based on the compilers' own past expertise as low-level field officers charged with criminal investigations.[8]

The first thing that stands out is the way these texts engage with history. History was a model form of writing factually about "events" (*shi*)—the term that in early imperial China was also the commonest one used to refer to the content of a case, encompassing beginning, middle, and end. Largely seen as a state function under the early empire, historical writing was a potent wellspring of the rhetoric of validity, exemplified in the formal structure of dynastic history writing that separated truthful narration of events (*shi*) from authorial commentary or judgment (*an*). The dynastic history, compiled by court-appointed scholars of the succeeding dynasty, was based on its predecessors' accumulated ministerial records and daily diaries of imperial "activity and repose" and constituted history's judgment on a completed era of imperial rule. The compilers of these first two Song dynasty printed legal collections used biographies of important officials compiled in such earlier dynastic histories as sources. Where these orthodox biographies included reports of cases as illustrations of their subjects' actions and achievements, now the cases stood alone.

As well as using these selected historic cases to construct a legal tradition based on antiquity, with lessons for the ethical "spirit of the laws," the compilers added other cases from recent local archives close to their own field experience. The result was a hybrid product where the deference of the specialist to the wisdom of the past tied these case narratives to classical forms of textual authority identified with the state and restricted the expert's contribution based on his own practice or experience. The reflections and advice of the judicial specialists who compiled these works were bracketed in the traditionally sanctioned form for interpretation in historical writing: as commentary.

The casebooks assembled by the Song dynasty "legalist school" provide insight into two important aspects of legal reasoning in criminal adjudication: the evaluation of evidence and the ideals of justice. Consider the following case, the first in the *Magic Mirror* collection.

> The crown prince of Wu, Sun Deng, once went out horseback riding, when a crossbow pellet flew by. His attendants searched and came upon a man grasping a bow, with pellets hanging at his waist. Everybody thought he was the culprit, but he would not admit it. Deng's followers wanted to beat him, but Deng would not allow it. He sent somebody to find the pellet that had flown by and compare them. They were not the same kind, and so the man was released.
>
> Comment (*an*): When someone suffers injustice, it is usually because of deceptive similarities. If the person hearing a case is not deliberate and attentive, but makes an angry show of his authority, he will end up inflicting a flood of wrongs. Though this was a small affair, it may serve to illustrate something large. This is why I put it at the beginning [of the collection].[9]

As this example shows, these Song compilations called attention to the role of the legal expert as detective. This makes these collections rich for the historical epistemologist who suspects that criminal law cases may be one of the oldest sources for everyday assumptions about evidence and proof, about the authority of the witness, and the nature of the clue. These Song collections, after all, are the locus classicus for the beginnings of the Chinese detective story tradition inspired by the fame of the eleventh-century magistrate Judge Bao (Bao Zheng). The historian Carlo Ginzburg has written about the European detective as practitioner of an ancient tradition of "conjectural knowledge" that must be gleaned from traces pieced together to make a whole that as a totality has been lost.[10] In Ginzburg's hands, it is essentially a historical method, whereby causes are inferred from effects by means of the visible signs left behind, as a hunter locates his quarry by examining the disturbances left by the animal's past movements in the forest. Like the story of the Prince of Wu above, many cases from the *Magic Mirror* and its companion volumes do pay attention to such external clues in the work of investigation. However, by contrast with the bias toward physical evidence in Ginzburg's evocation of Sherlock Holmes, with its nineteenth-century privileging of the scientific objectivity of material signs, the "legalist school" is more likely to portray magistrates skilled in psychology, able to see through deception or intimidation. Their strategies of interrogation and entrapment assume that emotions have a moral dimension, and investigators are shown countering the unreliability of both witnesses and physical evidence by making confession the centerpiece of the successful criminal investigation. Evidence of the sign weighs less than the verbal testimony of the only person with full knowledge of the crime—the perpetrator. A concern with the status and reputation of the witness as a sign of truth coexists, perhaps uneasily, with reliance on the problematic figure of the criminal himself as witness to his own deeds.

It is through commentary that the *Magic Mirror* in particular used historical cases to reflect not just on evidentiary fact, but also on the larger goals of justice. Although the original preface by the compiler Zheng Ke is lost, it is said that he was responding to an imperial edict of 1133 calling for officials to be more lenient in their sentencing.[11] Colin Hawes shows that through his commentary, Zheng Ke was able to introduce critical perspective on some famous historical legal decisions now deemed too harsh and to defend a consistent approach to jurisprudence, which, simply put, was to be as lenient as the law allowed. In advocating that the judge apply the criminal code strictly where the result is a more lenient sentence than some would like and that he resort to flexible interpretation when the code's penalty seems too severe, Zheng Ke was focusing on the inevitable gap between rules and their application in specific situations that thinking with legal cases reveals.[12] Interpreted this way, the *Magic Mirror* casebook may be seen as participating in an important Song debate over how the written legal code, which was inherited and adapted from the preceding Tang dynasty, and changing statutory precedents, which accumulated rapidly in the tenth and eleventh centuries, related to a normative moral order identified with the classics and the sages.

These jurisprudential issues are further illuminated by another legal case—a particularly controversial one before the Northern Song court in the eleventh century that pitted the famous rival ministers Wang Anshi and Sima Guang against one another. The defendant was a woman, Ayun, who was accused of attempting to murder her fiancé. When the case was debated before Emperor Shenzong in 1069, Wang Anshi wanted to use Ayun's prompt confession of her crime to mitigate her sentence, in keeping with statutes that rewarded freely volunteered confessions in this way. Sima Guang considered that hers was in fact a crime of a woman against her (in effect de facto) husband, which in the light of morality and ritual should be judged with the utmost severity, and argued for a capital sentence for a premeditated murder attempt. Their disagreements revolved around the relevance and coherence of statutory precedents in a case where the emotional human circumstances (*qing*) of the crime raised cardinal issues of morality. Sima Guang did not argue that statutory law should be ignored in the case, but that the court should use the ethical standards of the normative Confucian Way (Dao) in deciding which statutes applied. Wang Anshi tried to find a coherent rationale for a decision solely on the basis of the accumulated laws and precedents of the Song legal system. Although Wang Anshi won the day with the Shenzong emperor, in later centuries most commentators on the matter sided with Sima Guang.[13]

In sum, these Song deployments of legal cases were brought to bear on the most important jurisprudential issue in traditional Chinese law: how to decide on the appropriate level of punishment for a given crime. The provisions of the penal code, however detailed, were recognized as inadequate to deal with the inexhaustible variability of situations and the issues of morality and emotion (both *qing*) that surrounded any particular criminal act; yet it was here that the dialectic of judicial leniency versus severity had to be played out. The issue was not one of choosing between law and morality, but of understanding how morality should be brought to bear on matters of statutory interpretation. This was an issue for which legal cases were needed to provide models.

These issues illuminate but do not entirely explain the significance of the most famous surviving printed collection of Song legal cases, *The Enlightened Judgments by Famous Officials* (*Minggong shupan Qingming ji*), published in the middle of the thirteenth century. Unlike the earlier works of the Song "legalist school," this text featured only cases of contemporary jurists serving in the southeastern coastal province where the work was published.[14] The cases selected reflect the gamut of litigations likely to arrive at the bench of a working county-level local magistrate, with a heavy tilt toward disputes over property, inheritance, taxes, marriage, fraud, and official malfeasance as well as violent crimes—conflicts that in Europe would mostly be identified as "civil" but that in China were simply designated "minor matters" (*xishi*). *The Enlightened Judgments* shows magistrates writing in the first person, outlining for each case the circumstances and briefly explaining the evidence and legal reasoning behind their judgments. These judicial "verdicts" (*shupan*) belong to a genre of writing that may have owed something to the earlier Tang practice of asking examination candidates to write hypothetical judgments as a literary exercise.[15] Scholars disagree over how the readers of this collection and its successors went about the business of "thinking with cases" here. Internal evidence suggests some pragmatic reasons for the writing of such "verdicts." They were used when cases were appealed or otherwise sent forward to senior legal officials for review. Sometimes the case summaries were given to litigants as a record of a decision, or posted publicly to inform the community of it. But when the collection was published, it was meant to serve as what kind of a model? Were the cases meant for magistrates themselves, as models of the literary arts of persuasion, or of judicial reasoning balancing fidelity to code and the moral spirit of the classics? Were they read pragmatically by persons who had dealings at law, either as pettifoggers or litigants? Or were they, like the Song legalist anthologies, also seen as entertainment, fodder for the popular genres of detective fiction and drama, which by this period were commonly referred to as *gong'an*? With so eclectic a collection it is hard to say. *The Enlightened Judgments* does show a mature tradition of "thinking with cases" by magistrates as legal specialists. Their work required technical knowledge of the legal code and its accumulating supplements and substatutes and of the legal system's administrative procedures, while the written case justified the judge's personal verdict both in relation to the facts at hand and the application of code of punishments to specific circumstances. What has been hard to extract from the collection is any consistent approach to issues of legal interpretation of the kind that exercised experts on law earlier, in the Northern Song.

Looking at the Song dynasty, we can see an enormous expansion of the sphere of law that was characteristic of that era and put the growing popularity of legal casebooks in that larger context. But however they were read, cases never functioned in the style of Anglo-Saxon common law as direct precedents for later judicial decisions. A final complex question remains, however. How might case records, which accumulated in Song central and local government archives in massive numbers, have shaped the making of new law? According to Brian McKnight, it was in the Northern Song that the Board of Punishments systematized the practice of higher-level review of judicial verdicts in serious crimes and of issuing periodic supplements to the legal code (*lü*) in the form of substatutes or precedents (*li*;

or, as Jiang and Wu prefer to name them in chap. 1, "regulations"). It was understood that, in the manner of precedents, later rulings should supersede earlier ones. Although scholars see issues raised in specific cases in the background of many substatutes, this was by no means obvious or acknowledged. In the language of the substatute, the details of the original cases would be stripped away. Moreover, many other processes, such as official memo or imperial rescript (comment) or edict, could also inspire new substatutes. What is clear is that the proliferation of compilations summarizing supplementary legal rulings far outstripped the ability of working jurists to consult them, provoking a countervailing trend of looking directly to the emperor for ratification of decisions in difficult cases. In other words, however much case precedents may have played a background role in Song legal culture, the only one who could formally make law by deciding cases was the emperor.[16]

Western scholars have neglected the tradition of "thinking with cases" in Chinese law for several reasons. Failing to find Anglo-Saxon-style case precedents in a Chinese system of codified laws, they have underestimated the extent to which all law in practice involves interpretation—both of the facts on the ground and of the relevance of statute to these. Under the influence of positivist theories of law, they have tended to evaluate judgments like Sima Guang's above that invoke Confucian ethical norms as somehow extra-legal, lacking grounding—as examples of Confucian moralism overriding positive law. Further, they have tended to see the compressed, highly selective, and heterogeneous case narratives of legal anthologies and magistrates' handbooks as literary productions, shaped more by scholarly ideals of genteel culture than by a specialist's need to show off his craft. Certainly, the essay by Yasuhiko Karasawa in this volume (chap. 3) confirms the deep impact that both classical and vernacular models of good writing had on the construction of case reports, but Karasawa also shows literary skills being deployed according to models of validity that carried legal weight. And certainly, the essay by Jiang Yonglin and Wu Yanhong (chap. 1) on Ming dynasty case decisions as produced by both a local magistrate in the sixteenth century and the founding emperor in the fourteenth is rich with evidence of moralistic judgments, but it also illustrates a dialectic between statute and ideals of "fairness" where the play of legal interpretation is revealed.

Where lay this dialectic in the Ming dynasty? There is no doubt that the founding Ming emperor intended that the 460-section *Great Ming Code,* completed in 1397, be an entirely comprehensive successor to its Tang and Song prototypes. But this code also accumulated substatutes, decrees, and commands over the decades, while the attached *Grand Pronouncements,* made up of the imperial founder's verdicts in individual cases, gradually lost their status as precedents, most being judged too harsh or arbitrary by succeeding judicial authorities. Even more important, as Jiang and Wu's account of published "court opinions" by the sixteenth-century magistrate Mao Yilu shows, a great part of a working magistrate's docket consisted of everyday disputes and transgressions that required the magistrate to arrive at a fair verdict by keeping in mind the sometimes competing claims of "principle" or "reason" (*li*), "sentiment" (*qing*), and "law" (*fa*). Balancing these three was to engage in the same dialectic. If "law" came first in the form of the code and its supplements, "principle" invoked neo-Confucian philosophy ("the learning of the Way," or *lixue*), while "sentiment" focused on both the emotional and ethical components of human relationships—components that Confucian moral psychology ever since Mencius had taught were intertwined. However global the philosophical and ethical connotations of these ideas, in the context of adjudication they were also recognized as legitimate legal norms. If jurists had more latitude to treat statute elastically by appealing to the other two in the cases classified as "small matters" (*xiaoshi*) where penalties were light, exactly the same principles of reconciling "law" and "sentiment" could and did bear on capital crimes.

Cases, therefore, are where the work of interpretation in Chinese law can be seen. As such, case collections were not simply exercises in literary showmanship or official self-promotion, although they often were these. Nor were they even just models for emulation or study, though this function seems obvious, as fulsomely attested in prefatory introductions to printed collections. In cases lie traces of the practices of a legal community, including its assumptions about the ground of interpretation itself. Principles drawn from the classics and moral philosophy shaped that interpretation and were expected to provide the bridge between formal law and particular circumstances.[17] This idea of a legal system as a community of practice in the context of a historically derived interpretive culture is in accord with the legal theories of the contemporary Harvard scholar of jurisprudence Ronald Dworkin. It is interesting that Dworkin's modern anti-positivist theory of law, in rejecting the idea that law can ever be defined semantically by enunciating rules or defining their nature, turns to "hard cases" for explanation. In Dworkin's framework, law cases, with their capacity to instantiate principles in story and detail and to encode ethics in specific judgments, become the privileged ground of jurisprudential theory. While it is clear that traditional Chinese jurisprudence contained its own theory of "positive" law as code and edict emanating from the sovereign, it is tempting to imagine that magistrates, in compiling casebooks and making them significant bearers of legal knowledge, may have been implicitly offering a countervailing portrait of the law itself. "Thinking with cases," then, would become both an important dimension of the internal history of Chinese legal practice and a path to our better conceptualizing it from the outside.[18]

In this volume the essay by Pierre-Étienne Will (chap. 2) shows how after the seventeenth century, in the Qing dynasty (1644–1911), cases acquired a more formal kind of recognition in the imperial legal system. Some might be designated "leading cases" (*cheng'an*) by imperial rescript and circulated to supplement statutes and substatutes as a third level of codified instruction to magistrates. "Leading cases" could not be cited explicitly as precedents justifying a particular legal decision, but they were expected to suggest analogies to guide the magistrate toward suitable statutory interpretations. A wealth of published anthologies of "leading cases," indexed to statutes in the code or even grouped by type, attest to their usefulness. In Will's analysis of forensic cases, we do not see "leading cases" but quite ordinary ones compiled and circulated by legal experts in charge of autopsies (often lower-level law clerks). But their authors are entirely comfortable presenting these narratives of particulars as material designed to compensate for the rigidities of the official manual on forensics that was attached to the Qing code. The focus on bodily signs, material circumstances, and even physical anatomy in the cited forensic case records suggests to Will a spirit of evidentiary reasoning and problem solving aimed at improving knowledge, not just arriving at a correct verdict in an individual instance.

From the early Song "legalist school" to the "leading cases" of the Qing dynasty, cases at law were discussed and read by both experts and literate members of the public and reached into popular culture through performance and storytelling. In the Ming and Qing dynasties, diverse forms of written and published legal case records proliferated and were increasingly identified by the generic label *an*. These ranged from pettifoggers' handbooks (*song'an*), to magistrates' memoirs (*gong'an*), to the Qing-era "[Board of] Punishments cases" (*xing'an*), which were the case summaries that working local magistrates had to send forward to that central government ministry for review. Against this long historical background, the example of law, and in particular the metaphor of the judge, was readily available to be appealed to by late imperial specialists in other domains in explaining the inspiration behind their forms of the case. Both physicians and philosophers do this in the prefaces to their case collections discussed here.

Keeping notes on their patients and treatments was probably as old as literate medicine in China. We have seen how such notes figured in the famous biography of the second-century BCE physician Chunyu Yi in Sima Qian's history. But public written records of medical cases, like legal ones, first appeared embedded in the biographies of physicians that made their way into the dynastic histories, most often as third-person stories of marvelous cures. There are no surviving examples to compare with Chunyu Yi's case notes, for the traditions of hereditary physician households meant that craft secrets, like records of what pharmaceutical formulas doctors used, did not circulate to the outside. It was Song dynasty examination culture that provided a model for a new-style physician, learned in state-authorized medical classics, whose public persona was that of a scholar (*ruyi*), not a hereditary craftsman or religious specialist. And it was scholarly "literati physicians" who began in the thirteenth and fourteenth centuries to include brief narratives of their own cases in their medical treatises, and in some instances to add a separate case history section. In 1531, *The Medical Cases of Wang Ji* (*Shishan yi'an*) broke new ground as the first published medical case history collection by a single author. It was quickly followed by others. By end of the sixteenth century the medical case history collection was an established genre among learned physicians. In the eighteenth and nineteenth centuries, proponents of the revisionist "Warm Factor" (*wenbing*) school of therapists popularized a leaner, less discursive style of case history writing focused almost entirely on explaining the prescription formula used in a case. Anthologies also became popular, following the model of the late sixteenth-century collection *Classified Cases from Famous Doctors* (*Mingyi lei'an*) compiled by Jiang Guan.

In sum, public records of medical cases appeared in the first millennium CE embedded in historical narratives, and then in the Song and Yuan developed as illustrative anecdotes incorporated into the writings of learned physicians themselves. The record-keeping role of scholars, who circulated case notes supplied by physicians who treated their families, is illustrated in Ping-chen Hsiung's narrative of the pioneer twelfth-century pediatrician Qian Yi in chapter 5. The medical case history achieved a maturity of form in the Ming, when it became a record of a doctor's own experience, often constructed to convey a particular therapeutic strategy in pharmacy. In my essay on medicine in this volume (chap. 4), I argue that Ming casebooks reflected the emergence of competing styles of prescribing associated with different medical "lineages of learning." In this way the case history collections spoke to one another, while their prefaces make clear that authors imagined them as useful aids to diagnosis, part of an archive of past experience for physicians to draw upon at the bedside. This growth of the genre of medical case history writing and publication was fostered by the dilemmas of the new post-Song "literati physician," who was expected to model his learning on that of scholar-official graduates of imperial examinations, treating the ancient, thousand-year-old medical corpus as canonical, even as more recent medical masters increasingly emphasized the temporal and geographical mutability of disease. In the dialectic between text and experience, producing medical knowledge using cases privileged the latter, allowing physicians to bypass the traditional canon/commentary mode of thinking common in classics and historical learning for a direct consideration of clinical manifestations. Cases highlighted the doctor's skill at matching symptoms with pharmaceutical remedies, becoming a logical venue for teaching the hermeneutics of prescriptions.

If the medical case history belongs to a specialist domain that seems closest to that of a science in the modern sense, what are we to do with the Buddhist *gong'an*? Robert Sharf has argued that in the Tang and Song dynasties Chan *gong'an* were not enlightenment narratives designed to short-circuit intellection, as later Japanese-inspired Zen authorities claimed. Rather, they grew out of pedagogical performances designed to teach student monks the intricacies of doctrinal reasoning in a world of contingency. Such *gong'an* were part of a dense web of scholarly argument and counterargument designed to provide aspirants with scripts for dealing with the theological puzzles that were the inevitable consequence of Chan rejection of all timeless ethical or philosophical doctrines immune to paradox and logical contradiction. Through the "enlightened repartee" of the *gong'an*, the Chan believer learned to undermine any point of reference claiming to anchor belief. As such, famous *gong'an* were cases designed to serve as models for a group of religious specialists engaged in a creative game of scholastic argument.

In the late Ming, neo-Confucian philosophers developed their own version of thinking with cases in "cases of learning" (*xue'an*). Like Chan monks, these Confucian philosophers were looking for paths to self-cultivation and enlightenment. When a number of sixteenth- and seventeenth-century philosophers gathered their biographical narratives of Song and Ming Confucian sages and worthies under the rubric of "cases of learning," their format of recording "words and deeds" followed a standard pattern common to both Buddhist and Confucian hagiographical biography. Their writings also recall collected biographies of groups of people identified by moral or social type—the legions of "knights errant," "chaste women," "worthy officials," or "evil ministers" whose catalogued lives fill so many official histories. Certainly such collective biographical sets may be thought of as a form of "thinking with cases." Each life and its circumstances are different, yet collectively they point to a norm intended for moral instruction. They evoke the form of the case that in European historiography of casuistry is identified as the "exemplum"—an example carrying the didactic force of a religious teaching.

But *Cases of Learning of Ming Confucians* by Huang Zongxi (1610–1695), which followed an earlier collection by Geng Dingxiang (1524–1596) and another by Liu Yuanqing (1544–1609), requires a deeper reading of the generic form of model biographies. These works emerged in the context of the bitter debates inspired by the sixteenth-century philosopher Wang Yangming, whose radical critique of the officially approved doctrines handed down from the Song founders of the "Learning of the Way" associated with Zhu Xi had attracted a powerful following. "Cases of learning" began to be produced in the late Ming at a time when the "Learning of the Way" orthodoxy (*lixue*) was splintering into contending philosophical factions, and the very idea of a single doctrinal line of transmission from antiquity via the Song to the present Ming-era masters was increasingly hard to maintain. Hung-lam Chu's essay here (chap. 8) shows how each of the important sixteenth- and seventeenth-century collections of "cases of learning" took a position in the controversies surrounding the philosophy of Wang Yangming—offering its "dossier" on one or more individual philosophers, consisting of a biographical narrative and a selection of the subject's writings. Supporters and critics of Wang Yangming each produced their own casebooks. The work of genius among them, Huang Zongxi's *Cases of Learning of Ming Confucians,* looks for a way out of the dead end of, on the one hand, looking for a single orthodox line of transmission of the Way, or, on the other, the cul-de-sac of subjectivism that might follow a literal reading of Wang Yangming's democratization of sagehood. In Huang Zongxi's hands the "cases of learning" dissolve the One into the Many—the unitary Way can be seen only in the multiplicity and particularity of different sagely lives. By putting biography in the foreground, the "cases of learning" also encoded in the text Wang Yangming's central doctrine of the unity of knowledge and action.

In sum, in a late-Ming moment of social and intellectual crisis, the form of the case encouraged a different way of philosophizing. It accommodated debate among partisans who had to back their positions with evidence and who could rely on no transcendent or unquestioned authority of sagely transmission to fall back on. It also accommodated a philosophy that asserted the epistemological priority of personal action and experience, a Way that could be grasped only in the individual particularity of lives as lived. Rather than combing the records of Ming Confucians for the orthodox lineage of learning or measuring each scholar/sage against a fixed standard model/template of moral behavior, the seeker of the Way was invited to choose the path according to his own circumstances. "Cases of learning" pointed to situation ethics and to the necessity of individual judgment. The closest comparison in Western tradition may be to that of casuistry—the "cases of conscience" that taught how to translate Christian ethical norms into a Catholic priest's judgment of a sinner's individual confession.

The foregoing lays out a historical trajectory of all the major types of case collections that contributors to this volume examine. We can see that the legal case matured in the Song, the medical case matured in the Ming, and that the learned case was a product of the late Ming. Now I want to return to the scheme of "styles of reasoning" to see if we can find culturally specific inflections to the forms of the case in late imperial China.

THE FORMS OF THE CASE IN CHINA: "STYLES OF REASONING"

If thinking with cases is fundamentally about working with analogies, Forrester reminds us that there are a number of ways that analogy can be used and offers three types of analogical reasoning: 1) classification into kinds—taxonomy; 2) relating individual instances to a model, where models in turn might be defined differentially as exemplar, prototype, or model system; and 3) ordering by the historical relationship of precedent/descent.

Using cases to produce a taxonomy, or classification into groups of like kinds, is the method that seems closest to inductive method, aggregating like particulars and aspiring to find general patterns in them. Closest to the natural sciences, this strategy is also one that Forrester rejects as antithetical to the fidelity to the individual that he thinks essential to "thinking in cases." Classification of individual instances into types or kinds forces the similar to pose as the same: that is, it requires the erasure from view of nonconforming particularities. Chinese specialists resorted to classification for ordering knowledge of the "things" (*wu*) of both the natural and the social worlds, as found in numerous published encyclopedias or anthologies organized according to "classes" (*lei*). A common strategy for classifying the contents of both encyclopedias and more informal miscellanies (called *biji*) was to appeal to the cosmological hierarchy of Heaven, Earth, and Humanity, or the bibliographers' hierarchy of classics, histories, belles lettres, and monographs, or even to an order proceeding from the imperial center outward to the provinces, foreign parts, and the world of nonhuman nature beyond.

The same sort of value-laden eclecticism is found in plant classification, which would seem to be the most suitable for taxonomies resembling those of Western natural science. Robert Hymes has looked at a Song catalogue of chrysanthemum flowers, where the higher order classification into sets is cosmological (based on the symbolic hierarchy of color and season according to the cosmology of Five Phases [*wuxing*]), but where delight in variety produces descriptions of individual types that both cut across the hierarchy and are replete with attention to features not relevant to the overall ordering scheme.[19] In medicine, works on *materia medica* (*bencao*), mostly substances derived from plants, appealed to a cosmologically resonant three-part hierarchy of therapeutic value and potency as well as to natural categories such as grasses, fruits, and trees. Li Shizhen, the late sixteenth-century author of the famous *Classified Materia Medica* (*Bencao gangmu*), was innovative in providing a more complex, though still cosmologically ordered, hierarchy of nature in his organization of the major divisions of his work. But his intermediate-order framework of "classes" (*lei*) and, below them, "kinds" (*zhong*) ordered individual entries around folk-taxonomic concepts such as habitat, morphology, or use. In particular, his "classes" that grouped similar "kinds" only partially overlap modern botanical families, reflecting instead what George Metaille calls "tacit knowledge" that indigenous peoples have of their environment.[20] Here the overall laxness of taxonomic analysis in the production of empirical knowledge in China may have the richness of its case history tradition as a counterpart.

Ming medical case history collections were organized by topics, in books sometimes claiming to be ordered by "classes" (*leishu*). But the textual presentation of medical nosology did not produce species-like diseases, nor were cases classified according to the deep patterns believed to constitute the "root" (*ben*) of a disorder. As I argue in my chapter on medicine in this volume, the art of diagnosis was understood as one of recognizing the shifting dynamic of a small number of deep patterns of disorder while maintaining emphasis on the individual character of each clinical situation. Empirically, beyond broad categories like "medicine for women" (*fuke*) or "pediatrics" (*erke*) or "external medicine" (*waike*), casebooks organized entries around medical signs and symptoms or around parts of the body, allowing physicians to use them as clinical aids in diagnosis. The deeper dialectic of pattern and symptom did become an organizing principle for the eighteenth-century clinicians Yu Zhen and Ye Gui, who used cases to try and show how superficial similarities in symptoms could mask deep underlying differences in disease patterns. Legal collections most often organized cases according to categories of the legal code. In both medicine and law, then, classification ordinarily operated at the frankly eclectic level of an index or a table of contents, allowing users to find analogies to problems as they initially presented themselves for solution.

The idea of a case as a model was a natural one in China, where exemplary biographies were a time-honored form of didactic writing and where the metaphor of a carpenter's compass and square was a classical cliché for any example worthy of emulation. The commonplace rhetoric of imitating a model would suggest that here models are to be understood as closest to Forrester's "exemplar." But the "exemplar," which in today's philosophy of science points to standard experiments used to teach students of physics or chemistry, evokes the standardization of a blueprint rather than the human variation found in China's mainstream biographical tradition. Exemplary biographies of Confucian worthies, virtuous women, or wise rulers and ministers, and Buddhist and Daoist tales of salvation, immortals, or recluses all relate cases to a model as a form of moral instruction in keeping with the didactic form of the "exemplum." In this kind of moral discourse, the norms or rules of right conduct are implicit; they cannot be reduced to a code, but will be seen as embodied in virtuous persons. However rigid or formulaic the model cases may seem from an outsider's perspective, the model format carries with it the assumptions of situational ethics. Biographical detail invites comparison with readers' actual lives. What makes the late-Ming "cases of learning" that Hung-lam Chu explores stand out here is the degree to which the ideals of thought and conduct appealed to presented the student with real alternatives—not only a variety of philosophical paths, but the path of a life of action or of study, government service or private learning, discipleship, or the hermit's hut. This irreducibility of case to type distinguishes a model system from a more formulaic idea of a model as exemplar or exemplum and reveals the limitations of the more stereotypical collections of Chinese model biographies.

The third type is the historical relationship of precedent/descent. Here the ordering of cases requires consideration of the authority of history in the context of changing circumstances. As we have seen, in Chinese law, which was formally derived from the emperor and spelled out in the imperial penal code and administrative regulations, there was no theoretical place for precedent as the maker of law in the manner of decentralized Anglo-Saxon jurisprudence. Nonetheless, the record of substatutes or *li* beginning in the Song and of the Qing "leading case" (*cheng'an*) shows law adapting to changing times. As Pierre-Étienne Will's chapter here suggests, the Qing innovation of the "leading case" provided a context for his forensic specialists' use of cases to correct inadequacies in the legally binding official guidelines concerning autopsies.

In sum, we see cases in Chinese law, medicine, and philosophy as a strategy of modernists in an intellectual tradition that gave awesome weight to the authority of antiquity. With cases they negotiated the gap between classic and circumstances, code and crime, medical canon and therapeutic strategy. A record of a particular situation might provide a useful analogy with a later situation, equally particular. The intellectual link between one case and another led to a strategy of intervention in a particular crisis. Cases, then, were directed toward local, situated knowledge in a context where appeals to canonical authority were felt to be inadequate and the possibility of rival viewpoints was always implicitly present. It may be no accident that specialist writing on cases proliferated between the sixteenth and eighteenth centuries, when elite Chinese intellectual life was shifting away from earlier forms of classical orthodoxy toward the historicist, empiricist, and cumulative forms of classical scholarship called "Han learning" (*Hanxue*). If John Henderson is right that the tradition of commentary—a learned form that accommodated critique and innovation as long as it could still reference a sacralized canon—lost ground in the critical climate of the eighteenth century, then the form of the case itself may have played an innovative role.[21] Contributors to the Chinese-language volume on the case published in Taiwan (companion to this one) argue that "thinking with cases" not only fostered a spirit of empiricism, but one of independent thought as well.[22]

Finally, the Chinese inflection to "thinking with cases" is to me notable for the way practitioners understood it as linking knowledge and action. Whether philosopher making ethical choices, diagnostician selecting the prescription to use, or judge determining the punishment that fits the crime, the actors in case narratives must not only evaluate situations, but also intervene, not only interpret evidence, but also make facts on the ground by their power to shape events. This means that case narratives were likely to focus not just on evidence, but on judgment. Judgment calls attention to the gap between any rule and its instantiation in an individual set of circumstances. Rendering judgment goes beyond technical expertise, to a remainder that is insight and is personal. And it means that validity is tested above all by experience, by the efficacy of outcomes that, however astutely anticipated, cannot be predicted with certainty.

THE HISTORICAL SOCIOLOGY OF THE CASE

Throughout this introduction I have repeatedly associated the production of case narratives with specialist knowledge. Because that knowledge was linked to action, it is easy to see how "thinking with cases" facilitated a decision procedure important both in itself and as an underpinning for the specialist's authority. If we think about specialists in law, medicine, and religion/philosophy, in modern perspective we are talking about the emergence of what are commonly understood as the professions: the doctor, the lawyer, the priest. It is easy to see how the spread of printing, the emergence of examination culture, and the development of the late imperial economy provide a context for the increasing specialization of Chinese occupational roles and the development of bodies of learning appropriate for each. The scholar physician or the legal expert who was the magistrate's private secretary in the judicial bureaucracy fits this picture. Even for those whose working lives were passed in the imperial civil service, John Dardess has argued that as early as the formative decades of the Ming dynasty, scholar officials possessed a "professional" service ethos, a sense of group identity and self-policing bureaucratic criteria of performance.[23]

Of course, we cannot simply throw away the literati ideal of the classically educated man of letters that shaped the self-fashioning of almost all who were educated. The social prestige of the gentleman that permeated examination culture also has left fingerprints all over the writings defined here as "specialist." Judith Zeitlin's essay on the sixteenth-century physician Sun Yikui (chap. 6) argues that medical case history collections played the role of a doctor's literary works (*wenji*), while Yasuhiko Karasawa shows how literati ideas about good writing shaped the rhetoric and language of legal case narratives. Such habits of thought add an additional layer of complexity to the problem of trying to define the "professionalization" of specialist occupations in the late imperial period. Sociologists are divided on the theoretical issues: some emphasize "profession" as an ideal type, while others prefer to think about a historical process. If the ideal type encompasses formal qualifications for practice and autonomous institutions to police membership and standards, few Chinese occupations fit this pattern before the twentieth century.

Nonetheless, if the emphasis is upon a group identity based on a shared body of learning and socially recognized networks of affiliations and on specialized services provided in the context of a commercial exchange (salary or fee), it is easier to recognize that the vocational worlds of Qing medical, legal, and even religious experts were moving in that direction. The obscure legal experts on forensics discussed by Pierre-Étienne Will in his chapter here were among the ranks of "private secretaries" (*muyou*) whose technical knowledge in everything from law to financial administration was essential for the operation of Qing dynasty provincial and local government offices (yamen). As Will himself has shown in his massive bibliography of Chinese official handbooks, the manuals compiled specifically by and for private secretaries are testimony to the cumulative technical sophistication of specialist knowledge relevant to government as well as the persistent social distinctions between such specialists and ranking magistrates.[24] It was not so different with doctors. Even as nineteenth-century practitioners who saw their patients in urban clinics and earned income from the pharmaceutical trade found the moral image of "literati physician" invaluable, they depended upon networks of lineage, discipleship, and locality that created and sustained their reputations as effective physicians. As Volker Scheid has argued, the use of Western sociological categories can obscure the way these late imperial learned physicians and others imagined the communities that legitimated their technical knowledge and practice.[25] Thinking with cases is presented in this volume more as a kind of knowledge production than as sociological evidence. Nevertheless, it may be that reading, writing, and circulating cases itself may be taken as one marker of a professional orientation among certain individuals and groups in late imperial China.

Certainly, the lingering image of a Confucian "amateur ideal" keeps historians of China underestimating the degree to which working officials and their staffs deployed specialist knowledge in the administration of the empire. Robert Hymes has called attention to the use of history as an archive of cases in policy debates at the Northern Song court, including written materials for official examinations and those prepared for the education of the emperor. A generation ago, Robert Hartwell hypothesized that these sorts of materials, under the Song bibliographical category "*gushi*" (lit. "old events," translated by Hartwell as "historical models"), constituted a practice of using historical examples as case histories in a way that anticipates modern social science.[26] But as Hymes pointed out, the written records Hartwell appealed to were in fact much more heterogeneous, and even a history titled *A Mirror for Aid in Governing* (*Zizhi tongjian*), as Sima Guang's great work was, does not fit the form of the case.[27] Nonetheless, over the course of imperial history Chinese officials high and low produced hundreds of handbooks on administration, including in them specialist guides to defense and military training, famine relief, finance, water control, and much besides. The essays in this volume do not do much with these, but the hope is that our project will call attention to all sorts of sets of cases embedded in the vast archive scholars identify as magistrates' handbooks. These works in all their heterogeneity include a good number that manifest "thinking with cases."

But it is interesting that very few of these statecraft-oriented official handbooks were called *an*. Will's bibliography of official handbooks shows that in the writings of late imperial government experts and officials, *an* did not name an early form of social science, but a specifically legal and forensic kind of text. By the late Ming dynasty, the Chinese generic term *an* was embraced not only by doctors and legal experts, but also by the scholarly authors of some texts on theology and philosophy, while being ignored in the mainstream of a sophisticated tradition of statecraft. How do we explain this? Could it be that here the specialist label *an* appears as a sign policing the boundaries between more and less prestigious ways of writing about the craft of government? Or is it a subtle intellectual distinction? We would have to look at more statecraft manuals to begin to address this.

CONCLUSION: SCIENCE STUDIES, CHINESE SCIENCE, AND THE CASE

For most of the twentieth century, premodern China was assumed to lie outside the mainstream of world historical scientific development as defined by the achievements of Europe and North America since the seventeenth century. Among Western-educated Chinese reformers of the Republican period (1911–1949), public intellectuals like Hu Shi (1891–1962) argued that after the seventeenth century there had been an intuitively inductive indigenous "empirical" tradition in the historical, archeological, and philological studies pursued by Qing "evidential scholars" (*Hanxue, shixue*). These men were committed to authenticating the original texts of China's pre-imperial classics. In addition, Hu and other Chinese followers of John Dewey announced that this philosopher's view of science as a pragmatic method tested by concrete experience was well suited to long-standing Chinese conventions of inquiry, while a variety of Western-trained experts from the geologist Ding Wenjiang (1887–1936) to the chemist Ren Hongjun (1886–1961) found homegrown intellectual ancestors in the technical writings of explorers, technologists, and astronomers of the imperial past. Beginning in the 1950s, the wealth of such technical literature was made visible to the English-speaking world through the monumental scholarship of Sir Joseph Needham as documented in his multivolume *Science and Civilization in China*. However, all these undertakings carried the burden of a positivist model of science, reserving a privileged place for the European "scientific revolution" with its fixation on experimental procedures confirming universal and constant natural laws and the assumption that the validity of evidence is guaranteed only if it is uncontaminated by influences introduced by context or conditions of observation.

Over the past generation, the critical and deconstructive perspectives of contemporary science studies, with their emphasis on the plurality of sciences and their foundation in multiple practices, have provided space to reconsider the history of science in China. Building on Nathan Sivin's pioneering studies of ancient astronomy and medicine in context,[28] Benjamin Elman has documented a rich late-imperial tradition of "natural studies" or "natural philosophy" understood at the time as an application of the Song philosopher Zhu Xi's call for "investigating things and extending knowledge" (*gezhi*).[29] If this was not science as moderns understand it, neither was the Jesuit natural philosophy that invigorated Chinese natural studies in the seventeenth and eighteenth centuries—a body of knowledge that stimulated innovation in such fields as mathematics, computational astronomy, cartography, and engineering, while remaining constrained by religious and political agendas on both sides.

Seventeenth- and eighteenth-century Sino-Western "scientia," to use Elman's phrase, was a learned undertaking, carried out by men who were highly conscious of cosmological and philosophical worldviews bearing on their activities. If Elman makes his contribution by framing early modern scientific activities in both European and Chinese historical contexts, a specialist on Chinese agriculture, Francesca Bray, attacks the master narrative of modern science literally from the ground.[30] She argues that the science/technology distinction, although reified in standard academic disciplinary boundaries, is a recent epistemological artifact based on assumptions about the primacy of theory. If science is made up of declarations—claims about the natural order—and if technology must be seen as a sociomaterial system for producing effects in the world, both are mediated by what she calls "technique"—"skilled practices" of individuals that produce both knowledge and things. By pointing to the bricolage of artisanal work, the shaping role of available instruments (even in the modern laboratory), and the utilitarian agendas of practitioners everywhere, she makes a case for the tacit knowledge and manual labor that went into the "patterned manipulations of matter" of traditional Chinese agriculture. Focusing on this toolkit of "techniques" allows us to bring potters and navigators, bridge builders and plant breeders into a picture of the work of science where large-scale models of natural processes remain mostly invisible and where shaping sociopolitical regimes of knowledge must be part of the picture.

The study of cases adds a new dimension to this pluralistic picture of science as historically conditioned and heterogeneous in practice. Thinking with cases, as Forrester's work suggests, argues for a multiplicity of field-dependent methods as well as of practical techniques—epistemological pluralism, if you will. For the

Taiwanese scholars who worked on this project, the story of "thinking with cases" in China allowed them to pick up the early twentieth-century discussions of "Qing empiricism" and of the practical reason (*shixue*) characteristic of Chinese statecraft and to recuperate some methodological strategies implicit in these traditions. When the volume edited by Ping-chen Hsiung took as its title *Let the Evidence Speak*, it was a sign that scholars from China, still aware of lingering stereotypes of their civilization as scientifically lacking, are more interested in the phenomenon of thinking with cases as a container of evidence than as a rhetorical form. They also appreciate case-based reasoning as an open form, associating its capacity to accommodate change with freedom of thought as a sociopolitical value.

Looking back, it is not surprising that in China, with a strong tradition of statecraft but without a so-called scientific revolution, specialists never learned to divorce the legal case from other forms of "thinking with cases." The story of the "case" in the modern north Atlantic world has been one of ambivalence as law and other specialist domains gradually took separate paths. When, after the seventeenth-century, "thinking with cases" gradually came to be judged by the standards of natural science, law lost its relevance, while the experiential lessons of medical cases were gradually found wanting in comparison to the truth claims of experimental methods or statistical reasoning. In the twentieth century the case revived—first under the influence of psychoanalysis and then more broadly. It has ended up being bracketed with the modern "human sciences"—there is the social science "case study" or the case method of pedagogy in schools of law, medicine, and business.[31]

But the history of the case in China is clearly about the expertise needed to find proper grounds for action in a world of historical contingency. In its didactic aspect, it is in harmony with the robust contemporary manifestations of thinking with cases in the curricula of law, medical, and business schools, where the case history methods pioneered in Harvard classrooms in the early years of the twentieth century are still basic tools for teaching. In its moralistic concerns, it is in harmony with what Forrester calls "the new casuistry" of medical ethics—the application of moral judgments in specific clinical situations. In all these ways it brings into question the uneasy generalizations of contemporary social sciences in search of constants of social behavior identified with rationality independent of value. Thus the examples gathered here—the Chinese case writ large—throw light upon a perennial feature of "thinking with cases" that has been obscured by the modern obsession with the particular as a datum that gains significance only when aggregated into stable general patterns. Such patterns are valued in modern science as part of an epistemology that demands that explanation be about causes and follows Aristotle in claiming that such knowledge alone is universal. Thinking with cases evokes other paths—those connecting knowledge to experience and directed at outcomes, successful interventions in the world rather than law-like representations of it. In this way our exploration of the Chinese case has become an exercise in what has come to be called the social history of truth, one that may help recuperate the case as a mode of producing valid knowledge.

NOTES

1 *Zhangjiashan Han mu zhujian [ersiqi hao mu]*, 216. Archeologists believe the occupant of tomb 247 died around 186 BCE. My thanks to Michael Ludke for calling my attention to this archeological text and for assistance in interpreting it.

2 Sima Qian, *Shiji*, 9:105.2812–2813.

3 Chandler, *England in 1819*, 39, 198–209.

4 Hacking, "Styles of Scientific Reasoning"; Crombie, *Styles of Scientific Thinking*, vol. 1.

5 Forrester, "If p, then what? Thinking in Cases." By naming his essay "Thinking *in* Cases," Forrester artfully calls attention to the fact that his own essay instantiates his project, being organized around a number of case examples. Along with the other contributors to this volume, I am greatly indebted to Forrester's ideas. In the present volume, we have changed the preposition to *with* not because it adds anything new, but in order to mark his contribution as unique.

6 Ho Da-an, "Lunduan fuhao."

7 See SKQS, vol. 739. These Song works are grouped with the classics *Guanzi* and *Huainanzi.*

8 Through the translation by Van Gulik, the *Parallel Cases from under the Pear-tree* has until recently been the best known of the three collections. Its selection of cases for entertainment value has made it difficult to evaluate from a jurisprudential point of view, while Van Gulik's argument that the extant text of the earlier *Magic Mirror* is corrupt has discouraged scholars from its study. My account of these works relies on Hawes, "Reinterpreting Law," which critiques Van Gulik's textual judgments and analyzes the original commentary to the *Magic Mirror.*

9 Zheng Ke, comp., *Zheyu guijian, juan* 1, SKQS, 729:864.

10 Ginzburg, "Morelli, Freud, and Sherlock Holmes."

11 Hawes, "Reinterpreting Law," 25–26.

12 Ibid., 54, sums it up as follows: "The written laws may be interpreted flexibly when the result is a fairer and more lenient sentence, but they should be strictly applied when a flexible interpretation would result in a harsh, possibly unjust, sentence."

13 See the discussion in Langlois, "'Living Law,'" 200–217. Mine is a highly simplified summary of a protracted dispute. I am indebted here to Scogin, "Chinese Interest in Case Law," which offers a lucid discussion of issues of legal reasoning in the case.

14 Brian McKnight and James Liu provide an introduction and translation of about half the entries in the original, which was largely lost for many centuries before a copy was discovered in Japan in the 1980s. A modern, punctuated Chinese version of the original appeared in 1987.

15 In the Tang dynasty and Northern Song, examination candidates were asked to write *shupan* based on hypothetical cases. A Tang collection by Bo Juyi and Zhang Zhuo, *Dragon Sinew and Phoenix Marrow Judgments* (*Longjin fengsui pan*), assembled models of this essentially literary genre. Southern Song examinations dropped this category of question. See discussion in de Pee, "Cases of the New Terrace."

16 See McKnight, "From Statute to Precedent," 111–126. This is the gist of his revision of the Japanese scholarly view that the Song legal system passed from a "dependence on statutes to a dependence on Edicts, and then to a dependence on Precedents." Revisiting the issue in "How Did Cases Become Precedents," McKnight notes that Song legal documents often contained passing references to case precedents from the raw archive to which the working jurist had access, but only very rarely did they cite substatutes in a judgment.

17 Critiquing the Anglo-American scholarly search for "customary law" in the Qing, Bourgon in "Uncivil Dialogue" argues that magistrates' casebooks are where "model judgments . . . are often guided or framed through principles drawn from the Classics" (82), allowing one to see an equity-guided "juristic reasoning elaborated to resolve particular cases rationally" (68).

18 Dworkin, "The Model of Rules" and *Law's Empire.*

19 See Hymes, "Some Thoughts on 'Thinking in Cases.'" The work in question is *The Register of Chrysanthemums* (*Ju pu*) by Liu Meng (fl. 1104).

20 Metaille, "The *Bencao gangmu,*" 238. Metaille sees Li Shizhen as an important innovator in his own context of the neo-Confucian "investigation of things and extension of knowledge" (*gezhi*). He broke with the pharmacological tradition of thinking of *materia medica* primarily in terms of their therapeutic properties, and he combined philological research and field investigation to bring order into the multiplicity of historical and vernacular nomenclature, linking diverse "names" with identifiable plants and animals.

21 See Henderson, *Scripture, Canon and Commentary;* and Elman, *From Philosophy to Philology.*

22 See Hsiung, ed., *Rang zhengju shuohua: Zhongguo pian.*

23 Dardess, *Confucianism and Autocracy,* 13–84.

24 Will, "Official Handbooks and Anthologies of Imperial China." This giant, bibliographical work in progress had close to one thousand separate annotated titles as of the end of 2005.

25 Scheid, "Restructuring the Field of Chinese Medicine," 12–14.

26 Hartwell, "Historical Analogism."

27 Hymes, "Some Thoughts on 'Thinking in Cases.'" His examples of historical casebooks are *The Learning of Emperors* (*Di xue*) by Fan Zuyu (1041–1098), a work composed entirely of selected narratives about different emperors; and Zhen Dexiu's *Extended Meaning of the Great Learning* (*Daxue yanyi*), also intended for the moral education of the emperor.

28 Sivin, *Cosmos and Computation; Medicine, Philosophy, and Religion;* and *Science in Ancient China.* See also Sivin and Lloyd, *The Way and the Word.*

29 Elman, *On Their Own Terms.*

30 Bray, "Science, Technique, Technology."

31 Recent philosophers of science have suggested that a process of thinking with cases can be implicit in the natural as well as the human sciences. Thomas Kuhn's argument that science students learn rules not directly but from textbook-standard experiments that he calls exemplars brings physics and chemistry education in line with that in the medical or legal professions. Researchers in a historical, evolutionary science like biology, genetics, or ecology can be seen to map their subjects into "model systems" built out of accumulating cases arranged along an axis of variation susceptible to change over time. The idea that natural objects, whether clouds or DNA, are dynamic and never entirely predictable, while fascinating for its challenge to ontologies governing conventional notions of organic versus inorganic substance, is beyond the historical models of the case addressed in this volume.

PART ONE
THE CASE IN LAW

OVERLEAF: The legendary Judge Bao reviewing a court case. From *Bao Longtu gongan duan wai wupen zhuan*, 1472. Shanghai Museum collection. Facsimile reprint in *Ming Chenghua shuochang cihua congkan*, ed. Shanghai shi wenwu baoguan weiyuanhui and Shanghai bowuguan, vol. 5. Beijing: Wenwu chubanshe, 1979.

1

Satisfying Both Sentiment and Law

Fairness-Centered Judicial Reasoning as Seen in Late Ming Casebooks

JIANG YONGLIN AND WU YANHONG

In the last century of the Ming dynasty (1368–1644) lawsuits were common across the Chinese empire, judging from the large number of legal case collections that were published during this period. The case collections functioned to assist both specialists and laypeople in understanding legal matters and in participating in litigation. Such works may be categorized into several genres, ranging from the most private to the most official in authorship. The latter included collections drawn directly from the archives of either the central government agencies or local offices for circulation to the working magistrates of the various local courts.[1] At the private end of the spectrum were the so-called "Secret Handbooks of Litigation Masters" (*Songshi miben*) that provided hired legal specialists and their litigant clients with model indictments and verdicts derived from actual law cases.[2] Even more informal was the "court case fiction" genre (*gong'an xiaoshuo*), where tales of crime and punishment offered moral teachings as well as entertainment to the general public.[3] Collections of historical cases from previous dynasties, on the other hand, aimed to offer their readers, especially judicial officials, some ethical discipline and technical training drawn from the classical past.[4] Finally, a number of works, known as "judgments" or "court opinions" (*shenyu* or *yanyu*), were written by local judicial officials based on their personal legal practice. They were compiled and published by the officials themselves either as separate books or as parts of their collected writings. This last genre of law case collections, hereafter referred to as "court opinions," is the focus of this chapter.

"Court opinions" by individual Ming magistrates are well suited for exploring our central questions concerning the place of the case in legal theory and practice: first to show how judicial officials reasoned to reach their judgments, and second to indicate what role the archive of cases played in late Ming adjudication. "Court opinions" by late Ming judicial officials recorded the authors' original judgments, which were not court verdicts themselves but documents justifying the verdicts with reasoned opinions. In law enforcement, the judicial officials' goal was to "satisfy both sentiment and law" (*qingfa liangping*). Their judicial reasoning, then, was neither "case based" nor solely "rule based," but instead fairness centered. In forming their judgments, both legal rules and the specific circumstances of each case played a crucial role. While publishing such casebooks aimed at guiding other officials' legal practices, the authors intended these works to function as textbooks for moral and disciplinary education. They were not precedents with the legal power to guide future court rulings; rather, they were models illustrating how both formal law and the abstract principles of equity or fairness might be applied in individual situations.

THE CASEBOOKS OF "COURT OPINIONS"

In recent years, scholars have discovered six major casebooks from the late Ming dynasty, including Mao Yilu's *Court Opinions from Songjiang* (*Yunjian yanlüe*), the main subject of this essay. (For the other five casebooks, see the appendix at the end of the chapter). These casebooks record judgments drawn from the authors' stints as judicial officials in a variety of local areas. For the reader's convenience, each casebook has a "table of contents," listed by offenders, offenses, or both. Five of the six casebooks start each judgment with the phrase "It is heard that" (*shende*) or "It is observed that" (*kande*). In each entry, the authors narrate the circumstances, describe the offenders, analyze the case, and decide penalties. For difficult and serious cases, these prefectural judges or district magistrates would report to superior officials, and they often recorded the latter's responses.

What is the nature of these casebooks? What is their function in the local judicial process? There are several possibilities. They might be "collected writings" (*wenji*) by literati without any legal significance; or, at the other end of the spectrum, they could be seen as judicial "precedents" (*panli*) with legal binding force for their authors' contemporaries; or, in between, they could be considered judicial "archives" (*dang'an*), primarily historical in value but also with contemporary legal influence. In order to answer these questions, we need to examine the nature and function of "court opinions." In the local judicial process during the Ming, after judicial officials (prefectural judges or district magistrates) heard cases, they were required to compose court opinions—unless the matters involved were extremely minor.[5] Each court opinion would record the circumstances revealed by the hearings, provide an analysis regarding the offenses, and propose remedies—either naming penalties or requesting decisions from the superior offices.[6] For serious cases where heavy penalties were involved, these court opinions would have to be reported to superior offices. For cases that the officials could "handle by themselves" (*zili cisong*), court opinions could be written on the spot and announced to the litigants. After the trial, the responsible functionaries at government offices would compose the "verdicts" (*zhaoni*) on the basis of the court opinions.[7]

Court opinions and verdicts were related yet different judicial documents. The former constituted the basis of the latter, but they differed in content and format. Court opinions primarily contained the analysis of circumstances, interpretation of legal texts, and judicial reasoning supporting the application of sanctioning remedies. Their basic function was to justify the judicial decision, that is, to convince their readers (first the superior officials and litigants and then the general public after it was published) that the judicial rulings conformed to "sentiment, principle and law" (*qing li fa*). Consequently, a court opinion summed up case highlights rather than narrate the whole story. It pointed to general penalties (such as "penal servitude" or "beating with the heavy stick") rather than specifying them exactly. Verdicts, on the other hand, omitted the reasoning but narrated the details of the case and the specific penalties. As literary documents, court opinions followed no set form. The authors could use either ordinary classical prose or the more stylized antithetical rhetoric of parallel prose. Verdicts, however, were expected to use uniform language and follow a three-part pattern, that is, "description of facts" (*zhaoyou*), "application of legal stipulations" (*yiyou*), and "financial decision" (*zhaochu*).[8]

Although court opinions were not verdicts, as the summation of official judgments they formed the basis for verdicts. They were the official documents that were announced to plaintiffs and defendants and sent, when required, up to the superior officials together with the verdicts. Verdicts simply narrated the "facts," legal stipulations, and penalties; it was the court opinions that told readers why the judges believed the "facts" were true, that the selection of applicable law was correct, and that the penalties were appropriate. The late Ming magistrates' casebooks primarily contain such court opinions. In many instances, they also record superior officials' replies. They are literary "collected writings" in the sense that the judicial officials wrote, selected, and compiled them into personally authored books. These "writings," however, were original judicial documents. Since the casebooks are actually "collected court opinions," they can also be viewed as a part of judicial "archives" that record the actual legal practice at local courts.

MAO YILU AND HIS *COURT OPINIONS FROM SONGJIANG*

This chapter analyzes the role of law cases and the nature of judicial reasoning by focusing on a single casebook, Mao Yilu's *Court Opinions from Songjiang*, which contains the cases the author tried as the judge of Songjiang Prefecture in Nanzhili during the early seventeenth century.[9] Born to an old and prominent family in Sui'an, Zhejiang, he was appointed to the judgeship in Songjiang in 1604 after he passed the top level of the examinations and received the degree of palace graduate. During his tenure at Songjiang, he not only judged appellate cases, but also occasionally served as acting magistrate for the subordinate districts of Huating, Qingpu, and Shanghai.[10] In the only known biography of Mao, the author He Sanwei portrayed him as a model official with an impeccable reputation. Mao was honest in performing his official duties and rejected bribes from local functionaries.[11] He made district magistrates personally control account books of money and grain, thus eliminating possible fraud by scribes.[12] He also reformed the practice of transporting grain to the north, equalizing the burdens among the local areas.[13] But, according to He, Mao's major contributions to the government at Songjiang lay in education and law. In terms of education, Mao guided students at Confucian schools by commenting on their essays and supported them by donating his salary to improve school conditions. In 1622, fourteen candidates from Songjiang passed the metropolitan civil service examination and became palace graduates. Although by then Mao had left Songjiang, he was still credited as a success in "making scholars,"[14] and scholars in Shanghai erected a stele to eulogize Mao's virtues and achievements.[15] As for legal practice, Mao not only routinely tried and reviewed law cases from Songjiang and other prefectures, but also created the institution of "winter assizes" supplementing the "summer assizes" conducted in the hot months. These were occasions for the release of prisoners in doubtful cases or excusable circumstances.[16] In 1608, four years after Mao took up the office of prefectural judge, a succession of rainy days caused floods in the Wu area. Mao conducted the "summer assizes" one month early to release prisoners and severely punished those who committed crimes during the disaster period. Mao was credited with maintaining social order in Suzhou and Songjiang Prefectures, although all the crops were destroyed there.[17] It is interesting to note that when this laudatory biography was first published in 1623, Mao was near the height of his career. Although it is possible that the author intended to curry favor with him, the basic facts are confirmed by Mao's own official documents.

At the end of the Wanli reign (1573–1619), Mao served as transport-control censor (*xuncao yushi*),[18] involved in dredging the Jia River and maintaining the Grand Canal.[19] However, during the subsequent Tianqi reign (1621–1627), as the Grand Coordinator (*xunfu*)[20] of the Suzhou area, Mao was involved in the major court factional struggles between Donglin reformers and the powerful eunuch Wei Zhongxian (1568–1627).[21] As a supporter of Wei, Mao suppressed the unrest caused by the arrest of the upright scholar-official Zhou Shunchang (d. 1626)[22] and had a living shrine built for Wei at Suzhou.[23] In 1627, when the Chongzhen emperor (r. 1628–1644) took the throne and the Wei Zhongxian faction collapsed, Mao was incriminated as Wei's follower.[24] The shrine Mao built for Wei was then converted to a temple dedicated to the victims of Wei's terror. When Mao died suddenly in 1629 it was said he had been haunted by the ghosts of those victims.[25]

Court Opinions from Songjiang probably was published during the 1610s or early 1620s, well before the author's association with the eunuch dictator at court.[26] The text contains the court opinions that Mao Yilu wrote during his early career in Songjiang. The surviving text documents 183 law cases in no particular order. These involve a variety of issues from homicide, robbery, and salt smuggling to disputes over land ownership, debt, commerce, marriage, or bond servants, and cases of false accusation. Among these cases, most were submitted from district courts and retried by Mao at the appellate level. In turn, most cases were resubmitted by Mao to superior offices, petitioning for final judgment. Each entry starts with a title identifying the actual crime, the falsely charged crime, or the judge's task. A subheading names the superior office and its presiding official to whom the case was reported, together with the criminal/accuser's home district and personal name. The body of the opinion always opens with the phrase "It is heard in the preceding case that" (*qianjian shende*). It then briefly describes the criminals and narrates some key elements of the case. But the bulk of the text concentrates on analyzing the case by sorting out the facts, interpreting legal stipulations, and deliberating on special circumstances that would influence the selection of penalties. At the end the judge proposes a general penalty but without specifying the exact degree of punishment. In about fifty case entries, the written instructions from the superior offices are appended. Usually these instructions from above agree with Mao's judicial decisions and rule that the case can be closed. Occasionally, however, the superior officials modify Mao's rulings or remand a case back to him for retrial.

THE *CODE* AND *ITEMIZED REGULATIONS*: THE SOURCES OF RULE-BASED LEGAL REASONING

The Ming legal system was fundamentally rule based. Legal sources took the form of codified rules, which guided magistrates in solving legal problems. Rule-based legal reasoning entails deductive forms of argument. Imagined in the form of a syllogism, the codified rules serve as the first premise, while the facts of the law cases become the second premise. The basic formula appears as follows:

(A) Legal rule X, if violated, provides the remedy Y.
(B) Offender Z violates X

(C) Z, therefore, shall receive Y.

The judge's mission is to clarify the facts, select the rules, establish the relevant relationship between the facts and rules, and then reach a conclusion. In keeping with the principle that the ultimate source of law is the imperial command, the fundamental legal rules were laid out in the *Great Ming Code* (*Da Ming lü*) published in its final form in 1397, one year before the founding emperor's death.[27] Modeled after the codes of the previous Tang and Song dynasties and promulgated by the emperor Zhu Yuanzhang himself, this *Code* in 460 articles was expected to serve as the "constant law" of the land. Complementing the *Code* was the *Great Ming Commandment* (*Da Ming ling*), a body of codified rules issued in the first year of Zhu Yuanzhang's reign.[28] Over the course of the next two hundred years, adjustment of the law to fit changing circumstances took the form of successive supplementary "regulations" (*li*) often published under the rubric of "itemized regulations." (*tiaoli*). Because the *li* were issued in response to concrete situations, some Western scholars have imagined them as based on reasoning from cases and have therefore called them "precedents." Others, recognizing that the *li* had the force of supplementary law, have designated them as "substatutes." We believe that the word "regulations" best captures the normative tenor of this form of legislation.

Already during the Hongwu reign (1368–1398), the emperor Zhu Yuanzhang had promulgated a number of regulations to complement the *Code*. One of the most important was the *Itemized Regulations Regarding the Redemption of Punishments* (*Shuzui tiaoli*, 1397), which made most crimes in the *Code* redeemable with labor or money. In the subsequent reigns, more and more regulations were issued by the imperial court. During the Hongzhi reign (1488–1505), the court sorted out the existing regulations and compiled them into a single volume, *Itemized Regulations for Trying Penal Matters* (*Wenxing tiaoli*, 1500), which contained 281 articles.[29] Later on, during the Jiajing and Wanli reigns (1522–1566; 1573–1619), the *Itemized Regulations for Trying Penal Matters* was substantially revised (in 1555 and 1585), consisting of 385 and 382 articles, respectively.[30] In addition to this codified body of regulations, there were other separate regulations. An expanded *Itemized Regulations Regarding the Redemption of Punishments*, for example, was attached to the beginning of a number of commentaries to later editions of the *Great Ming Code*. These regulations not only stipulated new rules for the punishment of additional crimes not covered in the original 1397 *Code*, but also modified standing punishments in the *Code*.

What codified rules did Mao Yilu utilize in his legal reasoning and how did he present them? Conventional wisdom has it that by the late Ming, the *Great Ming Code* was little used in judicial process, almost becoming "a mere scrap of paper."[31] *Court Opinions from Songjiang* indicates the opposite. We find that Mao used the fundamental law extensively in his adjudication. In some cases, he directly quoted specific stipulations from the *Code*. In punishing a person who blinded his bondservant, for instance, Mao exactly quoted Article 337 of the *Code* on striking hired workers and incapacitating them (1.27a). To exonerate a person involved in a case of salt smuggling, Mao also directly quoted the rule that "only the persons and salt that are captured on the spot shall be handled" from Article 149 of the *Code* (1.2a).

In other cases, instead of quoting directly from the *Code,* Mao cited the crimes and punishments that are stipulated in it. In many cases involving false accusation (e.g., 7.29b), the judge stated that the criminals would be punished by "reciprocal punishment" (*fanzuo*) according to the *Code* (Art. 359).[32] In another example, when someone used fake silver, Mao sentenced him to penal servitude according to Article 383 of the *Code* on "counterfeiting silver" (3.39b).

In other cases, however, Mao simply meted out penalties according to the *Code* but did not specify which article he used. In one case, Mao sentenced a robber to "tattooing and penal servitude according to the *Code,*" which would be Article 291 (3.19a). In another case, Mao sentenced a so-called "rascal without resources" (*wuji guntu*) who defrauded others of their money and property to penal servitude "according to the *Code,*" which would be Article 297 (3.42a). In these cases, although Mao did not name the crimes in the language of the *Code,* we know from the context of his verdicts that he punished the robber for "taking away others' goods in daytime" and the rascal for "scheming and obtaining government or private property by deceit or cheating," respectively.

Sometimes Mao meted out punishments without mentioning the *Code.* For instance, some government functionaries extorted money from some commoners, and Mao judged that the former should "be punished by calculating the illicit goods" they received. Although Mao did not mention the legal basis of this ruling, we find that Article 371 of the *Code* states that if government officials or functionaries extort or borrow property from those within their areas of jurisdiction, they should be punished comparable to the crime of "accepting property without subverting the law" based on the value of the illicit goods. And Article 367 of the *Code* provides a table laying out the penalties for the given value of illicit goods. The *Great Ming Code,* therefore, served as an implied legal basis for making these judgments.

In a final pattern, Mao pointed out what was *not* stipulated in the *Code* and made his judgments accordingly. For instance, a bondservant named Zhang Feng died, leaving behind his wife and two sons. Feeling embarrassed to see his sister-in-law and nephews still working for their master, Zhang Feng's younger brother took them home. The master brought a lawsuit to the court, which sent runners to arrest the widow and her sons. The widow felt extremely humiliated and hanged herself at the master's house. Mao held that although the master did not kill the widow himself, he caused her to commit suicide; therefore, he was responsible for her death. Nevertheless, Mao continued, since the article titled "Using Coercion to Cause Others to Die" in the *Code* did not stipulate the crime and punishment for a master who caused his bondservant to die, the master should not be punished according to the *Code* (1.29b–30a). In this case, although the *Code* was not used to punish the wrongdoers, it still served as a key element in defining the crime and deciding the punishment.

In *Court Opinions from Songjiang,* we further find that Mao Yilu applied the *Itemized Regulations for Trying Penal Matters* to decide law cases in several ways.[33] First, he directly quoted the rules. When Mao doubted some circumstances in a forcible robbery case, he pointed out that the *Itemized Regulations for Trying Penal Matters* demanded that "In cases of forcible robbery . . . if illicit goods and weapons are not clear but seem doubtful, there is no harm in trying [the case] again."[34] Based on this procedural requirement, he reviewed the case and requested a reduced penalty for several defendants (3.5a–b). In another forcible robbery case, Mao quoted a regulation on "assailants carrying weapons and injuring others." He argued that this regulation specifically referred to the circumstance where offenders injured others; since here some offenders in the robbery case did not injure others, they should not be punished by the death penalty that was laid out in the *Itemized Regulations for Trying Penal Matters* (9.17b–18a).[35]

Furthermore, in another case involving a dispute over redeeming a piece of land, some people jointly struck the owner of the land and almost broke his finger. Mao cited the regulation on "wrangling" (*fenzheng*) and sentenced the leaders of the criminal gang to military exile (2.24a). Sometimes Mao simply punished criminals "according to regulations" without pointing out which specific regulation he used (9.5b).

The most extensive use of *Itemized Regulations for Trying Penal Matters* is seen in the "instructional replies" (*xiangpi*) attached to Mao's opinions. In *Court Opinions from Songjiang,* most of the extant 183 cases were sent to a superior office for instructional reply, which came from more than twenty officials in ten offices ranging from salt-control censor to river-patrol censor, regional inspector, and education inspector. To 50 cases Mao attached these "instructional replies," most of which seem to have constituted final decisions on those cases. In most of the 50 replies, the superior officials instructed Mao to "follow the suggested sentences" originally proposed. But they also converted the penalties, such as penal servitude or "beating with the heavy stick," into "redemption" by labor or money. Occasionally, the superior officials also added the penalty of the cangue or of an "extra" thirty or forty strokes of beating with the heavy stick (which could not be redeemed). All these measures were based on the *Itemized Regulations for Trying Penal Matters.*

In using the *Code* and the *Itemized Regulations for Trying Penal Matters,* Mao Yilu frequently analyzed and interpreted the intent, meaning, and elements of the rules and applied them to specific cases. In a case of homicide, Mr. Xia stabbed Mr. Ni with a knife, which caused Mr. Ni's death ten days later. At the district court, Mr. Xia was sentenced to decapitation for "deliberate killing" (*gusha*) according to the *Code* (Art. 313). In his appeal, however, Mr. Xia claimed that he only "injured" Mr. Ni "in play and by mistake" (*xiwu*) and should not be responsible for Mr. Ni's death, which occurred ten days later. Mao rejected the appeal in three steps. First, he refuted the assertion that Xia's intention was playful: a sharp knife was not a tool for practicing martial arts, and market streets were not the place for a contest of skills. Second, Mao inferred Mr. Xia's criminal intent from his acts. In Mr. Xia's original confession, he admitted that he "carried the knife and chased to stab" the victim. Mao pointed out that "carrying the knife" indicated the act of killing, and "chasing to stab" revealed that the victim was running away, not wrestling with the offender. In fact, after Mr. Xia injured Mr. Ni with the knife, he did not stop his assault. If the local constable had not taken away the knife, the victim would have died on the spot instead of lingering on for ten more days. This obviously suggested an intent to kill. In his final step, Mao made the judgment by connecting the intention of the defendant to the intent of the *Code*. He stated that the *Code*'s definition of "deliberate killing" focused on the perpetrator's "heart to kill." It had little to do with when the victim died. Mao, therefore, affirmed the original judgment (8.8a–9a).[36]

In short, *Court Opinions from Songjiang* shows that local judicial officials in the late Ming employed both the *Great Ming Code* and the *Itemized Regulations for Trying Penal Matters* in settling legal disputes. The judges and magistrates had to choose a specific rule in the law codes to define crimes and impose punishments, and they had to justify the choices by interpreting and analyzing the legal rules. In the two hundred years since its promulgation, the *Code* had not ceased to function as the basic legal source to promote justice among the populace. However, whether or not there were specific rules in the *Code*, judicial officials also looked to the *Itemized Regulations for Trying Penal Matters* either to find the extra remedies or to convert the punishments stipulated in the *Code* into redemptions listed in the *Itemized Regulations*. Working together, both the *Code* and the *Itemized Regulations for Trying Penal Matters* served as the basis for judicial officials' legal reasoning.

RULE-BASED ANALOGICAL REASONING

Ming law allowed legal reasoning by analogy but maintained the centrality of rules as the basis for analogical resemblance. While requiring that in deciding penalties it is imperative to cite the specific articles from the *Code* and the *Great Ming Commandment*,[37] the text of the *Code* admits that

> [t]he provisions in the *Code* and *Commandment* will not cover all matters. In cases where there is no specific statute for judging a crime, cite [a closely analogous statute in] the *Code* and decide the case by analogy. Propose whether the punishment shall be increased or reduced and submit it to the Ministry of Justice. After deliberation, it shall be memorialized to the throne. If someone decides the case without authorization and causes the punishment to be wrongly reduced or increased, he shall be punished on the basis of deliberately or negligently [reducing or increasing the punishment].[38]

Several interesting points can be found in this stipulation. The law admits that the scope of the established rules is limited in covering a complex world and thus permits judicial decision by analogy. The analogy, however, is not case based—it does not use previous law cases as precedents. Instead, it is still rule based, that is, what counts is the article from the *Code* that most closely resembles the circumstances. Furthermore, a case decided by analogy should be submitted to the central government and eventually obtain imperial approval. This procedural requirement, of course, aimed to curtail arbitrary decisions of judicial officials (by strengthening imperial authority), and it significantly reduced the possibility of the application of analogy in legal practice.

Indeed, to ensure the application of rule-based analogical reasoning, the *Code* particularly prohibits referring to specially decided cases to make legal judgments, even cases decided by the throne.

> The imperial decrees that decide penalties for individual cases as temporary expediencies and that are not promulgated as [a part of] the established *Code* shall not be cited analogically as [articles of] the *Code*. If they are cited analogically without authorization so that penalties are reduced or increased, [the officials] shall be punished on the basis of deliberately or negligently [exonerating the guilty or implicating the innocent].[39]

Within such a legal milieu, judges were discouraged from appealing to previous judicial decisions, even imperial ones.

The institution of rule-based analogical reasoning is broadened in the article "Doing What Ought Not to Be Done" (Buyingwei) in the *Code*. The article states that although a given act is not punished by either the *Code* or the *Commandment*, as long as it is considered inappropriate according to "principle" (*li*), it should be punished by either forty strokes of beating with the light stick or eighty strokes of beating with the heavy stick.[40] This catchall clause provided a flexible and practicable mechanism for judicial officials to settle legal disputes when they did not have fixed rules.

As shown in *Court Opinions from Songjiang,* the prefectural judge frequently could not find clear rules in either the *Code* or the *Itemized Regulations for Trying Penal Matters.* In this situation he neither searched for closely analogous articles from the law codes (a troublesome and wearying procedure) nor referred to any previous case decisions (as prohibited by the *Code*). Instead, he resorted to the article "Doing What Ought Not to Be Done" to make his judgments.

The case of Wang Xisi is illustrative of this. Wang and Mei Er, the bondservants of Qian Fenshan and Lu Shaozhuang, respectively, were often sent by their masters to cut wood and fish in coastal waters. One day, they joined some pirates and forcibly robbed a wheat merchant at Yangshan, one of the Zhoushan islands. After the crime came to light, both bondservants were sentenced to decapitation according to the *Code.* At the same time, their masters were accused of "harboring forcible robbers." But Mao found it difficult to convict the two masters, for the facts did not tally with the legal rules. In his analysis, he first stated the three defining characteristics of the crime as prescribed in the *Code* and *Itemized Regulations for Trying Penal Matters,* that is, formulating the plan, jointly plotting the act, and harboring two or more forcible robbers and sharing the illicit goods (*zang*) at home.[41] He then pointed out that in order to apply these rules, it was essential to find the accused guilty of formulating the plan or jointly plotting the robbery or of dividing the illicit goods after the act. But there was no evidence of such circumstances. For the masters, it was normal to send bondservants fishing and cutting wood. It was the bondservants' own decision to join the pirates and commit the crime; they did not discuss or plan the act with their masters at home. No illicit goods were ever found on the masters' property. Therefore, Mao ruled that he could not apply any one of the three circumstances to convict the two masters.

But Mao did not stop here. Although he found no legal rules to cite and no evidence of harboring forcible robbers, he was still deeply disturbed by the fact that these masters raised and housed criminal bondservants but could not restrain them. Eventually Mao punished them under the law "Doing What Ought Not to Be Done." They were sentenced to beating with the heavy stick according to the law, wearing the cangue, and compensating for the merchant's losses. In justifying his ruling, Mao noted that under the *Code,* were they accused of harboring forcible robbers, they could be charged only with formulating the plan or jointly plotting the act but not with acting themselves or sharing illicit goods. Under the *Code* such an offense was punishable by either penal servitude or beating with the heavy stick, both of which would be redeemed according to the *Itemized Regulations for Trying Penal Matters.* But if the masters were charged with "doing what ought not to be done," on the other hand, they could not only be sentenced to a (redeemable) beating, but could also be required to wear the cangue and pay heavily for the merchant's losses. By this, Mao concluded, the government could establish a "warning stone tablet" for those who allowed their bondservants to do wrong things or who knew about a robbery but did not report it to the authorities (2.1a–11a, esp. 8a–10b). Mao based both these judgments on a legal rule that allowed broad discretion to teach a lesson deemed beneficial to society.

In another dispute between relatives, the brothers Zhou Jin and Zhou Fang, in the course of an argument about land boundaries, started a fight over irrigation water one summer. Later, Zhou Jin's two sons and Zhou Fang's son joined the fight. When Zhou Fang's daughter-in-law saw that her husband was outnumbered, she tried to intervene but was "embarrassed and insulted." In her anger, she then hanged herself. Zhou Fang avenged his daughter-in-law's death by leading others to destroy Zhou Jin's house and compound. He also accused Zhou Jin of rape and homicide. Zhou Jin responded by charging Zhou Fang with looting his property. While Mao Yilu judged that neither the charge of rape nor that of looting was true, he held Zhou Jin's two sons responsible for the woman's death. Mao reasoned that the suicide was caused by their assault and battery. But Mao faced a problem: as relatives, the two sons' status was superior to that of their cousin's wife, and in the *Code,* there was no rule on "using coercion to cause others to die" where the aggressors were senior relatives of the victim. This meant that the two sons should not be tried as "ordinary persons." Mao, then, was caught in a dilemma: he did not have specific legal rules to handle the problem, but he could not release the two sons either. In the end, Mao again used the catch-all article of "Doing What Ought Not to Be Done" to settle the dispute. This way he could punish all sides: Zhou Jin and his two sons and their opponent Zhou Fang (Zhou Fang's son was spared, probably because he lost his wife). In addition, because Zhou Fang's family was in straitened circumstances but Zhou Jin's family was well to do, Mao ordered Zhou Jin to pay not only the burial expenses, but also five extra *liang* of silver to assist Zhou Fang's son's remarriage. By reconciling law and sentiment, Mao expressed the hope that his judgment would reach two goals: to preserve the harmony between the two brothers' families and to make fairness prevail so that Zhou Jin would accept the punishment from the bottom of his heart and Zhou Fang would also be satisfied with the decision (2.19b–2.21a).

SENTIMENT AND CIRCUMSTANCE: THE BASIS FOR PRACTICAL REASONING IN LEGAL CASES

As the previous two cases show, formal rules were not the only sources for judicial officials' reasoning. Use of the umbrella law on "Doing What Ought Not to Be Done" allowed the judge to consider the Confucian ethical implications of particular human relationships. Here the Ming legal system was also circumstance based. This was articulated in the rhetoric of *qing,* a word that can be rendered in

English as either "sentiment," as in "human sentiment" (*renqing*), or as "circumstances" in the sense of facts on the ground. In *Court Opinions from Songjiang,* the word *qing* refers both to legally pertinent circumstances and to particular human stipulations not specified in formal law. In the first sense it can mean the basic components of crime, such as the act of harboring robbers and the value of the illicit goods. Such facts (*qing*), which determine the degree of penalty the offenders will receive, are often anticipated in the codes. But the *qing* we discuss here refers to some human circumstances outside the law that generate special "sentiment." Such sentiment served as a factor that could alter the application of legal rules.

In his law enforcement, as *Court Opinions from Songjiang* shows, Mao Yilu appealed to *qing* as an essential factor in reaching his judgments. For example, one person falsely accused others after others falsely accused him. Should he receive a severe penalty according to the law? Or should he be punished leniently due to the circumstance that he was falsely accused first? Mao chose the latter (3.10a). In another example, a former functionary of the Huating District had just rented a piece of land. He wanted to drive away the former tenant and pull down his house, which was built on that field. Desperate, the former tenant falsely accused the former functionary of striking him. Mao held that although the former functionary was victimized by the false accusation and had the right to that piece of field as the new tenant, he was "beneath human sentiment" (*bujin renqing*) in the attempt to destroy the former tenant's house. Mao therefore sentenced both to beating with the heavy stick (3.12a–3.13a).

Ideally, sentiment and law should be in harmony: law should reflect sentiment, and sentiment as special circumstances was supposed to form one of the bases for legal norms. In the eyes of the Ming elite, the *Great Ming Code* embodied "Heavenly principle" and "human sentiment" when it established such principles as the "Ten Abominations," the "Eight Deliberations," and "remaining to support parents."[42] In reality, however, law and sentiment often conflicted. *Court Opinions from Songjiang* indicates that in the local judicial process, sentiment functioned in three ways vis-à-vis law codes.

First, sentiment supplemented law. When there were no applicable legal rules, sentiment was used to settle disputes. Mostly, sentiment incriminated litigants who would otherwise not be punished by law. The wealthy but stingy Wang Ren, for example, quarreled with his relatives and then was falsely accused by his uncle of harboring robbers. While Mao convicted the uncle of making false accusations as forbidden by law, he also condemned Wang Ren, the victim, for "treating kinsmen without affection which caused relatives to draw swords on each other." Both the false accuser and the falsely accused were sentenced to beating with the heavy stick (4.1a–4.4b). In another case, a Shanghai native named Cai sold some land. His former adopted son, named Xu, who had already returned to his own family and thus had nothing to do with the Cai family, redeemed the land with five *liang* of silver. However, Cai's nephew, who had been newly adopted to replace Xu, did not want to see the land fall into Xu's hands. So he falsely accused Xu of seizing tax grain. Xu argued that as Cai's former relative, it was not against "sentiment and principle" (*qingli*) for him to redeem Cai's abandoned property. Mao saw the matter differently. He concluded that both Xu, who redeemed his former adoptive father's land, and Cai's newly adopted son, who falsely accused Xu, acted out of greed. He ruled that Xu return the land to Cai's newly adopted son, but that he was entitled to a refund and would not need to perform any labor service based on the land (4.29b–4.30b). In the above two cases, both Wang and Xu were punished for violating the human relationships of kinship: neither unfeeling behavior toward kinsmen nor redeeming sold land was prohibited by law. Even though they were the victims of the original crimes of false accusation, they were seen as provoking that litigation and undermining social harmony. Where human relationships were concerned, considerations of sentiment provided alternatives to legal rules.

Second, sentiment was used to strengthen law by increasing the offenders' penalties. Take the case of Zhuang Ying as an example. Wanting to take his bondservant's wife, Zhuang blinded the bondservant. According to the *Code*, the household master who strikes hired workers to the point of incapacitation will be punished by penal servitude.[43] Mao believed that this penalty was far too lenient, as it could not match the cruelty of the crime. Since the law did not provide any other remedy, Mao imposed extra punishments on the basis of sentiment: Zhuang had to pay ten taels of silver to help the bondservant remarry, give ten *mu* (6,745 sq m) of land to support the victim, and allow him to return to the status of "respectable commoner" (*liang*) (1.25b–1.27b). In another example, one Li Yongbin not only committed adultery with the woman Yang, but also stole her deceased husband's property. According to law, Li was supposed to receive a beating with the heavy stick, which would then be redeemed. But Mao believed that such a penalty "was not severe enough to match the crime," so he proposed to add an extra beating that would actually be inflicted on the offender's body (8.23a–8.23b). In the above examples, Zhuang and Li saw their legally mandated penalties increased in the light of sentiment and circumstances.

Third, sometimes the appeal to sentiment counteracted the effects of the law code. A certain Zhang Er, for example, married another's man's wife who had the same surname as his own. To Mao, Zhang's act not only breached the law, but, more important, "violated the cardinal principles and virtues and bullied respectable people." According to the *Code*, such a marriage should be dissolved. Nevertheless, considering that Zhang and his illegitimate wife had already produced a child, Mao ruled that the couple keep their marital relationship. To compensate the victim for the loss of his wife, Mao further ordered that Zhang, together with the woman's father, who had assisted in this disposal of his daughter, pay eight *liang* of silver to the victim to cover the costs of remarrying (4.39a–4.40a). In another case, Jiang's bondservant Xue was so poor and sick that he had to sell his wife, Han, in order to survive. Jiang then asked another bondservant, Wang, to marry Han, because by matching two bondservants Jiang would not have to spend any money but be able to keep their labor. But the match between Wang and Han was not harmonious, which led to Han's suicide. Although Mao found no legal rules dealing with acts that led to another's suicide, he not only held Wang responsible for the death because he "did not treat her kindly," but also convicted the master, Jiang, for his "cruel heart" and "failure to take good care of Xue." This callousness had been the "incubator" (*tai*) of the tragedy. While Mao sentenced Wang and Jiang to beating with the heavy stick on the basis of sentiment, he acquitted Xue, the bondservant who had first sold his wife and then falsely accused his master of fornication with her. In spite of the fact that Xue had clearly broken the law against false accusations and wife sale, Mao's rationale was based on Xue's special circumstances. First, the bondservant sold his wife, undergoing the sorrow of "cutting out a piece of flesh to patch up a sore." Second, his ex-wife died, making him suffer the bitterness of "separating in life and parting in death." In addition, the illiterate bondservant's absurd complaint was drafted by a litigation specialist who "held the writing brush like a knife." Mao not only released Xue, but also ordered that the bondservant leave Jiang's household and become a "respectable person" because, since Xue had sued Jiang, the latter would certainly hate him (4.4b–4.6a). Here Mao's practical judgment aimed at restoring peace through addressing all sides of the human relationships that were caught up in the case.

Whether it supplemented, supported, or contradicted law, *qing* served alongside the legal code as one of the two basic elements in making judgments. Mao was, of course, clearly aware of the tension between sentiment and law. He viewed law as the "constant principle" (*jing*) and sentiment as "expediency" (*quan*). He admitted that from time to time he would have to modify legal rules in consideration of sentiment. This "violated 'constant principle' but enacted 'expediency'" (2.29b–2.30b).

Overriding legal rules by appealing to the practical reasoning implicit in the sentiment/circumstances of a case was in fact an age-old issue in Chinese legal culture. Even in pre-imperial times, Confucius (551–479 BCE) debated with his contemporaries regarding whether or not a son should turn in his father who stole their neighbor's sheep.[44] From the Han dynasty (206 BCE–220 CE) onwards, "human sentiment" gradually became an independent criterion for judicial officials to adopt in their adjudication.[45] To be sure, in the process of the Confucianization of law,[46] a number of statutes, such as "Eight Deliberations" and "Remaining to Support Parents," embedded specifically Confucian moral relationships into the statutory framework of law. Nevertheless, sentiment/circumstances continued to function as a strong factor that counterbalanced statute. In the early Ming dynasty, while the founding emperor Zhu Yuanzhang emphasized the significance of law in strengthening governmental institutions, he personally "sacrificed law to promote sentiment/human relationships" (*qufa shenqing*) by, for example, pardoning the criminal who was the only son of his old parents[47] and releasing the prisoner whose son petitioned to be allowed to be punished in his father's place.[48] Mao, together with his late-Ming colleagues, carried on the tradition when considerations of sentiment/circumstances seemed to them more appropriate than the resources of formal law.

In appealing to sentiment/circumstances, Mao often articulated particular purposes in justifying his decisions. Among these were the following types of moral considerations.

1. Retribution: Mao suggested that unless murderers were executed, "the dead would not rest in peace and the living would not close their mouths" (3.9b, 8.7a).
2. General deterrence: Mao petitioned to place the offenders in a cangue to establish "a warning" to those who formed gangs or who betrayed their household masters (3.21a, 7.33b, 9.23a).
3. Rehabilitation: Mao inflicted light penalties or applied the article "Doing What Ought Not to Be Done" in the *Code* (Art. 410) to offenders in the same lineage or family so as to maintain "lineage bonds" (*zuyi*), "natural ties" (*tianxing*), or "kinship" (*qinyi*) (7.19b, 7.25a, 7.29a). Mao also emphasized the rehabilitation of offenders to reform social mores. He aimed to eradicate so-called "wicked customs," especially the "custom" of false accusation (3.11b, 3.13a, 8.39a, 9.23a). He hoped to transform the so-called brutality and greed of offenders and replace them with a "human heart" (4.11a, 4.30a, 8.3a–8.3b).
4. Social stability: Mao would sacrifice the interests of the innocent and satisfy the demands of wrongdoers in order to "nip litigations in the bud" (1.32a, 1.39a, 2.29b, 3.11b, 3.13a, 4.26a, 4.30a, 8.39a, 9.20a).
5. Penal justice: Mao held that he paid special attention to the severity of punishment to ensure that his decisions would be neither "harsh" (*ke*, 2.36a–2.36b), "excessive" (*she*, 2.36a–2.36b), "wrong" (*yuan*, 2.25a, 3.7a), "unjust" (*wang*, 2.14a, 2.24b), nor "indulgent" (*zong*, 2.24b). Apparently, Mao did not believe that a reliance on legal rules alone would reach these practical goals of morality and fairness.

In turning to *qing* as the basis of legal reasoning, Mao emphasized the particularity of each case and paid close attention to individual situations. With considerable discretionary power, the prefectural judge proceeded to reach case-by-case judgments. Because of the specific circumstances, each case became a unique event, and the judicial result turned out to be flexible. Practical reasoning, then, sought not to apply legal rules strictly and mechanically but to achieve a social goal with flexible means. The general and fixed law codes were modified by particular and ever-changing circumstances.

"SATISFYING BOTH SENTIMENT AND LAW": FAIRNESS-CENTERED JUDICIAL REASONING

Although legal rules, as set forth in the *Code* and *Itemized Regulations for Trying Penal Matters,* and informal circumstances, as articulated in the rhetoric of "sentiment," were two different factors in Mao Yilu's judicial reasoning, they were not treated separately. In many cases in *Court Opinions from Songjiang,* Mao and his superiors tried actively to "adjudicate between sentiment and law" (*tiaoting yu qingfa zhijian,* 2.8a, 7.2b) and thus "satisfy both sentiment and law" (*qingfa liangping,* 2.6a, 3.29b). Their ultimate goal was to achieve harmony and fairness in society, and their judicial reasoning was based on both legal rules and sentiment/circumstances. In the case of the widow Xue, for instance, she, together with her young grandson, falsely accused a certain Tang of "destruction" (*jiaosha*). Her real intention, however, was to take back the land that her deceased husband had sold. At the initial trial, a judge commiserated with the lonely and helpless widow and boy and thus ruled that Xue be allowed to redeem all the land. Mao saw this lawsuit as "contravening both principle and law" (*yuli yufa juzuo*). From the law's point of view, the *Itemized Regulations for Trying Penal Matters* prohibits a complete redemption. From the point of view of principle, the land had been sold ten years earlier and had passed through three owners since then. If the land could be redeemed by Xue, it could also be redeemed by all the other owners. If land could be redeemed by any seller at any time, how could the interest of the buyer be protected and how could ownership rights be secured? Although the widow and boy deserved sympathy, Mao argued that "the *Code* and *Itemized Regulations* should not be violated, and wicked customs should not be encouraged." Nevertheless, desiring mercy for the widow and orphan, Mao "deliberated on the middle way between sentiment and law" (*can qingfa zhi zhong*) and ruled that Xue redeem half of the land and Tang keep the other half for his livelihood. But Mao's message to all other sellers was that Xue was able to redeem some of the land only because of her special circumstances and that due to legal regulations she was still not able to redeem all the land. This judgment, Mao believed, preserved the law and safeguarded people's property on the one hand and did not contradict the lower court's ruling providing succor for widows and youngsters (2.33a–2.34a). In this case, Mao acknowledged the tension between sentiment and law and intentionally adopted the "middle way" by partially sacrificing yet preserving both of them.

Indeed, balancing sentiment and law could be difficult, as these two elements often contradicted each other. Sometimes sentiment would weigh in to increase or reduce a penalty that was prescribed by law; on other occasions, after sentiment was considered, in the end legal remedies prevailed. The judge, however, seemed to have endeavored to locate the "happy medium" that could provide the sense of fairness to community members. In many cases, Mao first pointed to the legal rules relevant to a case and then provided alternative remedies by "only considering" or "reluctantly considering" sentiment and circumstances.

In balancing legal rules and sentiment/circumstances, however, Mao did not treat these two fundamental elements equally. Generally speaking, the former were more important than the latter. In every judicial decision, it was imperative to cite legal rules, whereas appeals to sentiment/circumstances were not required. More important, from time to time, when sentiment and law conflicted, judicial officials would override sentiment by sticking to legal rules. In the aforementioned case of Li Yongbin, the "seductive woman" Yang, over a period of ten years, engaged in adultery, changed husbands seven times, fornicated with bondservants, neighbors, and even strangers, and squandered her deceased husband's property. Mao ordered that she be driven out of her husband's family and be remarried under the direction of her younger brother. In Mao's eyes, Yang's "ludicrous acts" were too numerous to record; nevertheless, the judge admitted that "although the circumstances were most hateful, there were no other legal remedies that could be imposed" (*qing shen kehen, fa wu kejia*, 8.23a–8.24b). In this case, then, Mao on the one hand proposed to increase the penalty for Li (Yang's adulterer) due to consideration of sentiment; on the other hand, he left the ruling for Yang unchanged although sentiment pointed to grave culpability. While such inconsistency might suggest the judge's struggle in balancing sentiment and law, it could also reveal the importance he attached to legal regulations.

In an even clearer case, Xue Feng, in the initial trial, was sentenced to strangulation for committing a third robbery on the basis of the *Code*'s version of "three strikes and you're out." In the appellate trial, however, Mao pointed out that the use of the *Code* was mistaken. He argued that the *Code* explicitly provided that the "three strikes" limit should count only in cases where the offenders were tattooed.[49] Although Xue committed three robberies, he had not been tattooed as punishment for the second robbery because his mother returned the stolen items to the victim before Xue was seized by authorities. According to the *Code*, if the robbers' close relatives turn in the robbers or return the property to the owners, it shall be considered the same as if the robbers voluntarily confessed to the authorities in person.[50] For Xue, therefore, his mother's act reduced his penalty two degrees according to the *Code* and thus exempted him from tattooing according to the *Itemized Regulations for Trying Penal Matters.*[51] Since Xue had been tattooed only once before, the penalty of strangulation would not conform to law, although it might not contradict sentiment. Mao believed that the evidence for the robber's three crimes was irrefutable. As for considerations of sentiment, he found the offender "an habitual robber" unwilling to reform. This was precisely the very kind of criminal Mao would have liked to punish. Nevertheless, he weighed law against sentiment and eventually chose the former, proposing the *Code*'s penalty of penal servitude (4.19a–4.20b).

It is worth noting that although Mao, as a prefectural judge, enjoyed tremendous discretionary power, his reasoning was subject to review by his superiors. And occasionally Mao's opinions were overruled on the grounds that law should not be sacrificed. In the case of Wang Liu, for example, Wang He tried to redeem the land his father had sold to Wang Shan years earlier. Although it was against the law to redeem the land, Wang He insisted on his right to buy it back because his house and ancestral tombs were located there. At the district court, the magistrate had already ordered that Wang He be allowed to redeem four *mu* (2,698 sq m) of land. But Wang He was not satisfied. In order to obtain more, he let his brother Wang Liu falsely accuse Wang Shan of homicide. At the appellate court, Mao reconciled law and sentiment on the basis of two issues. First, on the redemption of land, Mao realized that it was contrary to law to redeem the land; to Wang He, therefore, receiving four *mu* had already been a "luxury." However, considering that the redeemed land did not include Wang He's residence and ancestral tombs, Mao was concerned that the dispute would not be settled. So he ruled that in addition to the four *mu*, Wang He be allowed to redeem half of the rest of the land so that he on the one hand could maintain his house and ancestral tombs, and on the other would not use the issue as an excuse to lodge further lawsuits. Wang Shan, the current owner of the land, would retain the rest of the property. Second, concerning Wang Liu's false accusation, it was clear to Mao that the accuser was subject to "reciprocal punishment" according to law. But the judge again considered that as Wang He's blood brother, Wang Liu's false accusation "involved sentiment and circumstance" (*qingzi xiangguan*). So Mao reduced the penalty from penal servitude to beating with the heavy stick. However, Mao's superior, the salt-control censor, disagreed with Mao's opinion: "The land dispute may be handled with appeal to sentiment; but the false accusation of homicide must be punished according to law." He remanded the judgment and urged Mao to decide the penalty on the basis of the *Code.* After retrial, Mao eventually sentenced Wang Liu to penal servitude according to the law code (1.38a–1.40b).

This case interests us in several respects. Clearly, the prefectural judge's discretionary power was limited; his reasoning to favor sentiment and circumstance or legal rules would be checked by other authorities in the judicial system. In this system, the dynamic interaction between the district magistrate, the prefectural judge, and the investigating censor seems often to have focused on the balance of sentiment and law. In Wang Liu's case there had been no question about the facts, but at each level, the adjudicating official made a different decision. Although each higher authority altered the judgment submitted from below, they all had the same mission: to balance sentiment and law properly. Even when the highest court, the investigating censor, ruled to ensure the enforcement of legal rules, its practice was based on a shared mission.

When sentiment and law were balanced in adjudication, the result was often a judgment punishing both plaintiffs and defendants in lawsuits, but also granting the offenders what they demanded. For example, Zhuang Qin, an estate manager, refused to extend the tenancy of a destitute bondservant, Dai Si, even though the latter claimed a right to use the land. When Dai Si's wife, Zhou, committed suicide due to a domestic quarrel, Dai Si went to court to accuse Zhuang of responsibility for her death.

Mao's adjudication in this case was based more on moral sentiment than legal statutes. No matter how "mean" the bondservant manager might have been, there was no indication that he broke any legal statute. On the contrary, he was not responsible for Zhou's death and so was a victim of a false accusation. And as the estate manager, he was probably entitled to make the decision regarding whether or not he would rent out land to tenants. However, in order to assist the destitute (enabling Dai to make a living) and promote a sense of fairness (comforting Zhou's soul in the netherworld), Mao punished the manager according to considerations of human sentiment, ordering him to pay Dai restitution money (for burying the dead and repairing his house) and accordingly also to rent the land to him. For the statutory criminal, Dai, who made the false accusation, Mao on the one hand punished him according to law with a beating with the heavy stick, and on the other hand granted him what he requested—rights to his nephew's tenancy of land and house. Here every consideration was aimed at maintaining a fair and harmonious society instead of enforcing legal rules strictly (3.28a–3.29b). This case resembles many others in late-Ming casebooks in that the judge ended up punishing litigants on both sides, while at the same time mediating the concrete claims to restore stable social relationships.

It should be noted that balancing sentiment and law was praised as a judicial virtue. In his preface to Mao's *Court Opinions from Songjiang*, the prefect of Songjiang, Zhang Jiude, followed many Ming administrative guidebooks when he emphasized the classical precedents for such jurisprudence. Quoting the statement from the *Book of Changes*—"[In deciding] major or minor cases, sentiment must be taken into account"—Zhang contended that there was no difference between law and sentiment. What Mao did, according to Zhang, was to gain an understanding of sentiment and circumstance from the litigants and accordingly punish them by law, only hoping that there would be no mistake and, ultimately, that punishments would cease to be used.[52] To make fairness prevail, the truly good judge sees the underlying harmony of law and sentiment and rules accordingly.

Legal rules, then, were only one aspect of fairness-centered judicial reasoning. Judicial officials were expected to deliberate on law, sentiment, and principle. The dependence on multiple elements weakened the authority of legal rules and made it difficult to predict the outcome of adjudication, which suggests judicial officials' tremendous discretionary power. Nevertheless, the lack of predictability in adjudication did not necessarily make people shy away from the courts. On the contrary, men and women, young and old, rich and poor, entered law courts, resorting to any means, legal or illegal, to seek entitlements. They were willing to risk the likelihood of punishment, hoping to achieve their goals in one way or another, because the essence of this fairness-centered adjudication focused on balancing the interests of all adjudicating parties. The plaintiff who brought a false accusation into court in fact was counting on the judge to see beyond the charge to a network of circumstances in light of which he or she deserved a remedy. It was rather ironic that while this system aimed at eliminating lawsuits in society, it instead might have encouraged people to generate lawsuits, with all the resulting tension in local communities and even families. Still, although fairness-centered reasoning confirmed the significance of officials' adjudicative authority, it did not necessarily lead to arbitrary decisions. For one thing, their choices and decisions would undergo review and require approval by the higher authorities in the system. For another, their adjudication was guided and checked by a shared legal culture across the empire. Solving legal problems by resorting to the triad of law, principle, and sentiment was what judicial officials were taught to do, and they felt proud of having achieved that. The casebooks, then, are the records of such achievements.

MEDIATION VERSUS ADJUDICATION IN MING LAW

How do we assess the nature of fairness-centered judicial reasoning? In his study of the civil judicial system in the Qing dynasty, Shiga Shūzō examines the application of law, sentiment, and principle in legal practice and asserts that magistrates engaged in "didactic conciliation" and that their judicial activity "was strongly colored by mediation."[53] Philip Huang, however, finds that in most of the Qing law cases he collected magistrates made their decisions according to law instead of finding "face-saving compromises." In other words, they acted like judges rather than mediators in the formal adjudication. Only occasionally, Huang says, did magistrates impose "compromises in the interest of 'harmony'" and become "indeed more mediators and administrators than judges." In such cases, "the magistrate's role was more administrative than adjudicatory," and "he was more a mediator than a judge applying the law. But such cases were clearly rare."[54]

While these two scholars deal primarily with the judicial system in the Qing, their arguments are pertinent to other time periods in Chinese history, including the Ming. Let us put the question of whether the Qing judicial system was "civil" aside in this chapter.[55] It seems to us that although they disagree with each other, Shiga and Huang share a common stance: they assume the Western dichotomy between adjudication and mediation. Looking at Chinese legal culture through such a lens, they must make an "either/or" choice: was legal practice in the Qing "mediatory" or "adjudicatory"? The difference between their arguments, then, lies primarily in quantity rather than quality. Namely, although Huang challenges Shiga's proposition, he still finds 11 cases, or 5 percent of the 221 cases in his sample, where magistrates did act as arbitrators.[56] But fairness-centered judicial reasoning as reflected in the late-Ming casebooks suggests a different approach, a holistic understanding of the Chinese judicial system. It was normal and desirable for judicial officials to reason on the basis of particular circumstances and the moral sentiments of human relationships as well as legal rules. They did not distinguish between "mediatory" and "adjudicatory" activities, but endeavored to make judgments by considering and balancing various elements. When human relations and circumstances were incorporated, the judicial officials' goal went well beyond "saving face" by employing "compromises"; instead, they intended to achieve fairness by deliberating on "sentiment." The bifurcation of "a formal system guided mainly by adjudication and an informal system guided mainly by compromise"[57] did not exist in the Ming. Ming adjudication, instead, combined both formal and informal, statutory and mediating functions. Mediation, if we do want to call it that, constituted an integral part of Ming court adjudication. Most cases in *Court Opinions from Songjiang* were adjudicated by reasoning on the basis of both statute and sentiment. It seems that there was a consensus in Ming judicial circles that the legal rules, in one way or another, were deficient in creating fair judgments. Combining and balancing various elements became the basic feature of the "formal justice system" practiced at local (and central) government offices. Furthermore, incorporating circumstantial elements into legal decisions did not necessarily mean that judicial officials would judge law cases arbitrarily. On the contrary, they were guided by a lofty ideal (of the Confucian Way, or Dao) to achieve fairness and harmony in society, and the third pillar of jurisprudence, principle (or *li*), alluded to this. They were also restrained by an elaborate judicial system. To be sure, as the cases in this chapter indicate, judicial officials often did not agree with each other on what elements they should consider and to what degree they should apply different criteria for judgment, but making different and even conflicting interpretations of rules has been a perennial feature in all legal cultures.

CONCLUDING REMARKS: THE ROLE OF THE CASE IN MING JURISPRUDENCE

Ming casebooks of "court opinions" are personally authored summaries of judgments in cases that came before a local judicial official. Though technically not "verdicts," they are part of the documentary record of individual cases and so can be viewed as actual legal archives. In these casebooks we can see that Ming legal practice was based on statutory rules, but also on the moral norms of "principle" and "sentiment" evaluated in the context of circumstance. Judgments aimed at fairness, which was not expediency, and not at some abstract universal justice, but rather a solution that would be recognized as equitable in a particular, historical legal culture.

In *Court Opinions from Songjiang,* some cases show legal reasoning as the matching of legal requirements; others appeal not to statutory rules but to Confucian moral norms and human relationships that were implicit standards for judgment. Legal reasoning appears impossible to divorce from the narrative of a set of legal circumstances. It is in keeping with this approach that we reject the thesis that the informal judgments invoking "principle" and "sentiment" are mediation rather than judicial decisions. Law cases, then, are where we see the judicial efforts to balance the ideal of harmony with the reality of conflict, written rules with the more general principle of fairness and specific circumstances of crimes.

To be sure, casebooks were not case laws. The authors of the extant late-Ming casebooks never cited a previous case decision as a precedent to settle legal disputes. In his recent article on the role of case precedent in the Qing judicial process, R. Randle Edwards observes that "[n]ot unlike judges in the Anglo-American common law system, Qing judges were obliged to 'treat like cases alike.'"[58] If case precedent is defined as previous court decisions with legal binding authority "for an identical or similar case afterwards arising or a similar question of law,"[59] the judicial obligation in the Qing as observed by Edwards cannot be found in Ming adjudication.

But those who compiled and published Ming casebooks did aim to influence judicial activities and educate the general public. Two prefaces to *Court Opinions from Songjiang* elaborate on Mao's mission "to rescue the world." The preface by Zhu Xun views court judgments as the "explications of Heavenly [Way]" (*tian zhi wei*). It praises Mao's judicial records as evidence of "acting by following the Heavenly way." If everybody followed Mao's example, punishments would be put aside and the realm pacified.[60] The other preface by the prefect of Songjiang, Zhang Jiude, also exalts Mao's efforts in making fair judgments, citing the Confucian ideal of a world where punishments will cease to be used.[61] If common people were supposed to learn good conduct from the cases, judicial officials were provided with examples of judgments that embodied fairness-centered judicial reasoning. In these ways casebook authors expected to influence their colleagues of the same or future generations by publishing their court opinions.

If Ming magistrates never turned to cases as precedents to guide judgment, did this mean, then, that Ming lawmakers were never engaged in "thinking with cases" to make new law? For a final exploration of this complicated question, we look at our late Ming judge's opinions in comparison with the pronouncements of the sovereign, the empire's supreme source of judicial authority. In the early years of the dynasty, it happened that the founding Hongwu emperor not only judged cases and decided on punishments for individual offenders, but also compiled a 236-article summary of his case rulings and promulgated it as the *Grand Pronouncements* (*Dagao*). Indeed, the *Grand Pronouncements,* the product of imperial legislation, became case law due to its authorship. When the first compilation of the text was published, Zhu Yuanzhang ordered that every household possess a copy of this law. Those who committed lesser crimes punishable by beating with the light or heavy stick, penal servitude, or life exile could have their penalties reduced by one degree if they had a copy of the legal text, and their punishments would be increased by one degree if they did not.[62] When the second and third compilations were finished, Zhu declared that those who did not respect and accept the text were not his "reformed" subjects and thus should be banished from the Chinese empire.[63] Zhu further made it clear that the text had to be studied in government schools and used in civil service examinations.[64] It is said that in 1392 more than 190,000 teachers and students who taught and studied the text were granted an audience at court and rewarded by the emperor.[65] Yang Yifan finds a number of articles in the *Grand Pronouncements* that show how the law was implemented and concludes that the *Grand Pronouncements* took effect with legally binding force on the very day it was issued.[66]

The contrast between imperial cases that made law and court opinions that merely made an individual case for a specific ruling can be seen by comparing the two texts from the perspective of legal discourse. In both collections we find three basic modes of legal discourse. The first is narrative discourse, giving an account of what happened in the case. The second is analysis discourse, which examines the truth or falsehood of the accusations and depositions, decides the rights and wrongs of the litigants, interprets legal rules, considers extra-legal circumstances, and explains why a particular penalty is inflicted. The third is policy discourse, which sets up rules for the audience to observe and thus transforms cases into law.[67]

Both *Court Opinions from Songjiang* and the *Grand Pronouncements* narrated the basic facts concerning the crime: they identified the offenders and the victims, described the offenses, and pointed out the social damage these caused. Both condemned the offenders and offenses with value-laden phrases such as "rascals" (*tu*), "villains" (*gun*), "good-for-nothings" (*wulai*), "fools" (*shuzi*), and "gangs" (*dang*). Nevertheless, compared to Zhu Yuanzhang, Mao Yilu was far more vehement in the pejorative rhetoric he used to denounce the offenders, regularly resorting to animal metaphors to characterize their persons and acts, such as "being covetous like wolves and quarrelsome like sparrows." By comparison, although the *Grand Pronouncements* is well known for its colloquial expressions, Zhu kept more to basic legal terms to define offenders and offenses. Obviously the rhetorical burden of proof lay more heavily on the magistrate than on the emperor.

The differences between *Court Opinions from Songjiang* and the *Grand Pronouncements* appear even more clearly in their use of analysis and policy discourses. In the former, analysis discourse constituted the lengthiest and most important part of each judgment. Its argument involved a variety of issues, including clarifying facts (especially from false accusations), selecting and interpreting legal rules, considering nonlegal factors, sorting out evidence, rebutting opposing opinions, and finding relevant relationships between rules and facts. To show his reader that he reached reasonable judgments, Mao emphasized the significance of evidence. Generally speaking, witnesses' testimonies were crucial (8.31b). For robbery, the illicit goods and the property owners' identification of them were most important (2.2a, 3.19b, 4.29a). For commercial transactions, contracts, account books, and other types of documents were essential (4.42a, 7.36b–7.39a, 8.28b). For marriages, marriage contracts or betrothal papers were to be examined (4.40b). Lengthily and extensively, then, Mao's analysis discourse explained and justified his judicial decisions. Through his careful choice of sources, use of evidence, and rationalization for a specific punishment, he hoped to win the approval of his superiors and the acceptance of the litigants.

The *Grand Pronouncements,* however, was largely indifferent to analysis discourse. Without offering any reasoning or analysis, the text reads like a collection of straightforward declarations or announcements. In particular, the *Grand Pronouncements* seldom quoted the *Code,* the fundamental law of the dynasty, to add legal legitimacy to its judgments. Even in cases where Zhu Yuanzhang might easily have used the *Code,* he neither mentioned the dynastic law nor specified any sources for his legal reasoning.[68] In addition, in most cases, Zhu ignored the *Code* and inflicted penalties on offenders based on his own understanding of the nature and social damage of the offenses, and his penalties were much harsher than what the *Code* provided.[69] The emperor claimed that the "extra-legal" punishments he employed were essential to eliminate social "evils" and promote Confucian values.[70] In essence, the justification for the judgments in the *Grand Pronouncements* derived not from any legal text or judicial reasoning, but straightforwardly from the imperial person's authority as its author. The legal decisions did not need any analysis to show how they were made or display any evidence for factual support. The truth of the facts and the correctness of the judgments did not need to be particularly justified and could not be questioned.

Finally, policy discourse is what lays out rules for the audience. Reversing the pattern we have seen with analysis discourse, policy discourse makes up the most important component in the *Grand Pronouncements* but is absent from *Court Opinions from Songjiang.* In the *Grand Pronouncements,* policy discourse is found in three forms. First, in all four imperial prefaces to the four compilations of the *Grand Pronouncements,* Zhu explicitly ordered that every subject (the audience of the first three compilations) and military officer (the audience of the fourth compilation) observe it as a "treasure for [their] happiness and longevity"[71] and accept its words as "my admonitions." These imperial prefaces defined the entire text as a set of coercive norms that were not to be violated. Second, many specific articles in the *Grand Pronouncements* laid down rules without any reference to a specific law case. Article 30 of the first compilation, for instance, does not mention any specific offenders, but simply states a rule prohibiting Buddhists and Daoists from associating themselves with secular or official society.[72]

In his third approach to policy discourse, Zhu used the *Grand Pronouncements* to make rules on the basis of law cases. The pattern of most articles of the text was first to describe the offenders and offenses and point out the social harm resulting from the crime, and then either explicitly to create a rule based on the case or to imply that the penalty inflicted should be used to punish similar crimes in the future. In *Court Opinions from Songjiang,* no entry sets up any rule for its audience to follow. The prefectural judge's mission was rather to understand and apply the existing rules than create new ones. To be sure, Mao also petitioned his superiors to allow certain special punishments as warnings to future criminals. When he believed that the penalties stipulated in the existing law were not severe enough, he would propose imposing the irregular method of "wearing the cangue" on the criminals so as to "generate warnings" for those who, in the future, would "help others do evil" (2.32b), "form a gang" (3.21a), "assist in striking others" (7.33b), "betray one's master" (9.23a), and so forth. These warnings, however, aimed only at compelling people to abide by the established *Code* and *Itemized Regulations for Trying Penal Matters;* the author would not expect that his proposals, if approved, would become standards for other judges and the general public to follow.

The *Grand Pronouncements* shows how cases that reached the emperor might inspire new laws, a process that indeed may have lain behind many of the supplementary "regulations" that accumulated over the course of the dynasty and had to be considered by magistrates like Mao. But Ming authorities who directed the imperial legal bureaucracy were uncomfortable with case-based jurisprudence, even when the emperor was the judge. Right after Zhu Yuanzhang's death the legitimacy and effectiveness of the *Grand Pronouncements* began to be questioned,[73] and by the mid-Ming, the legal relevance of the *Grand Pronouncements* lay only in the convention by which criminals would have their penalties reduced one degree if they possessed a copy of the text.[74] We have already noted the article in the *Code* itself forbidding magistrates to use imperial case rulings as precedents. Previous case decisions, imperial or otherwise, in order to attain binding legal force, would have to undergo a complex legislative process in which specific law case decisions would be turned into abstract legal rules (i.e., "regulations") that had to be followed by judicial officials across the empire.[75]

In short, the *Grand Pronouncements* shows not only how different the narrative and rhetorical organization of case narratives may be, but also how, considered by the center, cases may lie behind the making of new legal rules. From the other side, Mao's court opinions show how an individual judge's cases both reveal the limitations of the *Code* and are the only way to show how judicial officials dealt with them. Though previous case decisions were never mentioned in court opinions, the appeal to "sentiment" and "principle" became an integral part of the adjudication documented in case records while the need to balance both legal rules and nonlegal circumstances was adopted as a judicial principle and ethical standard. Emphasizing nonlegal "sentiment" yet downplaying early imperial legal decisions became a paradoxical feature of Ming adjudication.

APPENDIX: THE FIVE OTHER KNOWN MING CASEBOOKS

1. Li Qing (1602–1683). *New Words on Deciding Cases* (*Zheyu xinyu*). Composed when the author served as prefectural judge (*tuiguan*) in Ningbo Prefecture, Zhejiang. Ten *juan* (chapters), 200 cases under the follow headings: marriage, inheritance, property, fraud, fornication, robbery, money and grain, mistaken acts, serious offenses, and unjust verdicts.
2. Yan Junyan (*jinshi* 1628). *Court Opinions Drafted at Mengshui Studio* (*Mengshuizhai cundu*). Case decisions collected during the author's tenure as judge of Guangzhou Prefecture. Twenty-two *juan*, 1,438 cases under the following headings: investigation, judgment, reversal of verdicts, compassionate trial, and official dispatch.
3. Zhang Kentang (*jinshi* 1625). *Words of Deep Cultivation* (*Xunci*). Records the author's law enforcement efforts as magistrate of Xunxian, Beizhili, from 1625 to 1634. Twelve *juan*, 300 cases.
4. Qi Baojia (1602–1645, *jinshi* 1622). *Court Opinions from Puyang* (*Puyang yandu*). Written when the author served as judge of Xinghua Prefecture, Fujian, from 1622 to 1631. Thirteen hundred case judgments.

5. Qi Baojia. *Draft Court Opinions from Cases Personally Tried in the Wu Region* (*An Wu qinshen xigao*). Records the judgments by the author when he served as investigating censor in Suzhou and Songjiang between 1633 and 1635. More than 140 cases.

NOTES

This essay grew out of our papers presented at the Southern California China Colloquium "Looking for Cases in Song and Ming Law" held at UCLA, May 17, 2003. At that conference, organized by Prof. Charlotte Furth, Wu Yanhong delivered a paper titled "Case Collections as Legal Documents" and Jiang Yonglin a paper on "Discourse and Casebook Formation in the Late Ming Dynasty." We thank, among many others, Charlotte Furth, Bettine Birge, Brian McKnight, Hugh Scogin, Edward Farmer, and Ann Waltner for their insightful comments.

1 *Bibu zhaoni leichao* (Record of classified verdicts from the Ministry of Justice), e.g., contains the original verdicts presented by the Ministry of Justice for imperial decision during the Jiajing reign (1522–1566); *Sichuan gedi kan'an ji qita shiyi dangce* (Law cases and related archival records from various places in Sichuan) includes the original verdicts from a number of prefectures, subprefectures, and districts in Sichuan Province during the same period. Wu Yanhong has punctuated the latter text, which will be published in the series of Chinese casebooks edited by Yang Yifan at the Law Institute of the Chinese Academy of Social Sciences.

2 Fuma Susumu has found nearly twenty such texts from the late-Ming period, including *The Posthumous Writings of Xiao and Cao* (*Xiao-Cao yibi*) and *The Candle That Illuminates the Sky in the Legal Forest* (*Falin zhaotian zhu*). See Fuma, "Shōshi hihon *Xiaocao yibi*." For a brief discussion of such works, also see Macauley, *Social Power and Legal Culture.*

3 See, e.g., *Xinmin gong'an.*

4 See, e.g., Wu Ne's *Xiangxing yaolan* and Zhang Jiude's *Zheyu yaobian.*

5 She Ziqiang, *Zhipu,* 114.

6 Some late-Ming litigation masters' manuals, such as *Xiao-Cao yibi* and *Falin zhaotian zhu,* collected "model judgments" by magistrates or prefects as well as "model plaints" and "model replies."

7 She Ziqiang, *Zhipu,* 114.

8 Li Tianlin's *Shuwen huibian* provides "model writings" on these three parts of the verdicts. Also see Ju Huanwu, "Mingdai panjueshu"; and Yang Xuefeng, *Mingdai de shenpan,* 322–339.

9 Mao Yilu, *Yunjian yanlüe* (hereafter *YJYL*), published as a single book probably in the 1610s, now in the National Library of China, Beijing. Page numbers given in parentheses in the body of this chapter are keyed to this edition. Jiang Yonglin has punctuated the text, which will be published in the series of Chinese casebooks edited by Yang Yifan.

10 Huang Tiren, *Siranzhai canggao,* 3.1a–3.3a.

11 He Sanwei, "Jun sili," 396.

12 Ibid. Mao Yilu, "Yi xianzong bingjie" (Report on district scribes), in *YJYL*, 10.4a–10.10a.

13 He Sanwei, "Jun sili," 396; Mao Yilu, "Yi youxu beiyun gao" (On lenient treatment of transporting [grain] to the north), in *YJYL*, 10.10a–10.11b.

14 He Sanwei, "Jun sili," 398–399, 402.

15 Huang Tiren, *Siranzhai canggao*, 3.2a.

16 He Sanwei, "Jun sili," 397; Mao Yilu, "Shang lengshen zuiqiu bingtie" (Report on assizes of prisoners during the winter), in *YJYL*, 10.26a–10.27a.

17 He Sanwei, "Jun sili," 398; Mao Yilu, "Ni shuihuang bingjie gao" (Report on the floods), *YJYL*, 10.11b–10.12b.

18 For the duty of the office, see Hucker, *A Dictionary of Official Terms*, 256–257.

19 Zhang Tingyu et al., *Mingshi* (hereafter *MS*), 87.2128. Mao's activities were only sporadically mentioned in *MS*.

20 See Hucker, *A Dictionary of Official Terms*, 255.

21 *MS*, 305.7816–7825. For Wei Zhongxian, see *MS*, 305.7816–7823; and Arthur Hummel, ed., *Eminent Chinese*, 846–847.

22 *MS*, 245.6353–6355, 305.7820. Also see Goodrich and Fang, eds., *Dictionary of Ming Biography*, 274–277.

23 *MS*, 306.7868.

24 Ibid., 245.6355.

25 Goodrich and Fang, eds., *Dictionary of Ming Biography*, 276.

26 Two factors have led to such a speculation. First, we know that the book was published before 1626, because by that time Zhang Jiude had written his preface to the *Court Opinions from Songjiang* and Mao had been "inspecting" (*xun*) the Yulin area in Shaanxi, one of nine defense areas along the northern frontiers, with the official title of Censor-in-Chief (*duyushi*). See Zhang Jiude's preface and Lu Youzhu's postscript in the *Zheyu yaobian*. Second, the latest case that is recorded in *Court Opinions from Songjiang* occurred in 1608 (Wanli 36, see *YJYL*, 4.22a).

27 For the *Great Ming Code*, this chapter uses the edition in Gao Ju, *Minglü jijie fuli* (hereafter *JJFL*). For an English translation of the *Code*, see Jiang Yonglin, trans., *The Great Ming Code*.

28 Farmer, *Zhu Yuanzhang*, 150–194.

29 Wu Yanhong, *Mingdai chongjun*, 57.

30 Ibid., 79–81.

31 Zhang Jinfan, ed., *Zhongguo fazhi shi*, 277.

32 According to the principle of reciprocal punishment, the accuser will receive the penalty that would have been imposed on the accused had the accusation been true.

33 By the time Mao Yilu embarked on his official career, the Ming had promulgated the final version of the *Itemized Regulations for Trying Penal Matters*, i.e., the *Itemized Regulations for Trying Penal Matters of the Wanli Reign* (1585), a copy of which is found in *JJFL*. In *YJYL*, the term "Itemized Regulations" (*tiaoli*) is often shortened to "Regulations" (*li*).

34 This regulation was issued in Wanli 16 (1588). See *JJFL*, 1349–1350.

35 We have not been able to identify the source of the quoted regulation. It might refer to the second regulation under the category of "forcible robbery" (see *JJFL*, 1349). The regulation, however, stipulates that as long as the robbers carry weapons, regardless whether they injure others or not, they shall be executed according to the *Great Ming Code*. This is contrary to Mao's judgment that the robbers should not be sentenced to the death penalty since they did not injure other people. Here we leave the matter for future investigation.

36 The emphasis on the "heart to kill" for "deliberate killing" is also in the "incorporated commentary" (*zuanzhu*) to the *Code:* deliberate killing means that someone "first cherishes the heart to kill and then strikes and kills others." See *JJFL*, 1498.

37 *JJFL*, 2026. For an English version of the *Great Ming Commandment*, see Farmer, *Zhu Yuanzhang*, 150–194.

38 *JJFL*, 372.

39 Ibid., 2026.

40 Ibid., 1889.

41 Ibid., 1440, 1448.

42 In the *Great Ming Code*, the "Ten Abominations" refers to ten groups of the most heinous crimes, including plotting rebellion and lack of filial piety (Art. 2); the "Eight Deliberations" refers to eight groups of persons with special social status, such as emperor's relatives, who are entitled to special considerations (Art. 3); and "remaining to support parents" is a principle that allows criminals to stay home to support their disabled or old parents (Art. 18). See Jiang Yonglin, "The *Great Ming Code*: A Cosmological Instrument."

43 *JJFL*, 1591. It is not clear why Mao quoted the rule on "hired workers" instead of "bondservants."

44 Yang Bojun, ed., *Lunyu yizhu*, 139.

45 Haruhito Sadate, "Saiban kijun."

46 Ch'ü, *Law and Society.*

47 *Ming Taizu shilu*, 8:3519–3520.

48 Ibid., 4:1652.

49 *JJFL*, 1366.

50 Ibid., 305–308.

51 Ibid., 313–314.

52 *YJYL*, Zhang Jiude's preface, 1a–5b.

53 Shiga Shūzō, "Sindai soshō," 74, 96. Also see Philip Huang, *Civil Justice in China*, 77–78.

54 Philip Huang, 11–12, 77–78, 100–104. Also see Philip Huang [Huang Zongzhi], *Qingdai de falü*, 10–11.

55 Bourgon, "Uncivil Dialogue."

56 Philip Huang, *Civil Justice in China*, 104.

57 Ibid., 17.

58 Edwards, "The Role of Case Precedent," 182.

59 *Black's Law Dictionary*, 1176.

60 *YJYL*, Zhu Xun's Preface, 1a–5a.

61 Ibid., Zhang Jiude's Preface, 1a–5b.

62 *Dagao*, 252.

63 *Dagao xubian*, 337; *Dagao sanbian*, 419.

64 *Ming Taizu shilu*, 6:2676, 7:3141.

65 *MS*, 93.2284.

66 Yang Yifan, *Ming Dagao yanjiu*, 45–57.

67 Our classification of discourse patterns is inspired by Brady, *The Moral Bond*.

68 For instance, in denouncing the Mongol custom of "marrying brothers' widows or father's concubines," Zhu reiterated that "from now on, if there is any violation of the teachings of previous sage kings, even death cannot atone for the offense" (*Dagao*, Art. 22, p. 215). Although no specific legal authority was mentioned here, the penalty can be found in Article 115 of the *Code* (*JJFL*, 678).

69 Yang Yifan, *Ming Dagao yanjiu*, 58–79.

70 Ibid., 94–112.

71 *Dagao*, 197–198; *Dagao xubian*, 257; *Dagao sanbian*, 341–342; *Dagao wuchen*, 425–427.

72 *Dagao*, Art. 30, p. 221.

73 Huang Chang-chien, "Da Ming lü gao kao."

74 Wu Yanhong, "Mingdai liuxing kao." According to Wu, after the mid-Ming, criminals often had their penalties reduced under this imperial order regardless of whether they possessed a copy of the *Dagao*. For recourse to the *Dagao* as a method to reduce one degree of penalty, see the court verdicts collected in the *Sichuan gedi kan'an ji qita shiyi dangce*.

75 This process can be observed in Dai Jin et al., comp., *Huang Ming tiaofa shilei zuan*.

2

Developing Forensic Knowledge through Cases in the Qing Dynasty

PIERRE-ÉTIENNE WILL

If indeed "thinking with cases" has had a long specialist history in European law and medicine, much the same is true in China, making the topic of this chapter of particular interest to comparativists. Forensics, by definition, is at the junction of law and medicine: its object is to contribute to the solution of legal cases by using specialized knowledge and techniques borrowed from medical science and practice. Does the discipline of forensics "think with cases" in the same ways as law and medicine, in Europe as well as in China? As we shall see, in imperial China, at least, forensic theory and technique did fit in with the approaches favored by the legal-administrative and medical traditions. But interestingly, and not so paradoxically, it was closer to the former. The forensic literature that I will examine here was classified under law, not medicine; and indeed, the spirit of "scientific" inquiry based on examination of the facts, or even on experimentation, that one encounters in at least some of this literature is more in line with the practice of the more investigative judges of imperial China than with that of doctors belonging to the so-called "classical" tradition.

ADMINISTRATIVE HANDBOOKS AND THE ADMINISTRATION OF LAW

Being part of the judicial process, forensic practice (and therefore theory) needs to be considered within the larger framework of administrative practice.[1] Likewise forensic literature, in the form of cases or otherwise, belongs to the larger body of administrative literature. Within that body my research for the past several years has focused on what can be loosely called "handbooks," that is, works aimed at helping administrators to learn their trade or, more generally, to perform their duties in ways both ideologically correct and functionally efficient.

This is not the place to describe the many formats and genres that compose the category of "handbooks,"[2] except perhaps to recall that one can make a broad distinction between, on the one hand, prescriptive works (often called *guanzhen*, lit. "admonitions to officials"), and, on the other hand, works providing concrete examples, typically in the form of anthologies of administrative documents (*gongdu*). To be sure, a great many works feature a variable combination of the two aspects. More important for the present purpose is the fact that the distinction between the prescriptive and the concrete, which echoes that between ideological correctness and functional efficiency, also applies in the narrower domain of law and the administration of justice. As I see it, handbooks (or sections thereof) specializing in legal and judicial problems essentially include three categories. The first consists of expositions of the penal code and related regulations, using various degrees of explanation and rearrangement. This is of course purely prescriptive. A second category is composed of guides to the judicial procedure, providing advice on how to conduct investigations and interrogations, control subaltern personnel, handle tribunal audiences, and so forth; many of the treatises on forensics I will discuss later belong to this category. Such guides as a rule are more factual and concrete in content, reflecting as they do the personal experiences of their authors, and this is even truer of the third category, namely the anthologies of judicial opinions (*pi*) and sentences (*pan*), which constitute an important subset of the *gongdu* anthologies mentioned above. When they are contemporary publications, these anthologies are almost always by individual authors, but in form and intent they are not much different from the historical collections of judgments by "celebrated judges" of the more or less recent past.[3]

Where do "cases" fit in this configuration? Quite obviously, the anthologies of judgments just mentioned function as "casebooks" inasmuch as they propose variations on a common pattern—the reconstruction and interpretation by the judge of the circumstances of a criminal or a civil affair, and his conclusion in the form of a sentence based on the penal code—with a didactic aim. The same is true when what we have is not just the texts of judgments delivered by the courts, but literary reconstructions in the form of sometimes fairly extended narratives of entire affairs, including the initial complaint or accusation, the circumstances of the investigation, and the final judgment. Anecdotal narratives of a particular author's own experiences, adduced as examples, are occasionally found in what I have called guides to the judicial procedure (or parts of generalist administrative handbooks devoted to that topic). But there also exist anthologies entirely devoted to such narratives, recounting the experiences either of a group of past officials or of one single official.[4]

As with the anthologies of judgments, the accumulation of such narratives, whether in a single work or across a range of works, can be thought of as a "thesaurus of cases," based on which administrators were able to build their own understanding of how to manage judicial affairs. And indeed, this is why we may call these narratives "cases," not just anecdotes, as we would do, for example, referring to the stories collected in *biji* and other such genres. They are "cases" because both their individual substance and the cumulative process of which they are part participate in the buildup of a body of knowledge with a precise aim: enhancing the coverage, predictability, quality, and also flexibility of the judiciary decisions arrived at by imperial officials. Likewise, they are cases not only because they collectively focus on a well-defined specialized field, but also because they emanate from authors with the reputation and authority of experts. And finally, it should be emphasized that quite often these narratives of judicial cases are not simply about fact finding—about "solving the case," as in detective stories; they are equally important in their description of the correct procedure followed by the "judge," or even of the humanity he is able to display in his dealings with the people involved in the affair. In other words, the anthologies of judgments and judicial narratives present "model" cases in the sense that the officials who are their authors and/or subjects are shown to have conducted their investigations and pronounced their judgments in an exemplary fashion, and this is why such works belong to the didactic genres I have discussed.

Specialized forensic literature fits in the pattern just outlined. Its founding text, popularly known as *The Washing Away of Wrongs* (*Xiyuan lu*),[5] which started as a "how-to" kind of handbook, was transformed under the Qing into an officially sanctioned prescriptive manual, but at the same time the new Qing version gave rise to a series of recensions, typically titled *The Washing Away of Wrongs with Collected Evidence* (*Xiyuan lu jizheng*), which incorporated numerous cases; in the process these cases and others came to be published in separate anthologies, whose aim was to enhance the knowledge of specialists as well as introduce models of administrative efficiency. I will devote particular attention to one of these anthologies, the *Collected Evidence for Autopsies* (*Jianyan jizheng*) of 1829.

THE MEANING OF "CASES" IN CHINESE IMPERIAL LAW

To understand in what ways forensic cases are a particular example of how legal experts in the Qing used cases to advance specialist knowledge, however, we need first to go beyond the didactic genres described above and look at the general relationship between cases and the Penal Code in Qing practice. I just cited the anthologies of judgments by famous officials. Despite the similarity of contents, we have something rather different with other types of "cases" that are, basically, government documents and that emphasize not the person of the judge and his actions but the legal contents of the affair. These so-called *cheng'an* (leading cases) deserve some comments before proceeding further.[6]

Xu Lian—one of the important legal specialists of the nineteenth century and also the author of a major recension of the official treatise of forensics—wrote in a preface, "For what cannot be entirely dealt with based on the statutes [*lü*], we have the substatutes [*li*]; and for what cannot be entirely dealt with based on the substatutes, we have the leading cases [*cheng'an*]."[7] This captures nicely the hierarchy among these three types of authoritative texts in terms of their coverage—from the more general to the more particular. But there was also a hierarchy in terms of authority and, in fact, of nature. In theory the terse 436 statutes (*lü*) of the Qing code had the most authority: they were the immutable law bequeathed by the dynastic ancestors—essentially reproducing the Ming code, itself strongly inspired by the hallowed *Explanation of Tang Law* (*Tanglü shuyi*). But if the statutes could not be changed, they could be complemented or even set aside and superseded by substatutes (*li*)—it was a rule that when a *lü* and a *li* were in contradiction, it was the latter that applied. In this sense the substatutes, while they had less authority than the statutes in terms of historical legitimacy, definitely had more in terms of practical government. More important, the substatutes, contrary to the basic law, had their source in actual judicial cases that had occurred in a particular place and at a particular date: they were the end result of a process of formalization that started with affairs difficult to adjudicate that had been submitted to the court and yielded decisions thought to have the value of real "laws," enforceable whenever officials encountered similar situations.[8] In short, even though the text of a substatute in the code had the same abstract and general quality as that of a statute, it was grounded in one of those particular affairs that make the stuff of "cases."

By contrast, particular affairs and all their circumstances are preserved in the "leading cases." Leading cases were those that had been adjudicated by the central bureaus and sanctioned by imperial rescript (typically with the phrase *yiyi*, "follow their proposition"). They had less authority than the statutes and substatutes of the code, however, in the sense that it was not permissible to adduce a leading case in pronouncing a sentence: leading cases were only a cumulative and ever-expanding repository of judicial experience and decision making—a database, if you will—covering a vast array of possible circumstances in which judges would look for situations comparable to the actual situations they were confronting and from which they would draw suggestions as to which article of the code to invoke by using analogy (*bizhao*).

One of the basic problems in the administration of justice, especially in legal cultures based on codes, as in China, is reconciling the rigidity and limitations of written law with the infinite variety of situations occurring in real life; in other words, finding ways of achieving what in Chinese is called *biantong* (accommodation).[9] In China this sort of difficulty concerned much more than law and justice, however. Adapting contemporary observed realities to a set of received patterns has been a perennial problem for Chinese political thinkers and practitioners, due to the force of historical precedent in the Chinese tradition and to how indispensable a tool historical erudition was in the everyday practice of politics and government. There too "accommodation" was the question: to what extent was it legitimate to invoke changes in sociopolitical conditions to advocate new policies, and using what sort of rhetorical arguments was it possible at the same time to refer convincingly to the precedents found in the historical canon, failing which an argument would always be the weaker? That "thinking with cases" might be helpful in such circumstances is obvious, and indeed, some of the literature that was used as a repository of historical precedents was organized in formats that the "case" concept fits perfectly: the collections of exemplary biographies, with their tropes and variations, are typical in this respect, but there are other similar examples of compilations of historical materials rearranged in the form of self-contained anecdotes thematically brought together to make a point—or to help people to find a way to make a point.[10]

As we saw, the same problem of accommodating rigid patterns to an ever-changing reality was a central concern for judges and lawmakers alike. It was in a sense more central than in any other area of government, not only because of the rigidity, precision, and comparatively limited coverage of the Penal Code (even including the substatutes, which were about 2,000 at the end of the Qing, the code named no more than between 3,000 and 4,000 punishable offenses),[11] but also because of the very straightforward connection between crime, law, and punishment that was at its very foundation. Any serious crime or offense had to be named using the categories in the code, the relevant statute or substatute had to be adduced, and only this one, and only the corresponding punishment, could be applied by the judicial authorities. And this too was part of the problem: errors either in the establishment of the facts or in their penal designation would be systematically pinpointed by the reviewing judiciary offices at provincial or central level and lead to "rejection" (*bo*) and revision. In the case of justice, in other words, maladministration—deliberate or not—could be and often was dealt with in a much more systematic way than in other domains of government. Even if they did not end up with the judge being administratively sanctioned, rejections and demands for revision were a cause for endless trouble: fees had to be paid to the personnel of the reviewing bodies, investigations and interrogations had to be started anew, "criminals," witnesses, and evidence had to be moved from one government office (*yamen*) to another along the hierarchy of courts, new forensic investigations had to be conducted on remains that were more and more difficult to examine, and so on.

It is here that "leading cases" intervened as an essential tool for fine tuning a sentence proposal in a way that would not lead to rejection. To quote from just one statement, a certain Wu Guanghua, a private secretary who compiled an anthology of leading cases titled *Reference Materials for Those Who Make Plans in*

Cities (*Mouyi beikao*, 1758), remarked in his preface on their importance as examples of how to "find the right path between laxness and severity" (*kuanyan dezhong*); this was in response, he said, to those who consider that each case features unpredictable circumstances and therefore cannot be taken as a model to judge other cases. In fact, claimed Wu, leading cases were no more than "taking from within the Code to divine what is in the Code" (*lüli zhi zhong er shenming hu lüli*); discussing them regularly made it possible to interiorize the code's meaning and to be ready to adduce analogies when the need arose—hence the usefulness of having access to a large and well-selected database.

Publishing collections of leading cases appears to have been a thriving occupation for law specialists in the Qing, especially in the nineteenth century.[12] The criteria of selection could vary. For example, there were collections of "rejected cases" (*bo'an*), some of them ascribed to a particular official having served a long and authoritative tenure at the Board of Punishments. The collection assembled by Xu Lian, whose preface I quoted earlier, concentrated on cases in which the sentence originally proposed by the judge had been either augmented or diminished (*jiajian*) by the Board's resorting to analogy (*bizhao*).[13] It was meant to publicize leading cases that, in Xu's words, were "stored in the Board of Punishments only" (*du cang xingbu*) instead of being circulated in the provinces where they could help magistrates to write correct judgments. Compilations like Xu's were easy to consult because the cases were arranged according to the code's classification of offenses and because they were provided with detailed tables of contents. That consulting leading cases was a basic occupation for law specialists in the provinces is demonstrated by the way some such cases were repeatedly anthologized or recompiled in other types of legal handbooks.[14] Likewise, one finds manuscript collections of leading cases that had been compiled for future reference either by clerks or officials at the Board of Punishments or by private secretaries in the cabinets of provincial and local officials. They were drawn either from the actual archives when the compilers had access to them or from printed collections or possibly from cases published in the *Peking Gazette* and circulated by the central government among the provincial bureaucracies. Only a few remnants of such specialists' labors survive, however.[15]

Regarding the principles of analysis for cases suggested by Charlotte Furth in her introduction to this volume, it seems to me that among the different authoritative texts accessible to judges, the leading cases were the most compatible with what she calls analogical modeling. While the statutes and substatutes of the code had the quality of "blueprints" since they did not tolerate any interpretation or flexibility in their application, leading cases allowed for contingencies when they were used and in fact were meant to be used for their *resemblance* to the situations actually observed, rather than an impossibly exact identity: they were indeed an archive of possibilities from which one selects the best fit to the present circumstance.[16] In other words, not only do the cases collected in the specialized literature narrate discrete events, but they also narrate events and describe situations that do not correspond, or correspond imperfectly, to the situations provided for in the text of the code, and hence are situations that need to be compared with and related to the standard patterns enunciated in the code if a proper judicial solution—a proper punishment—is to be handed down. In short, they are more than simple examples or illustrations of a preexisting body of knowledge ready for use.

This is also what we find in the field of forensics. Despite their connection to what for lack of a better word we may call a "science"—medicine—the forensic cases I will discuss below should be seen as a subset of the judicial leading cases rather than of medical cases. Like leading cases, their aim was to reconcile forensic practice with an ideal of complete predictability and exactitude in the administration of justice—in other words, to reconcile it with the fantasy of a code that would encompass every conceivable situation and allow for no possible loophole. In the present case that particular "code" was the officially sanctioned prescriptive manual of forensics—*The Washing Away of Wrongs*—which in the eighteenth century came to be routinely published as an appendix to the Penal Code and to carry the same sort of authority.

As a matter of fact, the dominance of the Penal Code and *The Washing Away of Wrongs* as a cognitive principle of organization can be seen in the fact that the taxonomy at work in the collections of cases, either legal or forensic, is entirely dependent on the organization of the two master works. Most collections of leading cases are arranged by types of crime according to the definitions and in the order found in the code; likewise discussions of forensic problems arranged by cases follow more or less the order of the entries in *The Washing Away of Wrongs.* At the very least, they are grouped according to the same sort of categories, viz. the objects or actions responsible for the injuries and death of the victim. In both instances the connections between different cases are contained within preestablished categories, and cross-referencing, when it exists, is at best of marginal importance. But as we shall see, certain collections of forensic cases feature interesting variations.

In sum, there is a close connection, both formal and functional, between collections of judicial and of forensic cases. However, we still have to look more closely at the nature of forensics as it existed in China and at the contents of its founding treatise, *The Washing Away of Wrongs.* Then we will be in a position to deal with our central question, namely how "thinking with cases" furthered the development of forensic knowledge.

FORENSIC SCIENCE AND *THE WASHING AWAY OF WRONGS* IN CHINESE HISTORY

Forensic examination consists of inspecting the corpses of the victims of homicide or suspicious deaths in order to ascertain the exact causes and circumstances of their demise—in other words, performing an "autopsy," a term that etymologically means "looking for oneself." In China, at least, inspecting the wounds of surviving victims of homicide attempts or suspicious accidents was also part of the discipline. Examining the historical development of forensics in China involves several sorts of questions. First, there is the nature and history of Chinese forensic medicine per se, which includes, among other problems, the question of how it relates to the history and practice of Chinese classical medicine. Then, and importantly, there is the question of how forensic knowledge and practice articulated to the theory and practice of law in imperial China. And finally, there is the question of the place of forensics in administrative practice in general, and in particular how it figured among the professional requirements of the officials themselves. Indeed, as will be seen in the following sections, applying the concept of "thinking with cases" is of interest with respect to all three aspects.

The practice of forensic examination goes back a long way in the history of Chinese government. The first known document dealing with it is an untitled guide for local officials found in a tomb in Hubei and dating from the Qin dynasty (221–206 BC).[17] Part of this text is devoted to various techniques of judicial investigation, including the examination of corpses in order to ascertain the cause of death. For example, one entry discusses with remarkable detail a classic problem of later forensic science in China, namely determining whether a person found hanging has committed suicide or has been murdered.[18] From this point on important albeit indirect evidence of the recourse to forensics, of its techniques, and of the categories it used can be found in a variety of sources. The Tang Code contains several regulations on the punishment of officials who have not properly conducted the examination of wounded or dead victims, and anthologies of cases solved by celebrated judges of old composed during the Song often show them resorting to forensic examination.[19]

But the first known textual formalization of forensic science appeared at the very end of the Song: it is the original version of the aforementioned *Washing Away of Wrongs*, whose preface dates from 1247 and whose original title, in fact, is *A Collection of Records on the Washing Away of Wrongs* (*Xiyuan jilu*). This title clearly indicates, and the author Song Ci (1186–1249) also admits in the preface, that he was drawing from several older texts, which are no longer extant. Although other works on forensics were published in the following decades,[20] Song Ci's treatise and its sequels and commentaries were to dominate the field until the advent of modern (i.e., Western-inspired) forensic medicine.[21] In addition, the Song government formalized the use of certain documents directly related to forensic practice: they include formats for autopsy reports and also the representation of a corpse, front and back, called *shitu,* on which the magistrate was to indicate in red ink the wounds and other traumas he had observed on the victim. In fact, it is the development of forensic examination under the Song that explains, at least in part, the appearance at that time of a specialized and systematic treatise devoted to it—*A Collection of Records on the Washing Away of Wrongs.*

While in their everyday practice officials under the Yuan and Ming dynasties used a variety of unofficial versions, adaptations, and commentaries of the original *A Collection of Records on the Washing Away of Wrongs,* the Qing government was the first to impose an officially sanctioned text of *The Washing Away of Wrongs,* equal in authority to the statutes and substatutes in the Penal Code. This was the so-called *The Washing Away of Wrongs Collated by the Bureau of the Code [of the Board of Punishments]* (*Lüli guan jiaozheng Xiyuan lu*), which was published in 1694, in principle to be distributed to all the counties of the empire.[22] According to some Qing scholars, Song Ci's original text had become a rarity by the end of the Ming. The Qing compilers mobilized a number of specialized treatises to produce a text that directly reused only about 60 percent of the Song original. New materials and new knowledge contributed by Yuan and Ming authors were integrated, and material on procedure, in particular two important introductory essays, were added.

While such moves toward establishing a consistent standard in forensic practice made judicial investigation and decision making more dependable, they also raised certain problems. From its publication in 1694 to the end of the dynasty the official text on forensic medicine was never revised, while in fact practical and theoretical knowledge did change over these two centuries, as authors added to the stock of forensic experience based on their field practice. A particular aspect of this problem concerns the examination of bones—a domain where forensic science appears to have importantly complemented classic medical knowledge. Here experienced practitioners had to deal with an official blueprint that was being gradually outdated by actual observation. It was in 1770 that, following the request of a provincial judge, the court issued a couple of plates representing the skeleton (face and back), accompanied by a new description and checklist of the bones, where the magistrates were to indicate with red ink the traumas or other signs they had observed. (These plates with checklists were called *jiangu tuge.*) As a compulsory addition to all editions of *The Washing Away of Wrongs,* they remained the official description of the skeleton through the end of the Qing, even though almost from the time of their first publication they were criticized for their errors and contradictions. As a result, several authors published revised plates with commentaries, which described, counted, and sometimes named the bones differently, but they had to advise magistrates to keep these "modernized" plates for themselves and duly fill out the regular plates intended for the ministry, whose officials and clerks would reject any conclusions based on something different from the official standard. Against this background of an evolving "science" having to contend with a fixed official theory, the collection of forensic cases and the use that was made of them, discussed below, takes particular significance.

In any event, the felt insufficiency of the standard Board-approved text plus the 1770 skeleton plates explains why a fairly large number of enlarged private editions of *The Washing Away of Wrongs* were produced. These were enriched with a variety of commentaries, additions, annotations, systems of punctuation to make the text more user-friendly, plus examples of "leading cases," and mini-treatises on specific subjects. The initiator of this series of editions with commentaries was a well-known private secretary (*muyou*) from Zhejiang, Wang Youhuai—one of those unranked administrative specialists whose names are not likely to appear in the standard biographical compilations or in *Eminent Chinese of the Ch'ing Period*, but who enjoyed a considerable reputation among the bureaucratic circles of their time, and often long after their deaths.[23] Wang's *The Washing Away of Wrongs* recension, which enriched the basic text with notes and supplements, both in the upper margin and as appendices to certain sections, was called *The Washing Away of Wrongs with Collected Evidence* (*Xiyuan lu jizheng*); its preface is dated 1796, and it was constantly republished with new accretions through the early twentieth century.

The editorial history of *The Washing Away of Wrongs with Collected Evidence* would be too long to describe here in detail. To this date I have been able to identify about twenty-five different editions based on the original Wang Youhuai recension (the last was published in 1921). Each new publication was the occasion for new prefaces—by the compiler, by specialist colleagues, or by the high officials who encouraged the printing—which were again featured in most subsequent editions.[24] The titles added various markers to Wang's original title, such as "collective compilation" (*huizuan*), "complete compilation" (*quanzuan*), "with supplements and notes" (*buzhu*), "republished with supplements and notes" (*chongkan buzhu*), "with new supplements and with explanatory notes" (*zengbu zhushi*), and various combinations thereof;[25] several editions are in five or six *juan* as against the original four. The editions produced in the late Daoguang period, in particular, added a considerable quantity of commentaries and materials to those inserted by Wang himself, some of these materials being based on the personal forensic experience of the compilers. Many editions feature a system of punctuation in red ink (*jiadan*) that was introduced in 1837, and from 1843 at least we have several extremely well produced editions distinguishing the different strata of commentaries with inks of five different colors (*wuse pi*). One of these nineteenth-century versions of the Wang Youhuai recension served as the original for Herbert Giles's English translation of *The Washing Away of Wrongs,* first published in 1874 under the title "The 'Hsi Yüan Lu' or 'Instructions to Coroners.'"[26]

This English title is partly misleading, because the sophisticated and learned nineteenth-century recensions of the basic *Washing Away of Wrongs* text that I have just described were in fact not intended for the coroners—the forensic local specialists called *wuzuo*—who were subaltern personnel more often than not considered ignorant and unreliable. Rather, they were aimed at ranking administrators and at their technical advisors. And this leads to another problem raised by the Qing systematization and regulation of forensic practice, namely the frequently lamented insufficiencies of administrators in forensic literacy and competence.

Forensic examination featured prominently in the everyday administration of justice at the local level. By determining the exact causes and circumstances of any suspicious or violent death, it was to help to establish and allocate the exact degree of culpability of the defendant or defendants and thus decide on the appropriate punishments—in other words, "doing no injustice" (*wuyuan*) to either the victims or the criminals; or, if an injustice had been done, "washing it away" (*xiyuan*). An early eighteenth-century preface author comments on the phrase "getting the punishments clear" (*mingxing*), which features in the titles of a number of legal handbooks, saying, "If it is clear, then there is no injustice" (*ming ze wu yuan*).[27] And if it was important to avoid injustices, the reason was—apart from their possible social, political, or even religious consequences—the endless complication and trouble that was involved in the process of appeal and revision, not to mention, of course, the punishments meted out to officials convicted of a miscarriage of justice. On this last point, it may be recalled that, like in the Tang, irregularities in conducting a forensic examination—that is, negligence leading to errors in the examination report, or even deliberate tampering with the report—were considered a crime: the Qing code has an article in its "Punishments" (Xingbu) section titled "Not Being Sincere in Examining the Wounds on a Corpse" (Jianyan shishang bu yi shi), which is an enlarged version of an article in the Ming code and is followed by a long series of substatutes discussing various aspects of the forensic procedure.[28]

So, forensic knowledge was essential to a proper administration of justice, and yet if we are to believe several authors, despite regulations to the contrary, correct versions of *The Washing Away of Wrongs* were not as widely circulated among the concerned personnel as they should have been. For example, Qu Zhongrong compiled an influential critical edition of the Qing official text, *A Correction of Errors in the Washing Away of Wrongs* (*Xiyuan lu bianzheng*). In the 1827 preface he claims that while the Board's standard edition of *The Washing Away of Wrongs* should be available in every bureaucrat's headquarters, he has observed that all too often only "faulty small-sized commercial booklets" (*fangke elie xiaoce*) are used, which are kept like "talismans" (*hushenfu*) by the clerks and coroners. Indeed, the problem of forensic literacy was especially crucial in the case of the latter, since they were in principle the forensics experts in the local administrative apparatuses. They had no reason to be sloppy in their job: eighteenth-century regulations at least were very comprehensive and thorough concerning their training. The Penal Code has a long substatute on that subject whose different parts were handed down in 1728, 1740, and 1763, respectively, and then combined in 1788.[29] According to this text, the counties were to have from one to three coroners each (depending on their size), plus one or two apprentices. Each of the coroners and apprentices was to receive a copy of the official *Washing Away of Wrongs,* and a knowledgeable clerk from the local Office of Punishments would be appointed to explain carefully the text to them. Once a year they were to be examined by the prefects, who would ask them to comment on a passage from *The Washing Away of Wrongs* and reward or punish them according to their proficiency or lack thereof.

Such were the rules promulgated by the central government. Sometimes the provincial authorities at least attempted to have these regulations actually enforced. For example, in two circulars of 1758, the second of which cited the relevant substatute in the code, the provincial judge of Jiangxi claimed that a majority of the magistrates in the province were ignorant of the contents of *The Washing Away of Wrongs* and that a majority of the coroners were incompetent as well. He accordingly ordered the magistrates routinely to go over the text with the coroners, discussing how to distinguish suicides from homicides, how to examine wounds, how to identify lethal and nonlethal traumas, and so forth, so they might perform a competent and critical postmortem when the day did come.[30] At the end of the nineteenth century, the well-known law specialist and conservative politician Gangyi (1834–1900) complained that most magistrates did not care about selecting coroners and discussing *The Washing Away of Wrongs* with them, so that "the tradition of coroners was getting lost" (*wuzuo zhi chuan yi shi*) and that forensic reports were made haphazardly and against all rules.[31] Similarly, Xue Yunsheng, the famous legal scholar of the late Qing who compiled *Concentrating on Doubtful Matters when Reading the Substatutes* (*Duli cunyi*), states bluntly in his commentary to the above-mentioned substatute that these regulations were extremely comprehensive but that they were truly implemented only in exceptional cases—that in fact this substatute had become virtually empty. He adds that when in a province there was a "big case presenting difficulties" (*yinan da'an*), one usually had to look in another province to get a competent coroner.[32]

It is, to be sure, difficult to generalize. While Xue's remark dates from the very end of the Qing, one does come across mentions of the same kind of problem—

competent coroners are a rarity—much earlier. On the other hand, the already mentioned *Collected Evidence for Autopsies* of 1829, which I will introduce in more detail in a moment, features several coroners who discuss difficult forensic problems with much authority and erudition and obviously had their *Washing Away of Wrongs* at their fingertips. Still, coroners were routinely seen as mere instruments to whom, as we just saw, the contents of the basic textbook of their trade had to be fed by clerks and whose competence needed to be constantly checked by the officials. For all the authors who gave prefaces to the numerous recensions of *The Washing Away of Wrongs* published during the Qing, and for the authors of official handbooks in general, the officials, not the coroners, were to be the true possessors of forensic knowledge: only if they were perfectly conversant with forensic theory, and indeed with the practice itself,[33] would they avoid being manipulated by the "specialists"—the coroners, themselves in cahoots with the judicial clerks and of course open to receiving bribes from the parties involved. After all, the officials were the ones who assumed responsibility for forensic examinations and for the conclusions derived from them, which would in turn support their proposals for sentences.

Yet a basic problem deplored by the same authors was, precisely, the officials' frequent ignorance of even the basics of forensic examination. The following quotation, from a 1758 circular by the Jiangxi provincial judge, is typical.

> In ordinary times magistrates do not even cast an eye on the text of *The Washing Away of Wrongs,* so that when suddenly one day they have to go for a postmortem examination, they are at a loss and do not know what to do; as for determining which wounds have been caused by hands or feet, and which ones by other objects or by cutting blades, they are still less capable of making the distinction. They just listen to the announcements made by the coroner and note them one by one. And half of the coroners do not know their job, in addition to which they often accept bribes: is it then possible to say whether [the characterization of] the wounds is correct or wrong? And after they have returned to their offices they omit to check with *The Washing Away of Wrongs;* they just fill out the corpse diagram haphazardly, leave it to the clerks to put the seal on the statement, forward it, and consider that the process of examining and reporting is over.[34]

The target audience of the treatises on forensics included not only the magistrates, but also—and this is recalled in more than one preface—the private secretaries who specialized in law. Although the private secretaries were not authorized to participate in person in the autopsies,[35] when the official had returned to his headquarters he would discuss the case with them, and most of the time they were the ones who drafted the sentence proposal and the report to the higher authorities.

In fact, not a few authors of forensic treatises were private secretaries, beginning with Wang Youhuai himself and his colleague Li Guanlan, who provided some additions to the first *The Washing Away of Wrongs with Collected Evidence* of 1796 and wrote a preface to it.[36] Besides local practitioners, the intended readership also included the many law specialists in the various bureaucrats' headquarters in control of the judicial process higher up in the hierarchy and at the Board of Punishments: in short, all those distinguished people that one preface calls "the gentlemen of the judicial bureaus" (*yanju zhu junzi*) and "the erudites in law" (*dulüzhe*)[37]—among whom the coroners would certainly not be counted.

What is indeed remarkable in the history of the text and of all its additions and commentaries is the interplay we observe, reading the prefaces in particular, between textual erudition, personal observation, and the exchanges that must have taken place in the field with the coroners who were the manipulators of the actual bodies. All the knowledge thus accumulated found its way not only into treatises like the expanded editions of *The Washing Away of Wrongs with Collected Evidence,* but also into compilations set in the form of casebooks. One of these was the *Collected Evidence for Autopsies,* discussed in some detail in the next sections.

ADVANCING FORENSIC KNOWLEDGE THROUGH CASES

All the anthologies of judgments or cases mention as a matter of course forensic examination as a crucial technique of investigation and deduction in homicide cases. Forensic knowledge was part and parcel of the stock of experience recorded in compilations designed to enhance the individual expertise of officials as well as the efficiency of the judicial process in general. The important—albeit by no means absolute—distinction here might be between compilations of standard cases meant as examples, or models, and those meant to help solve unusual problems. The first aimed to nurture a culture of competence and dedication among administrators and were "handbooks" properly speaking; the second were intended to help administrators solve problems that at first glance could not be solved by the book, and this entailed introducing new knowledge. That new knowledge might consist of simple administrative tricks, but it could also be what we would call scientific knowledge.

The last description, as we shall see, better fits the works specializing in forensics—and after all this is not surprising if we remember that the discipline rested on medical knowledge. Concerning the other side of forensic practice—its being part of a standardized bureaucratic process and so raising problems of administrative behavior and procedural compliance—we find it in the compilations of cases, of whatever form, that deal with the entire judicial procedure. These cases did not necessarily involve rare or even sensational situations; it was rather a matter of providing local administrators with ordinary practical models to follow and, especially, to help them avoid making technical errors and being manipulated by persons interested in distorting the procedure.

FORENSICS AND THE ROUTINIZATION OF THE JUDICIAL PROCEDURE

Before turning to the problem-solving type of forensic literature, it may be of interest to introduce, by way of contrast, a good example of such routine accounts of the judicial system. This is a compilation of twenty cases published in 1838 by the governor general of Yunnan and Guizhou, Yilibu, under the title *Elementary Models for Studying Cases* (*Xue'an chumo*).[38] The aim of the work was to provide the magistrates of the two provinces, especially those who were beginners, with examples of how *ordinary* homicides and suicides should be dealt with. To use Yilibu's own terms in his preface, unlike the usual anthologies of leading cases selected for their difficulty, which "provide material for research" (*you zi yu kaohe*) but "are useless as models" (*wu yi yu fangmo*), the present compilation aimed merely to provide local officials with "standard models of investigation and decision" (*yankan xunduan zhi changfan*)—indeed, simple "patterns" (*chengshi*).[39] Studying these routine cases, all of which had been approved by the Board, Yunnan and Guizhou magistrates would know how to proceed to prevent injustices and mistrials from occurring, and also—and in fact especially—to avoid procedural errors likely to lead to a rejection of their conclusions. The text is composed of the files of twenty recent cases selected from the provincial archives of Yunnan, with only a few notes in the upper margin, and arranged by type of crime in the order of the code. Each step of the procedure is in evidence: the report by the local constable (*dibao*), the complaint filed by the victim's relatives, the declarations of the defendant, the official's responses (*pi*), the testimonies, the coroner's report, the sentence proposal, and the official's communications with the higher authorities. Everything in the file is quoted in its entirety, or nearly so: while this entails no little repetition, at the same time it allows us to see how new details or circumstances, sometimes quite significant, slip into the narrative from one testimony to the next until the judge's final summary. Reading through it one encounters, recounted in the language of the parties involved, the most banal of the tawdry transgressions that make up everyday life, like adulterous relationships, brawls during a banquet, fights, rapes, thefts, and so on—only these incidents happen to have ended with the homicide or the suicide of a man or a woman.

But of course, these glimpses of real life are not what the compilation was meant to offer: what was important was the unfolding of the procedure and how to present reports. Regarding the problem of incompetent forensic investigation discussed earlier, Yilibu's anthology leaves the impression that in early nineteenth-century Yunnan the coroners' task had become routinized and that there were no particular problems. This is in contrast to all the statements to the effect that autopsies were done haphazardly under the aegis of generally ignorant officials. The most one can say is that while it is possible that forensic examinations were often badly performed, at least they were always performed (this was the law), and the results, whatever their actual reliability may have been, were duly entered in the appropriate forms. In short, forensic practice and, hopefully, knowledge were embedded in the everyday practice of local government, and this obviously is why one finds such lengthy discussions of it in a large number of generalist magistrate handbooks.

But it does not seem to make much sense to speak of "thinking with cases" with a work like *Elementary Models for Studying Cases.* For one thing, there is not much thinking in it: there is no problem to solve, and no enhancement of the theoretical and technical knowledge available to the state and its officials is intended. These are "cases" (in the sense of judicial cases), to be sure, but it is essentially a question of listing examples useful to new officials for acquiring a basic knowledge of their trade.

THE WASHING AWAY OF WRONGS EXPANSIONS WITH CASES: LANG JINQI AND RUAN QIXIN

The situation is fairly different both with the more sophisticated versions of *The Washing Away of Wrongs with Collected Evidence*—the already mentioned late eighteenth-century expansion of the official Qing *Washing Away of Wrongs,* of which I will discuss the important edition published by Ruan Qixin in 1832—and with a casebook on the same subject, *Collected Evidence for Autopsies,* compiled by Lang Jinqi in 1829. Ruan's and Lang's works present an overlapping series of difficult forensic cases, albeit with important differences of organization and emphasis. That they cover similar ground is not surprising when one remarks that the two authors' careers appear to have much in common and appear to have in fact intersected; and, indeed, it seems to me worth devoting a few lines to their respective progresses.

Both appear to have been typical members of the elite of law and forensics specialists who put out scholarly editions and commentaries of the officially sanctioned *Washing Away of Wrongs* throughout the nineteenth century. We know that at the time he completed the *Collected Evidence for Autopsies* Lang Jinqi was prefect of Guilin, the capital of Guangxi (following a similar posting in Liuzhou in the same province); he already had thirty years of official career in the provinces behind him, during which he claimed to have solved "no less than thousands and hundreds of cases." This information is found in his preface (dated 1829) to a short illustrated treatise on the skeleton and on examining bones, *Collected References for Autopsies* (*Jianyan hecan*), to which in fact the *Collected Evidence for*

Autopsies served as a companion volume.[40] Lang's passion for forensic examinations and the discussion of forensic problems is readily apparent from this preface, and it is eloquently confirmed by the preface written for the 1849 edition of the work by his colleague Zhou Zuoji, who had known him in Guangxi. Of the 156 entries of *Collected Evidence for Autopsies* Lang tells us that they include first of all his own forensic observations in Guangxi, to which he added observations made by Ruan Qixin, as well as leading cases discussing various types of difficulties that he had asked his colleagues to retrieve for him from their private notes.

We actually do not know much about Ruan Qixin, except for the fact that he was also a *Washing Away of Wrongs* enthusiast and an important contributor to the body of forensic knowledge in the nineteenth century. He had discovered *The Washing Away of Wrongs,* he tells us, in the first years of the nineteenth century, while he was "learning the trade of Shen Buhai and Han Feizi" (in other words, training as a legal private secretary) and assisting a relative who was an official at the governor's office in Hangzhou;[41] later, he familiarized himself with forensic technique as a Warden's Office Commander in the South City district in Peking—a post that was especially entrusted with forensic examinations. After further encounters with *The Washing Away of Wrongs* specialists, he produced, as we saw, his own recension of *The Washing Away of Wrongs with Collected Evidence,* which added a quantity of important new materials: indeed, Ruan's recension can be said to be the "mother" of all later versions, which, like it, have the characters *buzhu* ("with supplements and notes") in their title. These supplementary materials were, essentially, cases.

These details are worth mentioning because, first, there is clearly a Guangxi connection. Ruan arrived in the province in 1823 as department magistrate of Hengzhou; in 1830 he assumed the post of prefect of Sicheng, and it was there that he compiled his edition of *The Washing Away of Wrongs with Collected Evidence,* whose preface (from which most of the above information is extracted) is dated 1832.[42] It is therefore highly probable that those two prefects, Lang and Ruan, knew each other and that they exchanged materials, as is indeed suggested in Lang's preface. The exchange apparently worked both ways, since many of the entries in Lang's *Collected Evidence for Autopsies* of 1829 are also found in the supplements introduced by Ruan in his 1832 *The Washing Away of Wrongs with Collected Evidence and Added Notes* (*Buzhu Xiyuan lu jizheng*), without our being able to decide who exactly supplied what.[43]

The second reason to mention all of this—and closer to the problem at hand—is that whatever the origin of the materials that the two works have in common, their usage and significance are not the same. They are the same "cases," without the smallest variant, but the way they are inserted in the two books is different, and this is first of all because the books themselves are completely different in form. To be sure, the peculiar categories of the official Qing *Washing Away of Wrongs* determine the content in both instances. In Ruan's *Washing Away of Wrongs with Collected Evidence and Added Notes* this goes without saying, since the cases figure in supplements (generally called *xuji*) inserted after several of the main divisions of the original text, such as, to cite some of the more important, "Examination of Female Corpses" (Yan funu shi) and "Examination of Bones" (Jiangu) in *juan* 1; "Wounds Caused by Hands, Feet and Other Objects" (Shou zu tawu shang), "Self-inflicted Wounds" (Zican), and other forms of suicide in *juan* 2; and "Various Considerations on Dubious Cases" (Yinan zashuo) or "On Wounds on Corpses" (Shishang zashuo), as well as "Unexpected Poisons" (Yiwai zhudu), in *juan* 3.[44] Lang's *Collected Evidence for Autopsies*, by contrast, is a mere list of cases (there is no explicit subdivision) loosely arranged by unspecified general categories that are in part (but only in part) those of *The Washing Away of Wrongs*, even if each individual case refers only to an entry in the latter.

The differences in arrangement are indeed interesting to observe. Quite often, Lang Jinqi quotes serially cases that Ruan Qixin has appended to different sections of *The Washing Away of Wrongs*. To give only one example, Lang gathers together cases of strangulation (by hands, rope, belt, stick, chains, or even the queue of the victim) and suffocation (by various objects, also including gas poisoning), which in *The Washing Away of Wrongs* are found under "hanging" (*ziyi*) or "faked hanging" (*jiazuo ziyi*) or "dubious cases" (a catch-all category) or "examination of bones," and several more. In other words, even though the underlying arrangement of Lang's casebook does have its own inconsistencies, he was able to a degree to free himself from the preestablished organization of *The Washing Away of Wrongs*. This was deliberate, as is suggested by Lang's complaint in his preface that even though the methods of forensic investigation "are all in *The Washing Away of Wrongs*," "its explanations are scattered in the text and confused in their arrangement, so that it is not easy to consult" (*qi shuo sanjian cuochu, jiangqiu fei yi*). It is a fact that in some of its parts *The Washing Away of Wrongs* seems uselessly complicated, one reason for this complication being, as I see it, that the late seventeenth-century editors of the official version, who set the pattern for the rest of the dynasty, were hopelessly caught between several principles of organization: by observable trauma on the body, both outside (bruises and wounds) and inside (traces on the bones), by agent of death (cuts, blows by various objects, poison, illness, etc.), by social cause of death (solitary accident, brawl, suicide, homicide, faked causes), by degree of uncertainty (the *yinan* category, and questions like whether wounds have been inflicted before or after the death), and so forth.

By definition, Ruan Qixin, the editor of *The Washing Away of Wrongs with Collected Evidence and Added Notes*, was tied to this organization: the numerous cases he introduced function as expansions of the preestablished categories of the work.

By contrast, in composing *Collected Evidence for Autopsies* Lang Jinqi was able more or less to ignore these categories. Insofar as a logic can be detected in the arrangement, it may be by type of trauma (strangulation, burns,[45] wounds by various objects and weapons, etc.), by external circumstances (e.g., deaths in prison or under torture),[46] by "cause" (e.g., falls or hanging, which is placed apart from the series on strangulation and suffocation), by problem set to the investigator (like the impossibility of direct examination[47] or the uncertainty about internal causes of death as against observable wounds)—occasionally requiring the collection of circumstantial, that is, nonforensic, evidence—and there may be other principles of arrangement that escape us.

What is important, at any rate, is that in the very layout of *Collected Evidence for Autopsies* the cases exist for and by themselves, independently of any theoretical exposition and not as "commentaries" to a canon. The work can be described as "reader-friendly," aimed at users in search of solutions to problems faced in the field, since the cases—whose titles are almost always explicit enough for the reader to guess the problem at hand—can be directly and rapidly found by browsing through the table of contents.

THE NATURE OF FORENSIC CASES

What do the "cases" collected in *The Washing Away of Wrongs with Collected Evidence and Added Notes* and *Collected Evidence for Autopsies* consist of exactly? First, each case record consists of, or includes, more or less extended fragments of autopsy reports: this determines not only the content of the entries, but also, to an extent, their form. Second, the forensic observations that make up the cases almost always introduce *problems,* even though they are not necessarily described as such in explicit terms. These problems range all the way from a bare description of evidence that does not, at first sight, correspond to the standard indications of the official *Washing Away of Wrongs* and therefore requires a minimum of interpretation or at least needs to be very carefully examined, to extended discussions of ambiguous or apparently indecisive situations.[48] Finally, the cases are always *practical* in the sense that they never deal with the sort of textual problems that were a favorite of *kaozheng* scholars—an approach that is found in many other forensic treatises, in fact, and in many notes enriching the basic *Washing Away of Wrongs* text in the nineteenth-century editions. The cases are meant to help forensic practitioners know how to interpret correctly what lies before their eyes, based on concrete situations, rather than adduce new textual evidence with a view to refining the normative corpus.

The fragments, as I said, are more or less extended.[49] Some are limited to a few lines reproducing the observations "shouted" (or "sung," *chang*) by the coroner in the course of his inspection: coroners enumerated a standard order of lethal (*zhiming*) and nonlethal (*bu zhiming*) spots on the front (*yangmian*) and back (*hemian*) of the body, each time describing the wounds or other traumas or absence of trauma when this absence was considered significant; they might add general observations on the position and aspect of the corpse, rigidity of the limbs or lack thereof, nature of the objects that caused the traumas, and so forth.[50] In the autopsy reports this enumeration, which can be extremely short, usually concludes with a summary introduced by the formula *weixi*, or just *xi*, meaning that "this is in fact" such-and-such a situation.

At the other extreme, we have lengthy narratives that are in the form of a formal magistrate's report, exactly of the sort found in *Elementary Models for Studying Cases* and in a large number of authors' anthologies of administrative papers (*gongdu*). In such documents, before introducing the coroner's observations, the magistrate recounts—with the usual conventional phrases stressing that everything was done according to procedure—how he received the information that a homicide was committed, went to the place with a coroner and a clerk, and, after having checked the environment, had the autopsy performed according to regulation and in the presence of the relatives of the victim; then he quoted the coroner's report, which of course he duly verified himself, discussed possible inconsistencies, and, when these were explained, delivered his conclusion. The more complex examples include lengthy discussions of inconsistencies or ambiguities, in the form either of a dialogue between the magistrate and the coroner or of exchanges between the higher courts and the magistrate, who in turn would ask the coroner to provide further explanations.[51] Occasionally the narrative adds depositions of relatives or witnesses when this is needed to explain forensic evidence that is either contradictory or insufficient to reach a conclusion.[52]

That these are "cases" (or "problems") of general interest, as opposed to narratives intended as concrete illustrations of a standard situation, is confirmed by the systematic terseness of the writing and by the fact that precise indications of name, age, place, or date are frequently replaced with indefinite words like *mou* (such-and-such) or *ruogan* (a certain number). The names and locale of the victim and, as the case may be, criminal are usually provided—which may be meant to recall that this is a *real* case, not an example in the abstract—but the age of the victim is almost always replaced with *mou*, the name of the coroner is practically never given, and only in a minority of instances is the date of the case provided.[53]

Although they remain anonymous most of the time, the coroners figure quite prominently in the more complex cases. In a few instances they are mere instruments, directed by a magistrate who obviously knows his forensics to proceed in such-and-such way and look for such-and-such detail.[54] In rare cases the coroner is reproached for having overlooked some important detail or for his lack of experience. But most coroners appear to know their job: they are able to argue when doubts or questions are put forward by the magistrate or by the higher courts, and their explanations are eventually accepted by the authorities.

This is not a trivial point if we remember that the cases assembled in *Collected Evidence for Autopsies* and similar collections were meant to contribute to the buildup of a specialized *knowledge.* The official *Washing Away of Wrongs* was the ultimate reference in any debate on a forensic problem, so that whenever it turned out to be deficient, or even wrong, a lot of evidence and debate needed to be mobilized to make the point. In this process the cases played an essential role. Studying them, we can see at the same time the profound influence of a fixed and legally binding body of science and a collective effort to refine and enlarge it, both for the sake of knowledge per se and for the sake of a sounder and more reliable application of the law.

Thus *The Washing Away of Wrongs,* its categories, and its contents are everywhere in the background of *Collected Evidence for Autopsies.* When *The Washing Away of Wrongs* is explicitly cited in the course of one of those debates in which the coroners were apparently active and generally respected participants, it is either to emphasize that the conclusions of a contested investigation actually fit (*xiangfu*) with a particular provision in the text or, on the contrary, to state that the circumstances observed are not found in it. In the first instance, the point of adducing the case is to show that a sufficiently expert and informed forensic examination can provide a reliable and authoritative interpretation of a situation that seemed unclear at first sight (or that the contesting parties tried to make unclear). In the second instance—of more interest to us—the point is to go beyond the received text and, in effect, improve the knowledge that it embodies.

PERFECTING *THE WASHING AWAY OF WRONGS*

Indeed, even though *The Washing Away of Wrongs* was routinely hailed as a superb tool to avoid injustices, the inadequacies of the official text appear to have been a constant worry for specialists. In his preface to *Collected References for Autopsies* (the companion volume to *Collected Evidence for Autopsies*), Lang Jingqi claimed, "I do not know how many cases there are that involve uncertainties and for which one cannot entirely trust the books" (*fan yu she yinan bu neng jin xin yu shu zhe bu zhi fanji*)—"the books" being *The Washing Away of Wrongs* and its various commentaries, as is made clear in the detailed discussion that precedes this statement. Lang was particularly straightforward here because the topic of his discussion (and of the book) was the understanding of the bones and skeleton, a domain in which, as we shall see, *The Washing Away of Wrongs* and its accompanying plates were found especially wanting.

To be sure, there are only a few cases in *Collected Evidence for Autopsies* where it is explicitly noted that the situation observed does not appear in *The Washing Away of Wrongs*, but these in general are fairly developed. In case 4, for example, the magistrate asked why it took almost a month for a man who had been stabbed by his brother to die, even though the knife had pierced the membranes (*toumo*),[55] and why the wound did not suppurate (*kuilan*). To the first question the coroner answered that the blade had not penetrated very deeply, hence the delay before death, and to the second that a "white scab" (*baijia*) had formed on the wound; however, "because *The Washing Away of Wrongs* does not mention scabs forming on a wound, I did not report it (*wei hebao*)." Interestingly, the magistrate asked a doctor to confirm the existence of such scab formations not described in the forensic literature.

We have a somewhat similar situation in case 41, where a man killed another with his fists. The problem was to determine which blows were lethal (the diagnosis can be made by examining the roots of the teeth and the top of the skull). The magistrate found the evidence offered insufficient and lengthily questioned the coroner, who provided fairly sophisticated answers. He noted that "*The Washing Away of Wrongs* does not say which bone must be examined in the case of blows to the ribs," and that the similar forensic effects of wounds to the stomach and to the scrotum posited by *The Washing Away of Wrongs* could not be invoked in the case of blows with fists. In other words, this was another case where insufficient detail and coverage in *The Washing Away of Wrongs* left room for argument.

The same can be said of case 5, but there the problem was no longer the absence of a particular pattern in the official guide, but, rather, discrepancies of detail. The problem at hand was the difference between the size of the actual wound and what it was expected to be according to *The Washing Away of Wrongs*, and again it required lengthy explanations on the coroner's part to explain it. The first examination concluded that the victim had committed suicide by cutting his throat with a razor, but the governor raised several questions based on *The Washing Away of Wrongs*. Not only were the clinical signs of suicide incomplete (one of the hands of the victim was relaxed, when according to the text both fists should have been clenched [*woquan*]), but the wound itself was much larger than described in the *Washing Away of Wrongs* entry devoted to self-mutilation with a "small knife": it was 4.2 inches long versus 2 inches at most. In addition, the coroner had omitted to mention the variations of depth from the left to the right end of the cut.[56] The magistrate's answer, also quoting from *The Washing Away of Wrongs*, maintained that only one hand (the one that held the knife) was supposed to be "curved" (*wanqu*). As for the size of the wound, he quoted the explanations of the coroner, according to whom it was due to the position of the head at the moment of the act, to the fact that a razor and not an ordinary knife had been used, and finally to the victim's "ardent wish to end his days" (*sizhe ji yu zijin*).[57] The direction and depth of the wound were correct—from right to left by a left-handed person: the detail had been forgotten in the first report because of the negligence of a clerk, already punished for it. But the governor again questioned the conclusions, citing the same entry of *The Washing Away of Wrongs* on using a "small knife." Cutting his throat from right to left, the man should have cut into his larynx at the start, causing such pain that the motion would have then weakened, so that the wound could not be as long and deep as reported. In his answer the magistrate again quoted *The Washing Away of Wrongs*, this time on the different energy and reactivity of the right and left hands, and provided a lengthy reconstruction of the victim's gesture, which again justified the inordinate size of the wound. After this the case was closed.

The argumentation in this particular case is interesting because it is a fact that the entries on "cutting one's throat"—termed either *zige houxia* or *ziwen*—in *The Washing Away of Wrongs* appear rather confusing in their descriptions, even more so when one takes into account the notes of the official text and those added later by Wang Youhuai in the upper margin.[58] This must have been the reason why Lang Jinqi included it in his collection: it illustrated how it was possible to extract different and sometimes conflicting arguments from the text of *The Washing Away of Wrongs* and with efficient reasoning make a point when superiors were contesting one's conclusions. And, once again, it confirmed that because *The Washing Away of Wrongs* could not possibly mention every sort of circumstance it was often necessary to distance oneself from the letter of the text in order to solve a problem. Thus, in this particular instance, the *Washing Away of Wrongs* entry quoted by the governor cites wound sizes only for the use of a "small knife" (*xiaodaozi*) (where the wound should not exceed two inches) or of a kitchen knife (*shidao*) (where one is allowed a wound four inches long). The victim in our case used a razor (*titou dao*), which was certainly "small," but also especially sharp. Collecting such examples of forensic creative thinking—even concerning small details—in the form of cases that had been successfully argued with the authorities was evidently an important factor in the continuous development of the discipline.

Case 9, also about a man who was reported to have committed suicide, this time by stabbing himself in the stomach, is of a different sort, in the sense that a conclusion could be reached only through nonforensic reasoning and circumstantial evidence. The problem was that the man, named Zhao, had also castrated himself and that his wife was arguing that in fact the deed had been done by a colleague of his, a certain Du (both were employed in a pawnshop and there had been a violent dispute over some business issues). All the investigations proved inconclusive because, despite clear clinical evidence of suicide, there was nothing in

The Washing Away of Wrongs on self-castration (*zixing zhage*) that would make it possible to draw a conclusion from forensic examination. After the wife appealed to the capital the emperor himself ordered new investigations—his assumption being that the man had stabbed himself to death but had been castrated by someone else. The truth was eventually established, but without any help from forensics: only a careful reconstruction of the dispute, based on the depositions of several witnesses, made it possible to establish beyond doubt (*an wu yiyi*) that after having been deeply humiliated by Du during a showdown that must have been quite dramatic indeed, Zhao castrated himself out of shame and eventually planted the knife in his own stomach when the other had refused to let him leave before they had settled their accounts. In short, this was a difficult case where "since one cannot rely on forensic examination one must entirely rely on the testimonies to reach a decision" (*kaijian ji bu zu ping, quan ping gongzheng dingyan*).[59]

Several other examples could be analyzed. Like the one just narrated, case 13 both finds *The Washing Away of Wrongs* wanting and proceeds through an exchange of reports by the magistrate and objections from his superiors. This was the classic situation of a woman having an affair and poisoning her husband with the help of her lover. The problem was to determine whether the death of the husband had actually been caused by the concoction that the culprits admitted to have prepared. The local authorities asked the authorization to proceed as one usually did in such cases, that is, by opening the coffin and submitting the bones of the victim to various manipulations in order to establish the cause of death (or, in shorthand, to "open and examine," *qijian*). All the authors are unanimous that such an operation, tantamount to dispersing and destroying the remains of the victim, should be performed only as a last resort, and this is also why there was so much insistence on doing the external examination as soon and as carefully as possible, so as to avoid having to do it again later, and in much more painful conditions.[60] And indeed, in the present case the provincial authorities remarked that the preparation in question was not on *The Washing Away of Wrongs*' list of poisons indicating their forensic effects and that therefore examining the bones of the victim (their color, in this particular instance) would be inconclusive. They consequently ordered the operation postponed until certain experiments—to which I shall return in a moment—had been performed.

That this case was adduced not as an illustration of a particular forensic technique but as an example of the stance to adopt when *The Washing Away of Wrongs* remains silent is confirmed by the fact that the narrative stops there: we are not told of the results of either the experiments or the autopsy that was presumably performed afterward. In other words, what is important here is the *method* for solving a particular type of problem, and this sort of method deserves a few more comments.

RESEARCH AND EXPERIMENTATION

All of the above cases feature the same type of problem, to wit, that all too often the official guide on forensics was insufficient to propose conclusions based on straightforward and indisputable evidence—conclusions, in other words, that would be rejection-proof and above all would render any injustice impossible.[61] *The Washing Away of Wrongs* was necessarily limited in its coverage and overlooked many configurations that could be observed in actual situations, it was too dogmatic in many of its details,[62] and it was badly organized and not free of contradictions. As a result, much ingenuity was required to find analogies acceptable to the authorities, to take advantage of the internal contradictions of the text, to apply careful reasoning to scarce or ambiguous evidence in order to square it with the authorized categories, and so on. Besides, since in the Qing *The Washing Away of Wrongs* was an official treatise, the "science" that it embodied could not be questioned. Even though it was rarely put in these terms, in the nineteenth century at least it is clear that some forensic scholars were growing impatient with this situation.

As a matter of fact, despite these constraints, in China at that time forensic medicine may well have been the occupation par excellence where scholars could cultivate a spirit of scientific research based on observation and experimentation. This may seem startling in an intellectual environment supposed to have been dominated by bookishness, cultural conformity, and bureaucratic routine. But it seems clear to me that the best minds and most militant administrators were ready to question, or at least improve and enlarge, a received body of knowledge. For one thing, the stakes were very high in criminal courts where the requirement, with implications both political and religious, was to avoid at all cost the smallest injustice. And then, the very nature of the discipline was an invitation to confront theory and reality and to qualify the theory when it did not fit with the reality.

Forensic medicine was, first of all, a *practice* that confronted its practitioners with the most concrete and physical (and, more often than not, unpalatable) realities. More than medical science, forensic science was grounded in the physical examination and direct manipulation of the body. Most of the authors of Qing treatises insist in their prefaces that they had personal experience of most of the situations they are introducing. Indeed, some state plainly that one cannot understand anything about forensic medicine without extensive participation in forensic examinations. Ruan Qixin, for example, says in his preface of 1832 that when he was first confronted with *The Washing Away of Wrongs* in the early 1800s, there was much that remained obscure to him, and it was only later in his career, when he was in charge of forensic examinations in one of the wards of Peking, that he began to understand exactly what it was about. It is clear from many of the cases cited in *Collected Evidence for Autopsies* and elsewhere that hands-on experience was essential to become a reliable forensic specialist.

What I have called a spirit of experimentation appears to have had a long tradition in Chinese forensics. The locus classicus might be the story, first found in the *Collection of Doubtful Cases* (*Yiyu ji*) of the early Song and reproduced in a note to the official Qing *Washing Away of Wrongs*, of a judge who was confronted with the corpse of a man found in a house that had burnt down. The man's wife maintained that he had died in the conflagration, but his brother accused her of having killed her husband and then set fire to the house. To get a clue the investigator had two pigs—one alive, one dead—burnt on a stack of wood and then compared them. The pig that had been burnt alive had ashes in its mouth; the dead pig did not. Then the judge examined the corpse of the man, who did not have ashes in his mouth: he was already dead when the house was set on fire.[63] We find some similar experimental tricks in the cases collected in *Collected Evidence for Autopsies*. In case 13, already referred to, the experiment was not on pigs but on chickens and dogs: the point was to feed them with the preparation that might have poisoned the deceased husband—an unlikely concoction of centipedes and bean roots—and look at the results, that is, at the color of their bones. The culprits were therefore ordered to dry it over a fire exactly as they had done before. The language used in the provincial judge's directive is rather striking: the official experimenter is urged to "check the aspect and estimate the principle at work, be meticulous in his investigating and careful in searching for evidence." (As we saw, the result of the experiment is not recorded in the source.)

As a matter of fact, experimental manipulations were part and parcel of the standard methodology recommended in *The Washing Away of Wrongs*. For example, bones were submitted to preparations and tests supposed to help in diagnosing the cause of death. Likewise, the method of "examining the ground" (*jiandi*) consisted of heating the ground and making it react with sesame oil to reveal the trace of a corpse that had been burnt and the position of the wounds, and then submitting it to further preparations involving intense heating, aspersion of a decoction of wine dregs (if this is the sense of *zaoshui*), and vinegar before covering it with a plate of Jinzhou lacquer (*jinqi zhuo*) on which any scars were supposed to appear. Interestingly, the corresponding methods in the original thirteenth-century *A Collection of Records on the Washing Away of Wrongs* use different ingredients and are far less sophisticated—and there is no separate entry on "examining the ground."[64] The "case" found in both *Collected Evidence for Autopsies* and the Ruan Qixin appendix to the relevant entry of *The Washing Away of Wrongs with Collected Evidence* does no more than cite *The Washing Away of Wrongs* entry and record a particular investigation that followed its instructions step-by-step—of course, successfully. So, in this case there is an experimental procedure but no creative thinking.

Research and experimentation are not just for finding methods, or tricks, to help pursue the ultimate end of forensics—revealing the true circumstances of deaths and ensuring a perfectly fair application of the law. They are also for enhancing the knowledge of the human body. I alluded earlier to the problems raised by an inaccurate description of the human skeleton in the official plates of 1770. Here the advances due to forensic specialists in the nineteenth century are most spectacularly in evidence. Why should it be so? Tentatively, I would suggest that the answer lies both in the relationship between forensic medicine and classical medicine in China and in the very specificity of forensic activity.

The relationship between forensic medicine and classical (or "elite") medicine is complex. In several respects, they are two completely different things. In principle, forensic examinations were performed not by doctors, but by the poorly paid coroners operating under the gaze of officials who were, first of all, administrators. The occupation of doctors was to cure people, while forensic practice dealt with dead people.[65] Whereas the former looked for symptoms of dysfunction in a living organism, the latter observed the signs of what had happened to what was now an object—a corpse. The main exception to this pattern is *juan* 4 of the Qing *Washing Away of Wrongs,* devoted to emergency treatments for the various sorts of wounds, accidents, and poisonings that are the stuff of forensic examination. The "cases" in *Collected Evidence for Autopsies* occasionally mention attempts to cure a wounded victim or calling a doctor, but it is extremely rare to have doctors called for help in establishing a forensic diagnosis. One example is case 4, already mentioned, where the conditions of the formation of a scab on a wound, as exposed by the coroner, were confirmed by a doctor who had been consulted on this point. Similarly, in case 12, the problem was to establish whether a man who fell in a cesspool in the course of a fight died because of the stuff he had ingested or because of the blows he had received before. The doctor who had been sent to take care of the victim was called before the magistrate to testify about what he saw and to offer his interpretation of the eventual death of the patient; he is cited in the conclusion of this rather long investigation: "Besides, we have the doctor's deposition on which we can rely" (*you yisheng gongzheng ke ping*).

If these examples are exceptional and if doctors were never called to perform an autopsy[66]—if, to use McKnight's words, "the Western marriage of professional medical knowledge and forensic practice was lacking in China"[67]—this does not mean that forensic science was completely cut from conventional medical knowledge. Quite the contrary, it can be seen in the more extended cases in our corpus that much of the reasoning behind the forensic interpretation of the traces observed by coroners is grounded in the representation of the body and its functions in classical medicine and that it uses the same concepts and terminology. This should not surprise us: the authors of forensic treatises were literati and thus had natural access to the medical elite tradition, with which most of them seem to have been quite conversant. Just as Song Ci in the Song cited several medical works as sources,[68] so in 1796 Wang Youhuai tells us in the preface to his *Washing Away of Wrongs with Collected Evidence* that he took notes not only from forensic treatises and collections of leading cases, but also from "reliable medical books" (*yishu kexin*).

What is remarkable in the *Collected Evidence for Autopsies* cases, in fact, is that quite often the coroners themselves "talk medicine" and even cite in support of their arguments the universal reference in medical science at the time, the imperially sponsored compilation titled *The Golden Mirror of Medicine* (*Yizong jinjian*, 1739). Indeed, many situations described in *The Washing Away of Wrongs* itself, and still more in the actual cases, are not just about broken bones, bodies burnt to ashes or hanging from beams, cut throats, and deadly poisons: they are complex configurations where many factors intersect, including not only the lesions immediately observable, but also the physical or even mental state of the victim before the fact, former illnesses, or pathologies manifesting themselves between an act of violence and the moment of death. Especially when death was delayed by several weeks, higher authorities raised questions. Determining the exact cause of death, and therefore the correct allocation of responsibilities, might entail reasoning about *internal* disorders beyond the scope of forensic science strictly speaking, which were problems for doctors. Yet these factors were extensively discussed by the persons involved in the forensic procedure, be they officials or coroners, and the conclusions were duly integrated into the final postmortem report.[69]

Chinese forensics concentrates on the external examination of the victims. With the exception of *kaijian*—cutting in the flesh to inspect the bones of decayed corpses whose surface is too damaged to reveal reliable traces—there is no dissection involved, and in particular there is no direct observation of the viscera.[70] That the study of bones, as opposed to viscera, should be the exception is not surprising: concern with and observation of the skeleton was a logical consequence of the nature of the discipline itself, since it had in many cases to deal with decayed corpses or with remains without any flesh left. This is not the place to discuss the respective influence of representations of the skeleton in medical treatises by doctors and in forensic treatises—the models appear to have operated in one or the other direction depending on the period, although in a general way the forensic scholars were the more influential. Of more interest to us for the present purpose are the efforts made by several nineteenth-century forensic specialists to improve the knowledge of bones through experimental observation, at a time when no advances had been made since the two chapters on bones in *The Golden Mirror of Medicine* and the faulty plates of the skeleton integrated into *The Washing Away of Wrongs* in 1770. They are of interest because they were part of a collective accumulation of knowledge, were based on serial observation within the framework of forensic practice, and are therefore related to the process of collecting cases.

One of the principal authors to have questioned the received description of the human skeleton is Lang Jinqi in his *Collected References for Autopsies,* the essay on bones to which *Collected Evidence for Autopsies* was a companion volume. The preface to the work is indeed very striking. Lang cites several cases investigated by him where there were contradictions between the standard text of *The Washing Away of Wrongs* and its appendices (the so-called *fukao,* quoting from various *Washing Away of Wrongs* studies), and where he himself had to look to find out which was wrong. In one example, the *fukao* mentioned three "small pin-bones" (*xiaochaigu*) at the back of the skull on which it was possible to observe traces in case of suicide by hanging, but *The Washing Away of Wrongs* proper had nothing about it. Lang examined the body carefully and did find the three bones with reddish lesions, but he was at a loss to fill out the standard forms because they did not mention them. His taste for the visual and the concrete is also illustrated by the fact that, to compensate for these insufficiencies, he managed after some frustration to have two wooden models carved that represented the external body and the skeleton, respectively, in all their details; the models were stored in his prefectural headquarters at Liuzhou so that in future investigations it would be possible to "argue based on the shape" (*yi xing lunbian*) instead of using incomplete and faulty plates. For his and his colleagues' use he also combined the checklist of bones (the *guge*) and the checklist of spots on the body (the *shige*) so that it would be easy to understand at first glance where there was "mutual clarification" (*huxiang faming*) and where "the inside and the outside differed somehow" (*neiwai shaoyi*).

Collected References for Autopsies proposes new plates representing the skeleton; the text consists of an updated list of the bones, with commentaries. Other authors in the nineteenth century—all of them well-known officials with a deep interest in law and forensics—were to continue the effort, with more and more precise pictures and descriptions: Xu Lian's impressive *Explanation of the Meaning of the Washing Away of Wrongs* (*Xiyuan lu xiangyi,* 1854) has a set of "actualized" (*xianni*) plates of the skeleton and bones, which may have been inspired by Western representations, even though the author claims they were drawn by artists who attended autopsies with him.[71] Likewise, in Gangyi's *Evidence on the Meaning of the Washing Away of Wrongs* (*Xiyuan lu yizheng,* 1891), Xu Lian's illustrations showing the bones (themselves updating the plates promulgated in 1770) are supplemented with Western-style (lit. "new pattern," *xinmo*) anatomical plates that constitute a striking stylistic break from the traditional drawings; however, Gangyi insists that the 1770 pattern and form (*tuge*) still needed to be used for reports and that any variant had to be carefully explained.

The results of all these efforts are not necessarily very scientific by our standards. There are many disagreements on the exact number of bones (even if in the prefaces the symbolic number of 365 bones, found in *The Washing Away of Wrongs*, is preserved), on the exact terminology, on the shape, and so on. But what is significant for our purpose is that this collective endeavor to perfect the knowledge of the human skeleton despite an imperially sanctioned fixed norm was almost always the work of men who availed themselves of extensive field experience, who displayed a feel for experimentation, research, and tinkering with concrete objects as well as for the accumulation of new evidence and new ideas, and who demonstrated a lively interest in whatever might modify—if not question radically—a codified knowledge that was sanctioned by a long and venerable tradition.

CONCLUSION

The original contribution of forensic medicine lies in the fact that in this instance "thinking with cases" applied to a field of knowledge where the ultimate validation could be found only in the precise observation of concrete objects and situations—the human body, the actions and aggressions that had an impact on it, and its component parts lying, as it were, in front of the observer. This was quite different from armchair textual *kaozheng*. A knowledge of the general principles written down in *The Washing Away of Wrongs* and grounded in classical medical theory was important, as was a knowledge of all the cases available for reference in the literature. But all the authors insisted that it would never replace the familiarity and experience acquired in the daily practice of the art—acquired through attending in person as many specific cases as possible.

As in the field of law and jurisprudence, the casebooks were a means of expanding such personal experience into collective databases that would acquaint each individual practitioner with a number of possibilities much larger than what he could expect to experience during his own career and influence in return his own practice and, perhaps, research. To be sure, this collective approach to building knowledge was not unique to the field of forensics—after all, the notion of a "community of scholars" exchanging ideas and findings existed in the traditional fields of erudition as well. But it seems to me that in their collective cognitive endeavor the attitude of the forensic specialists was influenced by the specific environment of an elite of militant bureaucrats, of which they were themselves members and which was united by a common goal—improving administrative practice and approaching an ideal of good government. One favorite locus for this elite to express itself and propagate its professional knowledge and values was of course the official handbooks of every description to which I alluded at the beginning of this chapter. The forensic treatises and casebooks definitely belong to this literature, and it is striking to see how in their prefaces—perhaps even more than in those to the regular official handbooks—the authors and sponsors are prone to speak of themselves as participants in a community of men united by their "common occupation" (*tongshi*), "common passion" (*tonghao*), and "common ideal" (*tongzhi*); a community, it should be added, whose members did not necessarily know each other and that in fact spanned the generations, as can be seen in some late nineteenth-century prefaces that recapitulate the entire history of writing and research in the field.

This group of people was an "elite" and considered itself to be so not only because they were experts respected and admired by their peers, but also because their ultimate goal was to bridge the gap between forensics as a science and forensics as a routine administrative activity—in other words, to inform the routine practice of forensic examination with the results of their research and experience. To accomplish this, assembling "cases" that confronted the received knowledge and basic regulations and making them widely known was clearly an important means.

NOTES

1 There exists a quantity of secondary literature on the history of forensics in China, especially in Chinese. The best-known synthesis in a Western language is Needham and Lu, "A History of Forensic Medicine," which draws heavily but uncritically from Chinese publications that tend to be outdated and repetitive and in fact have kept transmitting the same errors for decades: see Jia Jingtao, "Zhongguo fayixue." Jia himself is the author of a remarkable book on the history of Chinese forensic medicine, *Zhongguo gudai fayixue shi,* to which I am much indebted, and whose approach seems to me more balanced and, as it happens, less Sinocentric than that of his famous Cambridge colleague. Part of what follows is based on a seminar on *The Washing Away of Wrongs* held at Collège de France in 1997, which greatly benefited from the collaboration of my colleagues Jérôme Bourgon (for Chinese law) and Catherine Despeux and Frédéric Obringer (for Chinese medicine). Their contributions are indirectly reflected in this chapter.

2 On that topic see Pierre-Étienne Will [Wei Peixin], "Ming Qing shiqi de guanzhenshu," as well as my ongoing project, *Official Handbooks and Anthologies of Imperial China: A Descriptive and Critical Bibliography* (approx. 900 entries completed).

3 We have a famous example already in the Song. This is the *Minggong shupan qingming ji,* an anthology of judgments—here called *shupan,* with an emphasis on the textual aspect of the sentence—by Fujian officials during the first half of the thirteenth century. For the English translation of this collection, see Song Ci [Sung Tz'u], *The Enlightened Judgment.* Another famous collection is the playwright Li Yu's 1663 anthology

of administrative texts titled *Zizhi xinshu* (with a sequel of 1667). A large part of Li Yu's collection also consists of judgments (*panyu*, lit. "sentence words") by a great many different hands.

4 Here again the classic collections date back to the Song: they are He Ning and He Meng's *Yiyu ji* (10th century) and Zhen Ke's *Zheyu guijian* (early 12th century). Both of them deal with groups of historical figures, and contents extracted from these two works went into the equally famous *Parallel Cases from under the Pear-tree* (*Tangyin bishi*, 1211 preface). One well-known example devoted to a single official is *Cases Solved by Mr. Luzhou* (*Luzhou gong'an*, 1729 preface), of which the model official Lan Dingyuan (1680–1733) was both author and hero.

5 See Song Ci [Sung Tz'u], *The Washing Away of Wrongs.*

6 *Cheng'an* is sometimes rendered "established case." As a formal category in judicial administration it seems to have been a creation of the Qing.

7 See Xu Lian, preface to his *Xingbu bizhao jiajian cheng'an xubian* (1843). This was a new compilation (in 32 *juan*) taking into account the leading cases that had accumulated since the original compilation, published in 1834, for which Xu Lian had already written a preface.

8 Substatutes began to be appended to the statutes at the beginning of the sixteenth century; however, only with the Yongzheng and Qianlong codes did they acquire the same legal authority as the statutes (the 1740 code is the first to be titled *Da Qing lüli*).

9 The phrase is developed in a preface to a forensics treatise, which criticizes those who are "not able to exhaust all the variations [*bian*] in order to figure out the totality [or 'connecting principle,' *tong*]" (*bu neng qiong qi bian yi guan qi tong*). See Zhou Zuoji's 1849 preface to the *Jianyan hecan* (see below).

10 A number of examples could be cited that belong to the sphere of official handbooks inasmuch as they are explicitly intended as repositories of models for administrators.

11 See Bourgon, "Chine (culture juridique)," 189.

12 See the long but by no means exclusive list of works in Ch'ü, *Law and Society*, 300–301.

13 See note 7 above. Xu's preface illustrates how a sound knowledge of cases could be a pawn in the competition for influence and possibly bribes: such was the accumulation of leading cases (according to Xu, those from 1834 to 1843 assembled in the 32 *juan* of his compilation represented a pile several feet high) that officials in the Board offices would become familiar with the materials only after many years of service, and since most of them were transferred elsewhere as soon as they had mastered the job, if not before, the Board clerks were able to take advantage of the complexity and in fact disorder of the database, conceal archives if they were not properly bribed, and manipulate ignorant officials when a decision needed to be made. Even though complaints about clerks taking advantage of their knowledge of the precedents to manipulate their superiors are a topos in the literature and that officials probably tended to exaggerate the problem (as always, everything that went wrong was ascribed to the "vicious clerks"), Xu Lian's testimony confirms beyond doubt that it did exist.

14 Wu Guanghua's above-mentioned compilation, *Mouyi beikao* (The reference materials for those who make plans in cities), of 1758, is a good example of this process: it is said to have been derived from years of taking note of appropriate leading cases. Wu's employer, the prefect of Nanyang in Henan, who saw to it that the collection was printed, claimed that whoever was sitting on a court should keep a copy nearby.

15 One such example is a fascicle kept at the National Library of China under the title *Xingming zalan,* which collects leading cases dating mainly from the years 1813–1822 and covering a small number of categories from the *xingbu* section of the Penal Code; it was probably part of a larger set.

16 See Furth's introduction to this volume, pp. 4–5.

17 This guide—the first known official handbook—has been titled *The Way of the Official* (*Wei li zhi dao*) by its modern Chinese editors. For the text, see Hulsewé, *Remnants of Ch'in Law,* esp. 183–207. And see Bodde, "Forensic Medicine."

18 Suspicion that homicides might be camouflaged as suicides or vice versa is found everywhere in the literature, and at all times. For the Qing, see Huang Liuhong's *Fuhui quanshu,* 14.1a–b. Based on his experience in Shandong in the 1670s, he claims that of ten cases of homicide brought to the court, only one or two were authentic, the rest being suicides camouflaged as homicides. Likewise, citing his tenures as magistrate in Shandong and in north Jiangsu, Xu Lian claims in the preface to his *Xiyuan lu xiangyi* that suicide and its exploitation in false accusations were common in these regions.

19 See note 4 above.

20 Notably *A Record of No Wrongs* (*Wuyuan lu,* 1308 preface) and *A Record of Redressing the Wrongs* (*Pingyuan lu*). A large part of the contents of the latter (the original Song or Yuan text of which has been lost) seems to have been drawn from *A Collection of Records on the Washing Away of Wrongs,* while the rest was copied into *A Record of No Wrongs.*

21 Of a total forty-two works listed by Jia Jingtao's *Zhongguo gudai fayixue shi,* the vast majority are recensions of *The Washing Away of Wrongs,* or texts derived from it.

22 One can doubt that this was done, however. A memorial sent in by Ling Qiu, the provincial judge of Jiangxi, in 1738 complained that local administrators were using private editions and various other treatises all full of contradictions; an edict of 1732 ordering that the provincial governors send their local copies for examination and collation by the Bureau of the Code and that a definitive edition be promulgated had so far not been followed by any effect. In its response, the Board explained that the process had been delayed first by the destruction of the files in a fire, and then by the work of compiling the new Penal Code commissioned by Qianlong in 1736. An edict of 1738 again ordered the Bureau of the Code to edit a standard version of *The Washing Away of Wrongs* for distribution to the provinces as soon as the work on the new penal code was completed. See Ling Qiu, *Xijiang shinie jishi,* 1.8a–9b.

23 Apart from his *Washing Away of Wrongs* recension Wang compiled several works that were regularly reprinted during the nineteenth century. *Xingqian bilan* (Indispensable readings for legal and financial secretaries) and *Qiangu beiyao* (Essentials for financial secretaries), both of 1793, are handbooks for private secretaries; *Ban'an yaolue* (Important

points for handling cases) discusses the judicial procedure (originally included in Wang's compilation of didactic materials called *Zhizheng jiyao* [Essentials on government], dated 1794, which I have not been able to see); in 1792 Wang put out *Zengding zeli tuyao bianlan* (Essential tables of precedents for convenient consultation) in 49 *juan*, a presentation of the regulations on administrative sanctions (*chufen zeli*) in table form that revised and updated a work by the same title compiled by a certain Shi Zhongyin.

24 E.g., the 1892 Shanghai tushu jicheng yinshuju typeset edition has no less than eleven prefaces and two colophons, all but one borrowed from previous editions.

25 Although they do not mention Wang Youhuai as the original compiler, Xu Lian's *Explanation of the Meaning of the Washing Away of Wrongs* of 1854 and Gangyi's *Evidence on the Meaning of the Washing Away of Wrongs* of 1891 are very similar sorts of work.

26 See Giles, trans., "The 'Hsi Yüan Lu' or 'Instructions to Coroners,'" 1874 and 1924 versions. Giles, who tells us that he first heard of *The Washing Away of Wrongs* in Ningbo in 1873, apparently used the version edited in 1843 by Tong Lian (whose preface he translates). His translation of the work is by no means complete, however, and as it is not always accurate it should never be used without carefully checking with the original text.

27 Bulantai, preface to the *Jianshi kaoyao* (by Zhu Gang).

28 See Xue Yunsheng, *Duli cunyi*, 4:1266–1275, statute 412.

29 Ibid., statute 412, substatute 14.

30 See *Xijiang zhengyao*, 1.42b–1.43a, 47a–b.

31 Gangyi, postface to the 1892 Guangdong edition of his *Xiyuan lu yizheng*.

32 See above, notes 28 and 29.

33 Although the examination of the corpse was made by the coroner, who would "shout out" (*hebao*) his observations to the magistrate seated nearby, once the examination was over the magistrate was required to come by and check the results for himself; this might involve palpations, sniffing odors, and other unattractive manipulations from which many officials tended to recoil. In the preface to his *Explanation of the Meaning of the Washing Away of Wrongs* (1854), Xu Lian emphasizes that scholars who were selected to become magistrates on their proficiency in eight-legged essays were easy prey to the coroners' false reports, either because of their lack of experience or because they preferred to stay away from the filthiness of postmortem examinations.

34 *Xijiang zhengyao*, 1.42a–b.

35 The rule was that the magistrate had to go to the site where the autopsy would be performed—it was forbidden to move the corpse—accompanied by the coroner and one clerk from the Bureau of Punishments (i.e., a *xingshu*) only. Fang Ruqian, in the preface to his *Baojian Xiyuan lu* (1761), a popular adaptation of the basic text in rhymed verse, insists that autopsies could not be delegated to private secretaries.

36 Li Guanlan was also the chief compiler of an important edition of the Penal Code with commentaries, the *Da Qing lüli quanzuan jizheng* of 1799, and among his collaborators was Wang Youhuai.

37 1886 preface to *Jiangu buyi kaozheng* (Supplementary evidence for examining bones), an anonymous compilation of extracts from Xu Lian's *Explanation of the Meaning*

of the Washing Away of Wrongs. The so-called "judicial bureaus" were provincial courts that appeared at the time of the Tongzhi restoration in the 1860s.

38 Twenty more cases were published as a sequel in 1839 under the title *Xue'an chumo xubian;* each collection is composed of ten fascicles. Besides the original edition there is an 1881 new edition engraved at the offices of the Gansu provincial judge.

39 Yilibu cites two titles as examples of the collections of leading cases he criticizes, the *Cheng'an beikao,* which I have not seen so far, and the *Cheng'an xinbian,* of which I have seen a sequel titled *Cheng'an xinbian erji,* dating to 1763.

40 Except in a few instances where one or the other work is found appended to one of the later editions of *The Washing Away of Wrongs with Collected Evidence,* the *Collected References for Autopsies* and *Collected Evidence for Autopsies* were always published as a set, and in fact the preface can be said to introduce both. I do not know whether there actually was a printed 1829 edition, but I have been able to examine editions printed in 1835, 1847 (in Shaanxi), and 1883 (in Guizhou); we also know that there was a first Guizhou edition in 1849.

41 There is a short 1807 preface by him (written in Hangzhou) to a recension of *The Washing Away of Wrongs with Collected Evidence* that may be lost today, although the preface is reproduced in many later editions.

42 A preface of 1833, by the governor of Guangxi, tells us that Ruan had died in office earlier during the year.

43 I have not yet been able to examine a copy of the 1832 edition of *The Washing Away of Wrongs with Collected Evidence and Added Notes* (which was in fact printed in 1833 by the governor of Guangxi), but the later editions of the 1830s are all said to have been based on it. These editions of the 1830s were in turn reproduced, with some variations, by those of the 1840s and after. In other words, in all likelihood the materials I am discussing in this chapter, based on an 1864 edition available in Paris (titled *Chongkan buzhu Xiyuan lu jizheng*), go back to Ruan Qixin.

44 It happens that the same case is quoted twice, under two different headings. It should also be noted that there already were many cases cited in the pre-Ruan Qixin strata of the text, with indication of time and place, but these are not headed by a caption summarizing the problem at hand, like the Ruan (or Lang) cases.

45 Citing, in succession, cases of bones revealing that the victim's body was burnt after death, cases of scalding, of branding, and of burns by firearms and gunpowder.

46 This is an interesting example of what we might call "free association": the series of cases of death by strangulation or suffocation ends with the example of prisoners being strangled by their chains, whence the author proceeds to deaths under torture or after questioning. Incidentally, administrators were naturally reluctant to perform bona fide autopsies on persons who had perished in prison or during interrogation and tended to gloss over the circumstances and had the victims buried in haste. See the discussion in a long circular (*tongxing*) of 1832 quoted in Zhu Qingqi, comp., *Xuzeng Xing'an huilan,* 16.13b–16.14a.

47 E.g., when the corpse has been burnt, entailing an "examination of the ground" (*jiandi*) using certain chemical devices to make its shape appear with visible traces of the

wounds; these cases, quoted at the beginning of the work, are set apart from the cases of burning.

48 In his preface to the 1847 edition of *Collected References for Autopsies* and *Collected Evidence for Autopsies*, Jiang Rong, the editor, says that trifling errors in an autopsy could be of great consequence as far as the correct "naming of the crime" (*zuiming*) was concerned; therefore, one needed to "collect evidence" (*jizheng*) in order to feel secure in one's conclusions, and this is why Lang Jinqi's work was so useful to officials who did not themselves have extensive field experience.

49 Some entries include two or more affairs whose contents refer to the same problem.

50 In the case of suicides or suspicious deaths, e.g., there was a standard set of observations: on the eyes and mouth (open or closed), direction of eyeballs, condition of the hands and feet (stiff or relaxed), color of the face, etc.

51 In such instances the text is evidently a contraction of the original report, which would quote the higher authorities' remarks and the magistrate's reply at length, not omitting the conventional respectful phrases, and entailing much repetition along the way. Again, we find such reports quoted verbatim in *Elementary Models for Studying Cases*, whose point is not to focus on the relevant details but to reproduce the entire file as found in the provincial archives.

52 A typical example is case 8, where in the end the husband of a woman who had cut her own throat testified that she was left-handed; in this way the shape of the wound could be explained and, importantly, reconciled with *The Washing Away of Wrongs*' specifications. (The victim's father claimed she had not committed suicide but had been murdered, and he appealed to the capital, hence the importance of leaving no detail unexplained.) In a case of "strangulation with the hands" (*qiasi*), where a man had been killed by his opponent in the course of a fight, only the graphic description of the struggle by the surviving party made it possible to understand the forensic evidence correctly (case 69).

53 In the short entries consisting of a mere fragment of forensic report there is no identification whatsoever.

54 See, e.g., case 119, where the magistrate directs the coroner step-by-step in the preparation of the bones of a woman for examination after they had been extracted from her coffin. The forensic examination (interrupted at one point by the victim's relatives, who attempted to snatch the remains away) proves that she had drowned and that the wounds on some of her bones had been inflicted afterward in order to fake the accident as a homicide. Incidentally, this is one of only two cases in the entire collection with an indication of source, viz. *Yuexi cheng'an sanbian*. The other is case 26, which refers the reader to "Precedents of 1816, page 125."

55 The phrase *toumo* is frequently used in forensic literature, but absent from all the dictionaries. I am not sure of its exact meaning.

56 This was an important detail, of course: the pressure applied by the knife was supposed to be stronger at the start, therefore the cut would go from more to less deep; in the case of a left-handed person the direction would be the reverse from that in the case of the right-handed.

57 *The Washing Away of Wrongs* distinguishes between suicides committed in a state of anger, depression, fear of punishment, or because there is no other way out; in each instance the clinical manifestations (position of the eyes and mouth) are different. In the last instance mentioned the person "sees death as returning home, he ardently wishes to die in order to escape his responsibility." It may be that in our case the coroner was basing his explanation on some testimony not reproduced in the *Collected Evidence for Autopsies* extract.

58 In the 1864 edition that I used there are also several notes in different colors, which by definition are posterior to the affair described here. This was obviously a difficult topic. See [*Chongkan*] *Buzhu Xiyuan lu jizheng,* 2.27a–2.29b for the official text, 31a–35a for the cases appended by Ruan Qixin.

59 This case is dated 1817 and located in Zhili. It is also found in the Ruan Qixin appendix to the "Zican" section of *The Washing Away of Wrongs.*

60 Most authors consider that the two types of examination—external examination of the corpse and manipulation of the bones—correspond to the terms *yan* and *jian,* respectively, although there exist differing opinions. (*Jianyan* is routinely used to mean "forensic examination" in general.) When examination of the bones involves cutting through the flesh of the corpse, the term used is *kaijian.* A phrase frequently encountered (and used in the present example) to deplore the unpleasant aspects of bone examination from the point of view of the victim is *zhengshua zhi can* (the misfortune of having to experience steaming and scrubbing). *Juan* 1 of *The Washing Away of Wrongs* has a section called "Yangu," describing the bones and limited to their visual examination, and a section called "Jiangu," dealing with the fumigations and application of various products to which they may be submitted to make signs of lesions appear.

61 Note, however, that the difficulties recorded in the cases of *Collected Evidence for Autopsies* are not all due to the insufficiencies of *The Washing Away of Wrongs.* Some are ascribed to lack of evidence (corpses partially destroyed by fire or other causes: see, e.g., the learned argumentation of the coroner in case 49 who has to answer insistent questions about a corpse, most of which has been badly damaged by fire), to testimonies contradicting the forensic evidence, to negligence on the part of the coroner, or to lack of experience (e.g., case 137, about a man who "lost his *yang*" because of too-intense marital sex and whose death was hastily ascribed to poisoning by an inexperienced coroner who based himself on an ambiguity in the relevant entries of *The Washing Away of Wrongs*), etc.

62 We have seen the problem of the size typically ascribed to the wounds made with knives. Another example is the location of wounds on the body of people killed in a fall (*shidie shensi*), depending on whether they fell by themselves or were pushed by someone else. In two cases in *Collected Evidence for Autopsies* (10 and 11) it requires a great deal of argument to prove that the wounds of a man who fell without being pushed need not be limited to the list proposed by *The Washing Away of Wrongs* and could very well resemble those supposed to be characteristic of the victim of an attacker.

63 See He Ning and He Meng, *Yiyu ji,* 1; [*Chongkan*] *Buzhu Xiyuan lu jizheng,* 2.64b–2.65a, entry on "distinguishing in a blaze between persons who were alive and persons who

were already dead" (*yan huofen bian shengqian sihou*). The person who is being burnt alive opens his/her mouth to gasp for air, hence the ashes in the corpse's mouth.

64 For the mere paragraph on "death by burning" (*huosi*), see Song Ci, *Xiyuan jilu*, 62 (Sung Tz'u [Song Ci], *The Washing Away of Wrongs*, 132). Also see [*Chongkan*] *Buzhu Xiyuan lu jizheng*, 1.62a–b.

65 The catalogue of the private library of the famous collector and bibliographer Sun Xingyan (1753–1818) has one of its twelve sections devoted to "medicine and law" (*yilü*). In his preface (dated 1800), Sun explains that these two disciplines were "of great importance as to whether people will survive or be killed" (*shengren sharen suoguan shen zhong*). Forensic medicine was evidently an appendage to law: in the same catalogue *The Washing Away of Wrongs* and similar works are in the subsection on law, not medicine. See Sun Xingyan, *Sun shi citang shumu, neibian*, 3.18a–b. My thanks to Jérôme Bourgon for pointing out this source to me.

66 It may be interesting to note, though, that in a probably late-Ming handbook for pettifoggers titled *Falin jinjian, juan* 3, an autopsy report given as example is signed by the "doctor on duty" (*zhiri yisheng*).

67 McKnight, introduction to Sung Tz'u [Song Ci], *The Washing Away of Wrongs*, 26.

68 Sung Tz'u [Song Ci], *The Washing Away of Wrongs*, 28–29.

69 To cite one example among many others, in case 99 the problem was to determine why a man who was pushed by someone and merely fell on his behind died, when none of the expected wounds or traces on the bones were apparent; it required a lengthy and quasi-medical argument on the part of the coroner, supported by the testimony of the victim's wife, to establish that the victim had formerly suffered from an illness that explained his weakness.

70 Dissection seems to have been quite foreign to the Chinese medical tradition. One famous example is mentioned in the biography of the usurper Wang Mang at the beginning of the first century (to measure the length of the internal vessels), and one Han text in *Yellow Emperor's Inner Classic* (*Huangdi neijing*) states that it is permissible to dissect corpses for a better understanding of the viscera. Subsequently, it is only in the Northern Song that we again find mention of corpses of rebels being dissected with the help of doctors and of plates being drawn to represent the different organs. In a lesser-known example dating to the late sixteenth century, an army medical officer is said to have opened the stomach of corpses to observe their viscera and compare them with those of pigs. Finally, in his *Correcting Mistakes in the World of Medicine* (*Yilin gaicuo*) of 1830, Wang Qingren reported on his observations of the viscera from the corpses of child victims of an epidemic that had been partly devoured by dogs—not a case of dissection, strictly speaking—to criticize the descriptions in the medical treatises of his time. For this and for the next section I am greatly indebted to Catherine Despeux. On ancient Chinese dissection, see also Yamada Keiji, "Hakkōpa," and Wang Daohuan, "Lun *Yilin gaicuo de jie pouxue*." Commenting on Chinese medicine, Robert K. Douglas, a generally rather perceptive observer of China in the late nineteenth century, remarks that "Their [the Chinese] deeply-rooted repugnance to the use of the knife in surgery, or to post-mortem examinations, prevents the possibility of their acquiring any accurate knowledge of the

human frame." See Douglas, *China*, 230. And, importantly, dissection is absent from the discipline of forensics, where it could have been of much use. (The connection between the Northern Song examples of dissection and the publication of *A Collection of Records on the Washing Away of Wrongs*, made by some authors, is very unlikely; they proceeded from two very different approaches.)

71 Xu Lian's work on the bones also appears in an undated short treatise put together by an anonymous compiler and titled *Jiangu buyi kaozheng*.

3

From Oral Testimony to Written Records in Qing Legal Cases

YASUHIKO KARASAWA

A criminal case is an event before it is a case record. The written record, with its implicit claims to truthfulness, is in fact the result of a complex manipulation of the original process of investigation, interrogation, and analysis that constitutes court proceedings. In order to illuminate that process, this chapter examines one kind of document that was essential to the record of criminal cases in the Qing dynasty. These are the written records of oral testimony taken from defendants and key witnesses, which were written down separately based on the notes taken at their depositions and then woven into the case reports composed to explain the case and justify the magistrate's verdict. These documents, called "formal testimony," constituted key pieces of the evidence made available to the superior judicial officials who reviewed all serious crimes. The most important were likely to be criminal confessions.

I found two broad influences on criminal case recordings that derive from Qing-dynasty legal culture and literary convention. First, the requirements of judicial review of all serious felonies made legal specialists composing drafts of formal testimony strive for consistency in details, wording, and plot among the stories of different parties. In those obligatory judicial reviews, the credibility of testimony woven into the narrative of the case report played a decisive role in persuading senior authorities to accept the magistrate's suggested sentence. Second, the broader written culture of the Qing supplied models of narrative fashioning that played a crucial role in producing a highly formalized and concise style of reporting oral testimony. In particular, vernacular stories as a literary genre provided scribes who worked at county government offices (*yamens*) and who were part of its audience with the lexicon and other linguistic tools to take oral testimony originally uttered in local dialects or regional languages and record it in the uniform vernacular style derived from Mandarin speech (*guanhua*).

We usually find such formalized, concise style in the only surviving written records of oral testimony in local-level case records kept stored at the county offices.

These official case files do not include original depositions or drafts written prior to the final, decisive version, probably because it was not necessary to expose these documents to the eyes of senior authorities. However, one archive of local-level case records—the so-called "cases directly examined by the Board of Punishments" (*Xingbu xianshen,* referred to as "directly examined")—contained in Beijing's Board of Punishments archive reveals the process of revising drafts of written testimony into final form. "Directly examined" cases involved felonies that occurred in two counties surrounding Beijing and in Beijing itself.[1] The Board of Punishments, probably because it was the empire's supreme judicial authority responsible for the security of the emperor and court, left detailed records of the interrogation process of local cases that took place in the capital.

Because of their more detailed documentation, "directly examined" cases tell us how the interrogations were carried out and how the final draft of testimony was formalized. Through the process of recording depositions and producing successive drafts of testimony based on the interrogations, the raw dossier evolved into a polished, consistent final draft, without contradictions or ambiguity. The raw dossier itself never finalized the "truth" of the case; the valid legal case claimed truth when it arrived at a narrative that offered one and only one reconstruction of what actually happened. Using material from the Beijing Board of Punishments, this chapter shows how a legitimate legal case record of testimony was constructed, involving linguistic manipulation with the help of narrative devices derived from the written culture in the Qing.

THE STATUS OF DEPOSITIONS IN QING LEGAL PROCEDURE

Qing legal procedure is characterized by its well-organized system of obligatory reviews. Let me briefly summarize this system in order to show why witnesses' testimonies occupied a key position in legal case records. All legal cases, great and small, were first heard at the county office where the magistrate served as judge.[2] For serious cases requiring penalties including or exceeding temporary exile, a magistrate would file a formal case report including verified facts and the "suggested sentence" (*ni*) according to law. He sent this, along with the convicted criminal in person, to his senior official, the prefect. If the prefect verified the facts and found the suggested sentence reasonable, the case record, along with the criminal, was sent to his senior official, the judicial commissioner at the provincial capital. After investigating the documents and questioning the criminal, the judicial commissioner, if he found the suggested sentence proper, forwarded the case to the governor of the province. A noncapital case carrying a suggested sentence of temporary exile could be approved and carried out on the governor's authority. Homicide cases and those that required penalties of life exile or military servitude were sent to the Board of Punishments in Beijing. Only with its endorsement were the penalties finalized. Finally, cases requiring capital punishment had to be approved by the emperor. In this fashion, the establishment of penalties including and exceeding temporary exile required successive review at several levels of government.[3]

The obligatory review system served to check any errors in the judgment of the crime. At each stage of review, documents and the testimony of the criminal and witnesses were carefully examined. If any doubts arose, the case would be returned to a lower level with severe admonition. A mishandled case, if found, would damage a magistrate's future career. Thus the obligatory review system always placed pressure on the magistrate to be as careful as possible with all serious criminal procedures. (If a dissatisfied litigant appealed his case, a magistrate might even be ordered to send up to superiors the records of lesser "civil procedure" cases [*xishi*], which were not usually the subject of obligatory review.)[4] Therefore, in documenting a case, the primary requirement for a convincing case report was to provide consistent and firm testimony from the parties and witnesses.

But the reason testimony was so central requires further explanation. The legal historian Shiga Shūzō argues that in contrast to modern Western criminal procedure, in which factual issues are decided by "adjudication," Qing criminal procedure emphasized decisions based on the confession of the offender. This difference derives from differing expectations as to the role of the judge. "Adjudication" in the Western sense, according to Shiga,

> is simply a judgment or estimation, made by a chosen person or body of persons, which, once delivered, is accepted as a substitute for the truth itself. On the assumption that the truth itself can be grasped only by God, [Western] "adjudication" is intended to satisfy the social need to know the truth on a matter requiring prompt and adequate handling. . . . [T]he said judgment must be seen to come as close to the truth as human ability permits.

In contrast, in Qing China, the task of the judge (usually the magistrate) was to expose the truth itself. A judge in the Qing had to induce a defendant to tell the truth using any means, including trickery or torture, on the grounds that the person who committed the crime knows best what s/he did. Therefore, in Qing criminal procedure proof of guilt always had to include the criminal's written confession. "No one could be pronounced guilty of a crime he did not confess."[5]

Since guilt had to be established by a confession, the record of testimony constituted the most crucial part of the case report. Guidelines for producing written records of oral testimony were laid out in *A Complete Book Concerning Happiness and Benevolence* (*Fuhui quanshu*), a handbook for local magistrates compiled in the seventeenth century. Such testimony records consisted of two kinds: the "original deposition" (*gongzhuang* or *caogong*) and the "formal testimony" (*zhaozhuang*). The first is the record of what the parties and witnesses said during each interrogation. After several stages of interrogation, a magistrate would ascertain to his own satisfaction what had actually happened. The final draft, or "formal testimony," was composed to sum up these conclusions in the principals' own words. This formal testimony was read aloud in front of the criminal, who was expected to sign it (usually by a cross for men or a circle for women) to signify a guilty plea.[6]

Witnesses' statements were transcribed by scribes working at the government offices at each interrogation. "Original depositions" were the products of this stage. Then the draft testimony of each party was further composed either by scribes under the guidance of the magistrate's private secretaries or by the secretaries themselves.[7] These intermediate drafts are called "draft depositions" in this chapter. After revising these drafts, the secretaries crafted the formal testimony version to be used for the case report reviewed by superiors. The prospect of review encouraged private secretaries to pay attention to crucial requirements in composing testimony, such as the appropriate order of confessions, the consistency of events recounted in confessions, and skillful construction of the narrative plot or story. These conditions imposed by Qing judicial principles and procedure helped shape the social and cultural setting in which testimony was composed.

WRITING LEGAL TESTIMONY IN THE CONTEXT OF LITERARY CULTURE

Written testimony was full of administrative terms and legal clichés, but reading it as a technical language would fail to reveal the cultural context that also shaped it. The magistrates' private secretaries who composed testimony lived within the world of written culture that also produced examination and other literary essays and vernacular fiction. A number of guidebooks for legal private secretaries illuminate shared concepts of good literary style in Qing China.

One of these, *Important Points for Handling Cases* (*Ban'an yaolu*), a technical guide for legal specialists written in the eighteenth century, includes an essay titled "How to Compose Testimony" (Xugong) that may be taken as representative. It offered guidelines under six headings: 1) putting events in order (*qianhou cengci*); 2) logical development (*qichengzhuanghe*); 3) foreshadowing and correspondence between events (*maifu zhaoying*); 4) highlighting the key points and making a transition (*dianti guomai*); 5) summarizing points and adding supplementary accounts (*xiaona buwo*); and 6) writing with skill and laying out the story (*yunbi buju*).[8]

"Putting events in order" requires careful attention to the sequence of each party's testimony, to show clearly how an event developed and let the reviewing official grasp the point of the case. "Logical development" is about how to make all aspects of the description of an event consistent. This idea of consistency is encapsulated in three terms: *qing, xing,* and *jie.*[9] *Qing* indicates both the facts of the case and people's states of mind. *Xing* refers to the physical circumstances involved. *Jie* means the plot or the details of the story of the case. According to "How to Compose Testimony," every case must have its own facts (*qingjie*),[10] while each party must have his/her own circumstances (*qingxing*). The reason the two sides in the case came into conflict constitutes the facts (*qing*) of the case. The explanation of how the case developed forms the plot or the details (*jie*) of the story. The description of what each party thought and wished on the day of the crime explains the state of mind (*qing*) of the parties. The narration of how the parties got involved manifests the physical circumstances (*xing*) of each party. It is important that the plot (*qingjie*) of the case mirror the respective states of mind and physical circumstances (*qingxing*) of the parties involved. In other words, the narration of the plot of the case must logically organize (*canhe*) the different states of mind and physical circumstances of each party. The choice of elements used in narrating the testimony from beginning to end is made through the process of logical organization.

"Foreshadowing" (in guideline 3 above) warns against a sudden appearance of anybody in the testimony without prior identification to prepare the reader. The "correspondence of events" enjoins that such things as the words used to describe the event, dates and places, the location of injuries on a corpse, and the narration of circumstances should correspond in each witness' testimony without contradiction. However, since everybody involved has a different position and status, composing testimony also requires making distinctions in the order of events in each party's narration, in the language used, and in the manner of speech of different individuals.

The fourth technique, "highlighting the key points," is a skill of drawing attention to the core of the text. For example, in the description of a corpse, the phrase "it is determined that the cause of death was . . ." will lead to a description of the injuries. In a murder confession the criminal's description of his act should be followed by a statement of whether there was intent to kill. In "making a transition" the writer must make clear sequences such as how that event turned into this event, how an escaped criminal was caught and interrogated, and how the case first handled by one magistrate was taken over by his successor. "Summarizing points" (guideline 5) means condensing insignificant matters into a single phrase of only a few words. "Adding supplementary accounts" suggests that any doubtful points should be explained further at appropriate places within the record of testimony.

"Writing with skill" and "laying out the story" (guideline 6) are the keys to making a case report the kind of literary work that will satisfy reviewers. The language is clear and fluent. Not a single word is superfluous or rambling, and every sentence reveals a vigorous style. Testimony written in this way is well organized and coherent. An expert at "laying out the story" can keep in mind all aspects of the case; he can gather the threads of the various parties' testimonies in a consistent manner so that the narrative is concise, with no loose ends, yet complete, omitting nothing important. Summing up, the author of "How to Compose Testimony" insists that these guidelines are identical with those for composing literary essays. "This whole process is similar to that of reading and writing a literary essay, in that you need to ponder what is the main theme of the essay, which passage contains the main message, and which specific words convey its essence."[11]

This advice in fact contained many points of similarity with the guidelines for writing examination essays that had to be mastered by every candidate for a civil service position. Authors of guidelines for composing testimony were well aware of this. "How To Compose Testimony" begins: "Composing [literary] essays means writing meaningful opinions on behalf of the sages; composing a record of courtroom testimony means expressing views on behalf of mediocre plebeians" (*zuowen dai shengxian liyan, xugong dai yongsu dayi*).[12] "Literary essays" here means examination essays. This introductory sentence in elegant parallel prose style comparing the two types of writing lent prestige to the court scribe's work.

Tang Biao, author of two guidebooks for examination candidates, offered students advice closely echoing that in "How to Compose Testimony." A good examination essay should crystallize its theme in one summation.[13] Tang's "method of forward projection" (*yufu fa*), like "foreshadowing" in "How to Compose Testimony," recommended the use of foreshadowing to provide textual connections (*mailuo*) linking each part.[14] In addition, Tang's handbook discusses other methods such as "logical development," "highlighting the key points," and "making a transition," all of which emphasize interconnections within a text.[15] To highlight the importance of these integrative devices, Qing treatises on writing examination essays frequently used the metaphor of an "artery" (*mai*) to represent linkages within a text.[16] For Tang Biao, the method of "correspondence of events" was particularly crucial.[17] These points of similarity between the desired literary style of examination essays and that of records of court testimony would not surprise most legal secretaries, who in practice were likely to be people who had repeatedly failed to pass the examinations, becoming technical legal experts as a second-choice occupation.[18]

The aforementioned advice was meant for writing composed in classical Chinese. However, vernacular fiction also supplied models for legal composition, and it also was prized for criteria of internal consistency and integration of parts of a narrative into a thematic web. Qing champions of vernacular fiction even claimed their genre equaled the examination essay in sophistication of literary technique.[19] By showing that vernacular fiction could be analyzed and appreciated according to criteria developed for the prestigious essay, fiction critics argued for vernacular fiction as serious literature.

Traditional Chinese fiction criticism paid particular attention to the internal consistency within a text, employing such concepts as *lianguan* and *guanchuan* (both mean "internal consistency"). Fiction critics praised a work if each of its parts (or units of narrative) was systematically orchestrated to interconnect and shape the overall structure.[20] Narrative units had to be interwoven to form a "dense fabric."[21] As with the examination essay, the textual interconnections in a fictional narrative were metaphorically signified by the term *mai* (artery). "Logical development" and "foreshadowing" served the goal of integrating the sequence of units. Critics of vernacular fiction also cared about the linkage among narrative units that were located in different parts of the fiction, considering it necessary in helping the reader to grasp the entire structure. The ideal of "interconnection from start to finish" (*shouwei xiangying*), as Andrew Plaks explains, implied "the ability of the master narrator to arrange his narrative details so as to impart to his text the impression of a tight web of interrelated elements, each of which takes on its full significance only in the total context of all the other narrative units brought together in his coordinated structure."[22]

Thus we find that the lexicon of six guidelines found in "How to Compose Testimony" borrowed heavily from terminology used by fiction critics.[23] "Laying out the story," "highlighting the key points," "making a transition," "putting events in order"—all these techniques ensure that, like a fine work of fiction, the case text maintains a structural coherence as though it were a tightly woven fabric in which narrative threads (*xiansuo*), running inside like "arteries" (*mai*), interconnect to function as narrative units, ultimately shaping the entire text.[24]

RECORDS OF ORAL TESTIMONY WRITTEN IN THE VERNACULAR

Written testimony was supposed to be organized along lines closely resembling those of essays in classical Chinese, the written language commonly used for most purposes. Why, then, was the vernacular style of writing employed in composing testimony, instead of the classical style? "How to Compose Testimony" explains the reason.

> The style of testimony must not be classical. Every single statement must sound like a popular proverb and every single word must be understandable by everyone, so that the testimony can convey the tone of ordinary speech. I have seen testimony which included classical words such as *zhi, ji,* and *er* and passages from the [Confucian] Classics. Such testimony gives no sense of vulgar plebeian talk.[25]

In order to give a written record of testimony the appearance that it had actually been uttered by ordinary people, classical Chinese, which was linguistically distinct from spoken language, could not be employed. After all, "composing a record of courtroom testimony means expressing views on behalf of petty plebeians."[26]

Frequent use of popular proverbs in speech, in fact, enabled testimony to have the appearance of vulgar diction. In the famous eighteenth-century vernacular novel *The Dream of the Red Chamber* (*Honglou meng*), the speech of uncultured protagonists is full of vulgar proverbs. The author, Cao Xueqin, expressed his dissatisfaction with the artificiality of other novels in which utterances of maidservants were filled with the flavor of classic language.[27] Thus the use of proverbs in plebeian testimony came from a common linguistic practice conspicuous in the writings of both self-conscious authors of fiction and skilled legal secretaries. Behind the literary convention was an ideological principle nurtured by examination culture. Classical language expresses the spirit of the sages.[28] Therefore the speech of uneducated common people should not be expressed in sagely language, because such people were not supposed to have internalized the sages' virtue and spirit.[29] In sum, employment of the written vernacular for recording testimony was necessary to give testimony the realistic appearance of vulgar plebeian talk. In fact, written vernacular was much closer to what people actually spoke in daily life than the classic Chinese. However, the ideological basis of adopting the written vernacular was rooted in a linguistic ideal that the language of sages and of people who had a grasp of their spirit must be separated from the language of vulgar, uneducated people.[30]

Let us turn to the linguistic characteristics of testimony produced by the use of the written vernacular. When the oral mode of communication met the written one, the requirement of consistency meant that certain linguistic elements, such as marks of dialects and regional languages, disappeared from official documents. In addition, the record of testimony, though written in the vernacular style, had to avoid coarse use of language. "How to Compose Testimony" emphasizes,

> Testimony must not be too coarse. Slang expressions, such as profane and insulting remarks and obscene details in adultery and rape cases must not be transcribed verbatim. Those expressions and scenes can be summarized with simple words such as "to abuse and revile" (*hunma*), "to have illicit sex" (*chengjian*), and so on. Failure to do such summarizing will provoke the reproach of senior officials [who review the case].[31]

Testimony thus does not record what people actually said because the primary concern was the review process. The gap between speech and written records of testimony can be seen in surviving "formal testimony" documents from provincial archives in Sichuan and in Taiwan. Every example of testimony included in the Baxian archives (*Baxian dang'an*) and Danshui Subprefecture and Xinzhu County archives (*Danshuiting Xinzhuxian dang'an*, usually abbreviated as "Dan-Xin dang'an") is a final draft of composition. But no single example of written testimony in the Dan-Xin archives from nineteenth-century Taiwan is a verbatim record of Hakka or Southern Min languages, which were the major spoken languages on the island. Aside from a few rare examples, we cannot find remnants of those spoken languages in the written records of testimony in Dan-Xin cases.

Clerks, who usually were employed in their native counties, had no problem understanding what local people stated in their common mother tongue. But even prior to the stage of composing drafts in the written vernacular, it was necessary to simultaneously translate what people were saying in the courtroom into Mandarin in order to write their utterances down on paper.[32] First of all, many words in Hakka and Southern Min have no exact correspondents in Chinese logographs. Second, a scribe who recorded confessions at a county office might have chosen either of two approaches: he could record what his colleague orally translated into Mandarin for magistrates who understood neither Hakka nor Southern Min, or he could translate what he heard stated in these regional languages into Mandarin in his brain at the time of courtroom interrogation (not when he composed the written drafts).[33] Testimony composed for official preservation and for senior officials' review of the case, of course, was composed in the written vernacular. However, given that the vernacular style of written language based on Mandarin was the only available tool to record oral speech, initial recording of what people said during the interrogation was also inevitably done with the written Mandarin vernacular, thereby translating from one regional dialect to Mandarin in the scribe's brain.

In addition, local expressions from certain dialects or regional languages were a target of censorship in composing testimony. As drafts were composed, dialect elements might be eliminated. A suggestion from a Qing manual for private secretaries recommends,

> In testimony, although it is permissible to use vulgar language, it ought to be comprehensible to everybody. [Annotation:] Dialect (*fangyu*), patois (*tuyu*), and overly colloquial phrases (*shifen cunsu zhi yu*) must not be used. Only if a certain patois [phrase] is available [to express the situation] and cannot be deleted, a pertinent annotation must be added in the testimony so that the reader can understand what that phrase means.[34]

The fact that actual records of testimony in the Dan-Xin archive rarely reveal vestiges of dialect indicates that this suggestion was indeed followed by scribes and secretaries.[35]

Although technical barriers and censorial requirements interfered with the use of "patois" utterances, occasional remnants of dialect words can still be detected in Dan-Xin case records.[36] However, examples of "patois" are highly exceptional, and most of the vocabulary in written records of testimony is Mandarin. How, then, did scribes in the county offices learn Mandarin vocabulary? Aside from the tutelage of apprenticeship in the county offices itself, vernacular fiction was a logical model for representing dialogue in writing.[37] The occupation of clerks served to absorb semiliterate people with a limited ability to read and write as well as fully literate people who had failed the civil service examinations. Clerks in county offices in any region of China during the Qing period were exposed to Mandarin-based written vernacular through the reading of fiction.

As Patrick Hanan mentions in his pioneering work on Chinese vernacular stories, as popular fiction spread in late imperial China, its vernacular language became gradually standardized to reach an empire-wide audience, including readers whose mother tongues were not Mandarin. Thus although the written vernacular had its linguistic basis (grammar and syntax) in Beijing dialect, the so-called "normative power of genre" worked to eliminate locally flavored vocabulary, including that used only in the region of Beijing.[38] The normative power of genre also operated in the writing down of testimony in legal case records. The presumed readers of these records—senior imperial officials—came from different places throughout China. Written records of testimony had to use a standardized vocabulary in common use to be readily accessible to officials of various regional backgrounds.

Scribes and probably also the private secretaries supervising them were provided chances to acquire common vocabulary and Mandarin syntax through reading vernacular fiction aimed at such semi- and/or fully literate people throughout China. Using such lexicons in common use, these scribes and private secretaries could then exercise censorship over how the first draft record ought to be written and what vocabulary should be employed in successive drafts. The normative power over the choice of language—what Jack Goody would call one of the "consequences of literacy"—became available to exert pressure on testimony.[39]

In sum, records of testimony, though sometimes revealing "patois" vestiges that can be transcribed with Chinese logographs, are filled with Mandarin lexicon. The bulk of any given case record was written in the classical style with which any official would be familiar. But the complicated multilingual condition of Qing China made it necessary that even testimony recorded in spoken style be written in another common written language to provide for efficient understanding by officials from different parts of China.

COMPOSING TESTIMONY AT THE LOCAL LEVEL: A "DIRECTLY EXAMINED" CASE FROM BEIJING

The written records of testimony included in local-level case records heretofore available (such as the Dan-Xin archives, Baxian archives, Baodi County archives, and Taihuting archives) are all formal testimony. None of these archives appear to have preserved the original depositions, which were the primary records of confessions. The cases that were directly examined by the Board of Punishments in Beijing are an exception to this pattern. In order to maintain the security of the imperial capital, these local Beijing cases were investigated either by the Warden's Offices of the Five Wards Dividing the Imperial Capital (Wucheng bingmasi) or by the Offices of General-in-Chief Commander of Infantry and Five Police Brigades in the Imperial Capital (Tidu jiumen bujun xunbu wuying tongling yamen). If the suggested sentence included or exceeded temporary banishment, the case was sent directly to the Board of Punishments for further investigation and trial. A number of directly examined cases preserve records of original depositions, revised drafts of testimony in official format, and the final draft of testimony for judgment. Through these cases it is possible to trace exactly how private secretaries and scribes fashioned their written narratives out of what the parties in a case said at different stages of interrogation.

The process is best illuminated by following one case from beginning to end over a nine-month period in 1905.[40] On the eighteenth day of the second month of Guangxu 31 (1905), Wang Guocai (aged forty-five) filed a report in the Warden's Offices of the Five Wards located in Beijing, saying that his eldest son, Wang Qunzi (aged twelve), had been found dead on the previous day. On the twenty-ninth day of the same month, the murderer, Wang Tiegun (aged nineteen), was arrested based on another report from Wang Guocai in which he revealed that he had heard that Tiegun had been reproached by his mother, Mistress Wang Yang (aged forty-six), for his murder of Wang Qunzi.[41]

According to Tiegun's final formal testimony confessing to the crime, he and Wang Guocai's wife (that is, Qunzi's mother), Mistress Wang Yu (aged forty-five), had committed adultery. Their relationship was discovered by the boy Qunzi during the first month of the same year, and both of them were afraid that Qunzi would tell his father. They decided to kill Qunzi and carried out the premeditated murder on the fourteenth day of the second month. Although at first Mistress Wang Yu denied both adultery with Tiegun and conspiring in her son's murder, under interrogation she finally admitted that she had planned the murder of her son and had cooperated with Wang Tiegun to carry it out. Tiegun was sentenced to death by strangulation; the sentence of Mistress Wang Yu, which originally had been strangulation, was reduced to life imprisonment by the court assizes (*chaoshen*) of the same year.[42]

The first round of interrogations of Wang Tiegun was carried out over several weeks between the tenth day of the third month and the ninth day of the fourth month. Original depositions were drawn up on the basis of these sessions. Two preliminary drafts of Tiegun's testimony were written based on these. The second round of interrogations of Tiegun took place between the eighteenth day of the fourth month and the twelfth day of the fifth month. The third and final draft, Tiegun's formal testimony, was dated the twenty-eighth day of the fifth month. This draft was copied verbatim on the fourteenth and again on the twenty-second day of the sixth month, probably because they were produced for delivery to different officials.

The first round of interrogations of Mistress Wang Yu was conducted between the ninth day of the third month and the twelfth day of the fourth month. An original deposition based on her cumulative testimony (which covered everything she had confessed up to that point) was written some time in the fifth month. This first draft was revised to produce a second draft. Between the twenty-eighth day of the fourth month and the twenty-ninth day of the fifth month a second round of interrogations of Mistress Wang Yu was carried out. The final (third) draft, her formal testimony, was dated the twenty-ninth day of the fifth month and included her affirmation that all she had described on that date was true. Two verbatim copies of this formal testimony dated the fourteenth and the twenty-second days of the sixth month joined that of Wang Tiegun in the dossier.

But there is another set of records of testimony from Mistress Wang Yu in which she did not admit guilt. In one piece of this testimony, dated the twenty-ninth of the fourth month, she simply recounted how her son had disappeared and how the investigation had ensued, giving the impression that she had nothing to do with her son's death. In another piece of independent testimony dated the first day of the fifth month, she denied adultery and conspiracy to murder. Finally, there is testimony from her, based on a rough draft dated the same day, in which she admitted to adultery with Wang Tiegun. However, a month later (the twenty-ninth of the fifth month), Mistress Wang Yu signed a final "formal testimony" document admitting guilt and declaring that her earlier statements had been false.

This record shows that the stories told by the two principal offenders, Wang Tiegun and Mistress Wang Yu, differed subtly throughout their interrogations. But differences explicit in the original depositions were completely expurgated from the formal testimony records. This shows in a small matter, the date when Wang Qunzi discovered their adultery. Neither of the lovers was able to give a specific date. "I do not remember which day that was" (*buji riqi*) is usually used in their depositions. However, in both their formal testimonies, the specific date "the 25th day of the first month of this year" suddenly appears. Second, and more important, throughout their interrogations, the two lovers did not agree about who was responsible for initiating the plot. The conclusion of both formal testimonies was that Mistress Wang Yu was the instigator. But earlier drafts show each of the two denying responsibility. In her deposition recorded on the first day of the fifth month, Mistress Wang Yu claimed she tried to protect Qunzi from her lover's threats.

> Tiegun and I continued having illicit sex. We were accidentally discovered by Qunzi. It was the [blank] day of the first month. Tiegun threatened Qunzi. I told Qunzi, "You don't have to be frightened. I am here [to protect you]." From then on, Tiegun frequently asked me to help plan to kill Qunzi.[43]

A report from ten days later states that she again recounted the scene to emphasize that it was Wang Tiegun who had first proposed the murder.

> Discovering Tiegun lying in my room, Qunzi told Tiegun, "I will tell my dad." I told Qunzi, "Tiegun is just sleeping in my room. Don't get nervous. Nothing else is going on." Tiegun told me that [if Qunzi told my husband his life would be lost]. "Let's kill Qunzi." I told him "it is impossible for Qunzi to tell [his father]." Thereafter, Tiegun still tried to continue illicit sex, but I refused to do so. Tiegun told me, "I am still afraid that Qunzi will tell [his father]. I will kill Qunzi." I replied, "If you would like to continue having illicit sex [*xujian*] with me, please kill Qunzi."[44]

On the next day (the twelfth), she continued her testimony.

> Tiegun came to my house declaring that still he would like to kill Qunzi. I didn't agree at first. [But] Tiegun didn't agree [with me on letting Qunzi live]. I said, "If you want to kill [Qunzi], just do it." He asked me to give him a rope. I gave him two ropes. It was the evening of the 14th day. On the morning of the 15th day, after I told Qunzi to [go out to] buy noodles, Tiegun came to my house again and said, "I will kill Qunzi today. The idea [of murder] can be attributed to me alone." I also agreed with him. He told me to go with him to watch [whether the scene of the murder was being watched by others]. I didn't see Qunzi. When Tiegun followed Qunzi, I came home and combed my hair.[45]

In contrast, Wang Tiegun, at his interrogation on the eighteenth day of the fourth month, blamed his mistress.

> I continued illicit sex with Mistress Wang Yu as usual. One night I went out for a pee and was discovered by Wang Qunzi. When I entered the house, I forgot to lock the door. I went back to bed with Wang Yu. Wang Qunzi opened the door and came in and discovered [us]. He said he would tell Wang Guocai. Since Wang Yu was very afraid that Wang Guocai would find out about [her adultery], she proposed the idea of killing Wang Qunzi to prevent his telling. Originally she tried to kill [Qunzi] at home. Wang Yu bought two baked cakes and put poison in

them.... But because she was afraid that Qunzi would vomit, she didn't dare to have Qunzi eat them. In the evening of the 14th day of the second month, she told me, "Wang Guocai will be back pretty soon. It would be better to kill [Qunzi] as soon as possible."[46]

On the twenty-fourth day of the fourth month Wang Tiegun repeated the story, again emphasizing his own hesitation to commit murder.

> Wang Qunzi told me that he would tell Wang Guocai when Guocai came back. Therefore, Mistress Wang Yu decided to kill [Qunzi] and told me to carry out the murder. I didn't agree at first. Wang Yu told me to take Qunzi to the mountain when I carried coal on my back and push him over the cliff to die. I didn't agree.[47]

In his last deposition, dated the twelfth day of the fifth month, Wang Tiegun reconstructed the conversation between him and Mistress Wang Yu on the eve of the murders as follows:

> Because Qunzi discovered our illicit sex accidentally and Wang Guocai also was coming back soon, we were afraid that Qunzi would tell [Wang Guocai]. Wang Yu often consulted with me about how to kill Qunzi. [But] we hadn't yet committed murder. At that time, if we had delayed the murder any more, Qunzi would have tipped off [Wang Guocai] soon.... Wang Yu brought up her earlier adultery with Wang Fuling again [when her husband had beat her seriously]. She told me, "Since discovering our adultery, Qunzi has lost appetite and has not made any response to what I said. He just wishes to tell [his father] about our relationship." Wang Yu started to want me to kill Qunzi. I didn't agree at first. [But] I finally agreed [to kill Qunzi] when she said that Qunzi was her son and, therefore, she would be responsible for everything.[48]

Using these documents, we have no way to determine which of the lovers actually first proposed the murder or who took the lead in planning it. The Board's final case report on this case was lost from the archives, making it impossible to learn how the Board weighed the conflicting evidence on this important issue. Both a deposition and a formal testimony from the victim's father, Guocai, survive, in which he blamed his wife for being responsible for the murder of their son.[49] For whatever reason, a version closer to what Wang Tiegun had confessed was adopted as the official one. The conclusive formal testimony of Wang Tiegun (dated the twenty-eighth of the fifth month) says,

> On the 25th day of the first month of this year, I came out of her house to have a pee at sunrise. I forgot to lock the door when I went back to her room. I still lay relaxing under the quilt. Suddenly Wang Qunzi came in and discovered [us]. He declared that he would inform his father [of our illicit sex]. I immediately got up

and ran away. The next day I went to Mistress Wang Yu's house. She told me about her earlier illicit sex with Wang Fuling. She expressed her fear that if Wang Qunzi informed Wang Guocai [of our adultery], our lives would be lost. Therefore, she decided to slay Wang Qunzi to prevent him from informing and consulted with me. She asked me to abduct Wang Qunzi and put him in a box for carrying coal and throw him into the Hun River when I passed it. Before I consented to this idea, she also told me another idea—that she was going to put the powder of a poisonous insect in a cake and feed it to Wang Qunzi at home. I feared that after eating it Wang Qunzi might vomit from the poison. Neighbors would hear [his vomiting]. Thus, we didn't dare try this idea. On the evening of the 14th day of the second month, I went to her house again to have illicit sex with her and stayed there. Wang Yu told me, "Wang Qunzi, since discovering our illicit sex, has always felt anger in his heart, he refuses to answer me, and he shows no appetite. The day after tomorrow Wang Guocai is coming back. If he discovers [our illicit sex], he will tell your father. Both you and I will be ruined. It would be better to come up with a plan to kill Wang Qunzi to avoid a disaster." I asked her how we should kill him. Wang Yu consulted with me and decided that the next morning I would let my younger brother, Wang Tiechui, go home from my hut in Wopeng to have breakfast. She would give Qunzi one foreign *yuan* at sunrise and tell him to go to Wulitun to buy noodles. He would definitely pass by Wopeng. When Qunzi passed by, I would block him [on the path] and force him to eat the poisoned cake. If Qunzi ate it and lost consciousness, dying, I would tie up his corpse with a rope prepared on the way and carry him on my back to a remote place to dispose of it. If he wouldn't eat it, I would strangle him to death with the prepared rope. Hearing what she planned, I still hesitated. Mistress Wang Yu also said that Wang Qunzi was her son whom she had given birth to and she alone would take full responsibility if the murder were discovered. She told me not to be afraid. I was muddled temporarily [*yishi hutu*] and agreed to her plan.[50]

This is exactly the story that was told in Mistress Wang Yu's formal testimony dated the twenty-ninth day of the fifth month. The fact that in some parts of the two "final testimonies" not only the content of the story but also the wording are identical means that the person(s) responsible for composing the written record of testimony did not follow some specific instructions given in the essay "How to Compose Testimony." The essay states,

[S]ince everybody has a different position and status, composing testimony requires exercising the practice of imaginative identification with her or him [*sheshen chudi*] in order to give the impression that s/he is actually speaking. If the order of events varies in each party's narration, the language used and the manner of speech must be different from each other. Only a skilled composer of testimony can organize testimony in which each party speaks in a different manner without creating any contradictions with each other.[51]

Clearly the composer of testimony in this case failed to "give an impression that s/he is actually speaking." However, at the same time, the writer loyally employed the other part of the method of "correspondence of events" in the sense that all details of the stories told by the witnesses correspond with each other.

Following another method explicitly suggested by the essay "How to Compose Testimony," sexually graphic details in this case were indicated by the single word *jian* (illicit sex). Sexual acts were always referred to this way, not only in formal testimony, but also in all depositions given by Mistress Wang Yu and Wang Tiegun.[52] We have no clues about the exact language they used when they described their relations. Here we see that even the original depositions were subjected to standardization, eliminating vulgarisms that ordinary people might have used. Taken together with the standardization integral to literacy that mandated the employment of the written vernacular, these conventions helped blur local dialects and everyday idioms in records of testimony, making all language used in testimony throughout the empire look alike.

The belief that the crafts of writing vernacular fiction, successful examination essays, and records of testimony shared common ground shaped the cultural setting that conditioned the composition of testimony during the Qing period. All literate people shared the same theory and practice of writing, whether they used the literary or vernacular style. Although in theory writing depositions was supposed to imitate actual speech, in practice speech was transformed by linguistic manipulation to achieve consistency—an integral part of literacy. The cultural setting was characterized by the social domination of oral culture by written culture.

CONCLUSION

In the Qing legal tradition, what common people directly said did not primarily make up their "formal testimony." What commoners spoke was to be scrutinized to satisfy the literate culture's requirement of consistency. The state, which was the largest institution benefited by the ideological use of literacy, also imposed the requirement of consistency in order to satisfy legal categories. What commoners said should be transformed into written drafts with an emphasis on consistency in details of dates, action, and motivation of different parties. The original depositions of parties that exhibited internal contradictions, major and minor, were unified to produce a single version of the story.[53]

The requirement of consistency and the rejection of contradictions, first of all, derived from the Chinese legal tradition, in which the credibility of testimony played the most crucial role in establishing the truth of a case. Consistency in the written record of oral testimony was also derived from standards that were integral to literacy. By considering the interaction between oral and written modes of communication found in the process of composing testimony, we can locate that testimony in its larger social and cultural context.

As Jack Goody points out, one of the "consequences of literacy" was scrutiny.[54] For Goody, the ability to scrutinize written materials facilitated the growth of a spirit of criticism. However, he does not address the dominating power of literacy when it encountered oral culture.[55] The utterance produced by the oral mode of communication would fade immediately in such an encounter. Transcribing what was spoken gives us access to what was transmitted by oral communication. However, at the same time, the scrutinizing force, which is an integral part of literacy, tends to distort our view of oral culture.

The process of composing testimony in the Qing created an interface where the oral tradition met the written one. The spoken language was recorded in the written vernacular language. However, given the technological condition of Chinese languages in the late imperial period, it was impossible to record verbatim what witnesses said in court. Not all spoken vocabulary had corresponding logographs; in addition, spoken languages in south China were quite distinctive from Mandarin. Technological barriers were imposed by the nature of the Chinese language in writing down what was expressed orally. Linguistically standardizing effects (especially on the lexicon) were an inevitable result of the use of the written vernacular.

Packaging an event with a simple cliché was a common writing practice for those who composed written records of oral testimony in the Qing. This practice operated to draw a border around what had happened by dismissing details regarded as irrelevant by officials. As I stated earlier, in most parts of final drafts of written testimony not only the content of the story but the wording is also exactly the same. For the sake of establishing legal facts, both the writing practice and the employed style in written testimony served to make the case correspond with the codified category of crime. Molding what commoner defendants said into *one* uniform story was standard practice for judicial authorities.

However, the essay "How to Compose Testimony" states that "[t]he testimony must not be false. If the story has foundation, it will be firm. False words will be absolutely laid bare."[56] This advice means that Qing judicial authorities did not think they were falsely fabricating stories by fashioning the oral statements of defendants into a single written narrative version. The Qing legal tradition was based on the fundamental presupposition that the "truth" of the case could be discovered in the person who committed the crime.

Therefore, if we interpret the textuality found in the process of composing testimony as evidence of purposeful falsification of cases, we will fail to understand the way the Qing state tried to establish its ideological basis. Qing legal procedure was not constructed upon the "falsification" of what people said. Establishing consistent details in written testimony was an inevitable result when speech was converted to the written word. Textuality of recorded testimony, shaped through transforming speech into written narrative, involved the state's ritualistic use of commoners' voices to confirm the "truth" that it established.

The final draft of written testimony, which in essence describes exactly what people did, tends to render invisible the dominating forces exercised by the written mode of communication over the oral one. Written records of testimony used the writing skills that literate people were familiar with. Those skills included not only the writing patterns of examination essay style, but also those of vernacular fiction in that specific care was taken with both the form and content of protagonists' speech. Those who produced testimony records were people who were familiar with the form of the examination essay and with the literary devices and language employed in vernacular fiction. Composing testimony in Qing China meant a sharing of writing practices to reconstruct "reality" that once had been represented orally within the larger written culture.

NOTES

A different, longer Japanese version of this essay appeared in 1995 as "Hanasukoto to kakukoto no hazamade."

1 Shiga, "Criminal Procedure," pt. 1, 23; and *Shindai Chūgoku no hō*, 26–27. On the detailed procedure of handling cases arising within and around Beijing, see Na Silu, *Qingdai zhongyang sifa*, 295–380.

2 The following explanation of judicial procedure is based on Shiga, "Criminal Procedure," pt. 1. For the original Japanese version, see Shiga, *Shindai Chūgoku no hō*, chap. 1.

3 Buoye, in "Suddenly Murderous Intent Arose," gives a detailed analysis of homicide reports in eighteenth century China.

4 "Lesser" cases included disputes over land, debts, marriage, and inheritance. Magistrates' adjudication of these "civil" disputes was also part of the Qing justice system. For "civil justice" in the Qing, see Philip Huang, *Civil Justice in China.*

5 Shiga, "Criminal Procedure," pt. 2, 121–123. Citations come from 122. Also see Shiga, "Chūgoku hō bunka."

6 Shiga, "Criminal Procedure," pt. 2, 120–121. Shiga's original work in Japanese does not make a distinction between *gongzhuang* and *caogong.* See Shiga, *Shindai Chūgoku no hō*, 69. However, the English version translates *gongzhuang* as "original deposition," while *caogong* is translated as "draft deposition." I verified with actual records at the Number One Historical Archive in Beijing that original depositions were also called *caogong.* In this chapter, therefore, I do not make a distinction between *gongzhuang* and *caogong.*

7 See Reed, *Talons and Teeth,* for a detailed explanation of clerks' activities during the Qing. See Ch'ü T'ung-tsu, *Local Government in China,* 93–115, on the crucial role played by private secretaries in local administrations.

8 Wang Youhuai, *Ban'an yaolue,* 501–506. Other similar handbooks for private secretaries include the following titles: *Essentials for Handling Homicide Cases* (*Ming'an yaolue*); *On Sending a Copy of a Confession to Higher Authorities* (*Zhaojie shuo*); Mu Han, *My Limited Opinions on How to Clarify the Law* (*Mingxing guanjianlu*); Bai Yuanfeng, *Required Reading for Convening Courtrooms* (*Qintang bidu*); Wang Youhuai, *Indispensable Readings for Legal and Financial Secretaries* (*Xingqian bilan*); Wan Weihan, *Guidelines for Secretaries on Law and Taxation* (*Xingqian zhinan*); Gangyi, *Proposing Formulas for Investigating Cases* (*Shenkan nishi*); *Judicial Important Points* (*Yuanshu lunyao*); and *Essentials for Legal Secretaries* (*Xingmu yaolue*).

9 Most of the available guides explain consistency in testimony by using these three terms or some combination thereof.

10 Depending on context, *qingjie* can mean either of two distinct English words: "facts" and "plot."

11 Wang Youhuai, *Ban'an yaolue,* 501.

12 Ibid.

13 Tang Biao, *Fushi Shanyoufa,* 26b.

14 Tang Biao, *Dushu zuowenpu,* 7.91.

15 Ibid., 8.106, 9.130–9.131.

16 Wang Kaifu and Zhang Huien, eds., *Zhongguo gudai xiezuoxue,* 203–206. Tang Biao, *Dushu zuowenpu,* 7.91, 9.119. See also Liu Xizai, "Jingyi gai," 173–176. Liu was a scholar-official in the nineteenth century.

17 Tang Biao, *Dushu zuowenpu,* 7.87–7.88.

18 All literate people shared the training for classical essay writing in their elementary level education. In *A Cultural History of Civil Examinations,* Elman points out that preparation for examinations profoundly influenced the literate mentality in late imperial China.

19 Rolston, "Sources," 17–29.

20 Plaks, "Terminology," 90–91.

21 Ibid., 92–93, 95. Plaks points out that the metaphorical use of fabric and sewing was a major part of Chinese fiction criticism. The popular proverb *tianyi wufeng* (the clothes worn by people in Heaven are seamless) is used to describe a successful effort to "put events in order" (*qianhou cengci*). See Gangyi, *Shenkan nishi,* 7a; *Yuanshu lunyao,* the third page of "How to Compose Testimony."

22 Plaks, "Terminology," 95–97.

23 The "how to read" genre of fiction commentary (some examples of which are available in English in Rolston, ed., *How to Read the Chinese Novel*) includes a number of terms such as *zhaoying, xiansuo, buju, fu, mai, qichengzhuanghe, bi,* etc.

24 In guidelines for composing testimony, the idea of the narrative thread (*xiansuo*) provided a skill crucial to achieve structural integrity. "Once these threads are clear enough to be seen as one thread, all parties' mouths would be tuned to speak one voice"

(*ru yixian chuancheng, yikou tongsheng*). See Gangyi, *Shenkan nishi*, 7a; *Yuanshu lunyao*, the second page of "How to Compose Testimony."

25 Wang Youhuai, *Ban'an yaolue*, 506. This guideline was emphasized by almost all authors of handbooks. Bai Yuanfeng specifically warned not to use literary particles such as *hu, zhe*, and *ye*. See his *Qintang bidu*, 60a.

26 Wang Youhuai, *Ban'an yaolue*, 501.

27 Ōta, "'Kōrōmu' no gengo," 293.

28 This notion is emphasized in a seventeenth-century manual for education that aimed to train children eventually to pass the civil service examinations. See Cui Xuegu, *Shaoxue*, 6b.

29 Tang Biao repeatedly stresses this point in his *Dushu zuowenpu, juan* 7.

30 Li Tiaoyuan's *Danmo lu* introduces an episode about the use of patois in the civil service examination. In 1735 (Yongzheng 13), an examination candidate who participated in the Shaanxi provincial examination wrote a Sung dynasty-style edict praising sages (*songsheng biaowen*) with "Shaanxi patois" (*Shaanxi tuyu*), with the intention of making fun of Shaanxi native candidates. He received severe punishment for insulting the ceremonial civil service examination. See *Danmo lu*, 10.153–10.154.

31 Wang Youhuai, *Ban'an yaolue*, 506.

32 When Li Xiucheng, one of the leaders of the Taiping Rebellion, was seized by Zeng Guofang, Zeng's private secretaries could not understand Li's local patois (*tuyin*). They had to have Li himself write his answers to the questions they put to him during interrogation. See Luo Ergang, *Li Xiucheng*, 14. This example indicates that it was difficult for an interrogator to write down what local people said if he did not possess the skills to translate simultaneously between dialects and Mandarin.

33 Shiga, *Shindai Chūgoku no hō*, 57. In Zhangzhou Prefecture in Fujian, ordinary people did not understand Mandarin (*guanyin*), thus clerks at government offices served as translators during interrogation. Clerks presumably altered what people actually said. See *Zhangzhou fuzhi*, 38.9a. Considering this kind of abuse, Wang Huizu, an eighteenth-century private secretary and later an official, suggested that a newly appointed local magistrate should hire a native child to keep him company and allow the child to speak local patois (*tuyin*) freely. The magistrate thus would soon begin to understand the local dialect spoken by parties in the courtroom and not have to rely on clerks' translations. This, however, would not work unless the magistrate was as diligent as Wang Huizu. See his *Xuezhi yishuo*, 1.269–1.2670.

Acquiring a certain fluency in spoken Mandarin was required for officials, although such acquisition was not always at a level to satisfy the emperors. The Yongzheng emperor, in an edict, mentioned his difficulty in understanding the speech of officials from Guangdong and Fujian. A number of textbooks that taught spoken Mandarin were available during the Qing period. Shayizun's *Zhengyin juhua* (Appreciating the essence of the proper pronunciation), one of the popular titles, includes a section describing the scene of a trial, indicating that the author assumed that officials-to-be would be his main audience. For Yongzheng's edict, see *Qinding xuezheng quanshu, juan* 59 (Yongzheng 6), and *Daqing shilu, juan* 72 (Yongzheng 6).

34 "*Ban'an*" (Handling cases), in *Xingmu yaolue*, 1a. Bai Yuanfeng explicitly states that records of testimony should use only Mandarin. See his *Qintang bidu*, 61a.

35 Homicide reports to the upper authorities also had to avoid using dialect when referring to the fatal injuries on a body. See Zhang Wuwei, *Jiangqiu gongji lu*, 46a. This is a handbook left by a prefect of the early nineteenth century.

36 *Dan-Xin dang'an* 35506 leaves some Hakka vocabulary in the record of testimony. Hakka vocabulary in Xunzhou and Wuzhou (Guangxi) also appears in the writings of Li Xiucheng, one of the leaders of the Taiping Rebellion, most of whom came from Guangxi. See Luo Ergang, *Li Xiucheng*, 21–23, 45–47.

37 The courtroom scene in *Zhengyin juhua*, a Mandarin textbook, reads like a drama script: the story goes on with a successive pattern in which the magistrate questions and the witnesses answer. This vivid depiction not only provided officials-to-be with a useful example of what kind of language magistrates should use in the courtroom, but also supplied scribes at county offices with a tool to document courtroom records in Mandarin vernacular. It is possible that clerks at county offices also could learn Mandarin through these textbooks. See Shayizun, *Zhengyin juhua*, 75a–86a.

38 Hanan, *The Chinese Vernacular Story*, 8.

39 Goody and Watt, "The Consequences of Literacy"; Goody, *The Domestication of the Savage Mind*. Goody describes "consequences of literacy" as something positive that enables society to develop civilization. Rawski, in her seminal work on "functional literacy" in Qing China, seems to share Goody's perspective. See Rawski, *Education and Popular Literacy*. However, as my use of the term "censorship" shows, I see writing as assisting in the ideological reinforcement of domination. While Goody praises the spirit of criticism and cumulative knowledge enabled by scrutinizing writing, I would like to emphasize the ideological use of the scrutiny of written language. Goody's later important works do not alter his original idea on "consequences of literacy." See Goody, *The Logic of Writing* and *The Interface between the Written and the Oral*. For a criticism of Goody from this perspective, see Street, *Literacy in Theory and Practice*.

40 *Xingbu dang'an*, Sichuansi (Sichuan Bureau) section (abbreviated as XBDA/SC hereafter) 19961. Citations give the case file's serial number. A bureau with a prefix of one province name usually worked on examining felony cases that occurred in that particular province. Only a "directly examined" case forwarded to the Board, after each bureau drew a lot, was assigned to one of these bureaus. See Shiga, *Shindai Chūgoku no hō*, 58.

41 Although all parties in this case were surnamed Wang, this does not mean they belonged to the same family; rather, it is because they came from a single-lineage community.

42 XBDA/SC 19961.

43 Ibid., deposition of Mistress Wang Yu (first day of the fifth month, Guangxu 31).

44 Ibid., deposition of Mistress Wang Yu (eleventh day of the fifth month, Guangxu 31). The statement in parentheses was probably added by clerks (or any unknown superiors) as a "correction" in the margin of the document.

45 Ibid., deposition of Mistress Wang Yu (twelfth day of the fifth month, Guangxu 31).

46 Ibid., deposition of Wang Tiegun (eighteenth day of the fourth month, Guangxu 31).

47 Ibid., deposition of Wang Tiegun (twenty-fourth day of the fourth month, Guangxu 31).

48 Ibid., deposition of Wang Tiegun (twelfth day of the fifth month, Guangxu 31).

49 Ibid., deposition of Wang Guocai (twenty-fourth day of the fourth month, Guangxu 31); formal testimony of Wang Guocai (fourteenth day of the sixth month, Guangxu 31).

50 Ibid., formal testimony of Wang Tiegun (twenty-eighth day of the fifth month, Guangxu 31).

51 Wang Youhuai, *Ban'an yaolue,* 504. Jin Shengtan, a literary critic of the seventeenth century, insisted that protagonists in fictional stories should employ manners of speech suitable to their character and social condition. See Jin Shengtan, "Xu san," 10.

52 See Sommer, *Sex, Law, and Society,* on the boundary surrounding *jian* drawn by the Qing state and its ideological implications.

53 Ginzburg, in *Night Battles,* describes the dynamic process by which an agricultural cult rooted in peasants' oral traditions was transformed into witchcraft by the force of cultural hegemony, the inquisitors' perception, in sixteenth- and seventeenth-century Italy. Sabean, in "Peasant Voices and Bureaucratic Texts," analyzes the narrative structure of bureaucratic documents in early modern Germany that include records of courtroom interrogation, concluding that the bureaucratic narrative produced a single explanation of what happened. In the European field, historians have been successful in reconstructing the mental universe of oral culture by paying attention to the profound gap between interrogators and peasants—the gap that subtly appears in the inquisition records. See Ginzburg, *The Cheese and the Worms* and "The Inquisitor as Anthropologist"; Sabean, *Power in the Blood.* On the early use of confession records of those who participated in religious rebellions during the Qing, see Naquin, "True Confessions"; Perry, "When Peasants Speak."

54 Goody and Watt, "The Consequences of Literacy"; Goody, *The Domestication of the Savage Mind.*

55 Street, *Literacy in Theory and Practice;* Goody, *The Logic of Writing.*

56 Wang Youhuai, *Ban'an yaolue,* 507.

PART TWO

MEDICAL CASE HISTORIES

OVERLEAF: A senior doctor instructs two gentlemen—a scholar and another physician—while an attendant prepares medicines and healthy children frolic nearby. From Zhu Huiming, *Douzhen chuan xinlu,* first published in 1594. Reproduced from the 1786 edition held by the Gest Library, Princeton University.

4

Producing Medical Knowledge through Cases

History, Evidence, and Action

CHARLOTTE FURTH

How did Chinese physicians develop a tradition of thinking with cases? On one level, the answer to this question reveals a common human project of understanding ailment and cure. However, the forms of truth to which Chinese medical cases aspired were shaped by the culturally specific domains of China's classics, its official histories, and its law. The Chinese classics, both philosophical and medical, were works of high antiquity believed to express universal truths about the universe, human society, and ethics—truths that flowed inevitably from their status as canon. Orthodox dynastic history, for which the earliest Chinese models were court chronicles, was made up of officially commissioned narratives and essays about actual events in a changing world. Law, equally ancient in Chinese public life, was defined by imperially authorized statutory codes as interpreted by magistrates. If classics defined universals—the cosmologically grounded norms of nature and society—history's narratives of events provided models for establishing factual particulars (*shi*), while law was a domain of action, where official judgments based on evidence and code constituted grounds for active interventions in the world, not just representations of it. These particularities, the case of Chinese cases as it were, show evidential reasoning through a culturally inflected lens. By learning how medical cases did their work, we can place this tradition of knowledge production in a broader context of the history of Chinese scientific thinking and doing. We have long questioned the assumption that premodern Chinese thinkers managed only an "abortive empiricism"—as a famous American scholar of the 1960s once put it[1]—but we have only begun to show how indigenous Chinese sciences and technologies evolved "on their own terms."[2] Such inquiry helps us to understand the interplay of systems of natural knowledge, empirical methods, and artisanal practices that make premodern sciences globally comparable and to relativize a history too often reduced to the story of Europe's triumphant "scientific revolution."[3] The historical and cultural space opened up for imagining the antiquity and plurality of sciences pushes us toward new ground where the claims of universal reason and those of social and cultural constructionism must meet and carry on their perennial dialogue.

TRACES OF CASES IN EARLY IMPERIAL MEDICINE

A recent textbook published in the People's Republic of China offers a history of case records in Chinese medicine designed to help students apply an ancient tradition to contemporary clinical practice. Case histories are as old as medicine itself, it says, citing a couple of tales of royal illness from a sixth-century BCE court chronicle. The 297 prescriptions of the classic *Discourse on Cold Damage Disorders* (*Shanghan lun*, 2nd–3rd century CE) were matched to symptoms, and by implication to human sufferers. These are written traces of the cases of the Han dynasty medical master Zhang Ji. Over the first millennium anecdotes about famous doctors accumulated, until the four "Masters" of the Jin and Yuan dynasties (1115–1368 CE) began the practice of including narratives of their personal cases in their books as supporting evidence and so established the precedent for the mature Ming dynasty case narrative genre. This in turn laid the foundation for the standardized diagnostic path of twentieth-century practitioners of Chinese medicine (*bian zheng lun zhi*), documented in the cases of contemporary "senior doctors" (*lao Zhongyi*) in the People's Republic.[4]

Above all, modern accounts of the ancient foundations of the case history in medical reasoning find support in the biography of the royal physician Chunyu Yi as recorded in the most hallowed of ancient histories, Sima Qian's *Records of the Grand Historian* (*Shiji*) of the second century BCE. Chunyu Yi (fl. 175 BCE) was a literate doctor who reported to the emperor on twenty-five cases based on his "consultation records" (*zhenji*). As transmitted to posterity by the Grand Historian, Chunyu Yi's cases show his command of diagnosis by a patient's facial appearance and pulse readings of the condition of his or her internal circulation "channels" (*mai*) and his therapeutic use of acupuncture, moxibustion, and a familiar repertory of pharmaceutical strategies.

There is much that is quite reasonable about this textbook account of medical history. As reports on aliment and cure, medical writing will always bear traces of the clinical encounters between doctors and patients. Where there were written books, other kinds of handwritten records were likely to exist; in medicine, as in other fields, Chinese history displays a gradual evolution toward a more complex repertory of written works, powerfully assisted by the invention and spread of printing after the tenth century. However, in what senses are these early imperial accounts cases, either in the Chinese notion of *an* or in the English idiom of the "case history"?

To modern eyes Chunyu Yi's cases seem by far the most clinically rational of these ancient narratives of medical practice, and Ping-chen Hsiung's essay in this volume (chap. 5) stresses the inspiration they gave to late imperial clinicians. But in the earlier Han dynasty context, the text raises some cautionary questions. Li Jianmin's recent study of the origins of the medical concept of "channels" (*mai*) argues for an unfamiliar understanding of the familiar terminology: rather than originating as a purely medical term denoting river-like circulation channels streaming through the body, as it does today, the archaic concept of "channels" had cosmological roots in ancient astronomy, numerology, and geography so that early diagnosis by feeling a patient's pulses (also *mai*) was often a prognostication linking human ailment to macrocosmic patterns. In Sima Qian's history, Chunyu Yi's biography is bundled with that of Bian Que, an earlier, quasi-legendary healer said to have gained his medical knowledge as the result of drinking a magical elixir whose arts were frankly divinatory and whom myth depicted as possessing a bird's body, befitting a shaman-doctor immortal flown to Heaven. Bian Que was said to be the ancestral author of the learning about "channels" transmitted to Chunyu Yi, among others.[5] If, as Li Jianmin suggests, the study of archaic "channels" shows a cosmological order that doctors and shamans (*yi* and *wu*) shared, Chunyu Yi's medical diagnoses may have been understood more as divination than as a rational therapy compatible with modernist readings of the Chinese medical tradition. Twentieth-century practitioners of Chinese medicine as well as biomedical doctors have difficulty grasping the concept of a pulse in these texts.[6] In the record of Chunyu Yi's twenty-five cases, the doctor's first task was to determine "the frontier of life and death," and therapies—offered to those destined to live—were secondary.

Moreover, the reports about these cases were preserved by accident, embedded in a historian's narrative that also hints at the importance of oral traditions and of secret transmission of medical knowledge. Sima Qian told Chunyu Yi's story and Bian Que's together as accounts of famous doctors whose uncanny skills led them to misfortune. Accused of an unnamed crime (based on complaints against him brought by a patient), Chunyu Yi was pardoned but later was questioned about the sources of his knowledge by the monarch, who seemed particularly fascinated by the doctor's ability to predict his patients' fates. The record of the doctor's respectful reply is as follows.

> Nowadays, for each diagnosis I have made I have a "consultation record." The reason I am able to differentiate disorders is because of what I accomplished with my teacher. Since my teacher died, I have set out "consultation records" of disorders that I have diagnosed to predict the time [allotted] for life or death. I

observe where my predictions are accurate or amiss, and find the results in agreement with the pulse method. This is how I gain knowledge.

Here written records of past cases helped this doctor master his methods of diagnosis according to pulses, but they were a substitute for learning earlier transmitted directly from master to disciple. Moreover, contrary to the assumptions of the modern textbook, as of today neither the diagnostic principles nor the exact purpose and content of this doctor's ancient case records are known for sure.[7]

However they were remembered later, in the *Records of the Grand Historian,* Chunyu Yi's reports on his medical practice were not called "cases" (*an*). As Ho Da-an has shown, in other passages of the Grand Historian's work, *an* as a noun was a table or writing surface and, by extension, the written records that lay on them; and in its verbal aspect *an* was the act of writing or displaying such records. Further, early *an* were not everyday domestic pieces of furniture; together with *andu* (storage cabinets for documents), they were found in court and government bureaus, carrying connotations of official action. Producing *an* was the work of clerks carrying the force of government mandate.[8] The narratives of Bian Que and Chunyu Yi point in a different direction. They evoke a world in which paper was not yet in common use and books were rare and expensive artifacts of silk and wood. It was a world where medical learning depended upon the ties of masters and disciples, one of affinity between medical and shamanistic arts.

Other storied traces of medical practice that made their way into early histories and biographies turned on divinatory insight and magical legerdemain, on examples of clinical skill that retained an aura of the uncanny. There was Guo Yu, who could not be fooled when the Han emperor asked him to take the pulse of a male favorite disguised as a girl; there was the Tang palace physician whose acupuncture needle saved an empress in childbirth by forcing the fetus to let go of her vitals and be born, bearing the wounds on its palm as proof.[9] The third-century CE court physician Hua Tuo was particularly legendary, believed to cure by temporarily removing and washing the entrails of his patients. A more plausible narrative of Hua Tuo's medical practice is found in his biography in the *Chronicle of the Three Kingdoms* (*Sanguo zhi;* 222–264 CE). These stories of the doctor's ability to predict a person's death are found side by side with more prosaic accounts of his skill at curing headaches, purging worms, and healing insect bites.[10]

Thus side by side with legends are found traces of more naturalistic approaches to medicine. The ability to predict whether an illness will prove fatal is a useful medical skill well within the powers of many premodern healers, and several of Hua Tuo's exemplary cases turned on the patient's refusal to follow his sound health advice about food, drink, or sex. Even more ordinary is the story of how Wang Shuhe, author of the canonical *Pulse Classic* (*Maijing*), reassured a mother that her adolescent daughter's episodes of amenorrhea were not an illness and would correct themselves naturally. The seventh-century medical master Sun Simiao included in his writings several anecdotes about his own bouts of sickness as recommendations for the efficacy of a prescription, as well as a few stories about some of his patients.[11]

These early examples do not fail as medical case histories because they are implausible as stories, but because something about them is "merely anecdotal." They fit the literary/linguistic definition of a "case" as any instance bracketed off from surrounding text and presented as a set of particulars. If an anecdote is something of purely local import, these medical stories offered as examples illustrate some general point that is already given or assumed, here usually the doctor's amazing abilities. They are invitations to wonder, not raw material for problem solving. Even the most empirical clarify what is known on other grounds than the cases themselves.

Do these textual traces tell the whole story of medical record keeping in early Chinese history? Probably not. Much more relevant may be patterns of medical pedagogy in a world where master-disciple lineages and religious charisma were central to the production of medical knowledge and authority. Chunyu Yi spoke of private manuscript texts transmitted to him by his master, and their possession was proof of his claims to succession in a lineage whose code included the pledge of secret stewardship of medical wisdom. What is clear from Sima Qian's account is that Chunyu Yi *memorized* the texts of his treasured medical books and that he remembered many cases in his head. Where orality and literacy coexisted, the passage of knowledge into written form would be slow, and in Chinese medicine its traces were hidden by the practice of keeping expertise within the specialist lineage.

Sima Qian had said that Chunyu Yi was "secretive." When the People's Republic textbook picks up the story of written cases in the eleventh and twelfth centuries, after the invention of printing in the Song dynasty, it offers examples that better satisfy modern readers looking for textual evidence of clinical thinking with cases, while at the same time revealing how tensions between private and public knowledge shaped access. The surviving cases of Qian Yi (1032–1113) and those of Xu Shuwei (1079–ca. 1154) offer detailed narratives of the clinical encounter, the doctor's diagnosis, and the herbal formula or formulas prescribed as remedy. Each group of cases is a specialist set—Qian Yi was a pediatrician, and Xu Shuwei's cases all feature the large class of febrile disorders called "Cold Damage" (*shanghan*). Both sets showcase the art of prescription, the preeminent medical skill that formed the rhetorical and clinical climax of case history narratives in the mature Chinese medical tradition. Ping-chen Hsiung's chapter in this volume is testimony to the importance of Qian Yi's cases to later pediatric experts, who all looked back to this work as foundational for their medical specialty. But as Hsiung shows, the printed text of Qian Yi's *Proven Formulae of Medicine for Small Children* (*Xiao'er yaozheng zhijue*) was not produced by this doctor, who was suspicious of making his medical writings public, but by a literatus admirer, Yan Jizhong, who over a period of years painstakingly assembled materials in the possession of Qian Yi's clients and associates. Twenty-three cases were among the materials incorporated into *Proven Formulae,* penned by Yan Jizhong in formal classical style.[12] The fact that these cases were collected from clients points to an important function of cases as private writings: this is early evidence that literate doctors were expected to provide written explanations and recommendations to their patients or patients' families.

On the other hand, Xu Shuwei's *Ninety Discourses on Cold Damage Disorders* (*Shanghan jiushi lun*) would appear to be a model of personal case-based reasoning by an expert on Zhang Ji's *Discourse on Cold Damage Disorders,* considered a pharmaceutical classic by the Song state medical bureau. The text attributed to Xu Shuwei presented ninety narratives of his own cases, discussing the patients by name and social relationships, outlining their symptoms and his diagnoses and offering a brief commentary on the correct application of Zhang Ji's formulas and therapeutic strategies in each particular instance. Here the collection of cases appears clearly linked to the practical pedagogy of clinical decision making, directed at fellow experts. Although a number of Xu Shuwei's cases made their way into several important anthologies beginning in the sixteenth century, the collection itself remained an unpublished lineage document until the nineteenth century.[13]

While bearing witness to the sophistication of medical record keeping among some Song doctors, the examples of Xu Shuwei and Qian Yi show that conventions of secrecy helped protect the livelihoods of most Song physicians as they had their forebears. At the same time, these conventions were being challenged by state intervention in medical education, leading to imperially sponsored publication of newly codified medical classics and prescription manuals using print technology. For a while in the eleventh century there was even an imperially sponsored medical examination system in force that included test questions based on cases, while regulations promulgated in the capital envisioned a protocol whereby every year practicing physicians would bring their own case records to the authorities for vetting.[14] While policies of state supervision and regulation of medicine proved short lived, a longer-lasting trend was the greater integration of medicine into elite culture. As more literati amateurs took up medical learning, more physicians shifted away from technomagical models of expertise toward scholarly ones shaped by the ethical, social, and intellectual standards of the new neo-Confucian "Learning of the Way."[15] The relationship of the literatus Yan Jizhong and the doctor Qian Yi points to how these new social forces broadened the circulation of written cases. Well-to-do clients expected doctors to provide written records of their own family cases, which could be used at the bedside when a succession of physicians were brought in and which then easily became quasi-public, circulating informally among interested literati. If Yan Jizhong was one of many gentlemen who published medical formularies gathered this way as a charitable act,[16] medical case histories gradually became part of the repertory of text production favored by the new elite stratum of "literati physicians" (*ruyi*). In surviving printed works, one can trace a gradual evolution from small clusters of case narratives reported about a physician by outsiders, to case histories offered here and there as illustrations by the authors of medical treatises, to the production of single-authored works assembling a single physician's selected cases under his (or, very rarely, her) own name. Between the twelfth and fifteenth centuries, the case evolved from private to public record, from third-person to first-person narratives, and from functioning as an illustrative side dish or seasoning to serving as the main course.

MEDICAL CASE HISTORY COLLECTIONS IN THE MING: BETWEEN CLASSICS, HISTORY, AND LAW

Medical case histories, whether individual or in sets, began to be identified by their modern name of *yi'an* during the Ming dynasty. Contributors to the Chinese-language volume on the case that serves as a companion to this one conclude that this change in naming practices marked the emergence of a self-conscious genre of medical writing.[17] Christopher Cullen has attributed the steady rise in the number of titles from the sixteenth century onwards to the importance of authorship for the prestige of literati physicians in a prosperous and competitive late-Ming culture. Joanna Grant has put this growth in the context of the spreading communications networks linking doctors, merchants, and book dealers that fanned out from Huizhou Prefecture in Anhui, whose native sons authored many of the early volumes of *yi'an*.[18]

But the case history genre is about medical epistemology as well as the historical sociology of medical practice. In circulating and publishing cases, Ming authors looked back not to antiquity or the Song dynasty, but to the Four Masters of the Jin and Yuan. The most important of these, Zhang Congzheng (1156–1228), Li Gao (1180–1251), and Zhu Zhenheng (1282–1358), lived during the crisis-ridden thirteenth and fourteenth centuries when China was partitioned by the Jurchen (Jin) and Mongol (Yuan) invasions. Their revisionist treatises challenged the conventions of Song state medicine while grappling with their own growing sense of the geographical and temporal mutability of disease. The very success of the literati physician project encouraged doctors consciously to imitate the Song philosopher Zhu Xi's model of "transmission of the Way" in a single line of descent and to read medical classics through the lens of the cosmology of the "Learning of the

Way" identified with Zhu Xi's school of thought. But medical modernism—the belief shaped by their clinical experience that one cannot treat today's diseases with the prescriptions of ancient times—coexisted uneasily with literati physician reverence for learning from canonical ancient texts. Among the followers of the Four Masters, models of medical knowledge based on classical learning went hand in hand with diverging clinical doctrines identified with styles of prescribing favored by different groups of contemporary doctors.

Canon could not be abandoned, of course. Learned doctors could gloss their discourses with scriptural citations of the *Yellow Emperor's Inner Canon* (*Huangdi neijing*) and other classics or turn to commentary as a traditionally approved open form facilitating innovation. Ho Da-an has shown that the Chinese ideographs for "case" (*an*) and "commentary" (*an*) share a common origin.[19] A report on a case illuminating a point in a medical essay on the principles of diagnosis functions pretty much as an authorial commentary would. None of the Jin-Yuan masters themselves composed casebooks, but cases proliferated in their writings as illustrations—or comments—on their discourses. The openness of commentary lies in the way it both calls attention to a privileged authority and signals its own distance from that authority. But when cases stand alone, they break with the sacralized authority of canon or medical sages, providing a form amenable to even more open interpretations. The spreading circulation of medical case histories in the Ming dynasty went hand in hand with medical modernism as the innovations in prescription art of the Four Masters became more central to clinical practice. In this way differences among the followers of the Four Masters produced distinct and often contending "lineages of learning" or "scholarly currents" (*xuepai*).

The term "scholarly currents" evokes the fluid nature of the boundaries between distinct groupings of Ming dynasty doctors and their tendency to explain affiliations in terms of lineage and descent, personal discipleship, and common ideals, rather than more formal structures or definitive doctrines.[20] The slogans of the different masters identified preferences in the art of prescription—Zhang Congzheng's "sweat, purge, vomit"; Li Gao's "nourish Spleen-stomach"; Zhu Zhenheng's "nourish yin and make Fire descend." Each type of strategy was defended by a phalanx of citations from the canonical *Inner Canon* and other works. Each called attention to the challenge of ordering the bewildering multiplicity of clinical situations around manageable themes. The masters' treatises each defended its author's leading therapeutic preferences, while several generations of followers, in lineages scholarly or familial, branched out to forge what bedside strategies they could. There they found situations that seemed to call for exceptions to every rule of thumb. The case history, with its emphasis upon the particular, the contingent, and the situational, mediated the tension between canon and doctrine on the one hand and clinical practice on the other. A group of case histories could address the contention between medical "scholarly currents" in the context of one doctor's clinical preferences, implicitly supporting an associated lineage of practitioners. Cases attributed to the Jin-Yuan masters circulating in Ming medical circles extended far beyond those embedded in their medical essays as illustrations or commentary, and bit by bit many of these found their way independently into print.

Published case histories, then, were recognized as a novelty in the Ming, and early on their strangeness was mediated by thinking of them as part of works of history, preserving the deeds of famous doctors for their disciples and successors. After all, the pre-Qin Confucian classics had been complemented in the Han and succeeding dynasties by orthodox records of history beginning with Sima Qian's great work. If medicine required a canonical Confucian Way (Daotong) of its own, case histories might constitute the biographical chronicles of the deeds of doctors.

The first histories of medicine and the first anthology of historical cases were both produced in sixteenth-century Huizhou. The pioneer case anthology of Jiang Guan, side by side with the works of medical historians Xu Chunfu and Li Chan, showed historical thinking at work. Li Chan's *Introduction to Medical Learning* (*Yixue rumen;* first published in 1575) combined introductory essays on basic concepts and the historical evolution of medicine with a series of biographies of medical sages and worthies past and present. Modeling his structure on the Biographies section of the *Records of the Grand Historian,* Li presented six groups of historical physicians, arrayed in chronological order, but more important, according to a hierarchy of virtue from sages and Confucian doctors at the top down to Daoists and immortals below.[21] A more ambitious work was Xu Chunfu's *A Comprehensive Study of the Medical Tradition from Ancient to Modern Times* (*Gujin yitong daquan;* author's preface 1556), which aspired to document a tradition of orthodox lineage transmission in medicine. Around each medical topic (i.e., disease classification, or *lei*), Xu assembled historical excerpts beginning with the canonical *Inner Canon,* manipulating the selection and editing of later materials so as to lead readers toward what he believed were correct interpretations.[22]

In *Classified Cases from Famous Doctors* (*Mingyi lei'an;* author's preface 1549), historical principles shaped the selection and organization of a work made up entirely of case narratives.[23] Although the bulk of Jiang Guan's entries were culled from the medical writings of Song, Yuan, and Ming physicians, brief narratives about clinical encounters were included if they came from authoritative ancient works, as were unusual stories about famous ancient medical worthies and even anecdotes from contemporary essays (*biji*). All were presented in chronological order under each of 195 nosological classifications (*lei*). In Jiang's preface, as in the textbook from the People's Republic of China today, Chunyu Yi was named as the ancient founder of the case history tradition, "providing a measuring standard for the ages."[24]

A reported conversation between Jiang and one of his clients, a high official named Xu Guo, suggests how this medical author hoped to establish the significance of the case as history. Xu Guo, in the preface he graciously condescended to write for the completed volume, sketched a picture of the doctor's respectful question and his own reply.

> The old man [Jiang] once said to me, "Men of broad learning master the classics, but surely they do not neglect the histories either?" I said, "Didn't Confucius say 'If I wish to set forth my theoretical judgments, nothing is as good as illustrating them through the depth and clarity of actual events'?[25] So the Classics include histories like the *Spring and Autumn [Annals]*. The Classics are about principles [*yi*]; history is about events. One makes judgments [*duan*] about significance; one lays out cases [*an*] about events. One makes judgments based on principles; one draws up a case based on events. Without the Classics, where is the standard for judgments? Without history, how can cases have a foundation?" The old man said, "Right. I read the *Plain Questions* [i.e., *Inner Canon*] and the *Classic of Difficult Issues* to grasp their principles and respect them as classics. I study the biography of Chunyu Yi to grasp the events and find it trustworthy as history. Isn't this how physicians make judgments and set forth cases?"[26]

Jiang's effort at placing the case at the center of medicine drew on old and respected models of historical knowledge—models that assumed that classical moral norms were revealed in the scrupulous recording of historical events. As an orthodox public functionary, the historian (modeled on Confucius and Sima Qian) conveyed two types of truth—the moral universals revealed in the written words of the classics and the affairs of the world for which the prototype was court chronicles of events. As part of the recorded biography of a worthy physician, the case embodied good medical practice as an event, just as the acts of a government official entered the dynastic history as evidence of the transmission of the Way in action in the world.

Nonetheless, however prestigious as learning and however invested with the rhetoric of veracity, the methods of historical compilation turned out to be of limited value to physicians seeking to make cases clinically useful. A more successful pioneer work was *Medical Cases of Wang Ji* (*Shishan yi'an*) by another Huizhou physician, Wang Ji. This work, published around 1531, did more than any other to establish the model of the single-authored case history collection. These 123 cases, almost all his own, were compiled by his disciple Chen Jue under Wang Ji's personal supervision, and, as Wang's biographer Joanna Grant says, they present "an internally consistent depiction of his medical practice."[27]

The use of *yi'an* in the title suggests that this work offered a model of the case drawn from law. Like legal cases, medical cases constituted an archive of past experience in distinguishing between closely related instances and finding underlying patterns that would provide the key to successful problem solving—diagnosis in one domain, legal decision in the other. In his 1531 preface to the first edition, another follower of Wang Ji, Cheng Zeng, explained that medical reasoning was like legal reasoning: "When later men see this [casebook], won't it be like a legal expert having a record of decided cases, which allow him to draw analogies and extend kindness without end?"[28]

Following Wang Ji, a rhetorical appeal to a legal model became commonplace in succeeding works. Han Mao, a sixteenth-century advocate of case history record keeping, emphasized the bureaucratic orderliness of legal procedures, noting that a case was about documentation. "When you carefully examine [the patient] . . . that is like taking depositions. Taking the pulse is like interrogating the subject closely. And discussion of origins and treatment are like getting the confession and giving a verdict to finish off [the case]."[29] Sun Yikui compared the clarity and utility of a case record to a legal document "put in written form so that everyone can use it, just as a clerk judging a criminal case writes out the verdict that cannot be changed."[30] Others were more impressed with a judge's decision-making power. Xu Chunfu put it this way: "Using medicine is like using criminal penalties [*xing*]. A mistake makes the difference between life and death. But in the matter of penalties, the magistrate interrogates first, and then deliberates. Only after he has a decision does he write out the verdict. Once dead, a man cannot return to life, so one must be especially careful. Using drugs is the same."[31] In his essay on pulse diagnosis, Wu Kun compared the doctor pursuing a hidden malady with his drugs to "an old official hearing a case, who cites the law and sets the penalty [*yuanlü dingxing*] so that the guilty have no way to escape."[32] The idea of a case, in sum, was linked to a model of judicial reasoning and record keeping as setting a standard of validity and honesty. As persuasion, the metaphor of the judge also worked as a literary trope whereby the doctor rhetorically borrowed the mantle of official power. But these literary flourishes also pointed to something deeper: law provided the model of case documents as archives of precedents, of case-based reasoning by analogy, and of the judicial ruling as a mode of action.

YI'AN IN THE MING: CLASSIFICATION, ARGUMENT, AND JUDGMENT

The preceding discussion of Ming *yi'an* focuses on some of the epistemological implications of the forms of commentary, history, and law for thinking with cases in medicine. But it mattered how the preferred judicial model that authors rhetorically appealed to related to the specific demands of ordering cases to facilitate diagnosis and therapy. The question of how case records were to be composed and compared raised issues of disease classification and nosology that were specifically medical. According to Jiang Guan, Chunyu Yi, in recording his cases, had "distinguished the similar from the different." Jiang imagined his own work as a clinical reference tool as well a historical archive. This is seen in a former patient's recollection of Jiang's advice at a bedside consultation: "Among what I have collected, in such and such a chapter, is a prescription which is in accord with my diagnosis. Let's try out the case [*shi an zhi*]."[33] In sum, a work like Jiang's *Classified Cases from Famous Doctors,* as implied by its title, was a work of classification (*leishu*), encyclopedic, not narrative, in structure.

As they grappled with problems of nosology, doctors who wanted to think with cases had to struggle with the question of how their collections should identify the similarities and differences alluded to. One possible solution, taxonomic classification into species-like diseases, was difficult to implement using the received tradition, which was lavish in names that said very little about the deep patterns of disorder underlying the heterogeneity of symptoms. On the other hand, these patterns, which identified the quality, momentum, and location of a disorder in terms of a small number of cosmologically resonant concepts—yin-yang, Blood-qi, Heat-Cold, repletion-depletion, or Five Phases—were too broad to be useful if detached from the concrete manifestations of an individual's particular disorder. Received forms of classification—"Dividing by sections [*men;* lit. "gate"] and breaking up into classes [*lei*]" (*fen men xi lei*)—derived from ways of organizing the contents of books. Originally a *men* was a division in a bibliography; a *lei* was a topical section of an encyclopedia organized according to the prestige of textual genres. By the Ming dynasty the form of a *leishu* was increasingly used to order texts according to a cosmological hierarchy of Heaven, Earth, and Humanity into sections on natural and social topics, and encyclopedias were more and more practical in orientation. These received categories of the *leishu* were of little use in medicine, where the distinction between symptoms (a cough), syndromes (a cold), and taxonomic disease labels (cholera, diabetes) was weak, while the logic of practical use dictated that a medical reference work should be organized around presenting symptoms, convenient for bedside consultation.

Thus compilers of Ming casebooks worked with an eclectic terminological repertory inherited from classics and custom. Among the 91 "sections" in Xu Chunfu's general history or the 195 "classifications" in Jiang Guan's *Classified Cases from Famous Doctors,* groupings based on symptoms (*kesou* = coughing; *linbi* = urinary incontinence; *shuizhong* = edema; *outu* = vomiting) or alternatively based on parts of the body (*feiyu* = lung stasis; *xintong* = heart pain) form the largest number. Old names grown weighty due to their classical origins (*zhongfeng* = windstroke; *shanghan* = Cold Damage; *jiaoqi* = foot qi; *huoluan* = bowel uproar) came closer to functioning as taxonomic disease labels,[34] but were used so broadly as to call for further differentiation according to symptom or pattern dynamic. Although nosological classification was slowly changing over the course of late imperial Chinese history,[35] Ming case history collections were not major innovators here. Hsiung's chapter in this volume shows how Xue Kai grouped pediatric cases under standard prescription formulas that could be used on all the cases in a given set. Others also kept to pragmatic, symptom-based categories that facilitated bedside consultation. In their hands *men* and *lei* functioned with the straightforward eclecticism of the list, rather than indexing more complex diagnostic patterns in their material.[36]

Not surprisingly, then, some authors chose cases that were unusual. Nie Shangheng (b. 1572), a doctor and official in Fujian Province whose casebook tracked the ravages of smallpox there, selected his cases explicitly for their individual qualities.

> I have gathered some striking and successful cases from the past, which I narrate and record in detail. The facts of the illness and method of treatment are set forth fully so people can compare them. Readers may be able to know that when a certain disorder has reached a dangerous crisis a certain medicine is well suited to restoring tranquility, and when a certain sufferer is on brink of death, what medicine will restore life. I hope that from now on syndromes that are similar to one another may be "understood as connected categories" [*chu lei er tong*] and applied as fit.[37] If so later generations of sufferers from cruel and chronic disorders will not fail to benefit. This is my intention in composing "Medical Narratives."[38]

The title of Nie's book, *Medical Narratives of the Striking and Successful* (*Qi xiao yishu*), explained his principles of selection. Difficult cases, unusual successes—these could instruct the practitioner who did not need advice for routine illnesses. The bulk of cases in Jiang Guan's anthology were selected the same way: he chose the unusual, those of "surprising interest" (*chu qi*). While approving of a strategy of comparison, Nie was typical of case history authors in being interested in providing a range of examples likely to help solve the more difficult problems a doctor could face in his clinical practice. Like precedents in law, cases were most useful in problematic situations, not as data aggregating individual items into general taxonomic disease classes by induction.

To the modern eye the cases in collections potentially available to the Ming medical reader are often unsatisfactory. Our assumptions are shaped by experimental science, so we ask nagging questions that betray our preference for a standard product. We want case reports to follow a common format, consistently covering the full range of issues that are important for understanding and adequate comparison. One thing that kept Ming medical authors from accommodating these preferences was the literary construction of medical authority.[39] Given that a literate physician's prestige depended upon his class identification as a scholarly gentleman, Ming doctors taking up their pens valued refined language and allusion. The narrative structure of the clinical encounter further encouraged their tendency to see their cases as stories, revealing social relationships as well as diagnostic acumen. Poetical classical titles like *Pearls of Wisdom Retrieved from the Crimson Sea* (*Chishui xuan zhu*), *Notes from the Herb Garden* (*Zhiyuan yicao*), or *Record of Things Seen and Heard on Star-gazing Cliff* (*Fangxingyan jianxianlu*)[40] helped suggest that some case collections should be read as literature, padded with flattering prefaces from well-connected clients. Cheng Congzhou, a seventeenth-century doctor from Yangzhou, read drafts of his case narratives to his poetry club.[41]

Literary narrative also fleshed out accounts limited by the ad-hoc nature of much medical record keeping, as attested by the editorial comments of case history writers and compilers themselves. Some collections were assembled only late in life (Nie Shangheng, Yu Chang) or by disciples (Wang Ji, Wang Kentang); some were based on notes that were admittedly and probably deliberately left incomplete (Wang Kentang); sometimes records got lost or worm-eaten (Sun Yikui). A good number of volumes were compiled by disciples and junior relatives in a spirit of pious tribute that attested to a commemorative purpose or, more obliquely, to a desire to promote the reputation of a medical lineage (Sun Yikui, Wang Ji).

Nonetheless, late-Ming medical authors did sometimes discuss formal standards for a proper case narrative. Two early examples can be found in the medical writings of Han Mao (fl. 1522), a hereditary physician from Sichuan, and Wu Kun (1552–ca. 1620), an "enlightened physician" of Huizhou. Both authors offered model guidelines for a written record of a clinical case. Han Mao described six topics to be covered: the four standard diagnostic steps (looking, listening and smelling, asking, and feeling the pulse) plus a discourse on illness origin and, finally, the prescription therapies and the eventual outcome. Writing about his family's practice in a remote province, Han sketched for his readers standardized diagnostic forms that a physician could fill in. Wu Kun was much more explicit about how the information extracted would enable the physician to relate clinical evidence to classical doctrines about illness dynamics: the year, season, and date are keys to environmental configurations of qi circulation (*yun qi*); the symptoms of heat and cold by night and day are keys to the condition of Blood and qi; the patient's likes and dislikes reveal yin-yang patterns of the inner organ systems, while pulse patterns should correlate with the patient's age and physical appearance. Where Han made clear his belief that the value of such records was for the physician's own enlightenment, Wu said that "when the wealthy and learned are sick, you must definitely write out a case record" and sign it. This lets us know that in his practice, as in the Song dynasty, elite clients still expected documents of their cases from the attending doctors.[42]

Though neither Han Mao nor Wu Kun left published case records that conformed to these guidelines, their writings do point to increasing medical concern about system in record keeping bearing on cases. Sun Yikui's apologia for his case collection—which was put together by his two sons around 1596—shows some of this, as well as the cross-currents of competing narrative agendas.

> Doctors have produced many cases [*an*]; some are too brief to be clear about their methods; some use a frivolous style ill suited to therapeutic techniques. What do these have to do with making a case? What a shame! Now I write down those from my life experience that have hit the mark. I recount the symptoms, give details on the pulse, describe in full the method of treatment. For medicines I include the proportions according to the scale of Prince, Minister, Envoy, and Assistant;[43] I take note of cold, hot, warm or cool [weather], of earthen, red, black or white [facial color]. All is recorded in sequence to testify that my bedside conduct is not careless, and my prescribing not haphazard. Thus my modest learning can be rectified by those who know the Way, while novices in this craft of ours will open my book, which shows things as clearly as pointing to the palm of one's hand, and will instantly know how to proceed. These are my intentions [*yi*]; the reader must judge them.[44]

In fact, Sun was criticized for letting his storytelling impulses override his medical pedagogy in the case collection analyzed by Judith Zeitlin in this volume (chap. 6). As she shows, it was famous for lively anecdotes and personal digressions; moreover, it was organized to reflect the history of Sun's travels rather than the nature of the illnesses he treated.

Sun's attempt to defend himself from criticism is instructive. Like his contemporaries, his idea of how to reason with cases did not stress nosological classification into fixed kinds, but rather the use of analogy to locate individual precedents along a continuum of similarity and difference. However, given this model of case-based reasoning, late-Ming physicians did begin to judge individual case history narratives according to criteria of completeness and clarity that would facilitate adequate comparison.

But just as the influence of literary culture can explain only some of the discursiveness of Ming case histories, so carelessness, secretiveness, or accident can account for only some of their lacunae. Very few surviving case history narratives covered all of the diagnostic and therapeutic terrain found in the models provided by Han Mao and Wu Kun or the recommendations some doctors wrote out to guide their students in conducting and discussing a clinical encounter. For example, Yu Chang's (1585–1664) seventeenth-century version of these instructions listed sixteen areas of diagnostic inquiry, five essentials of pattern diagnosis, and seven features to define any prescription being used. Yu also implied that much of the actual discussion of cases among his medical disciples was done orally—giving us a glimpse of the vast world of medical knowledge that continued to rely on craft rather than textual learning.[45] Case histories, then, were highly selective—both about what cases to choose and what to say about them. To understand this selectivity, we have to think about case narratives as argument. This is where the skill of comparing cases was in fact to be practiced.

Individual cases showed diagnosis in particular situations but did not make explicit arguments for one style of therapy over another. In the hands of an individual author, however, a group of case histories could become a vehicle for promoting a given therapeutic strategy in the context of debate between medical "scholarly currents." Here the author's selection of cases to include in a set pointed to a pattern of resemblance between cases, not around the superficial labels for types of disorder conveyed by "section" or "class" (*lei*) but around the deeper functional patterns that gave symptoms significance. Understanding these patterns was considered the key to successful diagnosis and treatment. They explained the direction, path, momentum, and quality of a pathological process in terms of a few broadly resonant categories—repletion and depletion, heat and cold, inner and outer—all linked to the flow of bodily qi and Blood. As yin-yang Blood-qi pairs, these functional categories connected the body to the environment and macrocosm without and to circulation channels and visceral organ systems within; as markers of bodily humors of heat and cold, moisture and dryness, the patterning of pathology pointed to appropriate forms of drug action. The differences between various medical scholarly currents centered on pharmaceutical strategies that broadly speaking could be understood in the idiom of drug actions affecting these underlying functional patterns: drugs worked on yin factors or yang factors, Blood or qi; they replenished or drained, warmed or cooled, activated or tranquilized, released to the exterior or stabilized the center. A case narrative ideally could link symptoms and patterns while showcasing the customized prescriptions that experts and their clients saw as the key to "efficacy" (*yan*), that is, a successful outcome.

The Medical Cases of Wang Ji was a pioneer example of a group of case histories marshaled to serve this kind of medical debate.[46] Wang found himself at odds with the teachings of the great Yuan-dynasty innovator Zhu Zhenheng, whose therapeutic disciples, Wang thought, had followed too literally their master's doctrine that "yang is always in surplus and yin is always deficient." Using the language of bodily cosmology, Zhu's aphorism was a warning against the clinical dangers of strong purgatives and hot, drying drugs and encouraged a fail-safe strategy of always prescribing with an eye to protecting the body's fluids. In Wang's casebook an introductory essay interlarded with students' questions explored different facets of Zhu's "nourish yin Blood" strategy versus Wang's recommendation that at times one must also "replenish yang qi." Wang's arguments drew on both correlative cosmological theory and clinical observation. Concerning the first, he noted that in cosmology yang encompasses and leads yin, and Blood follows qi—a principle that plays out in the functioning of the *ying* (more yin) and *wei* (more yang) circulation channels that protect the body's surfaces from external invasion. Concerning the second, he pointed to examples where Zhu's practice was more flexible than his doctrine—in treating women's postpartum depletions, for example, where he taught "replenish qi and treat other disorders as secondary." Above all Wang pointed to his own clinical experience of yin depletions where patients had responded poorly to Zhu's yin boosters, while formulas tipped toward replenishing yang with ginseng and astragalus root (*huangqi*) had proven more effective. Some of these cases, characterized by emaciation, lassitude, periodic fevers, and bloody sputum, sound to moderns like consumptive syndromes.[47] Many, if not all, of the cases in Wang's collection turned on the use of ginseng and astragalus root, while an appended essay by a student criticized the aversion to ginseng in contemporary medical circles.[48]

Wang Ji and his students appear as revisionists concerned with modifying, rather than overthrowing, well-established therapeutic conventions. The case history format permitted this flexible approach, whereby a preferred strategy illustrated in a number of cases might be balanced against one or two useful for demonstrating exceptions to the rule. This model of compilation can also be seen in an early seventeenth-century collection where Wang's approach was extended to a more sweeping embrace of "warming and replenishing" strategies. *Medical Cases of Cheng Congzhou* (*Cheng Maoxian yi'an;* author's preface 1633) showed a particular concern with the proper treatment of the very large category of Cold-Damage disorders originally theorized in Zhang Ji's canonical work. That work presented the dynamics of disease process in terms of energy flow through yin and yang bodily channels, where early superficial yang stages of an illness, if not reversed, could lead to later, deeper, and more serious yin stages. Cheng Congzhou's cases drew a contrast between an initial phase governed by yang channels and dominated by hot, dry, external symptoms of the skin's surface—thirst, hectic flush, restlessness—and the later yin phase, marked by torpor, pallor, and a potentially life-threatening failure of vitality. Like Wang Ji, Cheng favored yang boosters under conditions of yin depletion, here applied as potentially lifesaving restoratives in emergencies. The pedagogical message of his cases was that doctors needed to learn to distinguish yin syndromes from yang ones in a variety of presentations and to trust the utility of ginseng and astragalus root (and in Cheng's practice also aconite [*fuzi*]) against the doubts and suspicions of patients and doctors alike.[49]

If case narratives like these constituted arguments, what did it take to win an argument? How did a case history collection convince? Collections like those of Wang Ji and Cheng Congzhou offered plenty of evidence that doubt and debate often surrounded the clinical encounter. Clients could be knowledgeable and opinionated, and, under pressure to achieve results, families easily shifted back and forth between home remedies and the recommendations of a variety of healers. The case history collection's claim to demonstrate "efficacy" operated at some remove from the tensions at the bedside, but traces of such tensions linger in the narratives. Accordingly, argument was sometimes polemical—few could resist an occasional jibe at "quacks" or a bit of hand wringing about the ignorant opportunists crowding the lower rungs of the medical hierarchy. Reputation, the other side of this equation, mattered, and fame as "an enlightened physician" according to Confucian standards of virtue vested medical authority in persons.

However, the appeal to evidence was relevant also, and it was provided by the prescriptions—the technical as well as the rhetorical climax of a case history narrative. Doctors knew that sick people sometimes recovered without medicines, and they knew that medicines sometimes failed. Case narratives, however, reported successes (or failures that showed the consequences of a flawed therapeutic strategy) and linked these to the doctor's skills as a pharmacist. The patient's recovery, of course, was one proof of a treatment's efficacy. But the argument that recovery was due to the doctor's remedies was of critical importance. This argument, ideally, lay in the correspondence revealed between the deep patterns detected in diagnosis and the drug actions of the various *materia medica* that made up the prescription. The relationship between disease and remedy was couched in cosmological language—that is, the deep yin-yang patterns of disorder should be complemented by the yin-yang qualities of the herbal ingredients, explaining the workings of the forces responsible for healing. Cosmology provided the idiom that made these affinities intelligible. Such explanations had their problems, of course. Since clinical experience had shown that remedies linked to any one configuration of yin-yang forces proved inefficacious sometimes, the debate between different doctors moved dialectically between the facts of the situation on the ground—what drugs were associated with medical success or failure—and questioning how yin-yang cosmological forces actually worked in different circumstances. Case-based reasoning here was neither purely empirical nor so bound by theory as to be unable to respond to evidence. Theory included broad, unstated assumptions about the natural and human worlds, while the test of "efficacy" produced successful results at least often enough to maintain those assumptions. The arguments for medical truth through case-based reasoning moved in the intellectual space allowed between these two. The deep structure of similarity/difference lay in presenting cases that showed deep pattern differences underlying surface similarities or deep pattern similarities masked by superficial differences.

Argument mattered, then. But thinking with medical cases was not just about argument. Just as there always remained a gap between the facts demonstrated in any given case and a general truth applicable to all similar cases, so doctors faced the contingency of each new clinical situation not just with thinking to do but with choices to make. Thinking about medicine as a form of action brought the authors of case histories back to the judicial metaphors that defined their cases as *an*. Cheng Congzhou expressed this in his 1633 preface to the collection by punning on the old philological associations of the word *an* (case) and *an* (to investigate based on facts), hence by extension "according to" or "commentary."

> Medicine is judgment [*yi zhe yi ye*]. A case is to make an investigation [*an zhe an ye*]. According to [*an*] the pivotal illness factors of repletion and depletion inquire into the warm or cold properties of drugs, look into the nature of human relationships and determine the character of the local environment. The reason for an illness may be inner or outer influences, or the coming and going of the seasons and weather, or it may be the perversities of the "seven emotions." By diagnosing [by pulse] within you may know what lies without [in the environment]; by looking at the external, the internal is made clear. If you don't concentrate your mind and use your resolve to form fairly detailed judgments, it won't be easy to grasp the situation.[50]

The word translated here as "judgment" is *yi*, which is pronounced the same as the Chinese word *yi* for "medicine." In saying "medicine is judgment," Cheng was repeating an aphoristic play on words common in Ming medical discourse—one that alluded to the Confucian classic the *Great Learning*'s injunction to integrity in thought and deed, conventionally translated as "make your intentions sincere [*cheng yi*]." To illustrate, medical authors often compared their decision making to the choices made on a battlefield, sometimes alluding to a famous anecdote from the biography of General Piaoqi in *Records of the Grand Historian*. All this appealed to their sense of the drama of the case—the heat and confusion of a medical crisis where life or death may depend not on scholarly learning but on swift appraisal and decisive action. Medical knowledge required integrity, which included the responsibility to intervene in a difficult and uncertain situation. In his own case history collection written around a decade after Cheng Congzhou, Yu Chang put it this way.

> I have heard it said that medicine is judgment [*yi*]. Faced with an illness, first one uses one's judgment to gain a "comprehensive understanding" of it; afterwards one tackles it with techniques and prescriptions. This is why the *Inner Canon* says that subtlety lies in judgment. What doctor fails to make judgments? Superficial or

profound are due to this; failing to match the hole to the peg is due to this; missing by a mile is due to this. The turning point of an illness leading to safety or danger, happiness or calamity, all are due to this. Depending on whether judgment is firm or wavering you have a verdict or undifferentiated chaos. Of course it is dangerous![51]

In naming the psychic faculty that produced medical decisions as "judgment," Ming physicians may seem to be talking about the limits of empirical knowledge, about hunches or guesswork, for example. But the constellation of meanings surrounding the term *yi* reached deep into classical philosophy and moral psychology. *Yi* was a "gut" feeling, to begin with. In the bodily system of correspondences familiar in medical thought, *yi* was associated with the Spleen-stomach system, midway between the active ratiocination of the faculty of the Heart, and *zhi*, the primal drive to live that was the faculty of the generative Kidney system. Often translated into English as "intention," "idea," "opinion," "wish," or even "will," *yi* calls attention to the volitional side of psychic life, to an individual's deepest commitments, especially those that form the ground for action. In naming his case history collection *Notes on My Judgment* (*Yuyi cao*),[52] Yu Chang constructed medical thinking in cases as both action oriented and personal, shaped by individual insight that is a matter of reflective judgment, and interventions that constitute the resulting judgments in action.

Yi as judgment implied something more as well. The practical imperative to make the right decision was also an ethical imperative. When the *Great Learning* spoke of "making one's intentions [*yi*] sincere," it carried the connotation of fidelity to the truth and responsibility to act.[53] Moreover, the *Great Learning* linked the ideal of a moral compass guiding one's intentions and actions with the scholar's project of study of the external world: "investigating things and extending knowledge" (*gewu zhizhi;* or, in shorthand, *gezhi*). While passionate debates in neo-Confucian metaphysics swirled around the deep meaning of this cryptic phrase from the Classic, scholars of "wide learning" (*boxue*)—which could range from antiquities, philology, and historical geography to plants and animals, foreign peoples, music, astronomy, and calendrical mathematics—appealed to the concept of "investigating things and extending knowledge" (*gezhi*) to bring their specialist knowledge into the framework of Zhu Xi's orthodox "Learning of the Way." The term, well enough established as about natural knowledge to serve as the Chinese translation of the Jesuit "scientia" in the seventeenth century, was applied to medical learning by a number of Ming literati physicians following the example of the Jin-Yuan master Zhu Zhenheng.[54] This is how Yu Chang integrated the ethical ideal of "sincere intentions" with the pursuit of natural knowledge of the body and the judgment of the doctor.

> In the *Great Learning* to "make your intentions sincere" is a matter of "investigating things and extending knowledge," and the strictest distinctions are between the paths of honesty and deceit. In general the turning point that leads to death comes from following the path of obscurantism, while holding onto simplicity will lead toward life.... How can we fail to "investigate" all the many things of the world? How can we fail to "extend" all that there is to know? Judgment is something that sprouts out of vacancy at the great foundation [of our beings]. How can we fail to make it sincere? To investigate a single thing is to extend one bit of knowledge. But if we fear to pursue things seeking to know, we will end our days investigating illness without knowing what kind of a thing illness is. Yet how hard it is when we wish to produce judgments that are both fitting and proper [according to the situation]![55]

The idea of the pursuit of technical knowledge as a moral enterprise came naturally to Yu Chang as a literatus physician. But this was not simply the result of a uniquely Chinese or Confucian "moralization of nature." Its separation from value is another one of those features of the modern fact of experimental science that has been mistaken as paradigmatic rather than historically contingent. Case-based reasoning accommodated the rhetorical associations of exactitude with fidelity, of validity with trustworthiness, of clarity with honesty—associations that are both very old and still persuasive in ordinary language. But when Yu talked about clinical reasoning and ethically inspired judgment in choosing what to do, he tells us how thinking in cases in the world of late Ming medicine linked knowledge and action at the level of moral ontology. Facts here are not discovered, but created; they are outcomes, authoritative because once made, they cannot be undone. In ways that recall the role of the judge or magistrate in a criminal trial, the doctor's empirical investigation has not really matured until it produces the judgment that may mean sickness or health, death or life for the patient. That judgment, because it is about a human being's fate and because it is irrevocable, calls upon psychic resources that are not a matter of learning alone and that we have to call spiritual.

LATER EVOLUTION OF THE CASE HISTORY GENRE: ANALYSIS AND VIRTUOSITY IN THE QING DYNASTY

Ming dynasty authors developed a rich tradition of case history writing shaped by both scholarly and legal models of learning and validity. Cases resisted classification into types or classes, narratives tended toward the literary and discursive, and issues of social reputation or lineage affiliation affected whose works got into print, while doctrinal controversies influenced the selection of cases included in them. In its stubborn individuality, the case reflected the laissez-faire institutional context of medicine, which between the sixteenth and eighteenth centuries continued to be studied through family, lineage, or master-disciple networks and which was practiced in an atmosphere of increasingly commercialized competition for clients. Nonetheless, over time in the Qing dynasty, case histories moved ever closer to the center of the production of medical knowledge. As a preferred vehicle for communicating the fruits of clinical experience, the case form was both a vehicle for medical innovation and a place where the personal virtuosity of individual doctors was celebrated. Innovations of eighteenth-century practitioners reflected these intellectual concerns.

One such innovator was Yu Zhen (fl. 1778). Reacting against the proliferation of anthologies of case histories, this late eighteenth-century doctor sought to create a contemporary meta-narrative about the archive itself. Culling from *Classified Cases from Famous Doctors* and its even bulkier successor volume, *Continued Classified Cases from Famous Doctors* (*Xu mingyi lei'an*, 1770), compiled by Wei Zhixiu (d. 1772), Yu chose over a thousand cases he deemed "artful." Under the title *Commentary on Medical Cases Old and New* (*Gujin yi'an an*), Yu arranged them by syndrome, following each selection with a record and each record with his own personal commentary (*an*). As he put it, "I distinguish true and false, separate good and bad, finding differences within sameness, displaying the indigo that surpasses the blue [figurative for pupils and successors exceeding their masters]. Sometimes I summarize many things with a few words, to show the broad outlines; sometimes I offer a complex narrative of old and new views, to supplement where the cases have not reached."[56] In Yu's hands, carefully selected old cases from famous doctors were literally like legal "leading cases" (*cheng'an*) compiled for later study.[57] However, this study did not lead to standardized therapeutic protocols. In Yu's thinking cases revealed a dialectic of "technique" (*fa*) and "art" (*qiao*)—that is, they helped capture the virtuosity of the doctor who knew how to play "fast and loose" with the rules of his craft. "The techniques of medicine are to be found in the numerous 'leading cases,' but the art behind the techniques is also here," he wrote. Following Yu's model of thinking, notable cases became the starting point for a discursive exploration that could be picked up and added to by others, as it was most notably by Wang Shixiong (1808–1867) in the mid-nineteenth century.[58] Yu's narrative was one of medical progress, with cases generating their own commentaries in an open-ended manner.

If Yu Zhen's work pondered the accumulating historical archive of famous cases, the admirers of Ye Gui (1666–1745) saw to it that after his death some of this legendary doctor's personal clinical records found their way into best-selling collections. Of these, *Medical Cases as a Guide to Clinical Practice* (*Lin zheng zhinan yi'an*), published in 1768, was the most authoritative and enduringly popular (there survive thirty-nine editions printed before the end of the imperial era).[59] A clinically oriented innovator from a hereditary medical family in Suzhou, Ye established a model style of case history that continues to be admired and imitated even today. Stripped of storytelling flourishes or social detail concerning the patients' identities, Ye's cases offered a laconic narrative that cut through the presenting symptoms to an underlying diagnostic pattern and concentrated on a customized prescription formula. The "Organizing Principles" (*Fanli*) that introduced the first edition of the collection help explain its thinking. They warn of the limitations of the nosological categories that constitute the surface organization of the section headings. By the selection and arrangement of cases within each category, the reader is being taught to distinguish between easily recognizable symptoms and syndromes (*zheng*, clusters of symptoms) and the more subtle "diagnostic patterns" (*zhenghou*) that identify the disorder at the most fundamental level.

Thus the nosological problem of pattern versus sign—of difference underlying similarity and similarity masking difference—is tackled head on.

> Diagnostic patterns are complex: if you wish to investigate them, it is difficult to generalize. Undeterred by my ignorance, I have divided cases into sections and classes [*fen men lei*]. But multiple patterns are common: for example "depletion-exhaustion," "cough," "spitting up blood" can all manifest one underlying diagnostic pattern. To divide these into different sections is to separate what belongs together. Then a cough may be a case of repletion or depletion, it may be a superficial symptom or a fundamental problem, or it may be caused by any one of the six seasonal forms of qi. To unite these into one section is to unite what should be separate. When "summer damp" is combined with "periodic fever and dysentery," or "Spleen function disorder" is combined with "vomiting and abdominal swelling" the overall problems multiply, and finding a satisfactory analytic category is not easy.[60]

Within each nosological label Ye's collection gathered a large selection of seemingly similar cases illustrating different underlying disease patterns. Even "small differences remaining [between cases] are full of significance and . . . if [the number of cases were] subtracted still more, one would not be able to show the master's unerring touch, or the beauty of the myriad variations in his prescription art."[61] Ye had a signature style of prescribing, preferring formulas featuring a relatively small number of mild and neutral ingredients, and he displeased traditionalists by dropping some old nosological categories like Fire, popular in the Ming dynasty. In particular he reorganized the venerable Cold Damage category, which he clearly believed overgeneralized a wide variety of syndromes marked by symptoms of heat and fever. What mattered most was the way these case histories showed distinct, deep diagnostic patterns at work in superficially similar cases and the way an informed expert could read those patterns back from the *materia medica* selected for a cure. Significantly, Ye's case records did not report outcomes, being content to demonstrate the underlying principles linking disorder and remedy in each instance. Cutting to the core this way, Ye's cases left out the discursive fabric of social life—the contingent situations and social relations of healing. It even left out the symptomatic noise—changing manifestations of a messy clinical encounter that a practitioner needed to consider in determining what clue mattered most to a diagnosis. The case was pared down to a demonstration of the hermeneutics of prescriptions themselves.[62]

Some of Ye's enduring prestige came from innovations that were later identified with a modernist school of Warm Factor disorders.[63] Some of the laconic quality of his cases reflected the Qing-dynasty setting where famous physicians more and more received patients in their clinics and had students and junior disciples take case notes that were copied for the client to take away (and therefore highlighted the prescription but did not record the outcome). His style of thinking with cases is also evidence for the increasing professionalization of medicine—a process no less genuine for being expressed through lineage affiliation, discipleship, and social networks of "scholarly currents" rather than the formal organizations of Western social theory.[64] While clients took away prescription formulas to be filled, these eighteenth-century case records demanded initiated readers who understood the deep structure of such formulas. Rather than pleading for more careful record keeping, Qing physicians expected an audience of specialists skilled at decoding medical shorthand. Medicine was still personal, the literati physician was still important as a moral ideal, and many case collections still featured anecdotes and stories. But as doctrinal controversies in the eighteenth century and after shifted to questions of the value of medical classicism itself, case history collections following those of Yu Zhen and Ye Gui can be seen as textual vehicles for busy clinicians and teachers, medical modernists and innovators. Further, in this way the record of medical cases themselves came gradually to represent medicine's recent history. The case genre, always especially well adapted to the model of disease as situational and of medical qualification as a kind of virtuosity vested in persons and revealed in action, in the long run was a mode of producing specialist knowledge that also fostered the modern twentieth-century definition of Chinese medicine as above all a "practice" whose essence was to be found in the clinical experience of eminent "senior physicians."[65]

NOTES

1 I am referring to Joseph Levenson's essay, "The Abortiveness of Empiricism in Early Ch'ing Thought," which was read by all graduate students in my generation. Levenson identified seventeenth-century science with Bacon's "inductive empiricism" and compared

it to the materialist ontologies of seventeenth-century Chinese philosophers like Huang Zongxi and Gu Yanwu, whom he labeled text-centered "nominalists."

2 The phrase is from the title of Benjamin Elman's book, *On Their Own Terms: Science in China, 1500–1900.*

3 For an overview of these themes, see ibid. See also Biagioli, ed., *The Science Studies Reader.*

4 Shi Qi and Xiao Mincai, eds., *Zhongyi bing'an xue,* 1–4, 137–151.

5 Bian Que may have been a composite figure or the presumed ancestral founder of a medical lineage, whereas Chunyu Yi was a historical contemporary of Sima Qian. *Shiji,* 9:105.2785–105.2817. See also Li Jianmin, *Si sheng zhi yu,* 299–302.

6 This is noted by Hsu, "Pulse Diagnostics," 61–62.

7 *Shiji,* 9:105.2813. The explanation quoted appears at the end of the biography as a reply to the monarch's query based on the cases submitted. But another quote, placed at the end of the twenty-five case narratives, hints at the role of memory: "Servant Yi said, 'there are many more [than the twenty-five] whom I examined and fixed the term for life or death, and others whom I cured after they were already sick, but over time I have forgotten them: without full knowledge I dare not reply [further].'"

8 Ho Da-an, "Lunduan fuhao," 320–337.

9 Chen Bangxian, ed., *Ershiliu shi yixue shiliao,* 60, 279.

10 For narratives about Hua Tuo, see Cullen, "Yi'an (case statements)," 305–307, citing *Chronicle of the Three Kingdoms.*

11 For Sun Simiao, see Sivin, "A Seventh-Century Chinese Medical Case History."

12 *Zhongguo yiji tongkao,* 3:4032–4039.

13 Xu Shuwei, *Shanghan jiushi lun,* in *Congshu jizheng xin bian,* 45:617; *Zhongguo yiji tongkao,* 1:279–280. Some of the cases were anthologized by Jiang Guan and Yu Zhen.

14 See Cullen, "Yi'an (case statements)," 304.

15 See Chen Yuanpeng, *Liang Song de "shang yi shiren" yu "ruyi"*; Leung, "Medical Learning from the Song to the Ming."

16 See Chen Yuanpeng, *Liang Song de "shang yi shiren" yu "ruyi,"* 134–149, for tables of publications sponsored by Song "gentleman admirers of medicine" (*shang yi shiren*).

17 Hsiung Pingchen, ed., *Rang zhengju shuohua: Zhongguo pian.*

18 Cullen, "Yi'an (case statements)," 310–321; Grant, *A Chinese Physician,* 21–50. The editors' general introduction to *Xin'anyiji congkan* asserts that one-half of the case collections published in the Ming dynasty were the work of Huizhou natives.

19 Ho Da-an, "Lunduan fuhao."

20 The translation of *xuepai* is from Scheid, "Restructuring the Field of Chinese Medicine," 14–15.

21 Li Chan, *Yixue rumen.*

22 Xu Chunfu, comp., *Gujin yitong daquan,* preface of 1556, but according to modern editors actually published between 1575 and 1578.

23 Jiang Guan, comp., *Mingyi lei'an.* Although the author's preface is dated 1549, the volume was edited by his sons and finally published in 1591.

24 Jiang Guan, preface to *Mingyi lei'an.*

25 The quote by Confucius appears in Sima Qian, "Taishigong zixu," chap. 130 of *Shiji.* The translation is from Watson, *Ss'u-ma Ch'ien,* 51.

26 Xu Guo, preface to *Mingyi lei'an,* dated 1586.

27 Grant, *A Chinese Physician,* 61.

28 Cheng Zheng, preface to *Shishan yi'an,* in Wang Ji, *Wang Shishan,* 59.

29 Han Mao, *Hanshi yitong,* 1.5–1.9, in *Zhongguo yixue dacheng,* 4:391.

30 Sun Yikui, preface to *Chi shui xuanzhu,* in *Zhongguo yiji tongkao,* 4:4949.

31 Xu Chunfu, *Gujin yitong daquan,* 3:212. According to his interlinear note, Xu here was quoting an earlier text titled *Classified Materia Medica* (*Bencao leishu*). It is no longer extant.

32 Wu Kun, "Mai'an geshi," in *Zhongguo yixue dacheng,* 2:651.

33 Zhang Yikui, preface to *Mingyi lei'an,* 7.

34 In the twentieth century these terms evolved into names for cerebral hemorrhage, typhoid, beri beri, and cholera in biomedicine.

35 Furth, *A Flourishing Yin,* 155–174, documents some streamlining of nosology in Ming dynasty "medicine for women" (*fuke*); Hanson, in "Robust Northerners and Delicate Southerners," shows how disagreements over the etiology of Cold Damage disorders led to a new class of Warm Factor (*wenbing*) fevers in the Qing.

36 These problems are being explored in Barbara Volkmar's work-in-progress on the case histories of Wan Quan, which argues for that physician's experimental agenda of using cases to document all the possible configurations of smallpox. At the end of his life Wan sighed that with more than one hundred configurations, he was still far from finished. See Volkmar, "The Notch in the River Boat."

37 This phrase is from the *Classic of Changes.*

38 Nie Shangheng, preface to *Qi xiao yishu,* in *Zhongguo yiji tongkao,* 4:4952–4953.

39 See Judith T. Zeitlin's chapter on the medical cases of Sun Yikui in this volume (chap. 6).

40 Xue Qinglu et al., eds., *Quanguo Zhongyi tushu lianhe mulu,* 630, 634.

41 Furth, *A Flourishing Yin,* 230–231.

42 Wu Kun, "Mai'an geshi," in *Zhonggui yixue dacheng,* 2:651; Han Mao, *Hanshi yitong,* in *Zhongguo yixue dacheng,* 4:391. See also Shi Qi and Xiao Mincai, eds., *Zhongyi bing'an xue,* 137–145.

43 This bureaucratic metaphor alludes to the relative importance of different drugs in a formula.

44 Sun Yikui, "Shengshengzi yi'an xiaoyin," in *Zhongguo yiji tongkao,* 4:4949.

45 See the section "A Model for Discussing Disorders with Disciples" (Yu menren ding yi bing shi), *Yuyi cao, juan* 1, in *Yu Jiayan yixue quanshu,* ed. Chen Yi et al., 375–376.

46 In *A Chinese Physician,* 106, Grant has tabulated thirty disease names spread over one hundred cases in Wang's compilation. Of the four categories including nine cases or more, one is itself the catchall category of "miscellaneous."

47 See particularly the sections on *nue* (periodic fevers; 22 cases), *tuxue* (spitting blood; 11 cases), and *tiaojing* (menstrual regulation; 9 cases).

48 For more on Wang Ji, see Grant, *A Chinese Physician.*

49 Cheng Congzhou, *Cheng Maoxian yi'an.* The collection contained ninety-three cases, not sorted by "classifications." See also Furth, *A Flourishing Yin,* chap. 7.

50 Cheng Congzhou, preface to *Cheng Maoxian yi'an,* in *Zhongguo yiji tongkao,* 4:4966.

51 Yu Chang, preface to *Yuyi cao* (dated 1643), 371. The phrase "comprehensive understanding" (*yunliang*) alludes to Zhuangzi's aphorism that the sage aspires to comprehend all the myriad things of the world (*yunliang wanwu*).

52 The title *Yuyi cao* is impossible to translate literally. *Yuyi* in classical usage refers to viewpoints or wishes expressed indirectly, implying a hidden level of meaning. *Cao,* or "running style of calligraphy," suggests informal thoughts spontaneously expressed.

53 Graham, *Disputers of the Tao,* 132–137.

54 See Elman, *On Their Own Terms,* chap. 1. Zhu Zhenheng, who was an initiated fourth-generation disciple of Zhu Xi as well as one of the medical "Four Masters," titled his most important medical treatise *A Further Discussion of "The Investigation of Things and the Extension of Knowledge"* (*Gezhi yulun*).

55 Yu Chang, preface to *Yuyi cao,* 371.

56 Yu Zhen, preface to *Gujin yi'an an.*

57 For the "leading case" in Qing law, see the chapter by Pierre-Étienne Will in this volume (chap. 2).

58 Wang Shixiong and Yu Zhen, *Gujin yi'an an xuan.* For further discussion, see the chapter by Hsiung in this volume (chap. 5).

59 Ye Gui, *Lin zheng zhinan yi'an.* This posthumous work is considered the most authoritative of the fifty-odd that were printed under Ye's name based on cases claiming to be his that surfaced gradually over time.

60 Hua Xiuyun, "Fanli," in Ye Gui, *Lin zheng zhinan yi'an,* 10. Hua was the medical colleague most responsible for the compilation and publication of the collection.

61 Ibid.

62 One of Ye's cases, reprinted in Shi Qi and Xiao Mincai, *Zhongyi bing'an xue,* 153, is translated and analyzed in Andrews, "From Case Records to Case Histories," 325–326.

63 See Hanson, "Robust Northerners and Delicate Southerners," 273–274, 276–279. She outlines the "four warps" model of febrile diseases, which Ye wanted to substitute for the traditional Cold Damage doctrine of "six warps."

64 See Scheid, "Restructuring the Field of Chinese Medicine," 11–15.

65 For the twentieth-century medical culture of "practice" and the "senior physician," see Farquhar, *Knowing Practice;* Lei, "How Did Chinese Medicine Become Experiential?" and Scheid, "Restructuring the Field of Chinese Medicine."

5

Facts in the Tale

Case Records and Pediatric Medicine in Late Imperial China

PING-CHEN HSIUNG

This essay looks at how the "case method" (as description, record, and analysis) evolved within one particular area of Chinese medicine—pediatrics—during the late imperial period. Focusing on four widely separated historical moments, it examines how the form, style, and authorship of case-based narratives and reasoning changed over time, from the earliest surviving examples in the second century BCE down to the eighteenth century. The classical precedent for the case-like medical story is found in the biography of the early Western Han physician Chunyu Yi as related by Sima Qian. In the Song dynasty, pediatric case records were important in establishing the reputation of Qian Yi, generally recognized as the founder of that medical specialty. In the Song period medical case narratives authored by literati also were found in other records that circulated about admired physicians. In the Ming period, when pediatrics flourished as a medical specialty, we have examples of pediatric case records based on direct clinical observation from two eminent practitioners. These show how practicing physicians were beginning to produce case records based on their personal experience and to classify them under nosological categories of pediatric disorder. Sometimes such classification extended to the recommendation of a common standard prescription formula for large sets of individual cases. Finally, by the early Qing, scholars were collecting, editing, and publishing anthologies of famous medical cases for the print market. Some medical authors added comments to famous earlier cases (called, confusingly, "comments" [*an*] on "cases" [*an*]). These medical records emerged from a distinct cultural tradition, showing that Chinese medicine had its own forms of "thinking in cases" in the sense of a "style of reasoning" as analyzed by John Forrester.[1]

Overall, as a form of specialized technical prose writing, case-based records appeared in China in a number of disciplines long before they acquired the typical name of "case" (*an*) in the Ming dynasty. Therefore, the close relationship between the case narrative, evidential reasoning, and the development of Chinese pediatrics does not necessarily rest on the categorical concept, set terms, or established genre of "case" (*an*). In fact, the linguistic idiom *yi'an* (medical case) came into use long after habits of case-based vocational reasoning and occupational learning had taken hold culturally. The language, writing style, and compositional features, as well as the characteristic content and organizational structure of this style of documentation, deserve special attention because they adopt a specific form of case-oriented thinking. Their use of narrative construction as a conceptual tool and rhetorical instrument in record keeping make them of particular interest in the comparative study of evidential reports.[2]

MEDICAL STORIES BEFORE PEDIATRICS

Most agree that China's first case-type medical narratives appeared in Sima Qian's *Records of the Grand Historian* (*Shiji*). These twenty-five brief accounts, retrospectively termed "consultation records" (*zhenji*), were inserted in the biographical section of China's early history as the testimony of Chunyu Yi (fl. 175 BCE), a presumably misjudged doctor speaking before the imperial court on his own behalf. In these short narratives Sima Qian shows a practicing healer recounting his own activities. Each tale includes the individual patient's name, occupation, and home area, as well as the symptoms, pulse reading, diagnosis, treatment, and outcome. Sima Qian's introduction to Chunyu Yi's biography, moreover, depicts a doctor who used his case reports to show why his apprenticeship (*shouxue*), practice (*zhenbing*), and efficacy (*yan*) in medicine often depended on texts (*fangshu*). Trained by old masters in reading pulses, Chenyu Yi purportedly used his case stories to show how his diagnoses depended upon information learned from reading the pulse. For therapy he is shown using moxa and acupuncture, as well as prescription recipes with set names, suggesting customarily known package treatments.[3]

One of these twenty-five case narratives concerns a child—the illness of a young prince of Qi. Called upon to help provide care for powerful patients, Chunyu Yi is depicted as the healing expert awaiting the demands of the rich and famous. Summoned to take the boy's pulse, Chunyu Yi prescribes energy-calming soup (*xiaqi tang*) to calm the young patient's qi and explains why a three-day dose of his medication should have taken care of the problem that was, as he saw it, caused by sadness and grief.[4] What is also evident from these itemized accounts is that in the clinical setting doctors shared knowledge "according to the classics" (*jingyue*) but did not always agree about either pulse diagnosis or physical or pharmaceutical therapy. In light of this tradition of dissent, case-based judgment could provide an on-the-spot basis for decision making, either as a countermeasure to fixed procedures or as a therapeutic alternative to abstract understanding.

CASE RECORDS AND THE ADVENT OF PEDIATRICS

As literary medicine continued to evolve after the Song dynasty (960–1279 CE), Chunyu Yi's cases, as represented in Sima Qian's record, were appreciated as a model form of case narrative. By the end of that era Sima Qian's chronicle was being copied, circulated, and consulted as an independent work by literary and medical scholars alike.[5] Like Chunyu Yi's accounts, the twenty-three notes on medical treatment contained within the three sections (*juan*) of *Proven Formulae of Medicine for Small Children* (*Xiao'er yaozheng zhijue;* 1119) documented the career of a physician, Qian Yi (1032–1113). Sandwiched between 47 short medical essays (*lun*) and 114 prescription recipes (*fang*), these pediatric notes are identified as "Records of Twenty-Three Illness Syndromes" (Ji changsuo zhibing ershisan zheng). Two out of the twenty-three case-based records may serve here as examples of the content and style. The first example has it that

> [t]hree children (boys) from the Zhang family came down with nausea. The eldest sweated till his entire body got wet; the second eldest [sweated] from the top of his head down to his chest. The youngest merely had some sweat on his forehead. Various practitioners [*zhongyi*] treated them with Wheat Sprout Powder [*maijian san*], yet with no effect. Dr. Qian said, "Treat the eldest with Melon Ball [*xianggua yuan*], the second eldest with Yihuang Powder [*yihuang san*], and the youngest with Plaster Soup [*shigao tang*]." These remedies were administered for five days, and [they] recovered.[6]

The second case is more elaborate.

> The five-year-old son of an official, Zhu, was feverish at night. When the boy awoke in the morning, he was normal. Various common practitioners treated it either as a case of "damage from cold"; or as a case of a "hot" disorder. They prescribed cooling drugs for the child to disperse the heat, but the child was not cured. His symptoms were excessive mucus and drowsiness. Other doctors used Powdered Iron Pills [*tiefen yuan*] to purge the mucus, but the child's illness worsened. On the fifth day he had a great craving for drink. Qian said, "One must not purge." Then he took one *liang* [fifty grams] of finely chopped White Atractylodes Rhizome [*baishu san*], boiled it until there were three *sheng* [liters] of juice, gave it to the child and let him drink as much as he desired. Zhu asked, "If he drinks a lot, won't he have diarrhea?" Qian replied, "Without un-boiled water one cannot develop diarrhea. Even if the child develops diarrhea, it should not be anything strange. But one must not purge." Zhu again asked, "What disorder should be treated first?" Qian replied, "[My medication is] to quench thirst, stop phlegm, reduce fever, and clean the insides all with this one prescription." When evening came, the prescribed dosage had been used up. Qian again examined the situation

and ordered, "He can take yet three more *sheng*." Three more *sheng* of Baishu Powder Drink were prepared and administered, whereupon there was some improvement. On the third day, [the patient received] yet another three *sheng* of the Baishu Powder Drink and the child was no longer thirsty, and also free of mucus. [Qian then] administered two doses of Donkey Glue Powder [*ajiao san*] and [the child] recovered.[7]

Qian Yi's cases remind readers of those of Chunyu Yi in many ways. Both identify the patient individually before they describe the symptoms, then they explain the medical history before concluding with diagnosis and treatment. Each case includes social information, such as the name and/or official title of the person in charge of the young patient (usually the father, but sometimes a grandfather or other close relative), the relationship between the family elder and the sick child (automatically revealing the gender of both parties), and the age of the patient. Next comes an account of the child's symptoms; then the physician's diagnosis, treatment protocol, pharmaceutical prescriptions (including ingredients, proportions, frequency, and period of application), and the outcome of the care are detailed. Both *Proven Formulae* and Sima Qian's biography of Chunyu Yi use classical language to combine "narrative storytelling with a built-in analytical voice" (*jiaxu jiayi*). Furthermore, like the testimonies Sima Qian constructed on behalf of Chunyu Yi, Qian Yi's case accounts and pediatric record were reconstructed later by an interested third party. In his original preface to *Proven Formulae*, the compiler, a minor official named Yan Jizhong, reveals that Qian had been engaged by Yan's own father to treat him when he was a boy of five or six. A Confucian official as an adult, Yan became increasingly aware of the difficult nature of pediatric medicine as well as the trail-blazing character of Qian's career, and this strengthened his desire to move beyond Qian's "unwillingness to transmit his knowledge casually" (*buken qingchuan qishu*). Collecting this specialized knowledge took place in four stages. First, Yan jotted down the initial ten or more prescriptions in his own family's possession as the result of their long acquaintance with the practitioner.[8] Next, he gathered several tens of instances (*shuozheng*) collected from Qian's associates as the master himself grew older.[9] Third, miscellaneous prescriptions were added. Finally, Yan compared, revised, and edited so as to improve upon his notes, consulting scattered records from other versions (*bieben*) of Qian's activities that were then circulating in the capital. The result is an observer's third-person narrative of an old master, representing Qian as one voice amid a spectrum of different opinions and competing activities.[10] But above all, Yan's efforts spoke eloquently about a time and place when an educated lay audience was interested in medicine as recorded, preserved, circulated, and discussed by means of the case method.

To choose a mere 23 cases out of a physician's career spanning half a century is, to say the least, highly selective. Fewer than 10 named illnesses are represented in these 23 cases, in contrast to the 47 medical essays (*yilun*) preceding them and the 117 prescription formulas (*zhufang*) following. In Yan's compilation, these specific cases were most probably read as explanatory sections supporting the preceding medical discussions (*lun*) and the therapeutic prescriptions (*fang*) that followed. Discussion, case, and prescription formed a crucial trilogy for the practitioner. The narrative is impressively detailed about the techniques of Qian's practice. During the Ming dynasty four centuries later, another famed medical author, Han Mao, in his *Master Han's Survey of Medicine* (*Hanshi yitong*, 1522) gave his view on how a medical case (*yi'an*) should be modeled on "all six principles" (*liufa jianbei*). That is, in addition to recording findings from the four basic diagnostic methods of "observing the appearance" (*wang xingse*), "listening to sounds" (*wen shengyin*), "asking about the condition" (*wen qingzhuang*), and "feeling the pulse" (*qie maili*), a medical case was also to "deliberate on the origins of the illness" (*lun bingyuan*) while displaying "the techniques of prescribing" (*zhifangshu*) in treatment.[11] By such latter-day standards, Yan's depiction of Qian's performance four centuries earlier was a clear achievement in evidential writing, all the more so as those cases were not selected for the mere purpose of self-promotion, and Qian's failures were observed alongside his successes.[12]

Here, it can be seen how medical cases combined literary narrative, technical documentation, and historical writing. When Qian Yi's twenty-three pediatric case records appeared, their compiler Yan Jizhong introduced them as "notes" (*ji*) on "illness syndromes treated" (*zheng*) rather than as "cases" (*an*). Yet as individual records about this or that patient cared for by a particular physician, they were explicitly and unequivocally separated from their earlier historiographical and bureaucratic contexts, to assume a textual and vocational integrity of their own. Case narratives also documented vocational competition and cultural negotiation. Yan portrayed Qian as waging one battle after another with rival doctors. In the accounts of the twenty-three cases, there are almost always "many doctors" (*zhuyi*), "various doctors" (*zhongyi*), or "numerous doctors" (*shuyi*) around the sickbed. Nor were debates among physicians the only forum for fierce competition, because they in turn were surrounded by distressed families, confronting each other with reams of different opinions, conflicting diagnoses, endless arguments, and often barefaced rivalry. In particular, parents and older relatives of the sick child, hardly short of ideas of their own, were all there to take part in the struggle. Readers, expert and amateur alike, were expected to judge Qian's crusade for themselves, albeit through the medium of Yan's representation, taking into account the circumstances and background that framed each case.

Rhetorically, then, when Yan explains the trouble he had to go through as a compiler to reveal the secrets of a practicing doctor with a habit of concealment, he is also asking his audience for a sympathetic hearing. In his preface, Yan mentions the existence of "other versions" (*bieben*), that is, different narratives dealing with Qian's methods—treatises, examples (*shuozheng*), and various prescriptions (*zafang*)—that were in circulation in the Song capital of Kaifeng. Like other doctors, Qian seemed ambivalent about "transmitting his knowledge casually" (*qingchuan qishu*), but Yan was convinced that publicizing the records was the best way to validate the authority of a worthy physician by marketing his expertise. In other words, to win the trust of patients and their families, potential disciples, or suspicious and jealous colleagues, actual cases of treatment might be the only instrument for substantiating one's ideas, promoting one's reputation, and guaranteeing one's lasting authority. As he appraised, catalogued, corrected, and elucidated his findings, therefore, Yan took pride in his public role, deliberately distancing his text from the disorderly bundles that "got distributed as soon as they were written."

Here we see that case documents were so highly valued both by experts and the uninitiated that both supply and demand were great. This also illustrates that a practical consequence of documenting Qian Yi's career with cases was to support his long-term reputation as the founder of Chinese pediatrics. His practice, methods, and reasoning, as documented in the case records, became increasingly popular as this vehicle came to play a vital role in facilitating the growth of pediatrics as a specialty.

Neither in their Song original (indirectly collected from secondary sources) nor in their extant Ming editions were Qian's pediatric cases referred to as *an* (cases). Instead, they were always called "Records of the Twenty-Three Illness Syndromes." Nor did the generic term "*yi'an*" permeate the entire medical literature market between the Song and Ming periods. The fact that important pediatric texts continued to use terms other than *yi'an* to name their case materials is an indication that the substance and narrative style of *yi'an* were widely popular before the appellation itself.

The picture had changed markedly, however, by the early Qing, when the concept and the term *yi'an* exercised overwhelming sway. By the eighteenth century the editors of the imperial library project *Complete Collection of the Four Treasuries* (*Siku quanshu*) identified Qian Yi's twenty-three records as the book's "medical cases."[13] In the late-Qing edition of *Proven Formulae* (1891), relied upon for production of modern reprints, at the end of prescription recipes or in between passages there are "comments" from its compiler, Zhou Xuehai. This shows that by the time of this later era of the nineteenth century, adding "commentary" on medical texts and calling them *an* was clearly in fashion.[14] The stages of bibliographic transformation that Qian's pediatric case record underwent show that the substance, narrative style, and generic name of medical cases were finally becoming one.

THE CONTEXT AND EFFECT OF A CASE STORY

In the four hundred or so years after Qian Yi, important developments were made in Chinese pediatrics in which case records played an indispensable role.[15] Documents from two Ming pediatricians of the sixteenth century serve as good examples: Wan Quan's (ca. 1495–1580) *Elaboration on Pediatric Medicine* (*Youke fahui*, 1549) and Xue Kai's (fl. 1488–1505) *Complete Text for the Protection of Infants* (*Baoying quanshu*, 1555). In contrast to those discussed in Qian Yi's *Proven Formulae*, the cases dealt with by Wan and Xue appear to be direct observations—that is, first-person narratives presented as if they came from an attending physician's personal journal. Moreover, by this time such individual cases were more likely to be grouped under classes of illness rather than assembled as overall proof of a doctor's personal achievements. As a result, the textual form and vocational implications of case histories changed. As printed texts were becoming more widespread, they in turn also fostered the reproduction and circulation of the medical corpus.

The four sections (*juan*) of Wan Quan's *Elaboration on Pediatric Medicine* contain 147 cases, arranged in 32 nosological classifications, each introduced by a general discussion (*lun*) to which one to twelve cases are appended. Read as a whole, these 32 discussions with attached cases represent the core of the text. Another 20 discussion topics did not have any cases appended to them.[16]

In terms of content and style, the cases in Wan's *Elaboration on Pediatric Medicine* are a mixed bag. About one-third of them (forty-nine cases) are terse "notes" on the health problems of an otherwise unidentified "child," summarized in no more than a dozen or so words. The following may serve as an example: "A child developed a rash on his face. His eyes appeared red and swollen. And he could not bear to be touched by hand. Dead on the third day" (9).

In contrast, a larger number of Wan's cases bear the complex and rich features of a story-like narrative, reminiscent of the classical accounts of Chunyu Yi in the Han or Song precedents from Qian Yi's *Proven Formulae.* Ninety-eight cases out of the 147 (or 67 percent of the total) include the following: information on the patient and family, prior history of the illness, description of the onset of symptoms, report of the doctor's physical examination using the four standard diagnostic procedures, and tentative judgments in the context of Wan's debates with other physicians and the patient's family. The reader learns the ingredients in the recommended prescriptions, the reasons for each, and their effects. Last, the final result is recorded, not without a display of compliments. For example, after successfully treating the daughter of a Huguang official named Sun, Wan claims to have been rewarded with ten taels of silver in addition to an inscribed plaque congratulating him as a "model scholar-doctor" (*guandai ruyi*) (77). The following is an example of this elaborate form.

> The Confucian instructor Mr. Tao from our district has an eight-month-old son suffering from vomiting. Many doctors came to treat him, with no result: medicinal decoctions and pills got thrown up as soon as they were swallowed. The various doctors said that vomiting right after swallowing is something caused by Fire, so they wanted to treat it as a problem related to Fire. Fire-draining medicines were administered, but with no effect. As the various practitioners failed to cure the problem, his vomiting worsened. I was then asked for my considered opinion. I said, [use] Internal Adjustment Soup [*lizhong tang*].
>
> The Master [the child's father] said that there was no way [for the child] to take this prescription. I said there was a different method of administering it. At the time, there was a lower-ranked student, Cai Yishang, present who had never had friendly relations with me. He stood beside us, laughing, and commented, "There is no need for so many words; just show us how your method might work." I responded, "You also need not waste so many words. Come tomorrow morning with your inquiry and you will see my ability. After all, this is not like imperial civil examination. Why the jealous fuss?"
>
> I then prepared the Internal Adjustment Soup according to the recipe, mixing in half a portion each of pig's gall bladder and urine from a young boy and roasting it until it was almost burnt; this I then boiled in water and it was taken. The symptoms stopped as soon as this medicine was received. The next morning, the student, Cai, came to ask about it. The Master said, "Indeed, it worked." He [Cai] then asked about the recipe and was told that it was the Internal Adjustment Soup. Mr. Cai then pressed [me] as to the specific approach. I told him, "[The method] was included under the recipe for "Baitong Soup [*baitong tang*] prepared with pig's gall bladder and human urine" as discussed in the *Discourse on Cold Damage Disorders*. You, sir, can go back and read it. I am sure you will understand the reasoning."
>
> The Master then asked me, "I had heard that Mr. Cai is often jealous of you, now I can believe it. Please enlighten me as to the method." I said, "Vomiting is basically a problem caused by a chill, which ought to be stopped with hot medicine such as the Internal Adjustment Soup. Yet as the chill inside worsens, there develops a rejection of yang elements. Thus, as hot medicine enters the throat, it is rejected by the coldness and finds no point of entry. Now, gall bladder is of a bitter-cold nature and a boy's urine of a salty-bitter character, so these two cold elements can join with the body's chill as they enter the [patient's] throat. There-

> fore [the medication] will not be regurgitated. In that short time, meanwhile, the yin element diminishes gradually, as the body's yang element is allowed to rise. This hot medicine should therefore be taken while chilled, to treat the kind of cold problems that reject [medication], so as to stop the throwing up. The Lizong emperor (1224–1264) of the Song dynasty once developed a vomiting that could not be stopped. Dr. Yang Jilao was summoned to treat it. He made an inquiry as to what medicine had been used, and was told that spicy hot medicine had been employed. The emperor said, "This was taken to no avail." Dr. Yang then respectfully reported, "Hot medicines should be taken at cold temperatures." Such medicine was then prepared and sunk down a well to chill for a long time before it was taken. One sip of this and the vomiting stopped. This was the same method [that I used here].
>
> Listening to this, the Master was pleased. After which [initial treatment], the Six Gentlemen Soup was prepared into balls to help facilitate [the recovery] (66–67).

As seen in this instance, long, discursive cases tend to include details of the physician's social involvement with the rich and powerful, as either an advertisement for his skill or a celebration of his status. This is not to say that all of Wan's cases were chosen for self-aggrandizement. Seven out of the eight cases that Wan treated for "abdominal pain" (*futong*) ended in death—a failure rate far exceeding that allowed in the imperial licensing examination for medical students, which required a 70-percent success rate (60–62). By now famous and confident, Wan decided to let the record stand.

With Wan's pediatric case records, we come close to having a practitioner's case-by-case observation, presumably noted by his own hand. Though not intended to suggest that such activity was taking place on the spot, the assumption of a direct authorship must have added to the impression of authenticity and authority of the knowledge conveyed. Moreover, as Wan's medical cases were grouped according to disease types and nosological categories, this, too, could be taken as a sign of further specialization. The inclusion of cases both of the long, discursive type on the one hand and short, laconic summaries on the other might be understood as proof of versatility. As time passed, we can see established authorities opted either for the short and simplified style as a form of further standardization or the long and elaborate kind as a style for deliberation. Wan Quan's records provide the profession and lay readers with an early sample of both as viable choices.

Most important, by keeping and printing his work, Wan spoke of his conviction that for specialist disciplines like pediatrics concrete evidence of experience persuaded like nothing else. Cases supplied a counter-voice against textbook authority. Vying with combative colleagues in treating a child having "seizures and choking on phlegm," Wan questioned even the revered name of Qian Yi, noting, "To follow the text literally can be worse than having no guidance at all" (*jinxinshu ze buru wushu*). To him, blind admiration for Qian rested on "nothing but flattering words from self-appointed disciples." Both these seemingly angry remarks, as well as Wan's mention of the Song precedent in the second case cited above, indicate that Wan was a practitioner who paid close attention to earlier cases and that cases from both general medical records and pediatric sources were at his disposal.[17] In fact, in a market where a doctor's ideas were but one quibbling voice amidst many, documented case reasoning was what Wan relied on to win in the end against either commonsensical street talk or noisy, confusing vocational debates. Thus his medical records often began by citing canonical works like *Yellow Emperor's Inner Canon* (*Huangdi neijing*) or Zhang Ji's *Discourse on Cold Damage Disorders* (*Shanghan lun*), followed by reverent mention of works from more recent Jin-Yuan masters like Zhu Zhenheng or Li Gao, before he would advance his own judgment. As he did so, moreover, he was portrayed as being constantly surrounded by challenging colleagues, opinionated families, and a thriving pediatric market filled with people who, he says, "would not trust my words" (*buxin yuyan*) (22). It was not uncommon for him to be surrounded, jeered at, and even overruled by his fellow practitioners. Furthermore, the families of Wan's more elite patients rarely had unequivocal trust in his reputation or skills. Indeed, amid the welter of comment and criticism, at times Wan's own father and the master to whom he had been apprenticed might also attend and freely offer their own ideas. Then, finally, there stood the pediatrician, Wan Quan, remembering the classics learned, the knowledge absorbed from past masters, and the pediatrics he had inherited as he attempted to make an intelligent decision.

He also had quite a bagful of therapeutic devices to choose from. Dozens of decoctions, pills, powders, and balls could be assembled according to a basic formula to be adjusted according to individual conditions. He also practiced massage, acupuncture, and moxibustion. Wan believed that medical writing and medical practice both demanded sound judgment, including precision in choosing therapies and exactitude in describing them. If expressions are inexact, they are only words. If a text is too complex or impenetrable, it is better to have no guidance at all. For this physician, writing up his cases was an important way to document, instruct, learn, establish a reputation, invite rewards, and, if necessary, fend off his opponents.[18]

THE POWER OF THE STANDARD

By contrast, the 1,528 case histories included in Xue Kai's *Complete Text for the Protection of Infants* give a different picture.[19] This pediatric text in 20 sections (*juan*) is organized into 220 classified childhood health problems. About 90 percent (197) have individual cases attached to them. In section fifteen on "miscellaneous complaints," 127 cases are listed regarding 14 different problems, including "continuous pain" (*zuotong buzhi*), "continuous vomiting" (*zuo'ou buzhi*), "difficulty urinating" (*xiaobian butong*), "taking of cleansing medication" (*fu baiduyao*), and the "application of cold and cooling medicine" (*fu hanliangyao*). On the other hand, section one, on pediatric theories and newborn care, contains the fewest cases (a mere 13). Other sections average a few dozen for each area of pediatric concern. The section on "symptoms related to the eye" (*munei zheng*) offers the largest number of cases—37—for a single classification.[20]

With rare exceptions (such as cases involving Xue's own children), almost all of Xue's pediatric cases are reported in the simple "generic" style, laconically identifying the patient as "a small child" (*yi xiao'er*) without further social detail. He summarizes the patient's symptoms, states the diagnosis in one or two phrases, and reports the treatments prescribed. Most, but not all, offer one or two words on the outcome, such as "well" (*an*), "since recovered" (*eryu*), or "failed to live" (*buqi*). Here is a typical example.

> A child. Fever, vomiting, diarrhea. Swollen belly. Refuses to feed. [Pulse] feels like falling beads. This is [due to] damage to the Spleen and Stomach system. Administer Fragrant Cinnabar Digestion Aid Paste [*xiangsha zhuwei gao*] first; then give Six Gentlemen Soup [*liujunzi tang*]. Completely recovered.[21]

As a whole, Xue's massive collection of pediatric cases represents a departure, and not just in terms of style. For one thing, he offers an unprecedented quantity of data from a single medical source. He emphasizes generic prescription formulas, in many instances placing instructions for favored prescription formulae at the end of the relevant section, not attached to individual cases as was done before. All of this suggests that by the sixteenth century clinical case reporting among experienced and respected physicians could be standardized as case reporting became an increasingly normal part of medical deliberations and as the circulation of cases called attention to aggregate patterns, not just individual instances. They could yield a "big picture" regarding changing vocational trends, disease patterns, and general health conditions. A further example of one of Xue's slightly longer case records will make clear the effect of this systematic documentation.

> A child, with chills and fever. Nausea. Unable to eat or drink. Cries as his belly is pressed. Pulse feels like a long string of beads. This is due to stagnation of food and drink [in the stomach]. Used Great Pacification Balls [*da'an wan*] [to induce] vomiting and diarrhea. Old accumulated stagnation resolved, and [the child] rests better. But the lip and eyes jerk; there are loose yellow stools. This is because the

> problem [of stagnation] has left, yet the fever encroaches in the vacancy. Administered Six Gentlemen Soup complemented with Uncaria Stem with Hooks [*diaotenggou*]. Recovered.[22]

Examined as a whole, Xue's pediatric case collection has the potential to give a modern researcher an idea of changing patterns in historical childhood diseases, including regional differences. At a microscopic level, these details also reveal the evolution of medical discourse because an actual case coming from a practicing specialist's direct observation conveys a new thought in progress. As a literary creation it continued to carry a field character like any case narrative would, thus interacting with the profession in a particularly direct fashion.

In their attention to both literary narrative and standardized therapies, Xue's pediatric cases were moving away from storytelling to a newly appreciated technical style. By sacrificing dramatic detail, anecdotes, or reports of conversation, this brief, detached, impersonal account would establish a model on its own. "Specialization" or "professionalization" may not be the appropriate term for such sixteenth-century developments, but this was expert knowledge that coincided with flourishing economic prosperity and a growing print culture that brought doctors, like others, into the commercial marketplace. These technical narratives did not replace the more elaborate or colorful case stories once and for all. But Xue's rank in the Imperial Academy of Medicine (Taiyiyuan) lent authority and prestige to his approach to case compilation. Large-scale aggregations of terse case narratives, with attention to classification, became increasingly popular.[23]

Nonetheless, as a father-son pair who enjoyed the prestige of professorial titles in pediatrics at the Imperial Academy of Medicine, Xue Kai and Xue Ji had stronger ties to the medical literary tradition than did a private physician like Wan Quan. In the preface to the officially sponsored edition of *Complete Text for the Protection of Infants,* for instance, its author, Wang Qi, put the publication of this work in a Confucian tradition of imperial beneficence and alluded directly to Chunyu Yi as a classical model. The Xues were assumed to share in a common elite culture based on classical education, which included the writings of Sima Qian.[24] Even in his streamlined case records, Xue often included classical quotations and showed vocational reverence for recent masters like Qian Yi. While aware of contemporary medical debates, Xue's case records projected the prestige of an elite physician who did not need to contend with the claims of rival practitioners.

So this case documentation of "effective treatments"[25] was there to serve a somewhat different purpose. It enhanced the authority and influence of its author by developing a "pattern." With its elegantly sparse technical language and terse individual documentation, therefore, the goal was more to lay a claim through the medium of public records than to negotiate one's way out of a heated debate. The circulation of case records guaranteed access so that people could follow or judge them according to their own reasoning. After the sixteenth century, experienced physicians could hardly practice without access to the case records of others. Medical cases became increasingly indispensable for vocational training and successful competition in medicine, and the composition and publication of the medical case genre developed a momentum of its own.[26]

CONCLUSION

The birth and development of pediatrics between the Song and the Ming dynasties took place in an era when Chinese medicine was wedded to the Confucian literary tradition. Furthermore, the unfolding of this medical subdiscipline took place as similar processes of branching out, diversification, or specialization were also happening in Chan Buddhism in the Chinese Buddhist tradition and in neo-Confucianism rooted in and evolving from classical Confucianism. Medical authors' and literary doctors' knowledge of earlier case records embedded in biographical or hagiographical literature may have spurred the production of evidence-related documentation. While the twenty-five "consultation records" preserved in Sima Qian's *Records of the Grand Historian* provided people with a particular narrative model to emulate, the twenty-three individual instances of treatment produced in testimony to Qian Yi's career represent a further use of this vehicle in which a particular Chinese style of prose composition for technical knowledge matured, weaving storytelling together with account keeping, case by case, to establish evidentiary substance.[27]

During the sixteenth century, physicians and medical authors of various persuasions experimented with different forms of this compositional style, terse or elaborate, as they circulated their textual products. Clearly, the sociocultural implications and vocational function of case studies depended as much on their content as upon their style of representation. To authenticate, deliberate, prove, debate, or produce pediatric knowledge, a case-by-case representation was not only useful but becoming imperative. In writing up the cases, medical authors like Wan or Xue folded their analytical opinions within the individual observation records so that it might be easier to work out thorny problems in their profession. From the reader's perspective, this new instrument allowed any bystander an opportunity to judge the relative merit of the respective physician-authors as preserved in the case records, one by one or as a whole.

By the eighteenth century, when Yu Zhen (1723–1795) published *Commentary on Medical Cases Old and New* (*Gujin yi'an an*, 1778), and the mid-nineteenth century, when this collection was redacted and embellished by Wang Shixiong as

Selections from "Commentary on Medical Cases Old and New" (*"Gujin yi'an an" xuan*, 1853), the compilation and application of case-related records in medicine had reached yet another stage. Here, we see commentators who took earlier collections of medical cases, in particular Jiang Guan's (1503–1565) *Classified Cases from Famous Doctors* (*Mingyi lei'an*) and its sequel, Wei Zhixiu's (1722–1772) *More Classified Cases from Famous Doctors* (*Xu mingyi lei'an*), as basic source materials while adding their own comments. This they did one after another, which resulted in a new work composed of a string of commentaries on medical case collections (and called so, as *yi'an*). In the *Selections* compiled by Wang Shixiong, several authors each added a different layer to the "nesting" effect of the case method. Jiang Guan and Wei Zhixu had gathered the original cases; Yu Zhen introduced commentaries; and Wang Shixiong selected from Yu Zhen's work and added further commentary.[28] In this 1853 collection the original cases often did not appear as part of the text. Rather, the commentators made it clear that since they were available in the originals compiled by Jiang and Wei, readers need only compare their analyses side by side with the primary case collection. In laying down the editorial views on those well-known case records, the commentators were thus working to agree or disagree with the physicians' judgment (as shown by the cases). Depending on particular instances, these two commentators from a still later era demonstrated their shared or widely divergent views on the collected case anthologies in different stages. Obviously, they operated in an environment where the reading, selection, and circulation of medical case records were an increasingly accepted form of exchange and deliberation. Moreover, this broadened interest in the case method in medicine also suggested that case narratives, by themselves, were not sufficient to exemplify or secure the real meaning or import of the outcome of those cases. Indeed, deliberations in a medical, as in a legal, setting depended as much upon context as they did upon styles of reasoning. In practice, both professional and educated lay consumers expected subsequent rounds of compiling, editing, and commenting to elucidate while confirming and enhancing the effect expected of a case. In other words, in its late imperial Chinese context, a case could best be set to work as a form of particularized commentary; and specialist commentaries worked at their best when shown together with specific cases of effective experiences documented in detail. The techniques they used were by no means unique to the medical field. Authors in Confucian classics, law, and Chan Buddhism, as well as writers from other semi-technical fields such as drama and fortune telling, had all employed similar skills to work with commentaries on exemplary cases.[29] The intellectual trend in philological studies during the Qing period (especially from the seventeenth to the nineteenth centuries) added particular force to this method of knowledge production. No doubt the active print industry and the widening reading public also helped to create a readership and consumer market for such an elaborate "chain effect" of accumulating case collections and their sibling commentaries. With the compilation and publication of collections of *an* (commentary) on *an* (cases), case-based reasoning in Chinese medicine reached a maturity at the very moment when these homophonic characters representing the old cultural milieu hit the late imperial readership.

Called the science of the individual, therefore, the case method has been used to demonstrate how any specific instance may operate according to or against the general rule. And for that matter, only effective experience may serve as a useful reference, precisely because "nothing goes by itself."[30] The long tradition that Chinese pediatrics established in working with and evolving alongside this case approach illustrates for us the true importance of the notion that "it all depends."[31] Reexamining the intellectual genealogy of this history, we are reminded of how it is also referred to as a "science of clues,"[32] as both its narratology and styles of reasoning were closely embedded in the cultural specificities of late imperial China.

NOTES

1 Forrester, "If *p*, then what? Thinking in Cases," 1–25.

2 For more on the relationship between narrative styles and the logic of scientific discovery, see Eco and Sebeok, eds., *The Sign of Three*, chaps. 1, 4, 7, 10.

3 Sima Qian, *Shiji*, 105:2794–2817. Prescription formulas include *xiaqi tang*, *rou tang*, and *huoqi tang*.

4 Ibid., 105:2798–2799.

5 *Canggong zhenji*, also known as *Qi Taicanggong mai'an*, began to be circulated as an individual work at least before the Yuan dynasty. See Xue Qinglu, ed., *Quanguo Zhongyi tushu lianhe mulu*, 627.

6 Qian Yi, *Xiao'er yaozheng zhijue*, 40.

7 Ibid.

8 These are gathered in the concluding *juan* of *Xiao'er yaozheng zhijue*, 45–80.

9 "Ji changsuo zhibing ershisan zheng," in ibid., 35–44.

10 See, e.g., case 2 and case 3 of the twenty-three instances. Ibid., 35–36.

11 Han Mao, *Hanshi yitong*, in *Zhongguo yixue dacheng*, 4:390–391. Also see Shi Zhongxu, *Zhongguo yixue shi*, 129.

12 In total, three death cases are recorded. See Qian Yi, *Xiao'er yaozheng zhijue*, 36–37, 39, 43.

13 See Yong Rong et al., ed., *Siku quanshu zongmu*.

14 These comments can be found in the 1982 reprint edition. See Qian Yi, *Xiao'er yaozheng zhijue*, 81–86.

15 For a historical overview of the emergence and development of pediatric medicine in the last thousand years of imperial Chinese history, see Hsiung Ping-chen, *Youyou*, 5–23, and *A Tender Voyage*, chap. 1.

16 Wan did not explain why no cases were attached to these twenty nosological classifications. A reader could surmise something from their descriptions. Some appear to be quaint or outdated categories, such as "sky-looking-approximating fits" (*tiandiao sixian*) or "white tiger symptoms-approximating fits" (*baihuzheng sixian*). Some appear to be variants of more substantive classifications. Under the broad rubric of Kidney-related deliberations, specific cases were placed under the topic of "Kidney disorders" (*shen suo shengbing*), rather than under the rubric of "disorders arising from the Kidney organ system" (*shenzang zhubing*) or "complications of syndromes arising from the Kidney organ system" (*shenzang jianzheng*). Disorders of Heart, Liver, Lung and Spleen organ systems were handled in the same way. Still, certain lacunae remain difficult to explain away. For example, Wan had much to say about ailments of the gallbladder (*dan*), yet left no illustrative cases whatsoever for that category of disorder. See *Youke fahui*, 16–17, 38–41, 52–58, 88, 94–100, 103–105. Hereafter, page references to this book will be given in parentheses.

17 In fact, Wan Quan inherited many of his pediatric theories from Qian Yi, including the model of infant growth called "changing and steaming" (*bianzheng*), and techniques of monitoring health problems from "facial symptoms" (*mianshang zheng*). He often referred to the cases and prescriptions of Qian Yi to lend force to his own opinions (ibid., 22–23, 86, 104–106).

18 See Wan's preface to his pediatric writings in *Youke fahui*, 3.

19 Xue Kai and Xue Ji. (ca. 1488–1558) were active during the Zhengde (1505–1521) and Jiajing (1521–1566) reigns of the Ming dynasty. Xue Ji was elected imperial professor of medicine and then administrative assistant of Nanjing (*Nanjing yuanpan*) during Zhengde's reign and later became medical commissioner under Jiajing's rule. As a result, his father, Xue Kai, was later given the honorary title of Commissioner of the Imperial Academy of Medicine (Taiyiyuanshi). The reputation of this father-son pair in medicine was enhanced greatly with the publication of *Xueshi yi'an shiliu zhong* (1529), *Baoying cuoyao* (1556), and *Baoying quanshu* (1555). See also Hsiung Pingchen, *Youyou*, 15–16.

20 The twenty-three nosological categories lacking any case record include theoretical subjects, such as the general discourse on "syndromes arising from the Heart system" (*xinzang zheng*), and discussions of the daily care of newborns and very young infants. There are very few cases attached to bookish syndromes like "lacquer boils" (*qichuang*). There are only two cases for "fetal fright" (*taijing*) and "late teething" (*chichi*), problems with which he presumably had only limited experience. Though there is no evidence of statistical thinking, the sheer volume of records is impressive. See Xue Kai, *Baoying quanshu*, 1.1–1.3, 8–23, 49–78; 2.168–2.171; 3.297–3.303; 4.365–4.411, 432–437; 5.448–5.450; 11.1116–11.1119; 15.1567–15.1593, 1646–1656, 1672–1691.

21 Ibid., 1.40.

22 Ibid., 1.40–1.41.

23 Here it is possible that in the operation of traditional Chinese medicine, general principles as represented by past classics and old authorities could have functioned as "incomplete theorized agreement." For a contemporary legal scholar's argument for the

value of incomplete theorization, see Sunstein, *Legal Reasoning and Political Conflict,* chaps. 1–2.

24 See Wang Ji's preface to *Baoying quanshu,* 1.1–1.11. See also Hsiung Pingchen, *Youyou,* 16–17.

25 See Xue Kai, *Baoying quanshu,* 1.40.

26 For further discussion, see Hsiung Pingchen, "Anju quezao," 201–252.

27 Before the mid-Ming dynasty, when medical case records appeared in the print market, there existed a few earlier precedents such as Luo Tianyi's *Luo Qianfu zhiyan an* (1281) and Zhu Zhenheng's *Guai'e dan* (1281). However, it was not until the late Ming that the term *yi'an* was married to the substance of medical case records and became widely used. See Hsiung Pingchen, "Anju quezao," 224–225.

28 Wang Shixiong and Yu Zhen, *Gujin yi'an an xuan.* See also Hsiung Pingchen, "Anju quezao," 229–230.

29 Further discussion is found in other chapters in this volume and in the companion volume edited by Hsiung Pingchen, *Rang zhengju shuohua: Zhongguo pian.*

30 Forrester, "If *p*, then what? Thinking in Cases," 9.

31 Ibid., quoting Lucas.

32 Ibid., 13, quoting Ginzburg.

6

The Literary Fashioning of Medical Authority

A Study of Sun Yikui's Case Histories

JUDITH T. ZEITLIN

This chapter examines the published casebook of a famous late-Ming physician, Sun Yikui (ca. 1522–1619), from the perspective of literary history. It has become commonplace in what we may call cultural studies of the European and American medical case to emphasize the narrative nature of this genre as part of a broader argument about the narrative structure of medical knowledge.[1] My study of Sun Yikui takes this insight as a basic point of departure but, in addition to exploring the narrative aspects of individual cases, analyzes the range of literary strategies and assumptions about the case's contribution to knowledge in the casebook as a whole. It is important to see the late-Ming medical casebook as a process of writing that was practiced, circulated, published, and read in a certain social and intellectual context as part of a well-developed print culture. Above all, because a late imperial doctor's status depended on class and culture rather than guild, professional, or imperial certification, the casebook was designed to appropriate for the literatus-physician the prestige and power of authorship in a society that prized the written word so highly.

Jiangnan, the prosperous region south of the Yangtze River where Sun Yikui established his practice, was a seat of both medical learning and the publishing industry during the sixteenth century. Sun himself is an excellent example of the physician as author, whose works, each covering a different genre of medical writing, were published during his lifetime. His casebook, published around 1599, was the last of his books to appear in print.[2] His discussion of selected issues in medical theory, *A Further Installment on the Purport of Medicine* (*Yizhi xuyu*) was published around 1590, followed by his medical encyclopedia *Pearls of Wisdom Retrieved from the Crimson Sea* (*Chishui xuan zhu*) around 1596.[3] The three books were written concurrently over the course of many years and were eventually published in Sun Yikui's old age as the capstone to a long and successful career as a clinical doctor.

Although Jiangnan was a major publishing center and medical works were recognized as a lucrative branch of the book trade, Sun Yikui's works were not, at least initially, published for profit.[4] Despite his reputation in the medical field, he could not find a publisher who was willing to finance the projects.[5] Eventually, the publication costs were underwritten through contributions and endorsements from his well-to-do and highly placed patients.[6] Both *The Crimson Sea* and the casebook are clearly identifiable as high-end private printing efforts rather than commercial ventures. The prestigious nature of this publishing mode in turn reinforced Sun's own authority and self-presentation as a learned doctor.

The increased publication of books on medicine in sixteenth-century Jiangnan is evident in the 178 titles listed in the bibliography of medical works Sun appended to *The Crimson Sea.* The itinerant habits of doctors such as Sun, who were required to travel frequently through the territories in which they maintained a practice, would also have facilitated getting hold of books and may have even helped disseminate them.[7] As printing made advances in medical knowledge formerly confined to the disciples of individual physicians or hereditary medical families available to a wider reading public of both specialists and laymen, doctors would have been expected to keep up-to-date. In *The Crimson Sea,* Sun takes his fellow physicians to task for sticking to outmoded and misguided medical theories, even after they have been persuasively refuted in print.

> *The Medical Casebook of Wang Ji* [*Shishan yi'an*] was published more than sixty years ago. The book's rebuttal of Wang Ruyan's injunction against the use of [yang-replenishing] ginseng and astralagus root is absolutely correct, yet doctors of our age still remain glued to the prejudice that one must "nourish yin and make Fire descend" and blithely forsake the use of ginseng and astralagus root.... Even when their stubbornness ... leads to the patient's death, they have no regrets. I myself have personally seen dozens or even a hundred such deaths with my own eyes!... Since Wang Ji's book has already been published, why are people still following the old practice? I expect it may be that contemporary doctors have not yet seen his book.[8]

To rectify this situation, Sun recopied the full text of Wang Ji's essay promoting ginseng and astralagus root in *The Crimson Sea* to make it available to a new generation of readers.

In fact, as the first important published collection of medical cases in China, Wang Ji's (1463–1539) casebook (published around 1531) is the *only* work of this genre to appear in Sun's bibliography. Sun's advocacy of Wang Ji's views is not surprising since he could claim membership in this renowned physician's lineage by having studied medicine for a time with one of Wang's disciples.[9] In addition, Sun, like Wang, was a native of Huizhou Prefecture in Anhui Province, where he also established a practice, and both men can be seen as products of Huizhou's distinctive medical culture and thriving publishing industry.[10] Still, the authority Sun appeals to in the above passage is Wang Ji as published expert rather than Wang Ji as personal teacher once removed. As revealed here, Sun's connection to Wang was mainly one of readership, established through the public medium of the printed word rather than through the private and primarily oral medium of discipleship and lineage.

The text of Sun's own casebook was jointly edited by two of his sons and two of his disciples. The book went through several editions during the Ming alone and was reprinted and excerpted throughout the next centuries, attesting to its popularity and importance in the medical literature. The casebook includes five chapters and covers 397 cases, a rather large number, it appears, judging from Joanna Grant's study of Wang Ji's casebook and Charlotte Furth's study of a comparable later casebook (published 1644).[11] Even so, these 397 cases by no means represent the total output of Sun's written cases. According to the notice of editorial principles (*fanli*), the published volume contains only about 20–30 percent of the original hefty manuscript. Some cases were involuntarily excised (part of the original manuscript was damaged); others were excluded on editorial policy: only cases resulting in a determinable method of cure were selected, while cases covering similar illnesses and treatments were omitted to avoid redundancy. The bulk of the cases included are success stories in which the patient makes a full recovery, but in a few cases the patient does die, either to bear out the astuteness of the physician's diagnosis of a fatal illness or as a result of a rival physician's blunder. As one of the earliest compilations of cases from a single physician's practice, Sun Yikui's work is particularly interesting from a literary point of view because he wrote when the case history genre was at a plastic stage and could still be composed with narrative flair and develop a personal voice.

DEFINING THE CASE

Like all genres of traditional Chinese medical writings, the case history was recorded in the classical language rather than the vernacular. In this, the medical literature is unexceptional, because with the exception of some fiction, drama, songs, teachings, sermons, and criminal confessions, all prose, even if it attempted to depict the reality of lived experience, was written in some form of classical Chinese up until the twentieth century. In terms of literary style, the case can be loosely classified as a type of reportage literature, belonging to the branch of "unofficial history" (*yeshi*). These are brief, anecdotal accounts of events, purportedly witnessed or heard about by the author, which are written in simple prose, mainly unadorned by literary figures such as allusion and metaphor. The narrative moves at a fast clip; dialogue is often included, and evaluative or interpretative comments are occasionally tacked on at the end. As short pieces, the expectation is that they will circulate in sets or collections, rather than singularly.

One of the most common and earliest genres of reportage writing is *zhiguai*, or "accounts of the strange." Medical anomalies and bizarre diseases were a staple of this literature, and some stories even included recipes for medical prescriptions. Early accounts of the strange were in turn featured as proof texts for anomalies in Ming medical reference books such as Li Shizhen's *Classified Materia Medica* (*Bencao gangmu*, late sixteenth century).[12] A number of cases in Jiang Guan's (1503–1565) influential *Classified Cases from Famous Doctors* (*Mingyi lei'an*, published 1591), particularly those that treat possession and other such syndromes, read like accounts of the strange, especially because in such anthologies of cases, the physician's first person is routinely changed to the third person and because the unusual was one of Jiang Guan's criteria for selection.[13] The similarities arise in part because the sources Jiang drew upon to compile his cases included not only specialist medical writings, but also actual *zhiguai* collections such as Hong Mai's (1123–1202) *Records of the Listener* (*Yijian zhi*).[14]

From a narratological view, what distinguishes the medical case history from an account of the strange is not primarily the concentration on one field of knowledge, the employment of technical language, or the repetition of a couple of basic plot types, but the fact that the author is presented as the main actor in the story. In other words, the author of the typical account of the strange is usually a heterodiegetic narrator—that is, he tells a story that happens to someone else, whereas the author of a typical medical case is a homodiegetic narrator, or someone who tells a story in which he is the chief protagonist. In that the medical case aims to contribute to a clearly defined domain of specialist knowledge, the physician-author's authority as an expert in the field reinforces both his role as chief protagonist in the story he tells and the factuality of his narrative. In accounts of the strange, the credibility of the events recounted is always at issue; to compensate, a narrative often attempts to provide internal proof attesting that the anomaly has indeed occurred; in certain stories, a lawsuit may even be brought, requiring the intervention of a court magistrate to investigate and verify the matter. By contrast, what is at stake in a physician's casebook is not normally the credibility of a particular case as fact, but whether the physician has followed the appropriate course of action in a specific situation; the case is offered as written evidence to prove that he has.

Sun Yikui prefaces his casebook with a definition of the medical case: "When a diagnosis and treatment have produced results and the recipe for a prescription is set, one then writes them down in a notebook so that they will be available for everyone to consult. It's like an experienced official having decided a lawsuit: once the written verdict is settled, it cannot be changed."[15] On a superficial level, the analogy enhances Sun's authority by equating what the physician does with the bureaucratic workings of the courtroom, just as likening medical records to legal documents does. On a deeper level, however, the analogy underscores the historical affinity between the medical and the legal case discussed at length in Charlotte Furth's essay in this volume (chap. 4). As she notes, the "consultation records" are included in Sima Qian's biography of Chunyu Yi as part of this early famous physician's attempt to acquit himself during an imperial interrogation into his medical practices.[16] Sun's preface indicates a similar defensive motive to set the record straight when he writes that his lifetime practice of noting down the symptoms, pulse diagnosis, and method of cure for each patient was partly intended to demonstrate to the world that "in attending the sick, I was not careless, and in prescribing drugs, I was not reckless."[17]

But *an* is not the only word we need to consider in sorting out the deeper parallels between the legal and medical case in China. As a noun, a case also becomes the object of certain verbs, whose implications are equally important for grasping the semantics of the case in a given language and culture. Summarizing André Jolles's ideas about the morphology of the case form, James Chandler writes, "The case has been repeatedly associated in many Indo-European languages with the metaphorics of scales and measures. In English we say that cases are "pondered" and "weighed"—that they "pend" or are "suspended," that they hang in the "balance." Chandler then cites Jolles directly: "The peculiarity of the case form lies precisely in that it poses a question without being able to give an answer, that it imposes on us the obligation to decide without containing the decision in itself—it is the place where a weighing of things is carried out, but not the result of that weighing."[18]

If we look at the verbs applied to the case in literary Chinese, we find the most common are *duan* (to decide), *pan* (to judge), and *ding* (to determine). *Duan*, the verb both Sun Yikui and Cheng Zeng employ in their prefaces and which is probably the broadest in covering any sort of case, is marked by the axe radical *jin*, while *pan*, which tends to be restricted to a purely judicial context, exhibits the knife radical *dao*. The metaphorics here relate to cutting off, cutting in two (in the sense of making a distinction and drawing a boundary), or fixing (in the sense of making a final determination). The semantics of the Chinese case that emerge here is one in which the deliberation entailed is expected to have a clear result, a verdict. It may be that to drive home his argument about the contradictory form of the case, Jolles emphasizes only the verbs of weighing and balancing and not other Indo-European verbs also commonly used with the case that stress outcome rather than process, such as decide, determine, and resolve. The Latin verb *dēcidēre*, from which the French *décider* and English *decide* come, is, in fact, derived from *caedere* (to cut) and means both "to cut off" and "to decide" in a fashion strikingly similar to the Chinese terms *duan* and *pan*. Still, an emphasis on result does not negate the importance of Jolles' argument for the form of the Chinese case—that it is, in Chandler's deft phrasing, "by virtue of judgment that [the case] offers formal mediation between the particular and the general, between instance and rule, between circumstance and principle."[19] It is rather that in the Chinese conception, only a clear judgment enabled a case to perform the work of mediation.

It is evident from Sun Yikui's preface that he understood a doctor's encounter with a patient to be a case only when it resulted in a clear outcome, one that followed a discernible trajectory of diagnosis-treatment-prescription. Sun's sons and disciples further reinforced this definition because, as they indicate in their notice of editorial principles, they selected from the manuscript only syndromes that exhibited a "fixed pattern" of cure (*dingshi*) to print as "leading cases" (*cheng'an*).[20] The assumption here is that only cases in which the mystery of the patient's illness has been solved by being diagnosed and cured could serve as precedents or reference points for the future.

From a narrative point of view, the analogy Sun draws between the medical case (*yi'an*) and the crime case (*gong'an*) is also significant since detective fiction and drama were an important literary subgenre in China, well developed by the thirteenth century and flourishing in the late Ming. Indeed, the medical case and crime case fiction of sixteenth-century China do share some obvious structural elements. I will pick out only a few of them here.

In her study of the case history as it is practiced in contemporary American medical education, Kathryn Hunter points out that the European and American medical case "developed [in the 19th century] along with that most modern of Western literary forms, the detective story."[21] Hunter draws parallels between the methods of observation and deduction employed by Sherlock Holmes in his detective work and those employed by doctors in their clinical reasoning.[22] The analogy may work even better for traditional Chinese detective fiction, however, because the official in charge of the case is detective, arresting officer, and judge all in one. In other words, the detective has full legal authority over the case he is investigating and, like a doctor, is not only supposed to diagnose the disorder and solve the mystery, but also remedy it once and for all. There are other structural similarities as well. A common convention of the crime case story or play, including some of those involving the famous Judge Bao, is for the detective-judge to enter onto the case only after several previous officials have already botched up the case and accused the wrong person, who is now imprisoned on death row. The judge's work consists largely of undoing the harm his predecessors have done before he can solve the crime and put the situation to rights. This convention may also have provided the structure for the medical case, especially those authored by a single physician. The doctor narrating a late-Ming medical case usually comes on the case only after several other doctors have already misdiagnosed the illness and compounded the patient's suffering by prescribing the wrong drugs. As in plots involving Judge Bao, the doctor-narrator-hero's correct diagnosis and successful cure thus shine forth all the more brightly against the background of the case's mismanagement by inept or crooked predecessors.

The catalogue of the eighteenth-century imperial library project, *Complete Collection of the Four Treasuries* (*Siku quanshu*), complains that although Sun Yikui was learned in medical theory, which he expounded upon in other works, his case histories sufferred from an excess of trivial detail and a disproportion of tangents to main text, partly because the chief aim of this work was to promote Sun's reputation as a successful clinical doctor.[23] Such criticisms are still repeated in modern reference works on Chinese medicine, though the latest edition of Sun's complete works does praise the case histories for their vividness and completeness.[24]

The imperial library's critique probably reveals more about the editors' neoclassical preference for economy in style and the greater rigidity of eighteenth-century case history conventions than it does about Sun Yikui's shortcomings. Nonetheless, the casebook's notice of editorial principles does show concern that readers might object to some of Sun's language in the cases. It defends the use of dialect, slang, and immodest praise of the doctor in these case histories on the grounds that this is how a patient's household actually talks in a crisis situation. Sun's own brief introduction to his casebook criticizes the case histories of previous doctors as being too laconic, taking them to task for omitting prescriptions and other crucial information. Sun doesn't mention any names, but as his main precedent, Wang Ji's casebook must have been among those he was critiquing. Wang Ji's casebook lacks the kind of details—both specifics such as personal names and vivid narrative touches—that are so striking in Sun's casebook.

The "problematic" aspects of Sun Yikui's case histories—the gossipy, lively detail and the internal preoccupation with the reception of the physician and his work, both of which appear extraneous to a strictly technical presentation of a treatment—provide the twin points of departure for my own study. The first part of the chapter provides an overview of this casebook's general orientation, mood, and working method. This provides a base and context for the analysis in the second half, which looks closely at three remarkable, richly textured cases, each of which raises literary issues of narrative technique in medical writing as well as social issues relating to gender and the clinical encounter.

My study deals mainly with the 154 cases included in the first two chapters covering the Sanwu region (Suzhou and Changzhou in Jiangsu Province, Huzhou in Zhejiang Province). Generally speaking, the cases that were the most dramatic and successful as stories were to be found in this section, and the first chapter in particular, when Sun must have been in the early process of establishing his career, sheds the most light on the social and literary function of the doctor's case history. On the whole, the cases in the last three chapters cover his practices in Xindu (Xin'an [Huizhou] in Anhui Province) and Yixing in Jiangsu Province and seem more routinized and perfunctory. Sun no longer incorporates much specific information about the writing or circulation of his case histories or details his patients' high opinion of him.

THE PREOCCUPATION WITH RECEPTION: SELF-PROMOTION AS SELF-FASHIONING

Sun Yikui was a perfect specimen of the literatus doctor type who relied primarily on the methods of pulse diagnosis and individually tailored prescriptions and who prided himself on his book learning and his social connections with the local elite. His case histories reflect this concern with status and place for they are grouped by the locality of his practice, rather than classified by symptom or organized in a strict chronology, as they are in many other casebooks. (According to the notice of editorial principles, within each locality the cases are said to be arranged in chronological order, but it is apparent from even a superficial reading that thematic considerations often played a part in determining the arrangement of cases too). With the typical literati disdain for narrow specialists and approval for broad knowledge in a field, Sun's cases range across a wide spectrum of patients and ailments; however, the majority concern the domains of *neike* ("internal" medicine), and *fuke* (medicine for women, particularly relating to reproduction), and his practice only rarely extended to the lower classes.[25] What links these disparate cases together is that they are framed around him as narrator and central character, a doctor who plays up a literati persona to enhance his medical aura and prestige.

Sun Yikui's status as the son of a degree-holding scholar was a crucial component of his self-presentation. In an autobiographical preface attached to *The Crimson Sea*, Sun recounts that he came from a family of scholars (rather than of hereditary doctors). When his father was only twenty and in weak health, he passed the first set of civil service examinations to qualify as a licentiate with a specialty in the *Classic of Changes* (*Yijing/I Ching*).[26] He studied hard for the next set of exams, which he took repeatedly but never passed. Each time he returned home after failing the examinations, he became demoralized and his health worsened. This profile of Sun's father was only too familiar throughout the late imperial period; indeed, unsuccessful examination candidates were also commonly understood to be perfect candidates for sickliness and were considered particularly vulnerable to serious illnesses such as stasis (*yu*), also translated as depression or melancholy.

Sun does not name his father's illness or describe his symptoms. Instead, he recollects the genesis of his desire to be a doctor: "I was only a little boy at the time. Waiting upon my father, I was really saddened by all this. I thought to myself: People say that to serve one's parents one must know medicine. How can I learn the secrets of medicine so that I can nurse my father back to health?"[27] Sun couches his career choice conventionally in terms of a filial imperative, but practical economic concerns are clearly motivating forces. Studying for the examinations like his father was apparently out of the question. His father first sends him off to learn to be a merchant; on the way he meets a Daoist who offers to reveal his secret prescriptions and teach him to be a doctor instead of wasting his time in search of profit. Sun does so, and then returns home to tell his father that he wants to practice medicine (here called the "technical arts"). His father readily agrees that medicine would be a better profession for his son than trade.

Sun's meeting with a mysterious figure who transmits esoteric technical knowledge to induct him into a profession is a trope of great antiquity in China. The biography of Bian Que, the legendary founder of medicine, included in *Records of the Grand Historian,* also begins with the future physician's meeting with a divine figure who gives him secret books of medical wisdom.[28] *Records of the Grand Historian* features a number of similar myths about the initiations of other great masters into the technical arts. As a rule, such episodes serve a metonymic as well as symbolic role in a biography; the acquisition of the secret book stands in for the whole of the person's early education and training.[29] Sun Yikui's account of how he became a doctor is more down-to-earth, however. The secret prescriptions he learned from the Daoist turn out to be "hard to put into practice." So he sets himself to studying the medical classics. But book learning proves insufficient too, so he leaves home to travel (a common form of medical apprenticeship), studying what and with whom he can. He finally settles and establishes a practice in the Sanwu region, where the first two chapters of the case histories are set. He concludes with an acknowledgment of his social and professional success; the renowned gentlemen of the Sanwu region considered him a knowledgeable man and befriended him despite the differences in their status, and in recognition of his accomplishments, one of them even helped defray the publication costs of his medical encyclopedia and distributed free of charge drugs made up according to Sun's prescriptions.

Although this personal account is attached to Sun's encyclopedia rather than to his casebook, his case histories can also be read as something of an autobiographical project, a cumulative work of self-representation and self-fashioning on the order of a *wenji,* the collected literary works of an individual scholar or official.[30] These case histories can be viewed as another expression of the concern to document the major events and accomplishments of one's own life that we find in the annalistic autobiographies (*zixu nianpu*) that were increasingly written in this period, although Sun's distinctive character and voice emerge more strongly than they do in any annalistic autobiography I know.[31] Indeed, his sons and disciples express this hope in their notice of editorial principles for Sun's casebook: "In perusing this work, it will also be possible for like-minded men to get a general sense of his life."[32]

The first edition of Sun Yikui's casebook is crowned with an entire volume of credentialing prefaces and laudatory poems and letters from prominent members of the local gentry, along with a portrait of the doctor himself accompanied by a series of encomia attributed to several of the same people. A portrait of the author was frequently included in a scholar's or official's literary collection as a visual counterpart to the literary documentation of the person provided in the text, reinforcing the biographical and commemorative nature of his "life's work." Sun's casebook resembles and even exceeds the prefatory materials of this kind customarily attached to a standard *bieji* of the period or to other Ming and Qing casebooks. (Though again his sons and disciples explain that they are printing only a fraction of the letters and endorsements Sun received from his patients over the course of his career). Some of the prefatory material to Sun's casebook is identified as contributions from prominent members of the local gentry (*zhu jinshen mingjia*), a subtitle that would never appear in a regular *bieji*. This explicit label serves to reinforce the status distinction between the contributors and the physician even as it endeavors to endorse the respectability and refinement of the volume as a whole.

Sun Yikui knew very well that case histories and testimonies by patients and their families were the raw materials out of which people from the earliest dynastic histories to his own day fashioned a physician's biography. He was acutely aware that only with the support of the local gentry could a doctor build up a practice, gain an audience for his writings, and become a leading figure in the field with a lasting reputation. He himself compiled a biographical essay on six famous doctors, ending with Zhu Zhenheng (1282–1358) and Hua Shou (Boren; 1304–1386). In the essay, Sun asserts that Hua Shou was in no way the inferior of Zhu Zhenheng, but regrettably, Zhu's reputation and influence in contemporary medicine vastly exceeds Hua's: "The reason is that Zhu was promoted by the members of the gentry of his time with whom he associated. And furthermore, the renowned physicians Dai Yuanli and Liu Zonghou were his students. This is why Zhu's name is so widespread, whereas despite the heights to which Hua took the art of medicine, his reputation lags behind." And this is why Sun also exclaims in the same essay, "Whenever I read *Records of the Grand Historian* and reach the part where the Grand Historian praises . . . Bo Yi, I always close the chapter and sigh over the fact that despite the heights of Hua Shou's art, no one afterwards helped publicize him and his work."[33] The Grand Historian's biography of the hermit Bo Yi, who starved himself to death, observes that although Bo Yi was a virtuous man, he left no writings behind and owed his fame entirely to Confucius' praise of him. In this particular essay, it is Sun who is serving as the biographer of other deserving physicians, but the Grand Historian's final lines of Bo Yi's biography could almost serve as a motto for Sun's own case history project: "People of humble origins living in village lanes strive to make perfect their actions and establish a name for virtue, but if they do not somehow ally themselves with a man of worth and importance, how can they hope that their fame will be handed down to posterity?"[34]

As in the case of other types of literary compositions, Sun Yikui circulated drafts of some of his encyclopedia chapters and medical cases to grateful clients, the way aspiring scholars might circulate their writings to admiring patrons. His cases concerning one particular patient, Dong Xun, an elderly gentleman with whom he was on close terms, is unusually forthcoming on this point. Sun first successfully treats Dong Xun for a stomach ailment; Sun concludes this first case with a long speech that Dong Xun made to someone else about his merits as a physician. In the speech, Dong quotes a line from a poem he had composed in praise of Sun, which he had copied onto a scroll as testimony to the doctor's merits (1.738 #7). In consecutive cases Sun treats Dong Xun's daughter-in-law, cook, married daughter, and, in the next chapter, his elderly wife. By the time Sun treats Dong Xun's cook, he is clearly on intimate terms with the old gentleman; the two are playing chess together when word comes that the cook is dying. "Such is my fate, such is my fate!" laments the unhappy gentleman, pushing aside the chessboard. To the doctor he explains that good cooks are hard to come by, and this one was the only one whose cooking he'd found to suit his taste. Sun magnanimously offers to attend to the cook. Dong demurs. "How can I bother a great man like you with such a humble fellow!" Sun replies, "A doctor is concerned with a person's life and death; what business has he to quibble over differences in status?" And he insists that he cannot stand idly by while someone in Dong's service needs help. He saves the cook's life, of course. When Dong Xun learns the news, he leaps to his feet in delight, exclaiming, "What I wrote about you in my poem . . . was not false praise!" (1.739 #9) The full text of this poem is, in fact, included in the "contributions from prominent members of the gentry."

After Sun cures Dong Xun's married daughter of cough and fatigue (1.739–1.740 #10), some greater expression of gratitude was evidently called for. The old gentleman sends him a letter of extravagant praise, which Sun quotes toward the end of this case. Of particular interest is this passage: "In the past Song Jinglian wrote a biography of Zhu Zhenheng. I'm certainly not so clever, but fortunately you have given me some accounts of cases you have cured. Allow me to write a preface for them in order to pass them on to posterity and provide an aid for other practitioners of this art." It is not clear whether Dong Xun ever actually read case histories or wrote such a preface, for no preface is included in the published edition of Sun's case histories. But what is important here is the evidence in the case histories themselves that Sun was passing along some of his cases in manuscript form as he wrote them to high-class patients with whom he enjoyed an ongoing relationship as physician and friend; important, too, is the *written* nature of the services such a patient could reciprocally perform on behalf of the physician. Clearly the highest literary tribute would be to write a biography or, barring that, a preface to the doctor's work, and below that still, the composition of a poem to spread his reputation. The delicate subject of monetary remuneration is never mentioned in the casebook (and in several cases, Dr. Sun takes pains to distinguish himself from mere medical apothecaries or shopkeepers). An offer to help finance publication of the doctor's work, however, could be acknowledged in print. In a letter included in the "contributions from prominent members of the gentry" but not in one of the case histories, another grateful patient of Sun's, Pan Jiansuo, writes of his regret that the doctor's published works are still incomplete and offers to underwrite the cost of publishing "his marvelous case histories" to make them widely available and make his name live forever like the famous doctors of old.[35]

In most of the cases where Sun cites praise of himself by others, the evaluation comes at the very end and serves the rhetorical function of providing closure to the narrative. In the case of Dong Xun's daughter, mentioned above, the quotation of the letter plays a more complex role. The letter is introduced close to the end of what appears to be a successful cure. The reader is already conditioned to take the laudatory evaluation as the conclusion of the case. But the closure of the letter, like the positive results of the treatment, turns out to be a false one, which heightens the plot twist. In the narrative, the letter is actually a pivotal device, which affords Sun the opportunity to issue a warning to the lady's husband that all is not as it seems to be, as he modestly shrugs off the father-in-law's effusive compliments. Sun reveals that the lady's pulse reading is still worrisome and that a relapse is possible if she becomes angry. (Of course, it's easy to read this as shrewdly hedging his bets, as seizing control of the narrative situation to prepare the family members and readers for the dramatic reversal in the case; and indeed at the end, this refusal to be so flattered that he will conceal or overlook the potential negative outcome of the lady's illness becomes an occasion for praise.) Once the warning has been issued, the narrative logic shifts to the rule that what someone (especially a doctor) warns against will come true. Sure enough, the lady does eventually grow angry with her husband—so angry that she stops taking the medicine Dr. Sun prescribed—and dies. Now when the doctor reports that everyone admired his straightforwardness and acumen, this final piece of praise really does mark the end of the case.

Two other entries specifically call attention to the practice of recording case histories. In the first (1.751 #46), a married woman, the daughter of another member of the gentry, is suffering from a digestive ailment and has for some time been under the misguided care of a specialist in women's medicine, a Dr. Chen (Chen *nüke*), with gradually worsening results. Finally Dr. Chen "comes to the end of his bag of tricks" and, preparing to leave, pronounces the illness to be a fatal one. At this juncture, our narrator is called in to treat her; he quickly finds that the lady's illness has been utterly misdiagnosed by Dr. Chen, the disaster compounded by the incorrect medicine he had prescribed for her. Step by step, Dr. Sun arrives at the correct prescriptions to eliminate each of the lady's symptoms and restore her completely to health.

In and of itself, there is nothing exceptional about this case. Competition with rival doctors is a staple of the Ming medical case. Furth has argued persuasively that this competition reveals the contingency of the doctor's medical authority and the precariousness of his professional position.[36] The physician himself was more likely to couch the problem in terms of the medical risks a patient exposed himself to through such fickleness and ignorance. As Sun complains elsewhere,

> Since a patient wants to find a quick remedy, he doesn't engage any one doctor long, but keeps switching from one physician to the next. The patient is especially ignorant that someone suffering from depletion has been robbed [*duo*] of essential vitality [*jingqi*] and must take quantities of replenishing drugs. The benefits of these are only visible after a period of months or years, but the patient, abominating how slow the therapy is to show results, switches to another physician for treatment. And so he keeps on changing doctors and trying new ones. A later physician, observing that the previous prescription didn't work, suspects that the syndrome has been misdiagnosed, and so he alters the drug therapy, little thinking that it is simply that the previous drug's capacity has not yet reached its full effect. From this, the patient's Spleen and Stomach are increasingly damaged, until he is beyond saving. And even then the patient deplores that there are no good doctors in this world![37]

From a narratological point of view, the entrance of the narrator-hero-doctor onto a case after it has already been bungled by a previous, incompetent doctor is one of the most common plot types in the Ming medical case. The hero-doctor's struggle over the disease is then dramatized as a struggle over the ignorance and chicanery of the other doctor. But what makes the above case of the lady with the digestive ailment remarkable is that it concludes with the *written* capitulation of the rival doctor: "The specialist turned red, marveled over my cure, and accepted his defeat. *Then he recorded [or copied?] the case and departed.*" The sign, practically and symbolically, that the rival doctor has bowed to Sun's superior authority is that he writes the case down. In this conclusion, recording a case history is portrayed primarily as a performative rather than informational act. We do not learn how Dr. Chen portrayed the events of the case or whether in fact he recorded only the prescriptions successfully used in the case. It doesn't matter. It is the gesture of recording a case that a rival doctor has successfully treated that flags the ignominy of Chen's defeat and Sun's triumph.

The other case (2.773–2.774 #150), involving a weird female genital disorder, sheds light on the intersection of medicine and book culture in Dr. Sun's view of knowledge. Distinctiveness—at least in the sense of relative uniqueness—was one of the criteria given for the selection of his published cases. But Sun's casebook seldom records "rare diseases" (*qiji*) or medical anomalies;[38] he rarely enters into the "discourse on the strange" or broader questions of epistemology. This subject, however, is addressed at some length in this particular case, not as an exposition of abstract principles, but contextualized within the social relations of healing, as part of the rhetorical arsenal a doctor had at his disposal. The case begins with an enigma. A man comes three times to the doctor's door, but each time he is so embarrassed that he leaves without saying what he's come for. The fourth time the man appears, blushing furiously, Dr. Sun takes the bull by the horns and delivers a long lecture.

> Everyone who comes to see me says I can diagnose curious illnesses and treat them. Now you've come three times—there must be something curious in it. If you don't divulge a word, even if you come one hundred times, I'll never be able to make a diagnosis, and the illness will never go away! Moreover, the universe is filled with strange things; nobody but a sage could be familiar with them all, or for that matter, cure them all. *In those collections of medical records, medical encyclopedias, medical theory, and so on, strange symptoms are as numerous as spines on a hedgehog. Unless someone perspicacious about such things can make a diagnosis and cure, how can we can expand the general knowledge of those who come after us?* (Italics mine.)

Once again we find the reflexive appeal to the function of the written medical record within a case that the doctor himself is recording. Striking also is the doctor's absolute confidence in books as a means of containing the frightening power of unknown phenomena—not because these books can explain anomalies and make them understandable, but simply because such books tame anomalies by incorporating them into the field of human knowledge.

In any event, the doctor's speech works. The man breaks down and confides the problem to the doctor: because of a strange growth in his wife's vagina, she is in such physical and mental anguish that she is ready to kill herself. After asking a few questions, the doctor makes his diagnosis: "Now generally what is considered strange is something that has never been seen or heard, or *something that has never been recorded in books.* Now what you've told me today is nothing but a symptom called "vaginal protrusion" [*yinting zheng*]. Since there's evidence of such a thing in books, surely it doesn't qualify as something strange!"[39] After assuring the man that his wife's condition is curable and unrelated to deeper reproductive disorders, the doctor gives him a prescription to take back to his wife, telling him the symptom should clear up in a month or so. Once again this seems like it should be the end of the story; once again there is a narrative twist. Three months later the husband appears at the doctor's doorstep again. He confirms that his wife had been cured just as the doctor had said. But he has returned to ask his advice about another matter concerning his wife's health. It's been more than a month since her last period; could the doctor tell him what illness she might be suffering from now? Amenorrhea was considered a grave problem for women in late imperial medical culture, a condition not only linked to reproductive capacities, but also indicative of a dangerous disruption of fundamental vitalities in the body.[40] But Dr. Sun does not even entertain this second line of reasoning for a moment. Instead he immediately replies, "Your wife is with child." The husband is incredulous. "But we thought she had only just recovered. It couldn't really be pregnancy, and we were afraid she might be suffering from another illness." The doctor is right, of course, and the case ends on the happy note that the woman carried the pregnancy to term and gave birth to a son. The birth of a child or eventual success at the examinations are two typical closures for Sun's cases, marking as they do the conjunction of two popular cultural happy endings with proof of a patient's complete return to health.

LITERARY ANALYSIS OF INDIVIDUAL CASES

So far I have argued that in packaging and positioning, Sun Yikui's published casebook, read as a collection, resembles a *bieji;* in its focus on the self-presentation of events in the author's life, I suggested that the casebook also had something in common with the annalistic autobiography. This section focuses on those characteristics his case histories shared with late-Ming classical fiction and drama. The three individual cases singled out for analysis are not particularly representative of the casebook as a whole. Even by the standards of Sun Yikui's other cases, these three are extraordinary in their appeal as stories and include variables not frequently found in the casebook at large. Two of the cases involve courtesans (there are only three in the entire five-chapter casebook, and it is rare even for concubines to be mentioned in case histories) and the last case is again one of only three in the book to involve a confrontation with a rival doctor who is a woman.[41]

Literature of this period abounds with romanticized stories about liaisons between young elite males and idealized courtesans. Indeed, the beautiful, talented, and morally superior courtesan is one of the staple themes of Chinese fiction through the late nineteenth century. Both of Sun's cases involving courtesans are more prosaic than the typical short story; still, the subject matter may have encouraged him to take greater narrative liberties than in other of his case histories. The first case I will discuss (1.747 #31) reads remarkably like a tale or anecdote from the period; indeed, with a little editing (omitting the detailed prescriptions and shifting the doctor's first-person pronoun to the third person), it could easily pass for one.

The case involves a courtesan incapacitated by an ailment called "wind-pain" (*tongfeng*), which, like rheumatism, results in symptoms such as aching and swollen joints. Her other symptoms include loss of appetite, weight loss, and amenorrhea. As in fiction and drama, this is no ordinary courtesan, however, but the crème de la crème of her profession, a woman of refinement who enjoys a reputation as the finest singer in the pleasure quarter. Since the courtesan's condition has already persisted for eight months, her avaricious and hard-hearted madam no longer sought medical help for her but accepted this as a chronic condition. The madam is another stock figure of fiction and drama, where her ugliness, moral and physical, is usually a foil to the goodness and beauty of the courtesan-heroine. The implication is that other doctors had been previously brought in, but all of them had failed. Dr. Sun is brought into the case by a friend and fellow townsman of his, a regular client of the courtesan's. It is here that the case departs from the norm. After taking her pulse and being asked by the friend for a prognosis, the doctor makes a joke. "If you can marry her, I can cure her." Marrying a courtesan, at least taking her as a concubine, was perfectly possible during the late Ming. Allan Barr has written about love affairs of this sort in late sixteenth-century literary circles.[42] And several of the most famous literary men in the 1630s and 1640s did take celebrated courtesans as concubines.[43]

The point of Dr. Sun's witticism is also to test the waters about his friend's feelings for her. It must already be apparent to the doctor that the friend calling him in signals more than a casual relationship. By bringing the doctor to see the courtesan, the friend has *already* assumed the role of male householder taking responsibility for a dependent female's illness. These social relationships of healing are simply ratified in the end when he actually becomes her husband. Nonetheless, the friend demurs at first, protesting that a love affair in the pleasure quarters leading to marriage is just a "cliché" that people like to tell stories about, not something people actually do. But the doctor presses on and affirms his approval of this particular courtesan as a wife; the friend soon admits that he had been wanting to marry her all along but was afraid it would be too expensive.

In fiction and drama, marriage between a young man of good family and a courtesan is usually opposed both by the boy's parents, who cut him off without a cent, and the girl's madam, who is loath to lose her "money tree." In this particular case, the doctor's friend is a widower of unidentified social background, presumably not of scholar status or Sun would have specified so; moreover, he is unlikely to be young and his parents are not a relevant factor, so how to get around the madam's avarice is the central problem. One of the most common subplots in scholar-courtesan romances in fiction and drama concerns the lovers' stratagems to raise the necessary purchase price to buy the woman out of service. The remarkable thing in this story is that it is the doctor himself who thinks up the scheme: take advantage of the courtesan's illness and swear an oath of marriage with her *now* to get a bargain from the madam. Thus the doctor *refrains* from treating the courtesan until *after* his friend has bought her out.

As a foregone conclusion, the actual treatment, though the prescriptions are given in detail, is definitely something of an anti-climax in the narrative. This is because the usual hermeneutic focus of a case history—the doctor's diagnosis of the deep structural disorder underlying the patient's surface symptoms and the logical assumptions determining his therapeutic course of action—is displaced from the medical plot to the marriage plot.[44] This displacement is borne out in the happy ending of the story, which finishes not simply with a report of the patient's full recovery, but also with the remarkable success of the match. In fact, the longevity of their union may be what Sun particularly congratulates himself upon, since marriages with courtesans appear to have been less stable on the whole than ordinary marriages.[45] The obligatory praise serving as closure for the case follows suit; what everyone praises is Sun's "judgment in people"—his ability to recognize the superior abilities and moral worth of this courtesan—rather than simply his medical expertise.

Another noteworthy thing in this case is the doctor's ability to detect the couple's true feelings for each other despite the fact that the illness the courtesan is diagnosed as suffering from—wind-pain—is not ordinarily linked with the manifestation of thwarted desires in either medical or fictional literature. The courtesan's other symptoms—loss of appetite, weight loss, and amenorrhea—on the other hand, are classic indicators of stasis in medical case histories; the same symptoms, minus the amenorrhea, are standard signs of lovesickness in fiction and drama.[46] Thus it is possible that these *other* symptoms, which accompany the courtesan's swelling and aching joints, are what lead the doctor to conclude that the patient "has set her heart on" his friend and that theirs may be a match made in Heaven. But this is something the doctor-narrator keeps from the reader, for he does not, unlike many other cases, reveal his diagnostic or therapeutic reasoning process. In any event, one obvious difference between a case history and a fictional narrative is that the latter would not tolerate such an asymmetry between the primary disease manifestation (wind-pain) and the significance the doctor reads into it (the patient is pining for marriage), but would be likely to rewrite the case by changing the disease to something else in order to squarely align sign and signifier.

An excellent example of the stricter degree of conformity between syndrome and meaning required in the plot of a tale than that of a case history is the story "Rui Yun" in *Liaozhai's Records of the Strange.* This collection of tales and anecdotes by Pu Songling was written about one hundred years after Sun Yikui's case histories but was not published until 1766. Sun's solution to the problem of how to marry a top-ranked courtesan on the cheap was so ingenious and so sensible that I figured it ought to be a common plot device in the scholar-courtesan romance. But the only story to turn up was this one, in which the intermediary figure of the doctor is replaced by a mysterious figure with magical powers, and the ailment the courtesan suffers from has an unmistakable moral significance.

Rui Yun is a beautiful and talented courtesan in Hangzhou who takes a shine to a poor scholar, the hero of the tale, who also falls deeply in love with her. She has persuaded her madam to let her bestow the honor of taking her cherry on the client of her own choice. She selects this poor scholar, who is deeply moved by her recognition of his true merits, but of course he has no way to raise the necessary sum and is forced to break off with her. A short time later, another man, also identified as a scholar, meets with the courtesan and touches her forehead with his finger, leaving behind a black stain. After he departs, she finds the stain cannot be washed off, and to her horror, similar black marks gradually spread across her face, completely disfiguring her. The madam strips the now useless courtesan of her finery and demotes her to the kitchen, where our hero, the poor scholar, finds her working as a scullery maid, hideous and miserable. Moved by her plight, he offers to buy her from the madam, who agrees. Although her purchase price is not very high, he must still sell his land and all of his belongings to raise it. He takes her home and marries her.

About a year later he happens to be introduced to a stranger, also a scholar, who abruptly brings up the courtesan Rui Yun and wonders whatever happened to her.

"She married someone," he replied.

"You don't happen to know what her purchase price was?" continued the stranger.

"Because she suffered from a rare disease, she actually went pretty cheaply," he admitted.[47]

It turns out, of course, that this is the very man responsible for inflicting the black mark in the first place. He had done so out of pity for the courtesan, to keep her "true value" hidden and intact until someone who "really loved talent" came along to appreciate her. "Well," says the poor scholar eagerly, "if you could stain her, can you also cleanse her?" The stranger prepares a basinful of water for him and tells him, "When she washes her face with this, she'll be cured. But she must come out and convey her thanks to the doctor in person."[48]

We can easily see that this is an idealized and allegorized version of Sun Yikui's plot in the case of the courtesan suffering from wind-pain. (My point in comparing these two narratives is to demonstrate their shared cultural background rather than any textual borrowing or direct literary influence.) In Pu Songling's tale, however, the relationship between the illness and its meaning is the opposite of arbitrary. The ailment is only *skin deep* to drive home the obvious lesson that the exemplary lover must be able to see past the surface and prize what lies beneath it. Moreover, the disfigurement relies on a not very subtle dialectic between a woman's true beauty and moral/sexual integrity, between a woman's true worth and her monetary value in the commercial market.

Causality has been strengthened to the point in this tale that not only the cure but the illness itself is the deliberate result of the intermediary figure. For this reason, this figure must be a magician of sorts, not simply an ordinary doctor, and the story speculates at the end that perhaps the stranger was an immortal (*xian*). Nonetheless, his basic affinity to a medical practitioner has earlier been affirmed when the narrative refers to him metaphorically as a doctor to be thanked. (The underlying medicalized view of the courtesan's predicament is also brought out by describing it as a "rare disease" that can be "cured.") The plot is motivated, as so many of Pu Songling's stories are, by the mechanics of requital and reversal. Because the courtesan at her peak valued the scholar in his poverty, he in turn values her when she is worthless. This is why, in contrast to the case history where the courtesan's lover is in cahoots with the doctor and prudently refrains from offering to buy her until he is confident she can be cured, Rui Yun's lover must be kept in a state of total ignorance so that he can prove the sincerity of his love and show himself worthy of such a prize. (Of course, Pu Songling is somewhat disingenuous, since the reward for unswerving devotion in the face of hideous disfigurement is the restoration of the beloved's beauty—but after all, his is a literature of wish fulfillment.)

The cultural ideal of *zhiren*—the ability to recognize another person's true worth—is the guiding force in both the tale and the case history. In the tale, as befits a romance, this recognition is distributed equally between the two lovers; the intermediary figure simply ratifies their mutual devotion and engineers the happy ending. In the case history, however, knowledge of human nature is represented as the monopoly of the doctor rather than the specific property of the lovers, so that it is he who is congratulated on his judgment in people. Thus despite the seemingly anomalous qualities of this case, on closer look we can see that it actually reinforces one of Sun's main themes. This case once again drives home the point that the knowledge he possesses as a medical practitioner is not "merely" a branch of specialized, technical, professional skill, but a component of the broad learning and insight expected of a true literatus who happens to be a physician. This point, somewhat paradoxically, lies at the heart of Sun's claim to medical authority.

Example 2: The Case of the Doomed Courtesan

The second case superficially resembles the previous one: a friend brings Dr. Sun to visit a courtesan and he diagnoses her illness. But the particular circumstances and the outcome are very different. The friend, Wu Xiaofeng, a scholar, is also Dr. Sun's patient and the medical subject of two case histories of his own in the book.[49] He takes Dr. Sun to meet the courtesan not in Sun's professional capacity as physician, but as a man-about-town at leisure. The two friends are traveling together, and as it is the mid-autumn festival, Wu proposes that they celebrate the holiday in the company of a courtesan he knows. Sun goes along with the idea and, when he meets the courtesan, concurs with his friend's view of her appeal. But soon she makes the mistake of coughing twice in succession. Wu now assumes the role of the friend in the previous case and begins to act the part of the man responsible for a sick woman in consultations with a male doctor. When she denies she is ill, he urges her to take advantage of Dr. Sun's presence and have him examine her. Xiaofeng's tone is half-bantering, as befits a drinking party, but the analogy of Sun to Bian Que, the legendary physician from antiquity, serves a more serious twofold purpose. The analogy is a standard compliment for a doctor, following Sun's usual technique of placing a positive assessment of himself in a third-party's mouth, but it also prepares the reader for the stunning feat of clinical reasoning that he will pull off in this case.

In contrast to the previous case, where the courtesan's illness was known and identified at the outset, here the process of detection and the solution to a puzzle—the hermeneutics of the medical plot—is everything, since the illness is diagnosed as terminal and a cure is out of the question. As clichéd as the Bian Que analogy is, it proves to be particularly apt in this case, because it describes the kind of preternatural ability to see the invisible and predict fate that Bian Que was proverbial for.[50] What is highlighted as extraordinary in this case is the fact that on the basis of a trivial clue (the two coughs in succession), one pulse examination, and a series of questions, the doctor is able to foresee the entire course of the patient's illness before she herself is even aware of being ill. (The extent of this tour de force is highlighted by the friend's interjection, "But she isn't even sick yet! How could you reach such a conclusion?") Picking up on the correlation between illness and crime as two manifestations of disorder, implicit in the analogy between the medical case and the crime case story, we may describe Sun's diagnosis of the courtesan's terminal illness as the equivalent of a magistrate's accurately predicting and solving a murder before it actually takes place without having the power or desire to prevent it.

The key fact for Sun in this case is that the woman who coughs is a courtesan, not a respectable woman, and a courtesan for him is coded as lustful. As he declares to his friend in the conclusion to the case, "A courtesan is ordinarily overcome with passionate desires." Such a statement is damning not only morally, but physically in the terms of the medical discourse of the time, which understood sexual moderation as a key to good health.[51] Sun's indifference (or even hostility) to this woman's plight contrasts sharply with his pity for the courtesan in the previous case. We might attribute the discrepancy to his view that Suqin did not possess the true nature of a courtesan, an interpretation borne out by the success of her marriage.

Upon closer reflection, however, one might also explain the discrepancy as the result of the very different circumstances and expectations of the doctor's visits to these two women. In the first case, he is brought in to see a patient bedridden for many months, suffering from a wasting disease. There is no question of attraction on the doctor's part. In the second case, however, he has come to attend a holiday drinking party with a pretty courtesan. His first reaction confirms his friend's high estimation of her charms ("I saw she did have a refined and charming air about her"). He has every expectation of enjoying a pleasant evening, perhaps even ending up in her bed. But she spoils everything by coughing. In the course of the examination, any lustful feelings that she might have aroused in him are now projected back onto her. Moreover, her lustfulness is now explicitly revealed to him as a sign of a pathological imbalance within the body, something above and beyond the "ordinarily" lecherous nature of a courtesan.

The information the doctor elicits when he questions her is tantamount to self-incrimination. Her odd pulse reading suggests to him that she suffers from "involuntary spending," a hypothesis that she herself later confirms. Although the doctor goes through the motions of addressing questions to his friend as the man in charge of a woman's illness, the courtesan is soon portrayed as replying to the doctor's questions herself without any intermediary. The courtesan's direct replies might simply be a literary expedient, to prevent the tedious back and forth of "he said, she said." But it is my impression from other cases that women are never represented as discussing their own illness or bodies with a doctor the way this courtesan does here. If so, then this is another way in which the doctor presents this particular courtesan as unseemly or "lacking the air of a lady of good family."

Mengyi, the syndrome he refers to, means "oneiric emissions or wet dreams" and is ordinarily applied to men. It is a common category in medical reference books and is also depicted in fiction, but not normally applied to women in Ming or Qing writings. Instead, when an equivalent for women is mentioned, it is usually called *meng jiao* (oneiric intercourse, usually with ghosts, gods, or demons). *The Crimson Sea* includes an entry for "oneiric emissions" (11.270–11.272), which Sun discusses exclusively as a male problem, mentioning the syndrome of "oneiric intercourse" for women only in passing, since he gives fuller attention to it in an entry titled "dreams of intercourse with ghosts" (*meng yu gui jiao,* 20.452) in the section of the encyclopedia devoted to female disorders.[52] Nonetheless, Sun apparently isn't puzzled at coming up with a pulse reading signifying "oneiric emissions" for a woman; what strikes him as inappropriate in this case is that the woman is a courtesan.

Sun's encyclopedia entry for oneiric emissions, which quotes extensively from Zhu Zhenheng's work, seems typical of the medical literature on the subject. Such emissions are considered a worrisome disorder, a sign of imbalance in the body that results in the squandering of finite resources of vitality. Medical compendia of the period indicate that sexual frustration or unrequited love were possible causes, but so was studying too hard or a weakened Kidney system. Early seventeenth-century physicians such as Zhang Jiebin ascribed the root cause of the disorder to the Heart or mind, for it was known that the Kidneys, which governed reproductive function, responded to emotional and mental stimuli by producing fluids. But erotic dreams were understood by doctors to be as likely to result from somatic as psychological imbalance—from the stirring of Essence or the stirring of amorous feelings—and so Zhang Jiebin argued that it was necessary to strengthen the Kidneys as well as purify the Heart, the system that governs consciousness, including thoughts and feelings.[53] Nonetheless, in view of Sun's surprise at coming upon a diagnosis of oneiric emissions for a courtesan, we can assume that at least for a woman he would expect to find this syndrome only among those suffering from sexual frustration with little opportunity for amorous encounters.

Particularly damning is the courtesan's confession that she suffers not only from involuntary spending at night, but even when she is in bed with a client. What this means for Sun is that her desires are out of control, hence his dark pronouncement, "When Heart and psyche have no regulating force, then the rule is there is no cure." This situation is especially grave considering the other signs of bodily imbalance he finds: amenorrhea, cold sweat, and exhaustion, which all indicate a deficiency of yin and a depletion of vitality.

The other key to the case is seasonal factors, which interact macrocosmically with the microcosm of the body. Sun records the month and year before the narrative proper begins ("Mid-autumn, 1572"), an unusual practice for him in the casebook. The time of year is then immediately explicitly narrativized within the case history: the arrival of the mid-autumn festival is the reason the doctor and his traveling companion decide to spend the evening with the courtesan. The timing of the doctor's examination of the courtesan is important because it is the unseasonable rampancy of her pulse that makes his reading so alarming. It is normal, he declares, for the pulse to be strung in the spring, when yang is increasing, but not in the autumn, when yin is increasing. Seasonal factors also play an important role in his application of Five-Phase reasoning to her case: "Now it is autumn, when the phase of Metal is increasing, and her pulse still so rampant. Imagine what will happen in the second month early next spring when the phase of Wood is increasing and Fire is the minister. Then her Lung Metal will be parched and impotent, and her reserves for ascending Water will already be used up."

In Five-Phase cosmology, Metal is the phase associated with autumn and the pulmonary system; Wood is the phase associated with spring and the hepatic system. Thus it sounds as though the courtesan has spring desires in autumn. Desire is appropriate for spring, the season of burgeoning, flowering, and ascending yang, but not in the autumn, when yang is waning and yin is waxing. In the autumn, *Inner Canon,* the foundational text of learned medicine, teaches one to sleep alone, to conserve and store primal qi vitalities. In the courtesan's case, she will not have stored primal qi but will have continued to dissipate it through sexual encounters and involuntary spending. Her reserves of Kidney Water (generative vitality) will be depleted, so that she will be especially vulnerable to the ascending yang fires of seasonal qi. The reference to water ascending alludes to the proper bodily func tioning relationship of Water (Kidney, generative vitality) and Fire (Heart, psychic functioning). In a healthy person, Water and Fire circulate, with Water ascending to cool the passions while Fire descends to its proper hiding place in the body's generative centers, available for use. Since her Water is exhausted, nothing will curb Fire's heat, which will be exacerbated next spring and burn all the brighter, especially because, as Sun insists, "courtesans are ordinarily overcome with desire."

A biomedical reading of this case is also possible. Such a reading would focus on Sun's attention to her cough, his discovery of her amenorrhea, his allusions to parched and impotent lungs and conclude he was diagnosing consumption.

Dr. Sun's tour de force of clinical reasoning not only completely exculpates the doctor for not helping the patient and elicits the reader's admiration for his diagnostic abilities, but also blames the patient for her own illness, since lustfulness is paradoxically labeled a standard attribute of a courtesan *and* singled out as a sign of pathology. Here the case pivots on the physician's command of a specialized discourse and his display of technical knowledge in contrast to the previous case, which developed the theme of the doctor's breadth of knowledge and his acumen in judging people as the key to practicing medicine. Nonetheless, the two cases share a similar model of medical knowledge and authority. On the basis of external signs, the physician shows himself able to divine the unknowable or to see what lies concealed inside a person. The early affiliation of doctors to diviners and magicians in Chinese historiography would have made the self-presentation of the physician as a "wizard of detection" in his case histories all the more expected and plausible to his patients and readers.[54]

Example 3: A Case of Postpartum Madness

The third case (1.746–1.747 #28), one of the longest in the book, involves the daughter-in-law of a high official who suffers a bout of life-threatening madness after a difficult delivery. Madness and related symptoms of vertigo, fainting, raving, or hallucination constituted a common postpartum syndrome in Chinese medical reference books. Sun's casebook includes about four or five related cases, though none of the others is detailed at such length. The syndrome appears at least as early as the influential Song dynasty classic *Complete Good Prescriptions for Women* (*Furen daquan liangfang*), by Chen Ziming (1190–1270), all the way up through eighteenth- and nineteenth-century works and probably later. *The Crimson Sea* is no exception; it contains four entries that describe postpartum symptoms of this sort.[55] In this particular case, the woman's crisis is precipitated by the birth of a girl when she had longed for a boy; shortly after, the girl died and the woman was left with no baby at all. (Sun does not mention whether she has other children; presumably not). After the news of the infant's death, the woman falls into a dead faint. When she comes to, she is having some sort of a fit and has lost her senses. Sun refrains from drawing explicit conclusions about the woman's mood and state of mind at the baby's death other than to say that she is "despondent," but he links events into a narrative sequence clearly enough for the reader to infer it. There are strong indications that the patient blames herself for her infant's death; in one of her subsequent crazy spells in her sleep she slaps herself in the face and pounds her chest, self-punishing behavior that clearly denotes self-reproach and remorse.

Sun does not attribute the woman's illness to her emotional state. Instead, he operates according to two related medical premises: First, since no "noxious dew" (*elu;* what biomedicine would call bloody vaginal discharge, or lochia) flowed at the time of the birth, she is suffering the ill effects of retaining this foul, stagnant fluid inside her body;[56] this postpartum blood is imagined as an obstruction within, rather like, or even interchangeable with, phlegm in the chest, which can block the Heart system and thus affect consciousness (*shen*). Second, she is suffering from a depletion of Blood in the Heart system. As Sun mentions in an encyclopedia entry on postpartum fright syndrome, quoting Xue Ji's sixteenth-century revision of *Complete Good Prescriptions for Women,* since the Heart is understood as the organ regulating the person as a whole, and since the Heart regulates Blood, once the Blood in the Heart is depleted, that person's psychic well-being is at risk.[57] Other postpartum entries in his encyclopedia rehearse variations on these two problems: obstructions of stagnant Blood/phlegm or a depletion of Blood. Both conditions have the effect of disabling the Heart system, which regulates consciousness, and thus can provoke a range of syndromes such as madness or hallucination. In the other cases of postpartum madness in the casebook, Sun tends to adopt one or the other (excess Blood, mainly in the form of unexpelled noxious dew, or Blood depletion in the Heart system, sometimes with excess heat or Fire).[58]

The therapeutic issue for Sun Yikui seems to have been whether to concentrate first on breaking up the stagnant Blood and stimulating the expulsion of the noxious dew or whether to concentrate first on replenishing strategies and deal with other problems later. In the late Ming, the strategy of first breaking up Blood was considered rather old-fashioned, while replenishing first, as advocated by physicians such as Zhu Zhenheng, was more up-to-date.[59] The complicating factor in this case, as usual, is that another medical practitioner has already preceded Sun on the scene. The unusual thing is that this doctor is a woman. She has already established a relation of trust with the patient, and most aggravating of all to Sun, as a woman, she has easy and intimate access to the patient's bedchamber.[60] This doctor has already gone the route of replenishing first: the ginseng she gives the patient is a powerful replenishing agent. Though ginseng alone without any balancing agents would have been considered rather crude pharmacology, Sun himself, as we have seen, was a strong advocate of ginseng in clinical treatment.[61] Here Sun is almost obliged to adopt the other tack: he insists upon the need to expel the noxious dew and phlegm first and takes his rival to task for administering such a strong replenishing agent right off the bat. (Later, after the patient has vomited up some phlegm and her postpartum discharge has begun to flow, he does include ginseng as one ingredient in a replenishing prescription.)

The other interesting thing about this case is that the patient's attack of postpartum madness includes not only loss of consciousness, bodily control, and reason, but also a bout of what looks like full-blown possession. At least that is what all the members of the household think when the patient begins fiercely declaring in elegant Mandarin that she is the bodhisattva Guanyin. This behavior is considered all the more aberrant because as a southerner born and bred to the Wu dialect, she would not be expected to have known Mandarin, which is a version of northern dialect. Add to that the characterization of this patient as a lady of high status, someone whose conversation had always been "proper and circumspect," a woman whose constitution had always been "frail" and who must be suffering from some form of postpartum exhaustion, and it is no wonder that the household members who knew her before the birth are convinced she must be possessed by the bodhisattva and address every manner of prayer to her. The doctor maintains himself as the lone voice of reason at this domestic scene of mayhem: "This is because the noxious dew was not completely expelled after the birth! Harboring all this blood has given rise to a syndrome that makes it seem as though she were seeing spirits. But in actuality, she is isn't being possessed by any god or Buddha."

After he shouts words of reason at her, she finally falls silent and he gives her some soul-calming powder mixed with talc and boy's urine. "Soul-calming powder" (*qinghun san*) as the prescription of choice here seems on the surface to potentially contradict the doctor's firm opposition to the possibility of an actual possession. But this prescription was an old remedy from *Complete Good Prescriptions for Women.* In *The Crimson Sea,* Sun lists this prescription as a cure for "postpartum Blood faintness" (*chanhou xueyun*); the recipe provided includes ginseng as well as ligusticum root (*chuanxiong*), a Blood harmonizer frequently used in prescriptions for women, and boy's urine is listed as one possible mixing agent (*diaofu*) to accompany the dose.[62]

Conspicuously absent from this scene is the female doctor. Sun conveniently blames both the patient's two relapses after he has taken over the case on medicines the female doctor had smuggled to her behind his back, and he naturally makes no mention of any alternate interpretation that his rival might give for the relapses. He does not lump the female doctor among the household members foolish enough to believe the patient was really possessed by a bodhisattva. In fact, he is unable to accuse the female doctor of following any healing practice deemed "unorthodox" from the point of view of Ming learned medicine, such as exorcism, ritual magic, or even acupuncture.[63] He finds no grounds to label his rival a "shaman" anywhere in the body of the case, but he is clearly deeply resentful to find himself in competition with a doctor who is a woman.

This is where the rhetorical structure of historical biography comes to his aid. It was conventional in both historical and fictionalized narrative for the author to append personal evaluative or interpretative comments after the conclusion of the story. The rhetorical and subjective cast of such comments was meant to contrast with the objective, relatively plain account of events found in the body of the text. The practice originated in early histories such as *Zuo's Commentary* (*Zuo zhuan*) or *Records of the Grand Historian,* where such comments were set apart under a distinct rubric such as "A gentleman remarks" or "The Grand Historian says." In late-Ming times, it was common practice in the classical tale for the author to invent a playful sobriquet as a rubric for his comments. Sun Yikui does not adopt a sobriquet or set his evaluation off under a clear rubric in this case, but the shift in tone and the rare employment of a historical allusion outside the realm of medicine clearly signals that he has moved to the territory of rhetorical comment.

> In the past, Bian Que said: "There are six illnesses which cannot be cured. Trusting a shaman and not a doctor is one of them." Formerly it was said that employing drugs is like employing an army. Despite the brilliance of the great General Guo Ziyi, because of [the terrible eunuch] Yu Chao'en's interference, he didn't succeed. I am certainly not in the same class as General Guo, but the errors that woman doctor committed were even worse than Yu Chao'en's treachery. Ah, one cannot be too cautious!"

In the comment, Sun can voice the sentiments he could not put into words in his narrative of the case. Although the woman doctor is not technically a shaman, she is the equivalent of one. The patient's mistake lay in not trusting in him, a true doctor, but in his rival, a false one. The analogy between the woman doctor and the treacherous Yu Chao'en is particularly apt in this case since Yu Chao'en was a eunuch, a nonman, the functional equivalent of a woman. In literati discourse, the eunuch was a despised category of person, the good Confucian official's traditional rival for the emperor's ear at court, and any participation by a eunuch in state affairs was by definition classified as evil and illegitimate.

The comment is also important because it lays bare one of the basic structuring mechanisms of the case history. The cliché "employing drugs is like employing an army" does more than simply imply that just as women and eunuchs don't belong in an army, so, too, women don't belong in the ranks of learned doctors.[64] Since the late Ming medical case is typically set up as a struggle with rival doctors, the narrating doctor's battle and eventual triumph over the patient's illness are often represented through or even replaced by his struggle with his rival. Sun's shift to a military rhetoric here underscores the point that in the case history, the rival doctor, rather than the illness itself, is frequently the doctor's chief adversary. In this particular case, the female doctor is clearly portrayed as an "internal enemy," one who has access to the trust of the patient and to her bedchamber and who can weasel her way in whenever the poor doctor's vigilance is relaxed for a moment. And finally, his rhetorical comment fits his usual self-promotional strategy for closure, since he is able to compare himself favorably with the brilliant, loyal Tang general Guo Ziyi and blame any miscalculations of his own in the treatment on the interference of a despicable adversary.

CONCLUSION

Sun Yikui was a talented storyteller with an eye for detail and an ear for dialogue. The liveliness of his style and his enjoyment of writing are evident throughout his work. Yet of course Sun's casebook was not published as a conglomeration of literary anecdotes but as a contribution to the specific field of medicine. To return to the starting premise of this volume—the style of case-based reasoning and its relation to specialist knowledge—we need to ask what precisely a case does in the casebook that it does not do in any of Sun's other writings. To address this question, we must first compare briefly all three of his published works, each of which follows a clear-cut intellectual division of labor.

The Crimson Sea includes only cases drawn from the works of other doctors. As a general medical encyclopedia, this longest of Sun's works is classified by nosology and further subdivided by syndrome, providing formulas for prescriptions used to treat a given ailment. Like many other reference books, it assembles the existing written wisdom on a general subject by excerpting relevant passages from previous works and authors. As an expert on his subject rather than a simple editor, Sun discusses these passages at length and offers his own opinions. But he confines himself to discussions of texts and does not bring in evidence from his own clinical practice.

The Purport of Medicine is a miscellaneous work that takes up individual topics in medicine. Sometimes individual cases drawn from Sun's own clinical experience are included as examples to explain certain problems or to illustrate certain views, but the name of the patient is usually omitted.[65] In this book, as in *The Crimson Sea,* Sun frequently refers to himself by his literary sobriquet, "Master of Generation" (Shengsheng zi), and follows the literary convention of placing his opinions as comments under the rubric of this sobriquet. Some of the cases he includes are even introduced by the words "The Master of Generation remarks."

When we turn back to Sun's casebook, certain aspects of the way he constructed his cases and what he hoped to achieve by grouping them together come into better relief. For a start, take names. Sun provides not only the full names of his patients, but their rank when applicable and how and where he came to treat them, in order to prove, as the notice of editorial principles explains, that "they were recorded based on fact" (*ju shi er lu*). Sun also avoids referring to himself by his literary sobriquet, since that would have the force of making a case seem more like an opinion being voiced than an event that had occurred. In this light, Sun's attitude toward names in the casebook, along with his decision not to classify his cases into medical categories, seems part of an overall strategy meant to distinguish a case from an example. After all, an example can be made up or synthesized because it is meant to flesh out a general theory or illustrate a specific point rather than to provide a narrative record of individual experience as a case does. The pithy definition Andreas Gailus proposes based on his synthesis of Forrester and Jolles seems particularly apt here: "a case occupies the logical space between example and anecdote—it is a set of events in other words that is reducible neither to an instance of a general pattern nor to an incident with only local significance."[66]

Chinese medicine did not subscribe to the idea of a general pattern of disease that would follow the identical course in each individual sufferer. Learned doctors in particular stressed the singularity of each person's disorder, which required the kind of complex diagnosis and individually tailored prescriptions that they alone could deliver. But there was also considerable pressure to provide standardized cures, to assume that certain drugs or drug combinations would always work for a given syndrome—to seek the very kind of short cuts the many set formulas in *The Crimson Sea* provided or that were even more accessible in the numerous books of prescriptions (*fang shu*) on the market.

Sun Yikui was a vocal opponent of rigidly adhering to any pharmaceutical formula, and he devotes an entire essay to this subject in *The Purport of Medicine.* Medical books may be used for reference, he cautions in this essay, but one cannot stubbornly follow them. A physician must approach each new patient with an open mind and find the real cause of his illness before composing a prescription—one must never force the illness to fit an already existing formula.[67] Sun's casebook was, in part, designed to show how a doctor adapts his therapeutic course of action to fit each new situation. As editors, Sun's sons and disciples sought to emphasize this quality of the book by adding the words *you faming*—"invention here"—in the table of contents after the title of any case where Sun had made some significant innovation.[68]

Sun's use of colorful narrative detail in his cases served the pedagogical function of showing how each encounter with a patient differed. In effect, Sun's casebook taught not only how to apply medical theory and prescriptions derived from a bewildering proliferation of books to an actual situation, but also how to cope with the complex social relations of a clinical practice. And he did so through a fusion of literary and personal authority. As he expressed the wish in his preface, he is making the casebook public so that "when practitioners of this profession who come after me open this book, it will be as though I am there guiding them."[69]

NOTES

Early drafts of this paper were presented at the Southern California China symposium on Chinese Medical Cases held at UCLA, January 1998, and the Berkeley conference on Cultural Studies of Chinese Science, Medicine, and Technology held February 1998. I am especially grateful to Charlotte Furth for helping me make sense of Sun's clinical reasoning. My thanks also to Yan Weikang, librarian at the Research Institute for Traditional Chinese Medicine in Bejing, for introducing me to Sun Yikui in the first place.

All references to Sun Yikui's writings are keyed to *Sun Yikui yixue quanshu.* The first number refers to the *juan,* the second to the page number; for the casebook, my calculation of the case number is also given.

1 Scholars have warned against confusing medical cases, even Freud's long cases, with fiction. See Marcus, "Freud and Dora"; Rothfield, *Vital Signs;* Hunter, *Doctors' Stories;* Epstein, *Altered Conditions;* Cohn, *The Distinction of Fiction.*

2 Chinese catalogues erroneously date the earliest published edition of the casebook, in the Research Institute of Chinese Medicine Library, to 1573 (*Quanguo Zhongyi tushu lianhe mulu,* 627) or to 1584 (*Zhongguo yiji tongkao,* 4949). My dating is based on internal evidence: a case dated 1593, and prefaces dated 1596 and 1599, which mention that the casebook is being published after Sun Yikui's other works.

3 The title refers to a parable about the legendary Yellow Emperor having left behind a "dark pearl" on a trip to a mythical Crimson Sea. For the allusion, see *Zhuangzi jinzhu jinyi,* "Tiandi," 302.

4 For a study of a medical publishing house operating in Hangzhou and Suzhou from the 1620s–1690s, see Widmer, "The Huangduzhai."

5 Sun's preface to *The Crimson Sea* describes the length and difficulty of the writing and publishing process. (In *Sun Yikui,* 13).

6 The list of readers and collators attached to *The Crimson Sea* most likely includes the names of some contributors in *Sun Yikui,* 14. The largest contributor to the casebook's publication was most likely Pan Jiansuo, a wealthy official in the Sanwu region. For Pan Jiansuo's offers to help finance the casebook's publication, see the letter he wrote to Sun ("Pan Jianshuo lao xiansheng ji"), which was printed in the earliest extant edition of the casebook in *Sun Yikui,* 723, and the account of a conversation in Sun Ye, "Zushu Shengsheng zi yi'an xiaoxu," in *Sun Yikui,* 712.

7 On the itinerant habits of doctors, see Grant, *A Chinese Physician,* though she links the dissemination of medical books to traveling merchants rather than to traveling doctors.

8 *The Crimson Sea,* in *Sun Yikui,* 12.232–12.233. On this therapeutic school of thought, see also Furth's chapter in this volume (chap. 4).

9 *The Purport of Medicine* (*Sun Yikui,* 2.677) includes a difficult case in which Sun goes to consult a teacher, taking his record of the patient's pulse diagnosis (*mai'an*) with him. Sun identifies the man as Huang Gutan, a disciple of Wang Ji and also from Anhui, but it is not clear how formally or for how long Sun studied with him. Sun does not mention having studied with this man in the autobiographical account in *The Crimson Sea,* suggesting that it was not a formal discipleship.

10 On Anhui medical culture, see Grant, *A Chinese Physician,* chap. 1. Chapter 4 of this volume (by Furth) points out that fully half of our published case histories in the Ming can be linked with men from this region. The first edition of *The Crimson Sea* was published by the famous Huang publishing house in Sheyi (Shexian), Anhui.

11 Wang Ji's *Shishan yi'an* included something over one hundred cases (Grant, *A Chinese Physician*); the casebook of Cheng Chongzhou, who practiced medicine in Yangzhou during the 1610s and 1620s, consisted of ninety-three cases in only two chapters (Furth, *A Flourishing Yin,* 226–265).

12 Zeitlin, *Historian of the Strange,* 3–4.

13 For examples, see Jiang Guan, comp., *Mingyi lei'an*, 8.242 and 2.74–2.75. Jiang's anthology of physicians' cases from antiquity to his own time was completed before his death in 1565 and circulated in manuscript form but wasn't published until 1591.

14 In fact, *Mingyi lei'an* is the sole source for nineteen otherwise lost entries from *Yijian zhi*, which are reprinted in Hong Mai, *Yijian zhi*, 4:1789–1796.

15 Sun Yikui, "Yi'an xiaoyin," in *Sun Yikui*, 713.

16 See Cullen, "Yi'an (case statements)," 304–305; and Sivin, *Medicine, Philosophy, and Religion*, 177–184.

17 Sun Yikui, "Yi'an xiaoyin," in *Sun Yikui*, 713.

18 Chandler, *England in 1819*, 208; and Jolles, *Formes Simples*, 137–158.

19 Chandler, *England in 1819*, 209.

20 "Fanli," in *Sun Yikui*, 724.

21 Hunter, *Doctors' Stories*, 21.

22 Ibid., 22–23.

23 Yong Rong et al., eds., *Siku quanshu zongmu*, 1:105.887.

24 For criticism, see *Zhongyi dacidian*, 93. For praise, see Han Xuejie and Zhang Yinsheng, "Sun Yikui yixue," 842.

25 A case in which he treats the wife of a bamboo craftsman is one of the few involving a lower-class patient (2.774 #151); the others involve mainly servants in the household of long-established patients.

26 The *Classic of Changes* is significant first because it is considered the foundational classic for the technical arts, and second, in Sun's first case friends introduce him to some patients because all of them share an interest in the *Classic of Changes*. This suggests that Sun regarded specialization in this classic as a family tradition that he participated in, both in a scholarly and medical capacity. The fourth essay in *The Purport of Medicine* (*Sun Yikui*, 648) is on the importance of the *Classic of Changes* for medicine and argues that any understanding of the one facilitates understanding of the other.

27 "Zixu" for *The Crimson Sea*, in *Sun Yikui*, 13.

28 Sima Qian, *Shiji*, chap. 105.

29 For example, the military genius of Chen Liang, later Marquis of Liu, is attributed to his being given a divine book as a boy in *Shiji*, chap. 55. On the "persistence of revelation" in accounts of the transmission of medical knowledge, see Sivin, *Medicine, Philosophy, and Religion*, 91–95.

30 *Bieji*, which could be published during a person's life as well as after his death, typically consisted of poetry, essays, and belles lettres; the book could be organized by genre or as an anthology of previous collections, but it usually followed some sort of rough chronological order.

31 For the term "annalistic autobiography," see Wu Pei-yi, *The Confucian's Progress*, 32–41. Works of this sort are composed in the form of year-by-year charts, but individual entries differ greatly as to length and detail. The earliest extant one dates from the thirteenth century, but the practice became more widespread in the sixteenth and seventeenth centuries and even more common during the eighteenth and nineteenth centuries.

32 *Sun Yikui,* 724.

33 "Zhang, Liu, Li, Zhu, Hua liu mingshi xiaozhuan," in *The Purport of Medicine, Sun Yikui,* 2.684.

34 Sima Qian, *Shiji,* 61.2127; Watson, trans., *Records of the Historian,* 11–15.

35 "Pan Jiansuo lao xiansheng ji," in *Sun Yikui,* 723. For a case history involving Pan, see 2.769 #137.

36 Furth, *A Flourishing Yin,* 242–244.

37 Cited in Han Xuejie and Zhang Yinsheng, "Sun Yikui yixue," 861.

38 An exception is case 149 (2.773), which Sun explicitly calls a "rare disease." Uncharacteristically, Sun says he has forgotten the name of the patient, a poor scholar, suggesting that it was the oddness of the illness that caused it to linger in his mind at all.

39 Indeed there are discussions of "vaginal protrusion" throughout the medical literature beginning with Chao Yuanfang, *Zhubing yuanhou lun* (610). An important reference for Sun in this case must have been the two cases of vaginal protrusion that Xue Ji (1487–1559) described in a commentary to his 1548 edited version of Chen Ziming's *Furen daquan liangfang.* (Yi-Li Wu, personal correspondence).

40 See Furth, "Body, Blood, and Gender"; and Bray, "A Deathly Disorder." Sun explicitly espouses this view in *The Crimson Sea.*

41 Leung, "Women Practicing Medicine," 119–120, discusses all three cases in which Sun competed with a female doctor in treating a patient. On the basis of this and other evidence, she argues that there was a considerable market not only for female midwives and popular female healers, but also for women doctors. On female doctors in the late Ming, see also Furth, *A Flourishing Yin,* chap. 8.

42 Barr, "The Wanli Context."

43 See, for instance, Chang, *The Late Ming Poet;* Ko, *Teachers of the Inner Chambers;* Wai-yee Li, "The Late Ming Courtesan."

44 I borrow the term "medical plot" from Hunter, *Doctors' Stories,* 65: "The medical plot, the narrative organization of the case, is shaped by the physician's quest for an understanding of the patient's illness: a diagnosis."

45 Barr, "The Wanli Context."

46 See Zeitlin, "The Life and Death of the Image."

47 Pu, *Liaozhai zhiyi,* 10.1389.

48 Ibid.

49 Sun treats him for an eye ailment in the first case in the book (1.735 #1) where he is introduced to Wu Xiaofeng and his brother by a clansman of Sun's because of their mutual interest in the *Classic of Changes.* In a later case (2.764 #121), Sun cures Wu of a digestive complaint, thereby leading to Wu's finally fathering a son at the age of fifty. Their friendship and professional relationship must have therefore been of some duration.

50 Sima Qian, *Shiji,* 105.2785–105.2794. On the close association between seeing and divining in early Chinese medicine, see Kuriyama, *The Expressiveness of the Body,* 178–179.

51 Furth, *A Flourishing Yin;* Bray, "A Deathly Disorder."

52 In the entry on *mengyi,* he mentions only one prescription that might be for women, because it is taken from the well-known medical work *Good Prescriptions for*

Women (*Furen liangfang*). But this reference occurs in an appendix to the *mengyi* category, labeled "spermatorrhea" (*jing hua bujin*), which again is ordinarily a male syndrome. Shapiro, in "The Puzzle of Spermatorrhea," 562, observes in his review of spermatorrhea and related syndromes in Chinese medical discourse that although "women's bodies also contained the vital essence jing, and as with men, it was regulated by the *shen* [Kidneys] . . . women fade from medical discussions of these disorders early on."

53 Zhang Jiebin, *Jingyue quanshu*, 19.357–19.359.

54 The phrase "wizard of detection" is from Hunter, *Doctors' Stories*, 22, where it is applied to Dr. Joe Bell, the Victorian physician whose lectures Arthur Conan Doyle attended while a medical student in Edinburgh. For the ancient Chinese doctor as "diviner," see Dewoskin, *Doctors, Diviners, and Magicians.*

55 These are "Postpartum Blood vertigo" (*chanhou xueyun;* 22.483), "Postpartum madness" (*chanhou diankuang;* 22.484), "Postpartum raving" (*chanhou kuangyan;* 22.484), and "Postpartum sudden hallucinations of ghosts or gods" (*chanhou zha jian guishen;* 23.486).

56 On the dangers of "noxious dew" for postpartum women and popular prescriptions for expelling and transforming this bloody vaginal discharge that were used to treat a variety of postpartum ailments, including raving or hallucination, see Yi-Li Wu, "Transmitted Secrets," 221–223.

57 "Postpartum Fright" (*chanhou xinshen jingji*), in *The Crimson Sea*, 23.486.

58 For example, see 2.756 #69, where too much heat enters the Blood Chamber, producing delirium as though the postpartum woman were seeing ghosts; or 1.751 #48, where a woman erroneously believed to be pregnant loses too much blood and becomes delirious; or 2.768 #135, where a postpartum young mother becomes delirious from not expelling noxious dew.

59 For a discussion of Sun's enormous debt to Zhu Zhenheng, see Han Xuejie and Zhang Yinsheng, "Sun Yikui yixue," 844–845.

60 Curiously, in this case Sun does not specifically mention any male relatives, such as husband or father-in-law, as involved in his dealings with the postpartum mother's treatment.

61 Recall his promotion of Wang Ji's essay refuting the taboo against ginseng quoted above. For a detailed discussion of Sun's views of ginseng, see Han Xuejie and Zhang Yinsheng, "Sun Yikui yixue," 844–845.

62 The entry describes "soul-calming powder" as something to be used when there is an abrupt postpartum loss of Blood and qi, or wild movements of depleted Fire with Blood following this Fire upward, resulting in a wild clouding of the senses, or when seeing sparks before one's eyes, and even losing consciousness altogether (*Sun Yikui*, 22.483). This powder is not part of the prescription given in the entry for "Postpartum suddenly seeing ghosts and spirits." There he suggests giving menstrual regulating powder (*diaojing san*) and cypress-nut powder (*boziren san*) instead (23.486).

63 Practioners of learned medicine during the Ming generally shunned acupuncture, preferring to rely instead on herbal cures. In Sun's *The Crimson Sea* entry for seeing ghosts or spirits postpartum (23.486), he cites a passage from Xue Ji, the reviser of *Complete Good*

Prescriptions for Women, that explains the syndrome at length in terms of either stagnant Blood or depleted Blood heating up, both of which will impair the workings of the Heart system and affect consciousness. Xue Ji's entry ends, "If this condition is really the result of haunting by a ghost, however, then it can be cured by using acupuncture on the 'ghost wailing point'" (*gui ku xue*) (20.452).

64 For other uses of the drugs as army metaphor in Sun's work, see his essay "Bu zhi fang shuo" (On not sticking to one formula), in *The Purport of Medicine* (*Sun Yikui,* 851–852).

65 For example, the beginning of *juan* 2 includes four cases: one involving his younger brother, one involving an unnamed woman, one involving a named clansman of his, and one involving an unnamed traveler (*Sun Yikui,* 676–679).

66 Gailus, "A Case of Individuality," 79.

67 "Bu zhi fang shuo," in *Sun Yikui,* 2.682–2.683.

68 See the "Fanli" to the casebook, in *Sun Yikui,* 724.

69 "Yian xiaoyin," in *Sun Yikui,* 713.

PART THREE
THE CASE IN RELIGION AND PHILOSOPHY

OVERLEAF: The eminent *gongan* Chan master Yuanwu Keqin and his two well-known disciples. Original illustration from *Yuanwu Chanshi Yulu,* 1298. Otani University collection. Image from *Chūgoku kodai hanga ten: Machida shisei 30-shūnen kinen, Nitchū Heiwa Yūkū Jōyaku teiketsu 10-shūnen kinen,* ed. Machida Shiritsu Kokusai Hanga Bijutsukan and Takimoto Hiroyuki. Machida-shi: Machida Shiritsu Kokusai Hanga Bijutsukan, 1988, p. 88.

7

How to Think with Chan *Gong'an*

ROBERT H. SHARF

A monk asked Zhaozhou: "Does a dog have buddha-nature?" Zhaozhou replied: "No."

This pithy exchange between an unidentified Buddhist monk and the Tang dynasty Chan master Zhaozhou Congshen (778–897) is perhaps the best-known example of a Chan *gong'an*, or "public case." Although the passage occurs in a collection of Zhaozhou's sayings supposedly compiled by his disciples, its notoriety is due to a Song dynasty master, Wumen Huikai (1183–1260), who placed this exchange at the beginning of his famous *gong'an* collection, *Gateless Barrier of the Chan Tradition* (*Chanzong wumen guan*, 1228).[1] Wumen's compilation, consisting of forty-four such exchanges and anecdotes accompanied by Wumen's comments, is one of the most important works of Chan literature. And as the first case in Wumen's collection, "Zhaozhou's dog" became the single most influential *gong'an* in the Chinese Chan, Korean Son, and Japanese Zen traditions. It is often the first and sometimes the only *gong'an* assigned to monks, and many traditional commentators claim, following Wumen's lead, that this single *gong'an* holds the key to all others.

Wumen's work was neither the earliest nor the most comprehensive compilation of Chan cases. Indeed, the *Gateless Barrier* is relatively short and straightforward in comparison to two earlier collections, the *Blue Cliff Record of Chan Master Foguo Yuanwu* (*Foguo Yuanwu Chanshi Biyan lu*), published in 1128, and the *Congrong Hermitage Record of the Commentaries by Old Wansong on the Case and Verse [Collection] by Reverend Jue of Tiantong [Mountain]* (*Wansong laoren pingzhang Tiantong Jue heshang songgu Congrongan lu*), published in 1224. The cases that make up these texts are each based on an individual anecdote, verbal exchange, or quandary known as the *benze* (original edict), to which has been added comments in prose and verse brushed by later masters. Whereas the *Gateless Barrier* contains forty-four such anecdotes accompanied by a brief comment and verse by Wumen, the *Blue Cliff Record* and *Congrong Hermitage Record* each contain one hundred cases including several layers of appended judgments, verses, and interlinear glosses. (The same "original edict" may appear in two or more collections, but the exegesis will invariably differ. More will be said about the structure of these collections below.) Many more *gong'an* collections gained currency in China, and the Chan tradition would come to speak of seventeen hundred authoritative cases (although this number was probably not meant to be taken literally). By the end of the Song the *gong'an* had assumed a central role in the ideological, literary, and institutional identity of the Chan school.

Popular books on Chan and Zen Buddhism present *gong'an* as intentionally incoherent or meaningless. They are, it is claimed, illogical paradoxes or unsolvable riddles intended to frustrate and short-circuit the intellect in order to quell thought and bring the practitioner to enlightenment. This understanding of *gong'an* is allied with a view of Chan as an iconoclastic and anti-intellectual tradition that rejects scripture, doctrine, philosophy, and indeed all forms of conceptual understanding in favor of unmediated or "pure" experience. *Gong'an* are intended, according to this view, not to communicate ideas so much as to induce a transformative experience. To grasp at the literal meaning of a Chan case is to miss its point.

Recently scholars have begun to question the instrumental view of Chan that underlies this approach to Chan cases, arguing that it is based on a misreading of the historical and ethnographic record.[2] Chan ranks among the most ritualistic forms of Buddhist monasticism, and a master's enlightenment is constituted within a prescribed set of institutional and ritual forms.[3] Moreover, the notion that Chan is designed to induce a nonconceptual or pure experience can be traced in part to late nineteenth- and early twentieth-century Japanese intellectuals such as D. T. Suzuki and Nishida Kitarō, who were culling from Western sources, notably William James.[4] The notion that Chan is anti-intellectual and repudiates "words and letters" is belied by the fact that the Chan tradition produced the largest literary corpus of any Buddhist school in East Asia.[5] This corpus consists in large part of "recorded sayings" (*yulu*) and "records of the transmission of the flame" (*chuandenglu*) texts—texts recounting the careers and teachings of past patriarchs from which the original edicts were drawn.

Scholars now appreciate that Chan is more complex than early apologists and enthusiasts cared to admit; it is no longer possible to reduce Chan practice and Chan literature to a mere means intended to engender a singular and ineffable spiritual experience. Accordingly, scholars of Chan *gong'an* have begun to attend to the institutional context and literary history of the genre,[6] and one scholar has devoted an entire monograph to the folkloric themes that appear in a single case.[7] Be that as it may, little progress has been made in deciphering the doctrinal and exegetical intent of Chan *gong'an;* it would appear that scholars remain reluctant to treat *gong'an* as a form of exegesis at all. This reluctance may be due to the enduring legacy of an earlier apologetic mystification of the *gong'an* literature. The primary objective of this chapter is to demonstrate that such reluctance is misguided and that it is indeed possible to recover the original meaning and doctrinal purport of at least some of the cases. The task is not easy, however, as the cases are philosophically subtle and hermeneutically sophisticated, and the authors of the collections delighted in obscure allusions, clever puns, and deft wordplay.

WHY "GONG'AN"?

The origins of the Buddhist use of the term *gong'an* remain obscure. The earliest references are associated with a handful of Chan masters from the Tang. Typical is the following anecdote from the biography of Chen Zunsu (780–877?)—a disciple of Huangbo Xiyun (d. ca. 850)—preserved in the *Jingde Era Record of the Transmission of the Lamp* (*Jingde chuandeng lu*).

> The master saw a monk coming and said: "[This] is an obvious case, but I spare you thirty blows." The monk said: "But this is the way that I am." The master said: "Why do the Vajra [guardians] at the monastery gate raise their fists?" The monk replied: "That is just the way they are." The master then hit him.[8]

The phrase "obvious case" (*xiancheng gong'an*) seems to mean "your guilt is written all over your face."[9] Coupled with the reference to a punishment of "thirty blows," the metaphor is clear: the master is figuratively positioned as a magistrate with the power to judge the defendant's "case" and to mete out appropriate punishment.

Tang references to *gong'an* are, however, rare. The phrase "[This] is an obvious case [*xiancheng gong'an*], but I spare you thirty blows" is repeated in the collected sayings of Yunmen Wenyan (864–949), where it is again attributed to Chen Zunsu.[10] The term *gong'an* appears twice again in Yunmen's text, referring in each instance to a legal or criminal case; for example, "Someone asked Yunmen: 'If a totally ignorant one comes, how do you help him?' The master replied: 'Both cases [his and yours] are taken care of by a single indictment'" (*liangchong gong'an yizhuan lingguo*).[11] There is no evidence in this or in any other ostensibly Tang work that *gong'an* referred to a particular anecdote, utterance, or literary genre.

I say "ostensibly Tang" since the texts in which these references appear were all redacted during the Song dynasty and thus must be used with caution. The *Jingde Record*—the text from which the Chen Zunsu anecdote was drawn—was not completed until 1004, and the oldest extant recension of Yunmen's collected sayings dates to 1267.[12] There is, to my knowledge, no conclusive evidence as to the pre-Song use, if any, of the term *gong'an* in a Buddhist context. That the term does not appear anywhere in the voluminous *Patriarchs Hall Anthology* (*Zutang ji*)—a comprehensive compilation of Chan biographies filled with *gong'an*-like anecdotes and dialogues published in 952—suggests that it was used rarely if at all in pre-Song Buddhism.

While the early history of the term *gong'an* is obscure, by the Southern Song it was commonly used in Buddhist sources to refer to a short anecdote or verbal exchange culled from the records of eminent patriarchs and subjected to written commentary—the "judgment"—in prose and verse. This use of *gong'an* was intended, it would seem, to liken these documents to the records of criminal cases that were set on a magistrate's desk (*an*) and used as legal precedents.[13] Such cases publicly attested to and were determinant of the magistrate's authority; in an analogous way the Chan *gong'an* came to embody and warrant the abbot's authority—his mastery of the tradition he inherited from his forebears—and to facilitate the instruction and evaluation of his students. The connection between the two sorts of *gong'an* is expressed eloquently in the Yuan-period preface to the *Blue Cliff Record* by Sanjiao Laoren dated 1304.[14]

> The practice of calling the writings of the teachings of the patriarchs "public cases" [*gong'an*] started during the Tang dynasty and became popular during the Song dynasty, so it has a long history. The two words ["public case"] are an expression referring to official documents of secular law. There are three uses. When the work of facing a wall [in meditation] is accomplished and the task of traveling by foot [in pilgrimage] is done, the zero point of the scale is hard to clarify, and it is easy to fall into the path of wild foxes. Perceptive people test for this, scolding and shouting to see the real extent of attainment, like an old magistrate reviewing a criminal case, seeing all the underlying facts, not missing a single point.
>
> Next, from the time of [Huineng] the waters of the Western River have still not been drunk,[15] and it is easy to despair over the sheep lost on the branching road.[16] Just as the compass needle always points south, out of compassion one is shown the way. Each blow of the staff, leaving a welt, is to bring about understanding. This is like an officer of the court reviewing a legal case and reversing the sentence, saving someone from death. This is the second use.
>
> Next after that, damaging crops is a serious concern, and hitching one's donkey is a weighty matter.[17] Students of chess need to concentrate, and it is easy to lament the color of dyed thread. For this reason the great teachers handed down instructions that the mind is to die on the [meditation] cushion. Each action, each inquiry is like an official promulgating an order, directing people to read the regulations and know the law, extinguishing bad thoughts as soon as they arise. This is the third use.

Providing written records of their case judgments, and setting out their circumstances and scope so that they might serve as standards and imperatives—from the very beginning [Chan cases] are no different than secular books of canon law. This seems to be why the patriarchal teachers established public cases and left them for the guidance of the monastic community.[18]

A similar analysis of the legal metaphor is found in *Evening Talks in a Mountain Hut* (*Shanfang yehua*) by Zhongfeng Mingben (1263–1323).

Someone asked: "Why is it that the [records of the teaching] devices and encounters of the buddhas and patriarchs are commonly called public cases [*gong'an*]?" Huan [Zhongfeng] replied: "Public cases" are likened to case documents of the public court [*gongfu zhi andu*]. They embody the law, and thus the control of disorder through the Kingly Way truly depends on them. "Public" [*gong*] pertains to the ultimate principle [*li*] by which the sages unify the wheel ruts and standardize the roads throughout the empire. "Cases" [*an*] are the authoritative writings recording the principles set forth by the sages. There has never been an empire without public courts, and there has never been a public court without case documents that are regarded as law and are used to eliminate impropriety throughout the empire. When public cases are utilized the principles and laws are put into effect; when principles and laws are put into effect the empire is rectified; when the empire is rectified the Kingly Way prevails. . . .

Those who are widely regarded as elders [i.e., Chan patriarchs] are the senior administrators of the monastic "court" [*conglin gongfu zhi zhangshi*]. Their collected records are the "case documents" [*andu*] that record their inspiring pronouncements. Occasionally, when men of old had some respite from teaching their disciples or when their private doors were shut, they would turn to [these documents] and select some out [*nian*], categorize them [*pan*], comment on them in verse [*song*], and supply alternate responses [*bie*] to them. Surely it was not just to show off their own erudition or to contradict the ancient worthies. Rather it was because they were pained to think that the great dharma might be misapprehended in the future. Thus they resorted to such expedients to open the wisdom eye of all who followed, with the hope that it would enable them all to realize it [for themselves].

They are called "public" [*gong*] because they mitigate private understanding, [and they are called] "cases" [*an*] because they are guaranteed to tally precisely with the buddhas and patriarchs. Thus when the public cases are penetrated, passion comes to an end; when passion comes to an end, birth and death are emptied; when birth and death are emptied, the buddha-way prevails. . . .

If ordinary people have some matter that they cannot resolve by themselves, they seek a decision from the public courts, and there the officials select [the appropriate] case records [*andu*] and, on the basis of them, settle the matter. Similarly, a student has something he wishes to understand but he cannot settle it himself, so questions his teacher about it, [and the teacher] selects the appropriate public case [*gong'an*] and settles it.

Now, the public case is the torch of wisdom that illuminates the darkness of the passions, the golden scraper that cuts away the film clouding the eye, the sharp ax that severs the life-root of birth and death, the divine mirror that reflects the original face of both the sage and the commoner. Through it the intention of the patriarchs is made abundantly clear, the buddha-mind is opened and revealed. For the essentials of complete transcendence, final emancipation, total penetration, and identical attainment, nothing surpasses the public case.[19]

These oft-quoted passages by Sanjiao Laoren and Zhongfeng Mingben attest to the salience of the legal metaphor in Chan literary circles. We will see below that the metaphor is apt: Chan *gong'an,* like the other forms of case writing explored in this volume, were intended to embody and facilitate an approach to knowledge that we call "thinking in cases." However, these Yuan-period texts have also been used by twentieth-century commentators to support the notion that *gong'an* were intended to evoke a mystical or spiritual experience. As such, before exploring just what "thinking in cases" means in a Chan context, it is necessary to put to rest once and for all the notion that *gong'an* were devoid of content or meaning. I will begin with a detailed analysis of a single *gong'an,* namely "Zhaozhou's dog." This case turns out to be a short but elegant commentary on a contentious medieval debate concerning the buddha-nature of insentient objects. While the recovery of this arcane debate will require an excursus into pre-Song Buddhist scholasticism, our efforts will pay off. For just as Chan masters promise, "Zhaozhou's dog" turns out to be the key that unlocks the entire *gong'an* tradition.

THE BUDDHA-NATURE OF INSENTIENT OBJECTS

In order to appreciate the original import of "Zhaozhou's dog" it is necessary to reconstruct the medieval debate over whether insentient objects possess buddha-nature. The doctrine of the buddha-nature of the insentient (*wuqing foxing*) first emerged during the seventh and eighth centuries and held that not only do all sentient beings inherently possess the nature of buddhahood, but so do plants and trees, stones and tiles, and even particles of dust. Stated in this manner it might appear as simply another expression of the familiar Mahayana teaching of emptiness: since the existence of something always depends on the existence of something else, there is nothing that possesses an abiding essence or "intrinsic-nature" (*zixing;* Sk. *svabhāva*), and thus everything is ultimately the same, inherently pure, and quiescent.

Nevertheless, the claim that insentient objects possess buddha-nature would have sounded odd, if not preposterous, to a medieval cleric. As early critics were quick to point out, the doctrine contravened well-known passages in authoritative Mahayana scriptures. Moreover, there were no recorded cases of an insentient object actually attaining enlightenment and becoming a buddha. In response, early proponents of the doctrine appealed to the notion of skillful means and to systems of "tenet classification" (*panjiao*) to defend themselves: they dismissed scriptural passages that contravened their position as provisional teachings for those of limited capacity. While the debate would continue throughout the medieval period, by the Song period the buddha-nature of the insentient had gained wide acceptance in both Tiantai and Chan circles, and it was embraced by many eminent Japanese monks as well.

To understand the doctrine we must go back to the fifth century, when the monk Daosheng (360–434) first advanced the position that all sentient beings, including *icchantika* (*yichanti*), possess buddha-nature.[20] The claim was contentious: the technical Sanskrit term *icchantika* refers to precisely those sentient beings who lack the potential for buddhahood, as stated explicitly in the six-fascicle version of the *Nirvāṇa-sūtra.* According to this text, translated sometime between 410 and 418, while buddha-nature is eternal, *icchantika* do not possess it.[21] Daosheng disagreed, insisting that *icchantika* also possess the seeds of buddha-nature and will one day attain buddhahood.

Daosheng's position was vindicated with the appearance of Dharmakṣema's translation of the *Nirvāṇa-sūtra* in 421. This so-called "northern recension" is not consistent on the topic, but it does contain a few passages indicating that all sentient beings—including *icchantika*—possess buddha-nature and will eventually attain enlightenment. This text is accordingly celebrated as the earliest and most important canonical statement of the universality of buddha-nature in China. However, the possession of buddha-nature is unambiguously restricted to the sentient: "'Non-buddha-nature' refers to insentient things such as walls and fences, tiles and stones. Everything apart from insentient things such as these is called 'buddha-nature.'"[22] This understanding prevailed throughout the Northern and Southern dynasties.

The developments that would lay the groundwork for the buddha-nature of the insentient position did not begin until over a century later. This is usually traced to the sixth-century monk Jingying Huiyuan (523–592), who was interested in the relationship between the buddha-nature doctrine set out in the *Nirvāṇa-sūtra* and the notion of "originally pure mind." In his *Essay on the Meaning of the Great Vehicle* (*Dacheng yizhang*), Huiyuan makes a pivotal distinction between the "buddha-nature that knows" (*nengzhi xing*) and the "buddha-nature that is known" (*suozhi xing*). The former is described as the "mind of true consciousness" (*zhenshi xin*) that is capable of awakening to buddha-nature through the elimination of ignorance. Huiyuan explains that "this nature is situated in sentient beings and does not extend to the insentient." Thus when the *Nirvāṇa-sūtra* restricts possession of buddha-nature to the sentient, it is referring to the "buddha-nature that knows." The latter, the "nature that is known," is identified with the dharma-realm, emptiness, ultimate truth, and so on. Huiyuan explicitly says that this aspect of buddha-nature is universal, penetrating everywhere, one implication being that it extends to insentient as well as to sentient things.[23]

This categorical bifurcation is in some respects structurally analogous to our distinction between epistemology and ontology, insofar as it distinguishes between buddha-nature as a rarefied and nondualistic mode of cognition or apprehension and buddha-nature as the ground of being that makes such a cognition possible. This conceptual structure will find its way into much of the subsequent theorizing on the subject.

While Huiyuan has all the pieces in place, he never actually states that insentient objects possess buddha-nature. The first to do so appears to have been the Sanlun exegete Jizang (549–623). Jizang takes a somewhat different approach to the issue. Rather than dividing buddha-nature into two aspects, one of which is associated with the insentient and one of which is not, Jizang argues that the distinction between sentient and insentient is itself empty.[24] Thus if you are going to deny buddha-nature to something,

> then not only are grasses and trees devoid of buddha-nature, but living beings are also devoid of buddha-nature. But if you hold to the existence of buddha-nature, then it is not only living beings that have buddha-nature, but grasses and trees must also have buddha-nature.... If we understand that all dharmas are equal and do not view the two marks of the contingent and the absolute, then in reality there are no marks of attainment or non-attainment. Since there is no non-attainment, we provisionally speak of attaining buddhahood. Thus at the moment when sentient beings attain buddhahood, all grasses and trees also attain buddhahood.[25]

For Jizang, the rubric of buddha-nature is merely another way of affirming emptiness, dependent origination, and the middle way, from which vantage point all distinctions disappear. Nonetheless, Jizang immediately goes on to qualify his thesis, conceding that his analysis proceeds from the perspective of "pervasiveness" (*tongmen*). From the perspective of "difference" (*biemen*), however, one can indeed distinguish between sentient and insentient.

> Because sentient beings have mental delusions, they can attain awakening. Grasses and trees have no mind, and thus they have no delusion. What would it mean for

> them to obtain awakening? It is like waking from a dream: if you are not dreaming, then you cannot wake up from it. Therefore it is said [in the *Nirvāṇa-sūtra*] that since sentient beings possess buddha-nature they can attain buddhahood, but since grasses and trees are devoid of buddha-nature they cannot attain buddhahood.[26]

Thus while Jizang is willing to come out and declare, perhaps for the first time, that insentient objects possess buddha-nature, he nevertheless strives to remain consistent with the teachings of the *Nirvāṇa-sūtra* by restricting the *attainment* of enlightenment to the sentient.

By the early Tang the doctrine of universal buddha-nature, or the ultimate identity of the Buddha and all beings, had become a hallmark of orthodoxy among most Chinese Buddhist commentators. But the urge toward increasingly comprehensive and expansive rhetorical formulations would inevitably run up against the scripturally sanctioned dichotomy between the sentient and the insentient. Exegetes were thus forced to reproduce the hermeneutic strategies pioneered by Huiyuan and Jizang. The renowned Huayan exegete Fazang (643–712), for example, much like Huiyuan, distinguishes between epistemology and ontology in order to assert the buddha-nature of the insentient without contravening the letter of the *Nirvāṇa-sūtra*.[27] And Jizang's distinction between the nondualistic perspective of the absolute versus the contingent perspective of the phenomenal realm amounts to much the same thing. In each case there is a palpable reluctance to contest scriptural authority.

The full development of the doctrine that insentient things have buddha-nature is usually associated with the Tiantai school, particularly with the ninth Tiantai patriarch Zhanran (711–782). We will see that this is misleading; Zhanran was following the lead of certain prominent Chan masters of his day. Be that as it may, Zhanran is one of the first to directly challenge the authority of the *Nirvāṇa-sūtra* on this issue.

As the self-conscious architect of Tiantai orthodoxy, Zhanran denies the originality of his position, claiming to find precedent in the *Great Calming and Discernment* (*Mohe zhiguan*).[28] In fact, we know that neither Zhiyi nor his student Guanding—the authors of the *Great Calming and Discernment*—countenanced the buddha-nature of the insentient.[29] In order to bring his own doctrine into line with the writings of his predecessors, Zhanran plays the *upāya* card: he insists that while Guanding understood that insentient objects possess buddha-nature, he couldn't say so as the times were not yet right.[30]

The most comprehensive presentation of Zhanran's views on this subject is found in his *Adamantine Scalpel* (*Jin'gang bei*), a short work written around 780, not long before his death, devoted exclusively to the defense and clarification of the buddha-nature of the insentient. His argument is simple: Mahayana doctrine 1) insists on the universality of buddha-nature, and 2) will not ultimately brook a distinction between sentient and insentient things. "The individual of the perfect [teaching] knows, from beginning to end, that the absolute principle is non-dual, and that there are no objects apart from mind. Who then is sentient? What then is insentient? Within the Assembly of the Lotus there are no differences."[31] According to Zhanran, statements to the contrary, such as the notorious passage in the *Nirvāṇa-sūtra,* must be understood as *pratipakṣa*—they are intended as expedient antidotes to particular misconceptions and thus must not be taken at face value.

Zhanran was the first to devote an entire treatise to the defense of buddha-nature of the insentient. The fact that *Adamantine Scalpel* was the only treatise (i.e., a *lun,* as opposed to a scriptural commentary) that he ever wrote and that it was his last composition suggests that the doctrine was of particular significance to him. Why would he have devoted so much energy to this single and somewhat idiosyncratic concern? While the available sources may be insufficient to provide a definitive answer, there is evidence that the doctrine had emerged as a pressing and controversial issue in eighth-century Buddhist circles. It seems that the immediate pretext for Zhanran's work was not the scholastic arguments advanced by earlier generations of Dilun, Sanlun, and Huayan commentators so much as the unorthodox positions touted by certain of Zhanran's contemporaries—contemporaries associated with early Chan.

BUDDHIST HERMENEUTICS

Before launching into the Tang Chan debate over the buddha-nature of the insentient, a few words are in order concerning what might be called the epistemological attitude of early Chan. Chan thought emerged, in part, out of an extended reflection by Buddhist philosophers on the contingency of knowledge, the vagaries of interpretation, and the nature of representation. This reflection gave rise to a version of linguistic relativism—to the perception of a gap between signifier and signified, between the contingent and the absolute, or, to use a common Buddhist motif, between the finger and the moon. At times such reflection threatened to destabilize Buddhist claims to truth, and notions such as the two truths, inherent buddha-nature, or matrix of buddhahood (Sk. *tathāgatagarbha*) might be seen as prophylactic contrivances used to shield the tradition from the ineludible force of its own dialectical and deconstructive logic.

This hermeneutic skepticism should not be mistaken for the modern problem of the historicization of truth; Chinese Buddhist exegetes, like their Confucian counterparts, were not drawn to parse "truth" and "history." Buddhists did not, in other words, hold to the modernist episteme that places the locus of historical truth in an impersonal "past" to which we no longer have immediate access.

Which is to say that they did not view the world through the metaphysical divide of constructed human knowledge versus objective reality, of value versus fact. Buddhist exegetes tended to appraise the veracity of historical truth not with respect to some value-neutral notion of past as such, but rather in terms of a transhistorical politico-ethical truth—the dharma or the Way—that is indeed knowable. (As many have noted, the distinctions between nature and culture, between fact and value, and between history and past have little purchase given the Chinese understanding of the interrelationship between heaven, earth, and the human realm.) Thus the perspective of the observer—one's humanity—is not something to be overcome in the interest of objectivity, since truth is a function of human concern. But this does not render truth relative, since human concern is woven into the fabric of the cosmos. Chinese Buddhist historical writing, like most forms of medieval Chinese historical exegesis, was, in short, a vehicle for moral suasion—the value of a historical narrative lay not in its fidelity to the inchoate otherness of the past but in its fidelity to an atemporal yet eminently knowable truth.

In short, the problem for Chinese Buddhists, and a recurring theme in Chan literature, was not that truth is historically contingent, but rather that truth, while immanent and unchanging, allows for no mediation or representation.

There are a number of Indian Buddhist doctrines to which we might turn in looking for the roots of this attitude. Early Buddhist texts likened the Buddha's teaching to a raft used to cross a river; having crossed the river the raft should be left behind lest it become a burden. Likewise, Chinese Buddhists spoke of a finger pointing toward the moon; one's attention should not dwell on the finger but rather on the moon to which it points. The teachings of the Buddha are like the raft or the finger—they are contrivances or "skillful means" (*fangbian;* Sk. *upāya*) indicating the Way. Any such contrivance will become an obstacle if mistaken for the truth itself.

In Mahayana Perfection of Wisdom (Prajñāpāramitā) texts we begin to find a far more powerful and all-encompassing attack on knowledge as such. Chan exegetes, as heirs to Perfection of Wisdom and Mādhyamika dialectic, pushed the notion of skillful means to its logical conclusion, becoming deeply skeptical of any and all constructs. They were radical contextualists who were, at times, willing to cast doubt on anything and everything, famously including the Buddha himself. Many well-known sayings (later to appear as *gong'an*) come to mind: "If you meet the Buddha, kill the Buddha; if you meet the patriarch, kill the patriarch" (*fengfo shafo, fengzu shazu*).[32] And "A monk asked Yunmen, 'What is Buddha?' Yunmen replied, 'A dry shit-stick.'"[33]

At the same time, the deconstructive rhetoric of Chan did not mitigate the imperative to practice. Monks continued to engage in the panoply of monastic rituals and ceremonies, including contemplation/invocation of the Buddha (*nianfo*), recitation of "magical" formulae (*dhāraṇī*) and scripture, image veneration, and so on. Chan doctrine, best exemplified by the *gong'an* genre, functioned not as a prescriptive model but as a metacritique that existed alongside orthodox monastic practice, serving as a reminder of the contingency of all forms, including the teachings of the Buddha himself. As we will see below, the "case method" turns out to be particularly well suited to a philosophical position that is distinguished by its suspicion of all positions, including its own.

EARLY CHAN AND THE BUDDHA-NATURE OF INSENTIENT OBJECTS

The *Record of the Masters and Disciples of the Laṅkāvatāra* (*Lengqie shizi ji*), a text recovered from the "library cave" at Dunhuang and attributed to Jingjue (683–ca. 750), is believed to date from the early years of the Kaiyuan period (713–742).[34] It consists of a string of biographies of the first seven generations of patriarchs associated with the Northern school of Chan. The issue of the buddha-nature of the insentient first appears in the biography of the fourth Chan patriarch Daoxin (580–651), who says, "The *Nirvāṇa-sūtra* says: 'All beings have buddha-nature.' If you say that walls, fences, tiles, and stones do not have buddha-nature, then how could they preach the dharma?"[35] And in the biography of the fifth patriarch Hongren (601–674) that immediately follows we find the following.

> [Hongren] said: "The Buddha has thirty-two marks. Do jars also have the thirty-two marks or not? Do pillars have the thirty-two marks or not? Proceeding in the same way we ask if earth, trees, tiles and stones have the thirty-two marks or not?" ... He also said: "At the moment when you are in the temple sitting in meditation, is your body also sitting in meditation beneath the trees of the mountain forests or not? Are earth, trees, tiles, and stones also able to sit in meditation or not? Are earth, trees, tiles, and stones able to see forms and hear sounds, wear a robe and carry a bowl, or not? When the *Laṅkāvatāra-sūtra* speaks of the dharma-body of the realm of objects, it [refers to] precisely this.[36]

Both Daoxin and Hongren allude to the nonduality of the subjective and objective realms, as well as to the doctrine, closely associated with the *Laṅkāvatāra-sūtra,* that "all is mind." This leads to the inference that even the inanimate objects of our perception can be said to possess buddha-nature and to preach the dharma. While we do not know whether this accurately depicts the teachings of either Daoxin or Hongren, the passages do attest to an interest in the issue among Chan monks in the first half of the eighth century.

The *Record of the Masters and Disciples* is not an isolated example. The *Treatise on the Transcendence of Cognition* (*Jueguan lun*) is a short text associated with the Ox-head lineage (Niutou zong), six manuscript copies of which were recovered from Dunhuang. It was likely composed by a later Ox-head teacher sometime during the third quarter of the eighth century, that is, just around the time that Zhanran was formulating his own position on the buddha-nature of the insentient.[37] The text takes the form of a conversation between a teacher named "Attainment" (Ruli) and his disciple "Gateway" (Yuanmen). About one-third of the way into the text we find the following exchange.

> Gateway asks, "Is the Way found only in embodied spiritual entities, or does it reside in grasses and trees as well?" Attainment says, "There is no place the Way does not pervade." [Gateway] asks, "If the Way is pervasive, why is it a crime to kill a person, whereas it is not a crime to kill grasses and trees?" [Attainment] answered, "Talk of whether it is a crime or not is a matter related to sentience and is thus not the true Way. It is only because worldly people have not attained the Way and falsely believe in a personal self that their murder entails mental [intent]. This intent bears karmic fruit, and thus we speak of it as a crime. Grasses and trees have no sentience and thus originally are in accord with the Way. As they are free of a self, there is no calculation involved in killing them, and thus we do not argue over whether it is a crime or not.
>
> Now one who is free of a self and is in accord with the Way looks at his own body as he would at grasses or at trees. He treats the cutting of his own body as do trees in a forest. . . .
>
> [Gateway] asks, "If grasses and trees have long been in accord with the Way, why do the scriptures not record instances of grasses or trees becoming buddhas but only of persons [becoming buddhas]?" [Attainment] answers, "They do not only record persons but record grasses and trees [becoming buddhas] as well. A scripture says, 'A single mote of dust contains all dharmas.' Another says, 'All dharmas are suchness; all sentient beings are also suchness.'[38] Suchness is devoid of any duality or discrimination."[39]

This work represents a significant departure from the arguments advanced by the Sanlun, Tiantai, and Huayan scholiasts discussed above. On the one hand, the *Treatise on the Transcendence of Cognition* accepts that, from a worldly perspective, grasses and trees are indeed insentient. But precisely because they lack mind and sentience and thus have no thought of "me" or "mine," grasses and trees are "in accord with the Way." The treatise goes so far as to claim scriptural support for the view that insentient things actually become buddhas. The way to buddhahood is the way of insentience: one must put an end to discernment and become mindless (*wuxin*). Then, like the grasses and trees, you will be one with the Way and utterly unconcerned with death.

A similar position is attributed to the Northern Chan master Shenxiu (605?–706) in the admittedly late *Record of the Mirror of the Tradition* (*Zongjing lu*), a text compiled by Yongming Yanshou (904–975) and published in 961. Shenxiu teaches that "when sentient beings cultivate realization, insentient beings also cultivate realization." There is ultimately no distinction between self and other, or consciousness and its objects.[40]

This fragmentary evidence suggests an interest among some early teachers associated with the Northern and the Ox-head Chan lineages in a somewhat radical version of the doctrine, in which insentient objects actually "cultivate realization" and "become buddhas."

However, not all of the early Chan leaders agreed; some prominent figures found the buddha-nature of the insentient position untenable. One of the more strident critiques of the doctrine is found in the record of Heze Shenhui (684–758)—the de facto "founder" of the Southern school of Chan—in which he debates a representative of the Ox-head lineage.

> Chan Master Yuan of Ox-Head Mountain asked: "[You say that] buddha-nature permeates all sentient things and does not permeate all insentient things. I heard a venerable elder say:
>
> Lush groves of emerald bamboos,
> Are wholly the dharma-body.
> Luxuriant clusters of chrysanthemums,
> Nothing is not gnosis [*prajñā*].[41]
>
> Now why do you say that [buddha-nature] only permeates sentient things and does not permeate insentient things?" [Shenhui] answered: "Surely you do not mean that the merit of groves of emerald bamboos equals that of the dharma-body, or that the wisdom of clusters of chrysanthemums is the same as gnosis? If the groves of bamboos and chrysanthemums are equal to the dharma-body and to gnosis, then in which sūtra does the Tathāgata record a case of an emerald bamboo or a chrysanthemum attaining awakening [*bodhi*]? The notion that emerald bamboos and chrysanthemums are the same as the dharma-body and gnosis is a heterodox doctrine. Why so? Because the *Nirvāṇa-sūtra* says: 'That which lacks buddha-nature is deemed an insentient thing.' "[42]

This exchange, as well as others to be discussed below, attest to the controversial status of the doctrine in the mid-eighth century.[43] Moreover, there is reason to believe that Shenhui and his followers flagged the doctrine as a means to distinguish themselves from their Northern Chan rivals. Recall that the *Record of the Masters and Disciples* depicts the fifth patriarch Hongren as a supporter of the buddha-nature of the insentient—Hongren suggests that even jars, pillars, tiles, and stones have the thirty-two marks of enlightenment. However, the *Platform Scripture of the*

Sixth Patriarch (*Liuzu tanjing*)—the Southern Chan scripture par excellence—has Hongren espousing the very opposite. In a list of "transmission verses" near the end of the Dunhuang version of the text, Hongren's verse is given as follows.

> Sentient beings come and lay down seeds,
> And insentient flowers grow.
> Without sentiency and without seeds,
> The ground of mind produces nothing.[44]

The doctrinal purport of the verse is not as clear as it might be, so it is not surprising that later versions of the verse found in the *Patriarchs Hall Anthology*,[45] the *Jingde Record*,[46] and the "vulgate" edition of the *Platform Scripture* published in 1291[47] modify the text so as to make Hongren's opposition to the doctrine unmistakable.

> Sentient beings come and lay down seeds,
> From the earth fruit is produced.
> Without sentiency and without seeds,
> There is no [buddha-]nature and nothing is produced.

Moreover, this altered verse no longer appears in the list of transmission verses appended somewhat haphazardly toward the end of the Dunhuang text. Instead, in later recensions it has been moved to the very heart of Huineng's autobiographical narrative; it figures in the secret transmission ceremony in which Huineng receives the dharma from Hongren. A transmission verse presumably exemplified the essence of a master's wisdom, as well as his distinctive "teaching style" (*feng*). It is thus significant that the core of Hongren's verse is a critique of the buddha-nature of the insentient doctrine. Shenhui and his heirs evidently viewed this as a "wedge issue" through which to distinguish themselves from their rivals. In the process they depict Hongren, whom they claimed as their own, as espousing a position contrary to that ascribed to him in the *Record of the Masters and Disciples*.

As the Southern school gained ascendancy in the mid-Tang, other masters would reiterate Shenhui's opposition to the buddha-nature of the insentient, including Dazhu Huihai (n.d.). The second fascicle of his *Essentials for Entering the Way of Sudden Enlightenment* (*Dunwu rudao yaomen*) contains a number of exchanges on the issue,[48] including the following.

> Deluded people do not know that the dharma-body has no appearance, but manifests form in response to things. Thus they say that, "Lush groves of emerald bamboos are wholly the dharma-body; luxuriant clusters of chrysanthemums, nothing is not gnosis [*prajñā*]." But if chrysanthemums were gnosis, gnosis would

> be the same as the insentient, and if emerald bamboos were the dharma-body, then the dharma-body would be the same as grasses and trees. Then when people munch on bamboo shoots, they must be munching on the dharma-body. . . .
>
> A master who lectured on the Huayan scripture asked: "Does the Chan Master believe that insentient things are buddha or not?" The Master said: "I don't believe it. For if insentient things were buddha, then living people would be inferior to the dead. Even dead donkeys and dead dogs would be superior to a living person. A scripture says: 'The buddha-body is precisely the dharma-body; it is born of the precepts, meditation, and wisdom; it is born from the three wisdoms and the six supernormal powers; it is born from all the excellent dharmas.' If you claim that insentient things are the Buddha, then were you, venerable one, to die right now, you would be a buddha."[49]

Note that Huihai is responding to the same aphorism that appears in Shenhui's work and that he advances similar arguments to dismiss the buddha-nature of the insentient doctrine as simply absurd. This was also the position of the Chan master Huangbo Xiyun (d. ca. 850), later celebrated for his doctrine that buddha and mind are one. Huangbo's logic is simple: since buddha is mind, only things that possess mind are buddha.[50]

Ironically, the identification of buddha and mind is the center of the most eloquent and influential Chan statement in *support* of the buddha-nature of the insentient, that by Nanyang Huizhong (675–775). Huizhong was a contemporary of Shenhui and is credited by the later Chan tradition with the teaching that insentient things not only possess buddha-nature, but also actually "preach the dharma." We have already seen that according to the *Record of the Masters and Disciples* the fourth patriarch may have beat him to it. Nevertheless, Huizhong's position on the subject is perhaps the most developed in the history of the debate, and I will, accordingly, quote a few representative passages from his writings.

> A Chan student asked: "What is the meaning of the saying 'the mind of an old buddha'?" The Master said: "Insentient things such as walls, fences, tiles, and stones are all the mind of an old buddha." The Chan student said: "But this is at odds with the scriptures. The *Nirvāṇa-sūtra* says: 'Everything apart from insentient things such as walls, fences, tiles and stones is called buddha-nature.' Now you say that all insentient things are the mind of buddha, but you have yet to consider the relationship between 'mind' and 'nature.' Are they different or not?" The Master said, "To the deluded they are different; to the enlightened they are not different."[51] . . .
>
> The student asked: "Within the teachings of the scriptures one only sees sentient beings receiving the prophecy of future perfect enlightenment and then, at

some future time, becoming a buddha named so-and-so. One never sees an insentient being receiving the prophecy of future perfect enlightenment and becoming a buddha. Among the thousand buddhas of the current Bhadra *kalpa,* if there is a single case of an insentient object becoming buddha, please show it to me." The Master said: "I now ask you, imagine a prince at the time of his coronation as king. Does the person of the prince receive the kingship [all at once], or must every territory in the kingdom be individually bestowed upon him?" [The student] replied: "When the prince is crowned king, everything in the kingdom becomes his. What need is there for him to receive anything else?" The Master said: "The present case is just the same: at the moment when sentient beings receive the prophecy of their future buddhahood, all the lands of the three-thousand great-thousand worlds are completely subsumed within the body of Vairocana Buddha. Beyond the body of the Buddha, could there still be some insentient object to receive the prophecy?"[52] . . .

[The student] asked: "A venerable elder has said:

> Lush groves of emerald bamboos,
> Are wholly suchness.
> Luxuriant clusters of chrysanthemums,
> Nothing is not gnosis.

Some people do not accept this teaching while others believe in it. The words are inconceivable, and I do not know what to make of it." The Master said: "This pertains to the realms of great beings such as Samantabhadra and Mañjusrī; it is not something that lesser men are able to believe and accept. This teaching is fully in accord with the intent of the superlative scriptures of the Mahayana. Thus the *Huayan Sūtra* says: 'The buddha-body fills the dharma-realm and manifests itself before all beings. It responds in accord with conditions, extending everywhere, yet it remains constantly ensconced on the seat of awakening.'[53] As emerald bamboos do not lie beyond the dharma-realm, are they not the dharma-body? Moreover, the *Mahāprajñāpāramitā-sūtra* says: 'Since matter is boundless, gnosis is also boundless.'[54] As chrysanthemums are but matter, are they not gnosis?"[55]

The last passage suggests that the aphorism about the bamboos and chrysanthemums was a focal point for the buddha-nature of the insentient controversy, and Huizhong may well have been responding to the teachings of Shenhui (or vice versa). In many respects, Huizhong's eloquent if intellectually diffuse position represents a logical terminus for the buddha-nature of the insentient position; it is difficult to know where one might go after invoking the notion that the universe itself is the body of Vairocana Buddha and that insentient things are constantly preaching the dharma. While others would weigh in on the issue throughout the latter years of the Tang, no one seems to have contributed much new to the debate.[56]

THE SINITIC CONTEXT

The Chinese preoccupation with the notion of inherent buddha-nature may well have been tied to the indigenous concern with humankind's *xing* (inherent nature), a philosophical theme that dates back to the Warring States period. The Mencian view that human nature is inherently good would have resonated, if not actually inspired, the claim, first articulated by Daosheng, that all beings possess the nature of buddhahood.

This is not to question the influence of Indian Buddhism in general, and Yogācāra and *tathāgatagarbha* (matrix of buddhahood) thought in particular, in the evolution of the doctrine. (If all is mind, and mind is buddha-nature, then nothing is devoid of buddha-nature.) Moreover, Indian texts such as the *Avataṃsaka-sūtra* do sometimes depict the cosmos as a single interconnected and resplendent whole. Nevertheless, the Indian rhetoric on the topic tends toward the abstract or transcendent—the perspective of a buddha rather than that of ordinary folk. I do not know of any Indian reference to mundane objects such as roof tiles or stones becoming buddhas and preaching the dharma. In other words, the extension of buddha-nature to the *insentient* appears to have been a distinctively Chinese innovation. One might interpret this doctrine as an attempt by Buddhists to appropriate the Mencian discourse from the Ruists and to trump them at the same time; in contrast to the expansive Mahayana vision of universal buddha-nature, extending even to walls and tiles, the Confucian discourse on *xing* appears uninspired and parochial.

Some also see the doctrine as a Buddhist expression of the holistic conception of the cosmos characteristic of early Chinese thought. I am referring to what Joseph Needham has called the "organismic" view of the world—the notion that the universe constitutes a single, organically connected and interdependent whole governed by the principle of "sympathetic resonance" (*ganying*) among the five phases, the ethers, and so on. Such a worldview does not seem to privilege metaphysical distinctions such as mind versus matter, immanent versus transcendent, or sentient versus insentient.

This is the approach taken by the Japanese scholar Kamata Shigeo, who has argued that the buddha-nature of the insentient represents a synthesis of the Indian Buddhist notion that all things are mind and the Chinese holistic view of all things as constituting a single body, particularly as articulated in certain early Daoist works.[57] There is certainly no shortage of Chinese precursors or analogues to the doctrine. Perhaps the most striking is the passage in chapter 22 of the *Zhuangzi*, where in response to the question "where does the Way exist?" Zhuangzi says that there is no place it doesn't exist, and then goes on to specify that it is in the ant, the panic grass, tiles and shards, and even piss and shit.[58]

Kamata is surely correct to draw attention to the Daoist antecedents of the doctrine. I would, however, make two observations: 1) while Kamata views the "holistic" tendencies in Daoism as valorizing nature, Zhuangzi, like the Buddhist exegetes examined above, does not distinguish between the products of civilization (tiles and shards) and the phenomena of the natural world (ants, grass, piss, and shit); 2) while the doctrine of the buddha-nature of the insentient may have been inspired by holistic Chinese cosmological ideas, it was initially articulated in the language of Sanlun, Huayan, and Tiantai scholasticism. The primary concern of early advocates of the doctrine was the coherent and consistent explication of the Indian materials at their disposal. These materials presented a host of hermeneutical difficulties, not least of which was how to harmonize *tathāgatagarbha* ontology with Mādhyamika dialectic. The pliable rhetoric of buddha-nature, which facilitated movement between epistemological and ontological perspectives, came to play a cardinal role in these intellectual struggles and generated, for better or worse, increasingly rarefied conceptual superstructures.

Chan forays into the controversy are, at first sight, less scholastic than those of their Sanlun, Huayan, and Tiantai counterparts. To the early Northern and Ox-head masters, the doctrine was logically and ideologically consonant with their emphasis on "no-mind," "extinguishing thought," and so on. Thus the doctrine was used not merely to express the radical nonduality of subject and object, but also to evoke a sense of perfect inner and outer quiescence, wherein one is indistinguishable from a tree or a wall.

Northern school support for the controversial buddha-nature of the insentient position presented Shenhui with a ready target for his polemical attacks. From Shenhui's point of view, the doctrine was more than merely contrary to scripture; it was morally and soteriologically pernicious. The identification of the physical world around us—the world of bamboos and chrysanthemums—with the world of enlightenment mitigates the need for rigorous monastic practice leading to buddhahood.[59]

It is difficult to determine to what extent Shenhui's attack was motivated by personal ambition and to what extent he was sincerely troubled by the ethical and doctrinal ramifications of the doctrine. But putting the question of motives aside, I would note that the arguments presented by Chan figures on both sides of the debate are eminently "discursive": Shenhui and his cohorts cite the authority of scripture, appeal to reason, logic, and common sense, make liberal (and sometimes questionable) use of analogy, and so on. And once you look beyond the distinctively "Channish" literary and stylistic peculiarities, you find that the underlying conceptual strategies are of a kind with their Sanlun, Tiantai, and Huayan counterparts. Take Huizhong's famous dictum that "insentient objects preach the dharma," for example. On the surface the notion seems hyperbolic, potentially antinomian, or simply fanciful. But when Huizhong is asked why, if insentient things are continually preaching the dharma, we can't hear it, he responds that only enlightened sages can hear them. Like Huiyuan, Jizang, Fazang, and other eminent scholiasts, Huizhong is forced to "save appearances" by reintroducing the slippery hermeneutic device of the two truths.[60]

As mentioned near the beginning of this chapter, Chan patriarchs are often presented as iconoclastic mavericks who eschewed scholastic pursuits in favor of rigorous meditation leading to enlightenment. Chan *gong'an* are accordingly viewed as devices intended to subvert discursive thought and bring about *satori*. But it should now be clear that the early architects of Chan thought remained beholden to scripture and tradition. They did, however, insist that their own hermeneutic practices were better suited to the Buddha's teachings than were the hermeneutics of their rivals. So it should come as no surprise to find that the most famous *gong'an* of all, Zhaozhou's dog, was originally set in the arcane intellectual context of the buddha-nature of the insentient controversy.

ZHAOZHOU'S DOG

While the "dog" *gong'an* became notorious as the first case of the thirteenth-century *Gateless Barrier,* the anecdote was culled from the writings of the ninth-century Chan master Zhaozhou. The full exchange, as found in the extant redaction of Zhaozhou's record (*Zhaozhou Zhenji Chanshi yulu*),[61] reads as follows.

> [A student] asked: "Does a dog also have buddha-nature or not?" The Master said: "It does not." The student said: "Everything from the buddhas above to the ants below has buddha-nature. Why does a dog not have it?" The Master said: "Because he has the nature of karmically conditioned consciousness."[62]

There is some evidence that the query concerning the buddha-nature of dogs was an oft-repeated challenge given to Chan masters—it is found in the biographies of other Tang masters as recorded in Song compilations.[63] At first glance, it might not be evident that the unstated context of this exchange was the buddha-nature of the insentient controversy. But look at another dialogue found later in Zhaozhou's record.

> [A student] asked: "Does an oak tree also have buddha-nature or not?" The Master said: "It has." [The student] said: "Then when will it become a buddha?" The Master said: "When the sky falls to the earth." [The student] said: "When will the sky fall to the earth?" The Master said: "When the oak tree becomes a buddha."[64]

Finally, note a third exchange in the same text, in which Zhaozhou is asked once again about the buddha-nature of dogs: "[A student] asked: 'Does a dog also have buddha-nature or not?' The Master said: 'The [road] in front of every house leads to Chang'an.'"[65]

Zhaozhou's response to the second question about the oak tree suggests that he will accept, at least provisionally, the buddha-nature of insentient things such as trees. And in the third exchange he has no trouble conceding buddha-nature to dogs as well. So why does he deny it to dogs the first time around?

The first questioner is fully aware, of course, that according to Buddhist teachings all sentient life has buddha-nature; no educated cleric would mistake the interlocutor's question as an expression of ignorance. The question makes sense only in the light of the buddha-nature of the insentient debates: it is a challenge to Zhaozhou to articulate his understanding of the controversy in a manner that remains true to Chan principles. Zhaozhou must respond in a fashion that does not express attachment to, or reify, the distinction between sentient and insentient, or between having and not having buddha-nature. At the same time he must avoid positing a third "medial" position—one that would affirm the nonduality of sentient and insentient, for example—since to do so would merely spawn a new conceptual dichotomy, this time between 1) the absolute wherein all distinctions are resolved and 2) the contingent realm of plurality. Zhaozhou's response—his unapologetic denial of buddha-nature to dogs—denotes his freedom from attachment to doctrine (i.e., his acknowledgment that no conventional formulation is ultimate) and at the same time his refusal to attempt to articulate a medial or transcendental position.

Wumen was familiar with the buddha-nature of the insentient context of these exchanges, as is evident in his commentary to the case.

> Wumen said: "To study Chan you must pass through the barrier of the patriarchal masters; to gain marvelous enlightenment you must completely sever the way of mind. If you have not passed through the barrier of the patriarchs, and not severed the way of mind, then you are no more than the spirit that haunts the grasses and the trees.[66]

This is a complex literary and philosophical gambit. On the one hand Wumen cleverly draws from a passage by the famous master Linji Yixuan (d. 866) that originally is unconnected to the debate: "For ten years, five seasons, there has not yet been one person [worthy of my teaching]. All have been mere spirits of bamboo and trees—haunting the grasses and leaves—or the specters of wild foxes. Happening upon a piece of shit they chew away frantically. Blind fools!"[67] Yet in the immediate context of the dog *gong'an*, Wumen's reference to the "spirits of grasses and trees" is a subtle allusion to the buddha-nature of the insentient controversy. Like Zhaozhou, Wumen refuses to countenance either side in the debate, while at the same time rejecting a medial position. Wumen does this through a literary reference that alludes to a *sentience* (*jingling*) abiding in grasses and trees, while the immediate context implicitly denies sentience to dogs. (Recall that according to the *Nirvāṇa-sūtra*, anything lacking buddha-nature is insentient.) In other words, Zhaozhou's emphatic insistence that dogs do not have buddha-nature would, one would suppose, make it even less likely that grasses and trees, which are insentient (devoid of spirit, or *ling*), possess buddha-nature. But in a twist characteristic of this genre, Wumen declares that if you do not grasp the import of Zhaozhou's denial of buddha-nature to dogs, then you are akin to the spirit—the sentience—that dwells in grasses and trees.

THE RHETORIC OF FREEDOM

It should be clear that Chan *gong'an* presupposed a high degree of familiarity with Buddhist literature, doctrine, and dialectic. Many of the *gong'an* reiterate the teaching that emptiness—the appreciation of the contingency of all percepts—is not attained through transcending the world of form. Rather, emptiness is the world of form properly apprehended. This venerable strand of Mahayana thought lies at the core of Zhaozhou's emphatic "no!" This "no" is not, in the end, a denial of buddha-nature to dogs so much as it is a rhetorical strategy for eluding the conceptual trap laid for him—Zhaozhou must neither affirm nor deny the doctrine of buddha-nature and at the same time must avoid postulating a third "transcendent" position.

A subset of Chan cases rehearses the notion that freedom lies in the realization that there is no freedom; transcendence lies in the understanding that there is no transcendence. These cases assume the logical structure of a paradox: x if and only if not x. Take, for example, Baizhang's (749–814) "wild fox" *gong'an*, case number 2 in the *Gateless Barrier*.

> Whenever Reverend Baizhang delivered a sermon, an old man always followed the congregation in to listen to the teaching. When the assembled people left, the old man left too. One day, however, he remained behind. The Master asked him, "Who are you who stand in front of me?" The old man replied, "I am not a human being. In the past, in the time of Kāśyapa Buddha, I resided on this mountain [as a monk]. On one occasion a student asked me, 'Is a person who has practiced great cultivation [i.e., an enlightened person] still subject to causation or not?' I answered, 'He is not subject to causation.' [Because of my answer] I was reborn as a fox for five hundred lifetimes. I now beseech you Reverend to say a transformative word on my behalf to free me from this fox body." Then [the old man] asked, "Is a person of attainment still subject to causation or not?" The Master an-

> swered, "He cannot evade causation." Upon hearing these words the old man was immediately enlightened. Making a bow he said, "I have now been released from the body of the fox which remains behind the mountain. I have been so bold as to tell this to the Reverend, and I ask that you perform a funeral for me as you would for a deceased monk." ... That evening [after performing the funeral for the fox] the Master convened an assembly and related the circumstances [behind the funeral]. Huangbo then asked, "The old man, failing to respond correctly, was reborn as a fox for five hundred lifetimes. Suppose that he gave the right answer every time; what would have happened then?" The Master said, "Come closer and I'll tell you." Huangbo approached [Baizhang] and gave the Master a slap. The Master clapped his hands and laughed, saying, "I had supposed that the barbarian had a red beard, and now here is a red-bearded barbarian!"[68]

According to Buddhist doctrine, rigorous practice leads to freedom from causation; the goal of the path—*nirvāṇa*—is the cessation of karmic activity and a final end to the cycle of life and death. Yet precisely because the old man gave this perfectly orthodox response he found himself bound to rebirth. This *gong'an* is then an elegant trap for those who would reify the notion of karma, just as Zhaozhou's dog is a trap for those who would reify the notion of buddha-nature. The challenge, then, is to respond in a manner that does not express attachment to the doctrine of causation and at the same time does not posit a new third position neither affirming nor denying causation. Like Zhaozhou, Baizhang escapes the trap through affirming what, in a conventional Buddhist context, is an outlandishly heterodox position, thereby signaling his liberation from any and all positions. The revelation that there is ultimately no escape from causation is precisely what frees the old man from causation. The resulting logical structure is that of a paradox: if you claim liberation is possible it is not; if you claim it is not possible it is. In other words, x if and only if not x.

Note that the final line of this case—"I had supposed that the barbarian had a red beard, and now here is a red-bearded barbarian"—involves a pun. In medieval times the word for "barbarian" (*hu*) was homophonous with the word for "fox" (*hu*).[69] Baizhang, delighted that his disciple has beaten him to the punch, compliments Huangbo by comparing him to the patriarch Bodhidharma—the wily barbarian who sports, according to iconographic convention, a full beard. But the red-bearded barbarian is simultaneously identified through the pun with the "red-haired" fox of the story, suggesting that the fox—a wily creature in China as in the West—may have been putting something over on Baizhang all along. The old man's tale is, after all, preposterous on the face of it. To take this one step further, Huangbo alone may have understood that Baizhang—perhaps the real "fox" of the story—should not be taken too seriously. This is precisely the intent of so many of the commentaries, interlinear glosses, and quips that are incorporated into the *gong'an* literature; each commentator strives to trump those who have gone before, thereby displacing any sense of hermeneutic security.

In saying that freedom lies in the realization that there is no freedom, have I said anything at all? In other words, is the assertion of the contingency of knowledge more veridical, epistemologically sound, or impervious to critique than other sorts of assertions? This is one of the central conundrums with which Chan writings struggle: if all truth claims are contingent or relational, how is it possible that Buddhism is transmitted intact across the cultural and linguistic divides that separate China from India? (This is a stumbling block for modern scholars of Buddhism as well: is medieval Chan commensurate with contemporary modes of Western thought and expression?)

This is the gist of case number 5 in the *Gateless Barrier* known as Xiangyan's (d. 898) "man up a tree." A man is stuck in a tree dangling from a branch by his teeth; his arms and legs cannot reach a limb. Someone comes along and asks, "Why did [the barbarian] come from the West?" (*wen xilai yi*). Just as the interlocutor in Zhaozhou's dog *gong'an* knows that dogs have buddha-nature and the old man who queried Baizhang knows that liberated beings are free from karma, any literate Chan monk is aware that the barbarian—Bodhidharma, the mythical progenitor of Chinese Chan—came from India to China to transmit the dharma. But the moment the man in the tree opens his mouth to respond in this or in any other fashion, he plunges to his death. Should he remain silent, however, he abrogates the duty incumbent on all Buddhists to transmit the teaching. So the underlying quandary is this: how is transmission possible in the first place? One traditional answer—the *tathāgatagarbha* approach—holds that transmission is accomplished by pointing to what already lies within, namely inherent buddha-nature or undefiled mind. This *gong'an,* like so many others, rejects this response. The critique, in short, is that the moon to which the finger points is another empty signifier. It is fingers all the way down.

"Xiangyan's man up a tree" captures the seeming paradox in the claim of an unbroken transmission passing from generation to generation. We would seem to be dealing with a transmission of the understanding that there is nothing to transmit. But, to paraphrase Zhuangzi, if we say that words don't say anything, have we said something or not? Was there anything for Bodhidharma to bring from the West? Why did he leave India?

In response, case after case reiterates, in entertaining and often dramatic fashion, that freedom lies in understanding that mediation is inescapable. Such cases turn back and devour themselves, like a snake eating its own tail, or "x if and only if not x." Case number 3 of the *Gateless Barrier,* for example, tells us that in response to any question the master Juzhi (n.d.) would simply raise one finger. One of Juzhi's acolytes, when asked by an outsider about his master's teaching, held up his own finger. When Juzhi heard this he took out a knife and cut off the boy's finger. As the boy ran screaming from the room, Juzhi "called him back, and when the boy turned his head, Juzhi raised his finger. The boy suddenly understood."[70] In other words, when the finger is rendered a "teaching"—a signifier—the master cuts it off. (Or to cite Linji, "If you meet the Buddha, kill the Buddha.") But lest the absence of a finger be mistaken for the Way, Juzhi again holds up his finger.

In the end, silence might seem to be the most appropriate response to the dilemma of ineludible mediation. This is the position of the *Vimalakīrti-sūtra,* an Indian Buddhist scripture popular in China and esteemed by many in the Chan tradition. When asked how to explicate nonduality, the hero, Vimalakīrti, remains silent, and his silence is lauded as the philosophical climax of the text.[71] And Wumen himself might be seen to countenance silence in his final commentarial verse on Zhaozhou's dog.

> The dog, buddha-nature,
> The authoritative pronouncement.
> The moment you implicate "has" or "has not,"
> Your body and life are lost.[72]

But many Chan cases insist that silence is merely another empty sign, and a particularly beguiling one at that. As we have seen, should Xiangyan's "man up a tree" remain silent to preserve life and limb, he reneges on his responsibilities and abandons the bodhisattva path. And Wumen explicitly rejects silence in case number 6 of his *gong'an* collection, in which Śākyamuni surprises his monks by silently holding up a flower rather than delivering a sermon. According to the story, only Mahākāsyapa smiles, signaling his comprehension of the Buddha's wordless gesture. Śākyamuni responds by praising Mahākāsyapa and entrusting him with his dharma. But Wumen, in his own caustic comment on the tale, castigates the Buddha as a "swindler" who "offers us dog's meat and calls it mutton." What if everyone smiled? Wumen asks sardonically.[73] Silence is no less contingent, no more sublime, no more direct than is any other sign, a point reiterated in Hakuin Ekaku's (1686–1769) famous case concerning the sound of one hand clapping.

THE ENACTMENT OF ENLIGHTENMENT

It should now be clear that Chan cases were not simply witty non-sequiturs designed to forestall intellection. They were, among other things, authoritative precedents and rhetorical models of how a Chan trainee was to respond to doctrinal quandaries and challenges. The structure of Chan case literature, which sanctions and incorporates layer upon layer of rejoinder and critique, was perfectly suited to a tradition that refused, at least on the surface, to espouse any doctrinal formulation as ultimate. A Chan case embodied not so much a position on a contested point, but rather a dialectical technique for dealing with existential issues of immediate import in Buddhist practice (causation, enlightenment, truth, death).

But how were *gong'an* actually incorporated into the monastic curriculum? Surviving *gong'an* collections offer little in the way of internal evidence. We know that the short anecdotes and dialogues that form the heart of each case—the "original edicts"—were culled from earlier literary genres, primarily the "recorded sayings" (*yulu*) collections associated with specific Chan masters, and the "records of the transmission of the lamp" (*chuandeng lu*) that consist of hagiographies of Chan patriarchs.[74] Both genres included copious anecdotes portraying the teaching styles of famous teachers. Later masters compiled personal collections of their favorite anecdotes along with layers of commentary and verse, a process that could yield a text of considerable complexity.

Take, for example, the *Blue Cliff Record*, one of most important early *gong'an* collections. The core of the work is a previous compilation, *Reverend Xuedou's Verse Commentaries on a Hundred Edicts* (*Xuedou heshang baize songgu*), which consists of one hundred *gong'an* compiled by Xuedou Chongxian (980–1052).[75] Most of Xuedou's hundred cases can be found in the earlier *Jingde Record*, with the exception of eighteen found in the *Extended Records of Chan Master Yunmen Kuangzhen* (*Yunmen Kuanzhen Chanshi guanglu*), but as any one anecdote can appear in multiple sources it is difficult to know with certainty the texts from which Xuedou drew. Xuedou, a noted poet, added his own comments and verse to each case. Years later, the master Yuanwu Keqin (1063–1135) delivered a series of lectures on Xuedou's collection, and the notes taken by Yuanwu's disciples were gathered and compiled by his student Puzhao (n.d.). The compilation was then edited by a lay disciple, Guan Wudang (n.d.), and published in 1128 as the *Blue Cliff Record*.

Each case in the *Blue Cliff Record* is prefaced with a short introduction, or "pointer" (*chuishi*), by Yuanwu, followed by the "original edict" (*benze*) set off with the term *ju*, meaning the case is "raised" for consideration. The case itself is interspersed with Yuanwu's short, interlinear glosses, often no more than a few pithy words. (Occasionally, Xuedou's laconic interlinear comments are also preserved under the heading *zhuyu*, or "appended phrase.") This is followed by a longer prose commentary (*pingchang*) by Yuanwu. Next comes Xuedou's verse (*song*), which is again interspersed with short glosses and quips by Yuanwu. The case ends with a concluding prose commentary (also called a *pingchang*) by Yuanwu on Xuedou's verse.

While we know something about the manner in which *gong'an* collections were assembled, it is more difficult to deduce the role of such collections in the actual training of Chan monks. One often hears that *gong'an* served as objects for formal meditation practice within the monastic community, but there is actually little evidence in support of this view, especially for the Song period when the *gong'an* collections first made their appearance.[76]

Scholars who insist that *gong'an* served as meditation devices in the Song have relied primarily on the writings of Dahui Zonggao (1089–1163). Dahui advocated a method of focusing the mind on the "critical phrase" (*huatou*) of a specific case, such as Zhaozhou's emphatic "no," giving rise to what is known as *kanhua chan*.[77] But even in the case of Dahui the situation is far from clear; while Dahui left us a massive oeuvre, passages advocating a "non-discursive" approach to the critical phrase are typically drawn from those few tracts, such as his "letters" (*Dahui shu*), that were directed specifically to lay literati disciples who had relatively little training in Buddhist scriptural and scholastic traditions. It is no secret that Dahui was actively competing against other Chan abbots of his day for lay patronage, and he appears to have devised his simplified *kanhua chan* specifically for the needs of his lay followers.[78] The legacy of Dahui's method in China is still not fully understood, but it did come into favor among some monastics in post-Song times. (This may have been because the dramatic decline in patronage led to a decline in Buddhist literary pursuits, making it increasingly difficult to appreciate the conceptual and literary complexities of the case genre.) More to the point, Dahui's technique was revived in the Tokugawa period by the Japanese priest Hakuin Ekaku, architect of the modern Rinzai monastic curriculum, who was similarly concerned with making *kōan* practice available to those who lacked proficiency in Chinese literature. The modern understanding of *gong'an* practice is inordinately influenced by contemporary Rinzai monastic training. Yet all this tells us little about how *gong'an* were approached by elite monks in Song monasteries.

Scholars who view *gong'an* as objects for nondiscursive meditation also make reference to Sanjiao Laoren's preface to the *Blue Cliff Record* as well as Zhongfeng Mingben's *Evening Talks in a Mountain Hut*—two texts composed in the Yuan and discussed at the beginning of this chapter. These two authors, as well as numerous other premodern commentators, rehearse, in a dense and highly literary diction, the usual Chan injunctions against grasping at the words; they remind us of the limitations of language and encourage us to see beyond the finger to the moon. Moreover, they suggest that understanding comes in a dramatic flash of insight and that insight is gained through intense and focused struggle with the case. (The same point is made by Wumen in his oft-quoted commentary on Zhaozhou's dog.) But the directive to go beyond words is in no way distinctive of

Chan; it is a venerable Buddhist teaching that, as we have seen, was itself subject to critique by authors of the case literature. Moreover, to my knowledge nowhere does Wumen, Sanjiao Laoren, Zhongfeng Mingben, or any other Song or Yuan commentator advocate the use of cases as objects for formal, nondiscursive meditation practice by ordained monks. Note that Zhongfeng's explanation of the term *gong'an* highlights, among other things, its use in *publicly* testing and validating a monk's understanding—a function that demands attending, at least in part, to the manifest content of the case.

In trying to reconstruct the place of *gong'an* in the intellectual and professional formation of Chan monks we must move beyond the internal evidence provided by the *gong'an* and *yulu* collections to the descriptions of Song monastic practice found in the Chan monastic codes known as "pure rules" (*qinggui*). Although these detailed prescriptive manuals make little explicit reference to the use of *gong'an* per se, they do provide a comprehensive picture of communal life within a Song Chan monastery. Specifically, we will attend to the institutional role of the abbot, since it is the abbot who, following the judicial metaphor, assumes the all-important role of magistrate and judge in wielding the *gong'an*.

The abbot of a public Buddhist monastery operated under the auspices of the imperial government and held jurisdiction over all monastic affairs. This was a major responsibility, since larger monasteries controlled significant wealth, including vast tracts of land, and housed upwards of hundreds and even thousands of monks. But our concern lies not with his administrative duties, but rather with his role as a living patriarch in a lineage stretching back to Śākyamuni. As scholars have shown, the Chan abbot was treated, by virtue of his office, his spiritual genealogy and bona fides, and his deportment, as an enlightened master and living buddha. But it would be a mistake to view the abbot's enlightenment as a nebulous quality abiding in the inner recesses of his mind. Enlightenment is better viewed as a "social fact" constituted through his monastic office—earned as it was through years of intense study and practice—and displayed and reaffirmed in an ongoing cycle of ritual performances.[79] In these performances the abbot was rendered the object of worship; monastics and laypersons would approach the abbot with prostrations and offerings in the same manner as they approached a consecrated icon.[80]

As there are several excellent studies now available on Song monastic ritual as described in the *qinggui* materials,[81] I will briefly mention only two rites that are of particular relevance to our study. In the first, called "Entering the Chamber" (*rushi*), the abbot met individually or in small groups with his senior disciples in a formal interview. In the second, called "Ascending the Hall" (*shangtang*), the abbot delivered a brief lecture to the entire monastic assembly from a ceremonial high seat in the dharma hall. In both instances the abbot's discourse focused on the sacred texts of the Chan tradition, namely the recorded sayings and transmission of the flame texts, as well as the *gong'an* collections.

Virtually all extant Chan codes devote space to the elaborate protocols governing the Entering the Chamber rite. The earliest and most influential code, *Rules of Purity for Chan Monasteries* (*Chanyuan qinggui*), compiled in 1103 by Changlu Zongze (d. 1107?), describes how the abbot's attendant first offers incense to the abbot and the precise manner in which the disciple or disciples are to enter the abbot's quarters. After making a series of prostrations and withdrawing to the southwest corner of the abbot's seat, the disciples are to "speak their minds frankly" (*tulu xiaoxi*), engaging in questions and dialogue with the abbot but avoiding any mention of "mundane troubles."[82] The topic of the encounter is not explicitly specified in the extant codes and appears to have been left up to the discretion of the monks.[83]

The ritual is, in the words of Griffith Foulk, a "re-enactment of the encounters between Chan masters and disciples that were contained in the flame histories. The brevity of the flame history anecdotes and the way in which they depict the expression of sacred truths in a few short words, were written into the ritual procedures."[84] Indeed, a comprehensive Yuan-period code, the *Imperial Edition of Baizhang's Rules of Purity* (*Chixiu Baizhang qinggui*), compiled between 1335 and 1338, states that an image of Bodhidharma was installed outside the entrance of the abbot's quarters to which the monks offered incense and prostrations prior to entering the abbot's room.[85] This likens the meeting with the abbot to the legendary encounter between Huike (487–593?) and Bodhidharma. According to this popular tale, Huike sat patiently outside Bodhidharma's cave for weeks on end to no avail. Finally, in a sincere if desperate attempt to gain the meditating master's attention, Huike cut off his arm and placed it before Bodhidharma. A brief verbal encounter ensued, leading to Huike's sudden enlightenment. Huike thus became the first person in China to receive the transmission and is celebrated as the second patriarch. In the Song this fictional encounter, appearing as case number 41 in the *Gateless Barrier* among other places, served as a prototype for Chan transmission in general and, more specifically, as the mythic frame for the ritual encounter between abbot and disciple in the Entering the Chamber rite.

While direct evidence is lacking, it seems reasonable to suppose that the dialogue between the abbot and his disciples would have focused, at least some of the time, on the interpretation of the sacred texts of the tradition, especially the collected sayings of the patriarchs found in the *yulu* and *gong'an* literature.[86] As such, the Entering the Chamber ritual would have prepared aspirants to the abbacy for the Ascending the Hall ritual, one of the most important events in the monastic cycle. In this grand rite, performed daily in the Northern Song but every five days or so later on,[87] the abbot ascends the central altar in the dharma hall and takes a seat on the "*dhyāna*-chair" (*chanyi*), a ceremonial "throne" that, like the imperial throne, faced south. He was situated, in other words, precisely as was the buddha icon enshrined on the central altar in the Buddha hall.

A detailed depiction is found at the beginning of fascicle 2 of the *Rules of Purity for Chan Monasteries,* which records the precise order in which the members of the clergy, in order of their rank, office, and seniority, enter the hall, make prostrations, and line up to listen to the abbot's sermon.[88] The rite is highly formalized, yet the detailed information on the movement and deportment of the participants provided by the *qinggui* materials stands in stark contrast to the lack of any information concerning the sermon's content.

However, the "recorded sayings" (*yulu*) of eminent Chan abbots provide us with literally thousands of examples of sermons delivered from the high seat during the Ascending the Hall ceremony. These sermons, usually called "ascending the hall" (*shangtang*) or "holding the whisk" (*bingfu*), are highly stylized and adhere closely to rhetorical models laid down in the recorded sayings of the patriarchs. Indeed, these short talks, sometimes no more than a few sentences, often open by raising (*ju*) a famous case, and in tone, content, and rhetorical form they look precisely like the sort of commentary found in well-known *gong'an* collections.

Despite the apparent routinization of these sermons, we may presume that it was no easy thing to pull them off; it required mastering a considerable body of canonical literature and internalizing the complex rhetorical logic of Buddhist dialectic. Documents such as the *Rules of Purity for Chan Monasteries* reveal that the study of scriptures, including the recorded sayings of past patriarchs, formed an important part of the monastic curriculum.[89] In addition to the study of texts, advanced disciples assimilated the distinctively "Channish" rhetorical style through regular exposure to the abbot's performance at Ascending the Hall and Entering the Chamber ceremonies. During the latter event, students were provided with the opportunity to hone their own oratorical skills in repartee with the master.

And this is where the *gong'an* literature would have come into play, for the private formal exchanges in the master's chamber were reenactments of the dialogues between famous masters and disciples of old that are featured in the *gong'an* literature. *Gong'an,* in short, functioned as "scripts" for the performance of mind-to-mind transmission that took place regularly in the abbot's quarters. The study of famous cases gave an advanced student of Chan the rhetorical tools required to engage in "enlightened repartee" with the master and prepared him for delivering formal sermons and engaging in ritual debate when he himself was ready to assume the role of enlightened patriarch on the high seat.

Chan cases constituted, among other things, exemplary models of "buddha-speak" for the Ascending the Hall ritual. That such talks were more routinized than is sometimes thought does not mean that the Chan master was acting in bad faith. The utterances and exchanges featured in the Ascending the Hall and Entering the Chamber rites were not lifeless substitutes for the "real thing," since, according to Chan dialectic, form and content—finger and moon—are ultimately inseparable. Which is to say that there is, in the end, no fixed or final referent to which terms like "patriarch," "buddha," or "enlightenment" can obtain. And this is precisely what the Chan aspirant was expected to appreciate and internalize through his engagement with the *gong'an* literature.

FINAL THOUGHTS

Like the civil judge, the Chan abbot's examination and final judgment is based on his mastery of an authorized corpus of prior cases. It may be no accident that Chan landed upon the "case method" as a means to propagate its particular brand of Buddhism. We have seen that Chan thought, following strands in Mahayana philosophy, regarded any and all doctrinal formulations as contingent, partial, and potentially deleterious. There was no set of timeless ethical or philosophical principles to which the Chan master could refer, at least not explicitly. Even the Buddha's words were not immune to critique; Zhaozhou calls the Buddha a swindler proffering dog meat as mutton. Chan teachings were disseminated not as a set of axiomatic truths, but rather as a dialectical method that could be applied to a wide range of doctrinal issues. The literary form of encounter dialogue was better suited than expository prose to such a teaching; the contrivance of spontaneous dialogue spared the master from the need to clarify his own position. Instead the master could sit back and trump whatever came his way, with an endless supply of aces in hand. Chan *gong'an* thus served as ideal topics for lectures from the high-seat—by critically engaging the cases and adding their own "capping phrases," living Chan abbots could enter into an ongoing game of rhetorical one-upmanship, ridiculing the masters of old while yet drawing on their authority.

Scholars of the case method in the West have suggested that it embodies a particular "style of reasoning," one that does not give pride of place to atemporal or universal principles but emphasizes instead the appropriate response to a specific contingency.[90] In Aristotelian terms, the case method inculcates *phronesis*—a kind of practical wisdom—as opposed to *episteme*, or theoretical or abstract understanding.[91] If this is true in the realms of law, medicine, or business, it may be even more true of Chan, since Chan explicitly disclaims any and all "eternal verities" from which a correct response or course of action might be deduced. Only when one relinquishes the search for universals can one respond to concrete situations with utter confidence and conviction—that is, with "no-mind" (*wuxin*). In other words, existential certainty can be attained only at the expense of abandoning a correspondence theory of truth.

Such an attitude has deep and extensive roots in Chinese Buddhism. Even in technical discussions of logic, Chinese Buddhist exegetes seem unconcerned with delineating a set of universal axioms with which to appraise the truth-value of a given proposition. Logic and syllogism were not a means to deduce or verify statements of truth so much as a means to persuade one's opponents. Buddhist logicians thus viewed the rules of argumentation and debate as contingent on the immediate social context; what was important was that both parties agree on the rules. As a result, in marked contrast to the Aristotelian project, in Chinese Buddhist logic an axiom or syllogism that was acceptable in one instance might well be unacceptable in another.[92] (Does a dog have buddha-nature? It depends on what day it is.)

There are many aspects of the Chan *gong'an* that suggest further parallels with the use of the case method in other cultural domains. To mention only a few: in Chan, as in medicine and law, cases were used in the formation of a specialized elite, since years of study and practice in debate were required to master the arcane *gong'an* repertoire. As a result, in China, as in the West, the case method contributed to a penchant for what Forrester calls "dogmatic bookishness."[93] Moreover, Chan cases, like their counterparts in medical and legal literature, delight in the unusual and the shocking;[94] I have already mentioned Juzhi cutting off a boy's finger and Yunmen calling the Buddha a "shit-stick," but the case that is most scandalizing in the monastic context is that of Nanquan (748–835) slitting the throat of a cat, in flagrant violation of the cardinal Buddhist precept against killing.[95] This aspect of case narratives is overdetermined: first, the method works precisely through forcing students to ponder exceptional and anomalous events that could serve as delimiting cases. The habitual and mundane have relatively little pedagogical value. Second, cases circulated as literary documents and as such were expected to entertain as well as to enlighten and authorize.

While the Chan use of *gong'an* during the Song and early Yuan displays many characteristics of the case method, the decline in literary learning and the disappearance of a bookish "specialized elite" in late imperial China transformed the Chan *gong'an* into something else altogether, a cipher of authority and mantra-like object of meditation. The *huatou* practice popularized by Dahui became the orthodox form of *gong'an* "study." Active participation in and appreciation of the dialectical logic, literary whimsy, and dense intertextuality characteristic of *gong'an* materials were either out of reach or out of fashion, and *gong'an* were wielded instead as indices of enlightenment. Further research is necessary to determine whether or not a coterie of Chan litterateurs continued to "think in cases" in later times. But it should now be clear that in the Song at least—the period when the major *gong'an* collections were compiled and redacted—an understanding of the literary, aesthetic, and discursive qualities of the genre was de rigueur for those aspiring to an abbotship in a public Chan monastery.

This chapter is no more than a preliminary foray into a few of the many hundreds of Chan cases that circulated in the Song. Even then, for lack of space, I have skipped much of the commentarial material in prose and verse that attends these same cases. There is much to be done in the literary and philosophical analysis of this sophisticated body of literature. It should now be evident that such an analysis is not only warranted but essential for those seeking to understand Song Chan.

NOTES

My thanks to Charlotte Furth and Elizabeth Horton Sharf for their comments and suggestions on earlier drafts of this chapter and to Ling Hon Lam for his meticulous editorial attention.

1 T 2005:48.292c20–24. The exchange is also featured in case no. 18 of the *Wansong Laoren pingzhang Tiantong Jue heshang songgu Congrongan lu*, T 2004:48.238b21–39a28. Textual details concerning Zhaozhou's recorded sayings (*Zhaozhou Zhenji Chanshi yulu*) will be found below.

2 Faure, *The Rhetoric of Immediacy* and *Chan Insights and Oversights;* Foulk, "Myth, Ritual, and Monastic Practice"; Sharf, "The Zen of Japanese Nationalism," "Whose Zen?" and "Experience."

3 Foulk and Sharf, "On the Ritual Use"; Sharf, "Ritual."

4 Sharf, "Whose Zen?"

5 On the sometimes controversial place of literary endeavors in the Song monastic institution, see esp. Gimello, "Mārga and Culture"; and Keyworth, "Transmitting the Lamp," 281–324.

6 See esp. Heine and Wright, eds., *The Kōan.*

7 Heine, *Shifting Shape.*

8 T 2076:51.291b17–19; cf. Miura and Sasaki, *Zen Dust,* 154, note 9; and Foulk, "The Form and Function," 19.

9 On *xiancheng gong'an,* see Iriya and Koga, eds., *Zengo jiten,* 112; and App, trans., *Master Yunmen,* 107, note 4.

10 *Yunmen Kuangzhen Chanshi guanglu,* T 1988:47.547a12; note that the Muzhou mentioned in the text refers to Chen Zunsu.

11 T 1988:47.551c28–29; App, trans., *Master Yunmen,* 143. See also T 1988:47.570c9.

12 App suggests that the first printed edition of this text appeared in 1035 (App, trans., *Master Yunmen,* 232–237), but this is still well after the death of Yunmen and the fall of the Tang. The term *gong'an* also appears associated with Huangbo in the *Wujia zhengzong zan* (ZZ 135.915:458a2), but here again we are dealing with a late text, published in 1254; see Miura and Sasaki, *Zen Dust,* 153–154, note 9.

13 On the etymological roots of the term *an* (case/table) and its relationship to *an* (examine/comment), see Ho Da-an, "Lunduan fuhao." On the evolution of the Chan *gong'an,* see also Li Yuzhen, "Dangtou banghe."

14 Sanjiao Laoren may be the pen name of Ruru jushi Yanbing; see Sueki, ed., *Gendaigoyaku Hekiganroku,* 1.20; and Komazawa, ed., *Zengaku daijiten,* 994a.

15 The phrase *xijiang weixi* is found in the *Mazu yulu:* "Layman Pang asked the patriarch: 'Who is it that does not keep company with the myriad dharmas?' The patriarch said: 'I will tell you when you swallow all the water of the West River in a single gulp'" See Iriya, trans., *Baso no goroku,* 35; Cheng Chien, *Sun-Face Buddha,* 87.

16 From the "Shuo fu" chapter of the *Liezi;* see Kobayashi, trans., *Resshi,* 406.

17 To hitch one's donkey is to be stuck on the path; see the *Linji lu,* T 1985:47.497c11; and Nakamura, ed., *Bukkyōgo daijiten,* 302a.

18 T 2003:48.139b29–c15; Cleary, trans., *The Blue Cliff Record,* 8–9, with changes, cf. Sueki, *Gendaigoyaku Hekiganroku,* 1.12–1.20.

19 My translation is based on the Songban jisha dazang jing edition, 37:419, register c, line 1–420, register a, line 12, and borrows liberally from the translations found in Miura and Sasaki, *Zen Dust,* 4–7; and Foulk, "The Form and Function," 43, note 15. On Zhongfeng Mingben, see esp. Yü Chün-fang, "Chung-feng Ming-pen."

20 On Daosheng and the early debates concerning the universality of buddha-nature, see Lai, "The *Mahāyānaparinirvāṇa Sūtra*"; Liebenthal, "The World Conception"; Link, "Tao-sheng"; Liu Ming-Wood, "The Doctrine of the Buddha-nature" and "The Problem of the *Icchantika*"; Penkower, "T'ien-t'ai during the T'ang Dynasty," 393–396, note 15; Tang Yongtong, *Han Wei liang Jin,* 2.601–2.676; and Tokiwa Daijo, *Busshō,* 178–193.

21 *Da banniyuan jing,* T 376:12.881b24 ff. and 893a9 ff.

22 Ibid., T 374:12.581a22–23.

23 See the *Dacheng yizhang,* T 1851:44.472c18–26.

24 *Dacheng xuanlun,* T 1853:45.40a–41a. On Jizang's theory of buddha-nature, see esp. Kamata, *Chūgoku bukkyō,* 43–46; Koseki, "Chi-tsang's '*Ta-ch'eng-hsuan-lun,*'" 186–268, and "Prajñāpāramitā"; Liu Ming-Wood, *Madhyamaka Thought,* 160–187; Tokiwa Daijo, *Busshō,* 217–219.

25 T 1853:45.40b18–20 and 40c13–18; cf. Liu Ming-Wood, *Madhyamaka Thought,* 186.

26 T 1853:45.40c24–27.

27 For example, in a discussion of the meaning of "dharma-nature" (*faxing*) in the *Dacheng qixin lun yiji,* Fazang explains that "true suchness [*zhenru*] pervades both the defiled and the pure, the sentient and the insentient." He then goes on to say that with regard to sentient beings suchness is called buddha-nature, and with regard to nonsentient beings it is called dharma-nature (T 1846:44.247c12–14). And in the *Huayan jing tan xuanji* he writes that "while the nature of true suchness taught by the three vehicles permeates both the sentient and the insentient, only sentient beings can awaken to buddha-nature" (T 1733:35.405c26–6a27; see the discussion in Penkower, "T'ien-t'ai during the T'ang Dynasty," 474–475). For a detailed discussion of Fazang's position, as well as the positions of other early Huayan exegetes including Chengguan, see Kamata, "Chūgoku zen," 443–445. Note that there is considerable speculation about the role that either Fazang or

Chengguan may have played as the unnamed foil in Zhanran's *Jin'gang bei;* see Penkower, "T'ien-t'ai during the T'ang Dynasty," 467–481, note 128, and "Making and Remaking Tradition," 47–48, note 101.

28 Specifically, he refers to a passage from Guanding's (561–632) preface to that work, a passage considered by the later tradition to represent the very essence of Tiantai teaching. Guanding writes, "When [the mind] is fixed on the dharma-realm—when [each] moment of thought [is one with] the dharma-realm—then there is not a single color nor a single smell that is not the middle way" (*Mohe zhiguan,* T 1911:46.1c24–25). Zhanran explains that this reference to the single color and the single smell refers to the universality of buddha-nature even among insentient things (*Zhiguan fuxing zhuanhong jue,* T 1912:46.151c26–28).

29 In his commentary on the *Nirvāṇa-sūtra,* for example, Guanding unambiguously states that insentient beings do not possess buddha-nature: "While there is buddha-nature in sentient beings, there is no buddha-nature in grasses and trees; rather, they have the nature of grass, trees, etc." (*Dabanniepan jing shu,* T 1767:38.184c22–23; see Penkower, "T'ien-t'ai during the T'ang Dynasty," 479, and "Making and Remaking Tradition," 49).

30 But there is evidence that Zhanran did recognize the novelty of his own position, at least within the Tiantai fold. The tacit acknowledgment is found in an autobiographical statement at the beginning of his *Adamantine Scalpel* explaining how the text came into being. One quiet night Zhanran was contemplating the sublime truths of the Tiantai teachings, and in the midst of his reverie he "fell into a trance-like sleep. From the depths of my consciousness, I proclaimed 'insentient things possess [buddha-]nature'" (T 1932:46.781a26–28, trans. Penkower, "Making and Remaking Tradition," 49). The rest of the text is presented as a transcript of the ensuing conversation with interlocutors that appear in his dream. The treatise closes abruptly with the following: "I suddenly awoke from my dream. The questioner, the respondent, the questions and answers, all were ungraspable" (T 1932:786b20–21). This would seem to be a remarkable admission: on the one hand, Zhanran presents his position on the buddha-nature of the insentient as emerging from reflection on cardinal Tiantai principles. On the other hand, that the doctrine occurs to him in the midst of a dream would seem to concede the originality of his thought. On the *Adamantine Scalpel,* see Kamata, *Chūgoku kegon,* 466–474; and Penkower, "T'ien-t'ai during the T'ang Dynasty."

31 T 1932:46.785b8–9, trans. Penkower, "T'ien-t'ai during the T'ang Dynasty," 525–528, with minor changes.

32 *Linji lu,* T 1985:47.500b22–23; this is cited by Wumen in his commentary to Zhaozhou's dog, T 2005:48.293a8–9.

33 This is case no. 21 in the *Gateless Barrier,* T 2005:48.295c6; cf. *Yunmen kuangzhen Chanshi guanglu,* T 1988:47.550b15.

34 On the question of authorship and dating of the *Record of the Masters and Disciples,* see esp. Barrett, "The Date," which argues that the text could not have been written later than 716; and Faure, *The Will to Orthodoxy,* 160–176.

35 T 2837:85.1289b8–9; Yanagida, *Shoki no zenshi,* 1:264.

36 T 2837:85.1290a4–6 and 14–18; Yanagida, *Shoki no zenshi,* 1:287–288.

37 On the Ox-head lineage in general and this text in particular, see McRae, "The Ox-head School." An edition of the *Jueguan lun*, along with Japanese and English translations, can be found in Tokiwa and Yanagida, trans., *Zekkanron.*

38 The first quotation may come from the *Avataṃsaka-sūtra* (T 278 and 279), which contains numerous statements to the same effect. The second quotation is a slightly modified version of a sentence from the *Vimalakīrti* (T 475:14.542b12–13).

39 Tokiwa and Yanagida, trans., *Zekkanron*, 91.

40 T 2016:48.943a24–28.

41 I have not been able to identify the source of this verse, although it appears repeatedly in discussions of the buddha-nature of the insentient doctrine; see, e.g., the *ZJ* records for Nanyang Huizhong (1.125.13), Dongshan Liangjie (2.65.3), and Dazhu Huihai (4.47.6), all of whom are discussed below.

42 *Shenhui yulu*, 139.

43 Another interesting Chinese text that explicitly castigates the doctrine that insentient objects have buddha-nature is the apocryphal *Śūraṃgama-sūtra* (*Shoulengyan jing*); see esp. T 945:19.153c9–14.

44 T 2007:48.344b9–10; cf. Yampolsky, *The Platform Sutra*, 177.

45 Yanagida, *Sodōshū sakuin*, 1.85.11–12.

46 T 2076:51.223a17–18.

47 T 2008:48.349a26–27.

48 While this text was not published until 1374, it agrees with the account of Huihai's teaching on the buddha-nature of the insentient found in the *ZJ* 4.47.6–11.

49 Hirano, trans., *Tongo yōmon*, 138 and 175; see also 155.

50 See the *Huangbo Duanji Chanshi wanling lu:* "The Master ascended the hall and said: 'This very mind is buddha. It reaches upward to all the buddhas and downward to things that slither on the ground; *everything that contains spirit* possesses buddha-nature and is equal with respect to the substance of the one mind. The reason that Bodhidharma came from India was only to transmit the dharma of one mind and to directly indicate that all beings are originally buddha'" (T 2012:48.386b2–5; emphasis mine). See also T 2012:48.381a28–29 for similar phrasing.

51 *ZJ* 1.121.10–122.14; cf. *Jingde chuandeng lu*, T 2076:51.438a9 ff.

52 *ZJ* 1.124.5–124.14; cf. *Jingde chuandeng lu*, T 2076:51.438b6–11.

53 T 279:10.30a6–7.

54 T 220:7.871c14–15.

55 *ZJ* 1.125.13–126.7 (this segment does not appear in the *Jingde Record*). See the discussion in Liu Ming-Wood, *Madhyamaka Thought*, 255.

56 While the controversy lost much of its steam in China following the Tang, in Japan it took on a life of its own. Innovative discussions of the issue can be found in the writings of numerous eminent Japanese monks, including Kūkai (774–835), Saichō (767–822), Annen (d. 889), Enchin (814–891), Ryōgen (912–985), Chūjin (1065–1138), Dōgen (1200–1253), and Nichiren (1222–1282), to name just a few. The controversy was also the focus of one of a series of spirited Hossō-Tendai debates held under imperial auspices in 963. Nor was the Japanese interest in the doctrine limited to exegetical works; it finds its way into

Japanese literature and performance arts as well. Sources on the buddha-nature of the insentient doctrine in Japan include Groner, *Ryōgen and Mount Hiei*, 337–339; LaFleur, "Saigyō"; Miyamoto, "Sōmoku kokudo"; Rambelli, *Vegetal Buddhas;* Sakamoto, "Hijō ni okeru busshō" and "On the 'Attainment of Buddhahood'"; Shively, "Buddhahood for the Nonsentient"; Sueki, "Annen *Shinjō sōmoku*" and "Annen: The Philosopher"; and Yoshizu, "Mujō busshōsetsu."

57 Kamata, "Chūgoku zen," 54, and *Chūgoku kegon*, 461–465.

58 See *Zhuangzi jinzhu jinyi*, 575; Watson, trans., *The Complete Works of Chuang Tzu*, 240–241. A. C. Graham views the twenty-second chapter as part of a cycle dating to the late third or second century BC, a period when "the Yellow Emperor and the Lao-tzu of the book which bears his name have become the acknowledged representatives of Daoism" (Graham, *Chuang-tzu*, 158). These dialogues are notable for raising themes that would be foregrounded in later Chinese Buddhism.

59 Shenhui's critique, in other words, has much in common with the later attacks by the Song master Dahui Zonggao (1089–1163) against the "silent illumination Chan" (*mozhao Chan*) of his Caodong lineage rivals, or with later Japanese Rinzai critiques of Sōtō doctrine. I would also note that Shenhui's concerns resonate with those of contemporary exponents of "critical Buddhism" (*hihan bukkyō*): just as the buddha-nature of the insentient mitigates the need for personal realization, it obviates the need for social, political, and environmental transformation.

60 For an insightful analysis of the Chan deployment of the two truths, see Faure, *The Rhetoric of Immediacy*, 53–78.

61 The *Zhaozhou Zhenji Chanshi yulu* is believed to have been in circulation by the end of the tenth century; the earliest extant recension is that preserved as fascicle 13 in the *Guzunsu yulu*, published in 1144. Thus while the extant text is in no way reliable as a guide to Zhaozhou's teaching, it is likely close to the version Wumen had at his disposal.

62 ZZ 118.314:157c8–10; Akizuki, trans., *Jōshū roku*, 130–131.

63 See, e.g., the *Jingde Record* biography of Xingshan Weikuan (755–817), a student of Mazu Daoyi.

> [A student] asked: "Does a dog also have buddha-nature or not?" The Master said: "It does." The monk said: "Does the Reverend also have it or not?" The Master said: "I don't have it." The monk said: "All sentient beings have buddha-nature. Why does the Reverend alone not possess it?" The Master said: "I am not all sentient beings." The monk said: "Since you are not a sentient being, are you a buddha or not?" The Master said: "I am not a buddha." The monk asked: "Ultimately what sort of thing is it?" The Master said: "It is also not a thing." The monk said: "Can it be seen or thought?" The Master said: "If you think of it you won't reach it; if you deliberate on it you won't get it. Therefore it is called inconceivable" (T 2076:51.255a18–24).

64 ZZ 118.321:161b14–16; Akizuki, trans., *Jōshū roku*, 255–256. This exchange suggests that case no. 37 in the *Gateless Barrier*, "Zhaozhou's oak tree," must also be revisited in the light of the buddha-nature of the insentient controversy.

65 ZZ 118.324:162c6–7; Akizuki, trans., *Jōshū roku*, 294.

66 T 2005:48.292c25–27.

67 *Linji lu,* T 47.500c1–4; Sasaki, trans., *The Recorded Sayings of Ch'an Master Lin-chi,* 25. Cf. Iriya, trans., *Rinzai roku,* 98; and Watson, trans., *The Zen Teachings of Master Lin-chi,* 53. The phrase "the spirit that haunts the grasses and the trees" (*yicao fumu jingling*) is also found in the *Yuanwu Foguo Chanshi yulu,* T 1997:47.758c23–24; cf. ibid. 760b12.

68 *Wumen guan,* T 2005:48.293a15–b3. Cf. Yamada Kōun, trans., *Gateless Gate,* 19–20; and Cleary, *No Barrier,* 9–10. The *gong'an* also appears as case no. 8 in the *Congrong Hermitage Record;* for a full account of its textual history, see Heine, *Shifting Shape,* 201–202.

69 Pulleyblank, *Lexicon of Reconstructed Pronunciation,* 126–127.

70 T 2005:48.293b10–16; cf. *Blue Cliff Record* case no. 19.

71 *Vimalakīrtinirdesa-sūtra,* trans. Kumārajīva, T 475:14.551c22.

72 T 2005:48.293a13–14.

73 T 2005:48.293c17–21.

74 English sources on the evolution of *gong'an* literature in the Song include Yanagida, "The 'Recorded Sayings' "; McRae, "Encounter Dialogue"; Yü Chün-fang, "Ch'an Education"; Hsieh, "A Study of the Evolution"; Keyworth, "Transmitting the Lamp"; and Foulk, "The Form and Function."

75 Today the (reconstructed?) text can be found in Fujita, ed., *Zudokko,* a modern compilation intended for Rinzai monastic training.

76 It is true that they came to be used as such in Tokugawa Japan, but this should not be taken as evidence of Chinese practice. As Rinzai monasticism spread in medieval Japan it became necessary to adapt the literary tradition for the growing number of monks with only limited skills in classical Chinese. In part inspired by Dahui, influential Rinzai figures such as Shūhō Myōchō (1282–1338) and Hakuin Ekaku (1686–1769) developed and eventually routinized a *gong'an* "curriculum" that allowed Japanese students with limited skill in literary Chinese to ritually participate in the Rinzai literary tradition. In the process, *gong'an* came to function, for some at least, as nondiscursive icons of awakening, rather than conceptually sophisticated instantiations of Mahayana dialectic.

77 See, e.g., the discussions in Buswell, "The 'Short-cut' Approach"; Foulk, "The Form and Function"; Hsieh, "A Study of the Evolution" and "Yuan-Wu K'o-Ch'in's (1063–1135) Teaching"; Keyworth, "Transmitting the Lamp"; Miura and Sasaki, *Zen Dust;* and Yü Chün-fang, "Ta-Hui Tsung-Kao."

78 On Dahui and the role of lay patronage, see esp. Levering, "Ch'an Enlightenment"; Schlütter, "Chan Buddhism," "Silent Illumination," and "Before the Empty Eon."

79 On the performative role of a Chan abbot, see Faure, *The Rhetoric of Immediacy;* Foulk, "Myth, Ritual, and Monastic Practice"; Foulk and Sharf, "On the Ritual Use"; Sharf, "The Idolization of Enlightenment" and "Ritual." For a critique of "enlightenment" as a subjective experience or state of consciousness, see also Sharf, "Experience."

80 On the ritual status of the Chan abbot, see esp. the *Regulations for Chan Practice* (*Chanmen guishi*), a monastic code appended to the biography of Baizhang found in the *Jingde Record* (T 2067:51.251a6–9; see also the comments in Collcutt, *Five Mountains,* 197; and Foulk, "Myth, Ritual, and Monastic Practice," 157–158).

81 See esp. Foulk, "The Form and Function"; and Yifa, *The Origins of Buddhist Monastic Codes.*

82 Kagamishima, Satō, and Kosaka, trans., *Yakuchū: Zen'en shingi,* 66–69; Yifa, *The Origins of Buddhist Monastic Codes,* 132–134.

83 In a parenthetical comment Zongze notes that the monk might raise a subject for conversation (*juhua*), continue a previous conversation (*tonghua*), or simply request instruction (*qingyi*). Yifa interprets the first term—*juhua*—as referring explicitly to *gong'an* (*The Origins of Buddhist Monastic Codes,* 134), but she may be reading too much into the phrase, especially as the term *gong'an* never appears in the *Rules of Purity for Chan Monasteries.* Nor does the term *gong'an* appear in connection with the *rushi* rite in other "canonical" Chan codes, such as the *Conglin jiaoding qinggui zongyao* of 1274, or the *Chixiu Baizhang qinggui* of 1338; see ZZ 112.31:16b12–c15 and T 2025:48.1120c15–1121a7, respectively. However, *juhua* may refer more generically to raising famous anecdotes or sayings of the patriarchs culled from a variety of literary genres.

84 Foulk "Myth, Ritual, and Monastic Practice," 181.

85 T 2025:48.1120c21ff.; cf. ZZ 112.32:16a8–10.

86 See note 83 above.

87 Collcutt, *Five Mountains,* 180–181; Yifa, *The Origins of Buddhist Monastic Codes,* 266–267, note 1.

88 See the description in Kagamishima, Satō, and Kosaka, trans., *Yakuchū: Zen'en shingi,* 71–75; Yifa, *The Origins of Buddhist Monastic Codes,* 135–136; and Sharf, "Ritual."

89 Foulk, "The Form and Function," 187.

90 On styles of reasoning, see esp. Hacking, "Styles of Scientific Reasoning"; on the case method, see Forrester, "If *p*, then what?"

91 Jonsen and Toulmin, *The Abuse of Casuistry,* 59–74.

92 Harbsmeier, *Logic and Language,* 376–379.

93 Forrester, "If *p*, then what?" 15.

94 Furth, "Producing Medical Knowledge," 4.

95 Note that this case is included in virtually every major *gong'an* collection, including the *Gateless Barrier* (case no. 14), the *Blue Cliff Record* (case no. 63), and the *Congrong Hermitage Record* (case no. 9).

8

Confucian "Case Learning"

The Genre of Xue'an *Writings*

HUNG-LAM CHU

Xue'an were latecomers to the family of cased-based and *an*-titled writings. The binome *xue'an* translates literally as "learning" and "case," making a generic title for a specific kind of text, the "case of learning." It usually took the form of a collection that paired biographies of scholars with selected excerpts from their writings. The earliest known *xue'an* work was written in the late sixteenth century by a Confucian master about the learning of a couple of earlier Confucian masters, to further the understanding of interested Confucian students. Thereafter, *xue'an* works about Confucian learning continued to appear down into the twentieth century.

The generic title apparently gained its popularity because of the publication of Huang Zongxi's (1610–1695) *Cases of Learning of Ming Confucians* (*Mingru xue'an*,[1] hereafter *Cases of Ming Confucians*) around 1680.[2] The vitality of the genre is attested to by the fact that *xue'an*-titled works known and accessible to us now abound in number. Several lengthy ones, some even bearing no relevance to Confucian learning at all, were published as late as the last decade.[3]

Xue'an works are about individual scholars and philosophical schools of thought, often organized by dynastic period. Works in the latter category are as a rule massive. The seminal *Cases of Ming Confucians*, which collects biographies of 212 Confucian masters together with selections from their writings, has a text of about one million characters. Other examples include the *Cases of Learning from the Song and Yuan* (*Song-Yuan xue'an*), a work begun by Huang Zongxi and completed by Quan Zuwang (1705–1755) and first published in 1838. In 1914 *Cases of Learning of the Two Han Dynasties and the Three Kingdoms* (*Liang Han Sanguo xue'an*) appeared, with a preface by Tang Yan (1857–1920). It was followed in 1938 by *Cases of Learning of the Qing Confucians* (*Qingru xue'an*), prefaced by Xu Shichang (1858–1939). With the last publication, every era in which Confucianism was a sanctioned state ideology and in which Confucian learning actually flourished had been analyzed in the *xue'an* genre of writing. The genre thus appears to have been considered appropriate for writing about the history of thought and philosophy, although the question remains as to whether it was originally conceived as a genre for historical writing.

Xue'an writings had no standard format, but one inspired by and modified from the *Cases of Ming Confucians* was frequently used. It consisted of a biography of the scholar concerned, some commentary by the biographer on the scholar's words and deeds, followed by selections from the scholar's writings and possibly from other historical documents concerning him. Such selections might include letters, notes, prefaces, essays, diaries, autobiographical accounts, or records of debates or conversations. Sometimes, as in the twentieth-century compilations of Tang Yan and Xu Shichang, the subject's exegeses and commentaries on the Confucian classics are also included.

Collections that survey the learning of a whole dynasty reveal complexities both of the period and of the author-compiler himself. The reader becomes aware of the philosophical views of individual Confucians, of trends of thought, and of the rise and decline of schools. The scope of coverage varied, but few *xue'an* works stepped outside the boundary of Confucianism to deal with other philosophies. The author-compilers were keen to show their own scholarly views on how Confucianism should be studied and practiced, which differed according to their intellectual persuasions. But all were immediately concerned with how their *xue'an* collections should be used.

Of all the *xue'an* works known to us, Huang Zongxi's *Cases of Ming Confucians* is indisputably the classic exemplar of the genre and a landmark in its development. It influenced later works in terms of the scholarly rigor demanded for the writing as well as format and style. Scholars have written widely on Huang's masterpiece and have discussed its organization as well as its philosophical assumptions and relevance to the history of neo-Confucian thought.[4] Nonetheless, a fuller understanding of the nature of the work as Huang himself saw it and the uses he intended for it may emerge from placing it in the context of the *xue'an* as a genre.[5]

This chapter is an inquiry into the nature of *xue'an* works and the intellectual orientations manifested in them. I offer a comparative study of all known and extant early *xue'an* works, with the *Cases of Ming Confucians* at the center. By asking what kind of works they were supposed to be, what it meant to have them so titled, what uses they served in the context of late Ming and early Qing thought, we may gain insight into philosophical dimensions of "thinking with cases" and into concepts of the substance and method of Confucian learning of Huang Zongxi and his contemporaries.

DEFINITION OF THE TERM *XUE'AN* AND CLASSIFICATION OF *XUE'AN* WORKS

It is curious that, despite the popularity of the term *xue'an* in sixteenth- and seventeenth-century writings on Confucian philosophy, neither Huang Zongxi nor any other contemporary author gave the term any definition.[6] Their silence denies us any ready understanding of the problem. Only more recently do we see scholars engaged in serious discussions of the meaning of the term and its early implications.

Recent scholars have proposed two definitions, both essentially based on reading *Cases of Ming Confucians*. One takes the "archival" view and regards *xue'an* as the scholarly records, files, or dossier of a scholar or a school of thought. This definition rests on the etymology of the key word "*an*."[7] The other definition takes a "cultural" view, seeing the term as the Confucian equivalent or version of the Chan Buddhist *gong'an* (*koan*). Here *xue'an* are seen as a kind of "scholarly *gong'an*," which differs from the Chan *gong'an* only in that the doctrinal teaching is expounded in literary form rather than through paradoxical sayings. Advocates of this definition point to the intellectual culture of the late Ming period, when it was popular for master Confucians to be versed in Chan Buddhism.[8] Both these definitions are the result of legitimate inferences, although their merit has yet to be determined.

A second issue concerns bibliographical classification. Modern scholars have been widely influenced by Liang Qichao (1873–1929) and see *xue'an* works as historical writings. This is because in his *History of Chinese Learning and Scholarship in the Last Three Hundred Years* (*Zhongguo jin sanbai nian xueshu shi*), Liang pointed to *Cases of Ming Confucians* as the first formal and complete "history of learning and scholarship" (*xueshushi*) ever written by a Chinese scholar.[9] But it is doubtful that *xue'an* were originally designed as intellectual history in the modern sense. Few scholars on the subject recall that Liang had also stated in his earlier *Abridged Version of Cases of Learning of Ming Confucians* (*Jieben Mingru xue'an*) that *Cases of Ming Confucians* was "a book on the Way." So Liang with equal clarity claimed that Huang Zongxi intended his book "to show the scholar a gate to the Way" and that his own abridgement was "solely about the essentials of governing one's own mind and body."[10] Here Liang treated *Cases of Ming Confucians* as a guide to self-cultivation practice.

Nonetheless, even when Liang Qichao spoke of *Cases of Ming Confucians* as a historical work, he was not only responding to Western historiographical influence,[11] but also appealing to traditional Chinese bibliographical classifications of learning. In the Han dynasty, collected biographies of ancient and modern philosophers were gathered together by Sima Qian (145–ca. 86 BCE) in the *Records of the Grand Historian* (*Shiji*), which also includes an authoritative discourse on the gist of six major schools of thought by the author's father, Sima Tan. Surviving works by or attributed to the philosophers were cataloged by Ban Gu (32–92 CE) in the *History of the Han Dynasty* (*Hanshu*). These sets of biographies and Ban's bibliographic essays offer analytical accounts of key doctrines of the various ancient schools and of the origins and development of their philosophies.[12] When *Cases of Ming Confucians* arranged biographies and words of the Ming Confucians according to the schools of thought they belonged to, it could be considered to follow this model.[13]

Aspects of its format would also allow *Cases of Ming Confucians* to be considered a kind of "record of words and deeds" (*yanxing lu*)—another recognized genre of historical writings in traditional bibliographic classification. An exemplary work of the "record of words and deeds" type was Zhu Xi's (1130–1200) *Record of Words and Deeds of Eminent Officials of the Five Reigns* (*Wuchao mingchen yanxing lu*) and its sequel, *Record of Words and Deeds of Eminent Officials of the Three Reigns* (*Sanchao mingchen yanxing lu*). These companion texts recorded entry by entry the deeds and words of eminent officials of the Northern Song dynasty. Other scholars have regarded another work by Zhu Xi on Cheng Hao (1032–1085) and Cheng Yi (1033–1107), the *Sources of the Yi-Luo School* (*Yi-Luo yuanyuan lu*), as the actual prototype of the *xue'an* type of compilation.[14] This book explores the *lixue* or *daoxue* tradition of neo-Confucianism through the two Cheng brothers, including their teacher, friends, and students. But this is also a particular kind of "record of words and deeds," except that there is a "social biography" for each figure it included.[15] These works by Zhu Xi, meant to complement one another,[16] are actually "records of deeds" in the main, because the words so recorded were those spoken in the course of concrete events rather than in philosophic writings.

The *Cases of Ming Confucians* differs from Zhu Xi's prototypes not so much because it offers a full narrative biography of each Ming Confucian, incorporating occasional quotations of the subject's words and also critical and evaluative comments from the biographer, Huang Zongxi; it differs categorically in the inclusion of the subject's written words or recorded sayings after the biography. The relationship between the biography and the appended selections is such that without the latter the function and the force of a biography still is kept intact, but without the former the selections are only a decontextualized cluster of excerpts. In this hybrid form the biographical narrative and the documentary selections from the subject's own words were meant to have special implications in relationship to one another. In other words, *Cases of Ming Confucians* could be viewed as a documentary record "of words and deeds" but must have been meant to be more than that.[17]

There are two further problems with treating the Ming and Qing *xue'an* discussed in this chapter as historical works. The first is that Huang Zongxi himself, as well as *xue'an* authors before and after him, do not leave the impression that they considered their books works of history. The second is that in the standard Qing bibliograhies, most early *xue'an* were not classified under history. As a matter of fact, of the six *xue'an*-titled works included in the eighteenth-century imperial library's *Complete Collection of the Four Treasuries* (*Siku quanshu*) and reviewed in its catalogue (*Siku quanshu zongmu,* hereafter *Analytical Bibliography*),[18] only *Cases of Ming Confiucians* was classified in the Division of History. It appears under the "Section of Biographical Collections in the Subdivision of Biographies" (Shibu zhuanji lei zonglu zhi shu).[19] The rest were classified under one or another of the sections devoted to the Confucian Classics and philosophers.

The eighteenth-century imperial cataloguers were working within accepted understandings of the distinctions between history and philosophy that were reflected in their classification of famous works of the past. History was presumed to narrate events and to value objectivity, and biographies as history quoted the words of their subjects as matters of record of events. This was the pattern in such classics as the *Sayings of the States* (*Guoyu*), the *Book of Documents* (*Shujing*), and in Zhu Xi's aforementioned *Sources of the Yi-Luo School,* where a collection of biographical sketches presented the words and deeds of the masters who had contributed to the rise of the Cheng brothers' school of neo-Confucianism in the Northern Song dynasty.

Philosophy was defined as the teachings of the "masters" (*zi*), sages, and worthies of the past and comprised texts that presented the philosopher's thought in his own words or that offered those words supplemented by exegetical commentary. Zhu Xi's *Reflections on Things at Hand* (*Jinsi lu*) made the anthology of topically arranged sayings and writings of several Confucian masters a popular form of philosophical textbook. In this format the carefully ordered compilation of selections from past philosophers served to advance a theory (*lishuo*), in this case Zhu Xi's own doctrine of the learning of nature and principle.

But these boundaries required interpretation. The narration of a past Confucian's words, put in the context of his deeds, that is, biography, could be regarded as history. On the other hand, the life as recorded in a Confucian's biography revealed his philosophy in action. Understanding the person of the philosopher—his biography—matters most. Moreover, when a number of biographies were gathered together, systematic networks of schools and evolving transmissions of teachings could be seen in cross reference—revealing history. When the compilers of the *Four Treasuries* looked at early *xue'an* with these issues in mind, classification was decided by the compilers' judgement about each author's intended purpose for writing. But whether their understanding of the nature of the works in question was in accord with those of the authors is a matter for us to judge. To make that judgment, it will be useful to consider them together as belonging to a previously unrecognized genre, the *xue'an.*

THE FIRST *XUE'AN* AND LATE MING THOUGHT

In the hundred years preceeding the publication of Huang Zongxi's *Cases of Ming Confucians* around 1680, five related works were produced that called themselves *xue'an,* all later included in the eighteenth-century *Four Treasuries.* They were *The Case of Learning from the Analects* (*Lunyu xue'an*), written in 1617 by Huang Zongxi's teacher, Liu Zongzhou (1578–1645); *Cases of Learning of the Confucians* (*Zhuru xue'an*) by Liu Yuanqing (1544–1609), written around 1596; *Cases of Learning* (*Xue'an*), written by Wang Shen (fl. 1660s) shortly before *Cases of Ming Confucians; Cases of Learning of the Two Cheng Brothers* (*Er-Cheng xue'an*), a work by Huang Zongxi that was completed by his son, Huang Baijia (1643–1709); and *The Case of Learning of [Chen Jian from] Dongguan* (*Dongguan xue'an*), written by Wu Ding (fl. 1750s) in the mid-eighteenth century. These works are thematically related. In addition to claiming the form of the "case," all were engaged to various degrees in the debates over the controversial philosophy of Wang Yangming (1472–1529).

I begin, however, with the earliest text known to have used the term *xue'an* as a title—Geng Dingxiang's (1524–1596) "Cases of Learning of Mr. Lu Jiuyuan and Mr. Yang Jian" (Lu-Yang er xiansheng xue'an). This piece, being an essay in Geng's *Collected Works,* was not singled out for review in the *Analytical Bibliography of the Four Treasuries.* But discussion concerning the *xue'an* genre must start here because it obviously inspired the earliest known book-length *xue'an,* the *Cases of Learning of the Confucians* by Liu Yuanqing, who was Geng's devoted student.[20]

Geng's piece is found in the "Biography" section of his collected writings (*juan* 13). It consists of two biographies—of the Song Confucians Lu Jiuyuan (1139–1193) and Yang Jian (1141–1226)—and a concluding note. The career and sayings of Lu are presented chronologically, in separate entries. This presentation makes the account somewhat similar to that of the "records of words and deeds of eminent officials" genre of writing. But the career information and philosophical expressions included are highly selective. The format of the biography of Yang Jian is similar, except that the sources are even more focused on Yang's enlightenment as a result of his discussion with Lu. In sum, these two biographies include only words and deeds bearing on the paths to enlightenment followed by these two Southern Song worthies. The accounts do allow Lu and Yang each to speak for his own philosophical orientation. But Geng Dingxiang seems to want to present his subjects' learning as much through the observation of conduct as through a mere knowledge of words. In the cases of Lu Jiuyuan and Yang Jian, the truth of their learning is to be known only by an observation of their actions.

Geng's postscript is particularly illuminating for our understanding of why he adopted the term *xue'an.* It reveals that he wrote the biographies of Lu and Yang to correct what he considered a misunderstanding of the learning of these two Confucian masters. Believing that their learning was arrived at through some kind of sudden enlightenment, scholars in their school of thought erred in "talking lavishly about [the greatness of] subtle enlightenment and mysterious comprehension but slighting solid cultivation." Geng wrote their biographies to show the contrary. The record of their actions and words was evidence that Lu and Yang had arrived at their learning through a gradual process, and the correct way to learn from them was for the student to follow a similar slow path: identify his own intention, know his own heart, and correct his mistakes, all the while not insisting upon his personal views but yielding to the opinions of others.[21]

What Geng Dingxiang did here was to reexamine and refute a current opinion. The term *xue'an* here carries the connotation of a legal "case." It is as if his aim was to reverse the verdict. What he actually did was state the facts and judge the matter simultaneously. The evidence of his "case" was the words and deeds of his two subjects, from which he also drew his conclusion. Geng's *xue'an* had the double function of filing a case and passing a verdict on it. The ultimate aim of this case was to present a correct path of learning for the potential followers of the teachings of Lu and Yang. Note that in terms of philosophical lineage Geng Dingxiang's philosophy was derived from the Taizhou school,[22] which in turn was derived from the Yaojiang school of Wang Yangming, whose philosophy was deemed close to that of Lu and Yang. Belonging to this lineage of learning, Geng would consider Lu and Yang as philosophical ancestors. Ultimately his *xue'an* piece aimed to guide Confucians along the right path of learning. Hence it did not stop at the judgment of the right and wrong or the superiority and inferiority of a certain theory or doctrine, but rather aimed to show a path of practice. In this sense, *xue'an* bore the meaning of plan, and learning pointed to a way of living.[23]

Geng Dingxiang's work inspired his student Liu Yuanqing's *Cases of Learning of the Confucians.*[24] The extant text of the latter has a total of twenty-five *juan*, each one for a major Confucian philosopher. The chapter heading for each *juan* always reads the "important sayings [*yaoyu*] of Mr. So and So." Altogether twelve Song Confucians and thirteen Ming Confucians were included, concluding with Liu's teacher, Geng Dingxiang himself.[25] Each *juan* was standardized to include a fairly long biography of the Confucian, followed by a selection of the subject's words drawn from essays or recorded conversations whose sources were not indicated. Liu Yuanqing offered no commentary on his compilation.

Some of the biographies in the book were actually written by Geng Dingxiang and were taken directly from Geng's works. These biographies included Geng's comments wherever available. By means of this borrowing, Liu showed his respect for his teacher.[26] But the "important sayings" of these Confucians appear to have been selected by Liu himself. Although he did not speak of it explicitly, it is clear that Liu inherited Geng's doctrine and meant for his own compilation to expand on it.

Liu did clearly explain his intention in his preface: to reveal the fact that the learning of both Confucius and Mencius was based on the understanding of human nature. According to Liu, neither Confucius nor Mencius had elaborated on the term "nature." Instead, Confucius regarded realization of one's nature in "learning with a constant perseverance and application,"[27] whereas Mencius considered "giving full realization to one's heart" in order for one to understand his own nature.[28] These aphorisms spoke only of learning and practice and of exertion of one's inborn capacities (which meant for Mencius the development and maturation of the four germs in one's heart—benevolence, dutifulness, observance of the rites, and wisdom).[29] For Liu, human nature could be known through lived experience, but not through philosophical verbalization.

Later Confucians, however, obscured this doctrine of learning. According to Liu, they tried to define human nature in terms of things seen and heard, describing and explaining it only by means of words and perceptual knowledge. Thus their theories were not universal but changed with the times. All new doctrines arose as a result of the demands of change.[30] In fact, the evolution of Confucian learning introduced defects like the partiality and passivity of a Lu Jiuyuan or the incoherence and irrelevance of a Zhu Xi. This process, which saw the rise of one doctrine and the fall of another, was one of internal struggles like those of men "fighting inside a cave" (*xuezhong zhi dou*). For now, those who advocated "imperceptible agreement in the internal" (the school of Mind) were carrying the day. But there was no guarantee that those who advocated "further seeking from the outside" (the school of Principle) would not make a comeback. As long as learning remained a matter of words and opinions but not genuine practice, there was no way to achieve the kind of learning that had been taught and demonstrated by Confucius and Mencius.

Liu Yuanqing's preface ends by offering his endeavor as a proposed solution to the perennial problem. The key lines read,

> Would this fight inside the cave never end? Only now do I understand the greatness of the learning of Confucius and Mencius. [The sages knew that] one may talk about nature or not; and that to speak of what is external [to one's nature] does not negate the internal, and to speak of what is internal does not negate the external. Should this not perhaps be what makes a sage [*sheng*] different from a worthy Confucian [*ru*]? Nevertheless, as all the [Song and Ming] Confucians were surely seeking the light of the path of the sages, how am I to assess [their achievement] when there are no Confucius and Mencius in the world [to be the standard]? Thus I can only "prepare the cases" [*ju'an*] of these Confucians [whose ac-

counts are included in this book]. As for a judgment [*panduan*] of who among them were sages and who were worthy Confucians, so that my long-standing doubts might be cleared up, perhaps I can still come up with one before long, even though I am now old.

To put an end to the internal struggle of the Confucians, Liu tried to point out the sages' way of learning by "preparing the cases" of those Confucians who had sought the light of the sages in their lives. The biographies and "important sayings" of each of them offered models or ways of learning of these past Confucians. The interested student could decide which of them had accomplished the "learning of a sage" and which only the "learning of a worthy Confucian" and accordingly choose who deserved his emulation. It is clear, then, that his aim of producing a *xue'an* was to present for the interested scholars the ways or models of learning of some master Confucians through their own words and the knowledge of their lives. But as the reader could judge simply on the basis of his own study, the strength of abiding adherence to a master-disciple way of learning was bound to be largely reduced.

Liu Yuanqing appeared to be judgmentally neutral, as he merely "prepared the cases" but did not attempt to promote any particular Confucians. But this neutrality was actually superficial. In reality, he thought that some Ming Confucians (e.g., Wang Yangming and his followers) had attained the wisdom of a sage, while the Song Confucians remained at the level of Confucian worthies. This judgment was very mildly and indirectly expressed in this work, but appeared clearer in two other related pieces of writing. One of them, the "Preface to the Biographical Sketches of Song Confucians" (Songru zhuanlue xu), written for a book that in effect was the Song portion of *Cases of Learning of Confucians*, helps reveal the hidden intention of the latter work.[31] A key passage from this preface alerts us to the fact that although Liu Quanqing "prepared the cases" of the Song Confucians in his *Cases of Learning of Confucians*, he did not see them alone as the best models to follow. Liu cited Geng, saying, "This is because the way [of learning] chosen [*zeshu*] by Song Confucians is slightly different [from that chosen by Confucius and Mencius]." Geng's metaphor of a lamp shining different measures of space according to its position is used to illustrate the point Mencius emphasized that "making careful choice [*shenshu*]"[32] is all important in learning. The sages' way is to be preferred because their words, "though plain, are not estranged from human experience and are boundless in meaning." The Song Confucian "theories are not independent of personal viewpoints [*jian*], which, though profound, are limited in meaning." But, "although Song Confucians surely did not succeed in seeking to illuminate the way of Confucius, as personages they were often men of lofty stature and renowned accomplishments ... far outshining those styled as Confucian scholars in recent ages but superficially learned, unprincipled and pedantic." Their accomplishments were to be taken as a reflection of their learning.

Liu's greater regard for some Ming Confucians was expressed in another preface, "Preface to Sketches of Confucian Masters of the Present Dynasty" (Zhaodai ruzong jilue xu), written for a biographical collection by Geng Dingxiang, in which the biographies of Wang Yangming and his disciples, Zou Shouyi, Wang Gen, and Luo Hongxian, were included. As the title of the book suggests, these four figures were considered the only true Confucian masters of the Ming dynasty up to the time of the compilation. Liu more than concurred with Geng's judgement on this when he said, "In the past, the learning of Song Confucians split and was daily transmitted erroneously. Scholars analyzed terms and examined sentences in textual commentaries.... [But] when Yuyao [Wang Yangming] emerged to raise the doctrine of innate knowledge, [the heart of learning] became thoroughly visible like the sun at noon." Liu also lauded Wang Yangming and his disciples for the right choice in learning they made (*zeshu*), which enabled one to make good his nature.[33]

Clearly, Liu Yuanqing and his teacher Geng Dingxiang favored the philosophy of Wang Yangming. Hence the critical review introducing *Cases of Learning of Confucians* in the *Analytical Bibliography* is correct in saying of Liu, "because his learning took root in that of Wang Shouren [Yangming], when it came to writings of the Cheng-Zhu school he chose only those having affinity with the doctrines of Lu Jiuyuan."[34] More important for this analysis is that, as revealed in the two passages quoted above, the ultimate aim of a *xue'an* was to offer a path for "choosing a way" of learning.

Liu Zongzhou's *The Case of Learning from the Analects* is a commentary that elucidates Confucius' canonical text entry by entry. Liu's goal was to expound on the meaning of the sayings and events recorded in each entry and to illuminate their philosophical subtleties. Here the term *xue'an* connotes the author's examination, verification, and judgment of the meaning of the canonical text, a task traditionally addressed in classical commentary, here reinforced by the inclusion of earlier commentators' remarks alongside his own. Accordingly, the *Four Treasuries* classified this work in the subdivision of the *Four Books* in the division of Confucian Canons, thus considering it a classical commentary.[35]

However, Liu's work lay on the far side of the fine line between commentary as classical exegesis and commentary as philosophical interpretation. Liu used analogy and his own reasoning for his explanations and elucidations.[36] As the critical abstract (*tiyao*) of this work in the *Analytical Bibliography* puts it, "Liu in this book gave his own opinions candidly. His arguments are not flawless, but they are nonetheless all expressions of his own solid understanding. They are unlike those Confucian classical commentaries which, though plagarisms of Buddhist doctrines, are boastfully promoted as the attainment of unsurpassable truth." Furthermore, there are also places where by means of his exposition he "criticized the later [and decadent] adherents of the doctrine of innate knowledge."[37] Liu's work exposes the difficulty of achieving a clear-cut categorical distinction between classical and philosophical writing or between commentary and interpretation.

Cases of Learning (*Xue'an*) by Wang Shen is a work that gathered together selections from the pre-Qin classics and the Song neo-Confucian masters.[38] They include the *Four Books,* Zhu Xi's *Regulations for Learning from the White Deer Hollow Academy* (*Bailudong [xue]gui*) and "Admonitions from the Studio of Reverence" (Jingzhai zhen), as well as *School Rules* (*Xueze*) by Cheng Duanmeng (1143–1191) and Dong Zhu (1152–1214). The *Analytical Bibliography* maintains that Wang's work expanded on a work of the same nature by Rao Lu (fl. 1256) and "mainly aimed at correcting the faults of the later adherents of the Yaojiang school [of Wang Yangming]."[39] This comment found agreement in Fang Bao's undated preface to the work. But Fang also said that the book "includes the articles [of learning] set by Rao Lu and Zhen Dexiu (1178–1235) as well as the protocols of the meetings of the Donglin Academy set by Gu Xiancheng (1550–1612) and Gao Panlong (1562–1626)."[40]

The texts of the *Four Books* selected by Wang Shen in effect include only sayings attributed to Confucius, Yanzi, Zengzi, Zisi, and Mencius. These sayings were meant to demonstrate the learning of the sages. Zhu Xi's *Regulations for Learning* and Cheng Duanmeng and Dong Zhu's *School Rules* were meant to elucidate the teachings of later advanced learning and elementary learning, respectively. The excerpts from these two books were listed in separate entries, under each of which elucidating notes and rules and regulations were furnished to make the content concrete. These added comments seem to have come from the works of Rao Lu and Zhen Dexiu. The substance of Wang Shen's Cases of Learning was conceived as a plan of teaching from the teacher's point of view and as a plan of learning (*xue'an*) from the student's. The connotation of "a plan" for the word *an* followed the usage in the writings of Geng Dingxiang and Liu Yuanqing, only it appears even more clearly in this case, as clear-cut and concise as the title of the book itself. The heart of Wang Shen's argument is equally clear: only by following the steps and articles of learning—the plan of learning—as presented in his book could one achieve the learning that would enable him to become a sage.

One early *xue'an, Cases of Learning of the Two Cheng Brothers,* was written early on by Huang Zongxi himself and completed by his son Huang Baijia after Zongxi's death.[41] The *Annotated Bibliography* states the reason for this work thus: "This work holds that the Cheng brothers differed in their attainment of virtues. So it compiled the sayings of the two Chengs and discussions about them by former Confucians into two separate *juan,* one for each of the brothers."[42] This description of the book's format suggests that the word *an* implied the meanings of making a classification, setting up a file, and passing a judgment. To use the legal metaphor again, the text presented a case in law and proposed a verdict for it. The sayings of the Cheng brothers and the comments on their persons and words were evidence for the verdict. Like Geng Dingxiang's "Cases of the Learning of Mr. Yang and Mr. Lu," the verdict followed from the judge's own argument. Huang Zongxi, the compiler-cum-judge, was arguing that the doctrines of the two Cheng brothers were different and that "Zhu Xi gained his [intellectual] strength mainly from Cheng Yi and might not have thoroughly learned the teaching of Cheng Hao."[43] Likewise, "scholars must be careful to take note that the two Cheng masters guided students in different ways."[44] The implication was that Zhu Xi could not represent the whole of orthodox Confucianism.

The final early *xue'an* to be included in the *Annotated Bibliography* was Wu Ding's *The Case of Learning of [Chen Jian] from Dongguan*, completed in the mid-eighteenth century. This book was specifically written to defend Wang Yangming's interpretation of Song neo-Confucianism by refuting one of his late Ming critics—Chen Jian's (1497–1567) *A General Discussion of Defects of Learning* (*Xuebu tongbian*), which was dedicated to critiquing Wang Yangming's *Master Zhu's Final Conclusions Arrived at Late in Life* (*Zhuzi wannian dinglun*).[45] Wang's book, by means of a chronological arrangement of Zhu Xi's letters to his friends and students, had concluded that Zhu Xi's philosophy differed from that of Lu Jiuyuan in his younger years but converged with Lu's thought in his old age. Chen Jian, by his own chronological study of Zhu Xi's letters, reached the opposite conclusion and charged that Lu Jiuyuan's version of Confucian learning was not Confucianism but Chan Buddhism. Wu Ding disagreed. "He therefore listed Chen Jian's statements and made his own argument against them one by one."[46] The term *xue'an* here implied a use of documentary evidence to reexamine and repudiate an accepted theory or formulation. As in a litigation case, both evidential statements and judgment are provided.

In these early *xue'an*-titled works we have discussed so far, the purpose of "making a case" for a Confucian was to allow him to "make an argument" or "advance a theory" of his own. The *xue'an* writings drew upon the established neo-Confucian traditions of recording the "words and deeds" of masters, with or without commentary, to teach the learning of the Way. In the hands of a skillful scholar-compiler, the selection, arrangement, and classification of these documentary materials, together with commentary on them, had always constituted a hermeneutics. When these late-Ming scholars began to speak of their compilations as "*an*," the judicial metaphor suggested a subtle shift in assumptions about how the reader was expected to find the truth. A master's words and deeds, instead of being seen as canon or history, were defined as evidence, and the body of the text on him called for the reader's evaluative judgment (verdict) of the case put together by the author-compiler. To weigh evidence to decide for or against the truth of philosophical claims was particularly called for in the late-Ming context of fierce debate over the ideas of Wang Yangming and his followers. Each of the early *xue'an* weighed in on one side or the other of these debates, justifying the eighteenth-century imperial cataloguers' classification of such works as philosophy. Of these works, those written by Geng Dingxiang and Liu Yuanqing had the deeper meaning of providing models or plans of learning—that is, documenting for the reader records on a variety of masters. Huang Zongxi's *Cases of Ming Confucians* can profitably be examined and understood in the context of these pioneering works that experimented with the forms of a *xue'an*.[47]

THE AIM AND NATURE OF *CASES OF MING CONFUCIANS*

How, then, do we understand *Cases of Ming Confucians* in this intellectual context? First of all, being published around 1680, it was able to look back on the whole Ming dynasty and its philosophical polemics as things of the past. The eighteenth-century *Four Treasuries* compilers, seeing that the work grouped philosophers around regional lineages of masters and disciples, including Huang Zongxi's own teachers, understood the work's organizing principle to be based on tracing philosophical schools of thought. They interpreted the book's structural principles and the implications of Huang's arguments in terms of school rivalries in which he had taken a clear side. Thus they charged that the book was a manifestation of intellectual partisanship inherited from the late Ming, but "not exclusively written for the discussion of learning [*jiangxue*]."[48] In sum, their classification of the work as history allowed readers to avoid the contentious issue of philosophical endorsement of controversial Ming personages. Was that the intention of Huang Zongxi? What about the views of Huang himself and his other readers?

Our examination begins with the two prefaces and the "Organizing Principles" (Fafan) Huang Zongxi wrote for *Cases of Ming Confucians*.[49] These two prefaces, both written in 1693, share common themes but differ in language and ideas. The first preface was written while Huang was gravely ill. It is not as clear and cogent as the revised one he completed after recovering from his illness. However, the first preface is important in that it betrays Huang's immediate concerns while writing.

In both prefaces Huang Zongxi expressed the same opposition to the prevalent scholarly practice of doctrinal partisanship. The revised preface lamented "present-day scholars who insist upon going only one way, forcibly construing the statements [of Zhu Xi] as the standard by which to assess the ancients and the moderns, and slandering as wayward and rebellious whoever slightly differs from them." But he also predicted scornfully that the one-way-only scholars were tilling a ground full of "yellow cogon grass and white reeds [*huangmao baiwei*]"—a phrase coined by the great Su Shi (1037–1101) to describe the lackluster performance of infertile soil.[50] Conformity stunted development, as far as Confucian learning was concerned. In opposition to this, Huang emphasized the importance of diversity in approaches to learning, using the analogy of travelers arriving at the same destination by different paths, or of all rivers finding the sea as their final destination. In this spirit he presented the original doctrines of serious Ming Confucians and let the student make his own choice of whom to follow. The Confucians selected were serious because, as the first preface put it, "whether their attainment was profound or shallow, perfect or faulty, they had all given their best efforts, and had exhausted the myriad dimensions of their minds before becoming masters of their own schools." Huang's contribution, as stated in both prefaces, was to "distinguish between the sources and tributaries [of their learning] to make clear their essential doctrines." In both prefaces, Huang used the metaphor of a filled water pot to show how *Cases of Ming Confucians* should be used. The student should imagine "a water pot placed at the main thoroughfare. If one carries only a bowl or a wooden ladle there and takes the water, he will not go away unsatiated." *Cases of Ming Confucians* was a resevoir of learning—a single source, divisible as the thirsty student selects what he needs according to his own measure. A useful sourcebook or reader is apportioned like water into bowls, but water itself is not a divisible thing.

It is also noteworthy that both prefaces quoted Tang Bin's comments on the book: "The doctrines contained in the *Cases of Ming Confucians* are complex and various, but if you know how to read them, you will find that they are not without some unifying thread."[51] The revised preface also quoted Chen Xigu (1634–1687),[52] who compared the text to a famous Tang painting: "The *Xue'an* is like the *Picture of the King's Audience* [*Wanghui tu*],[53] the sight of which pierces one's mind and startles his eyes. For only in this does one see the greatness of the King, who embraces all in the universe." These comments conveyed that this book had a broad coverage of rich materials as well as a unifying theme; it was not a grab bag of selections but communicated a doctrine of the author's own.

The first preface included a lengthy critique of Yun Richu (1602–1679), who along with Huang was also an eminent disciple of Liu Zongzhou. In 1669 Yun was residing in Shaoxing editing the many works of Liu into a comprehensive reader, *Essentials of Master Liu's Teachings* (*Liuzi jieyao*). This collection "took Zhu Xi's *Reflections on Things at Hand* as a model, and compiled Liu's works into classifications."[54] Huang's preface criticized Yun for bias. "Concerning a learning which could be arrived at by different paths and ways of consideration, he still has not been able to move beyond some fixed positions." Yun was evaluating Liu's theory of "sincerity of the mind"—a theory Huang insisted was highly original—based on Zhu Xi's interpretation. Believing that Yun was unable to see the core of Liu's doctrine, much less to expound on it, Huang declined to write a preface to Yun's work.[55] In his own preface Huang said that *Cases of Ming Confucians* by contrast offered a faithful presentation of Liu: "I based my argument on [the doctrine of] our late teacher, not daring to alter it." The fact that Huang went to great lengths to address this issue suggests that in the course of its writing, *Cases of Ming Confucians* had been shaped as a response to Yun's interpretation of their teacher's learning.

Why were these matters dropped from the revised preface? The main reason seems to be related to Huang's emphasis on a scholar's personal choice in his way of learning. There is no doubt Huang believed in loyalty to his teacher and felt reverence for his teacher's learning. But on principle, he did not want to present Liu's philosophy and practice from the vantage point of his own membership in Liu's lineage of learning. As philosophically the universe was made up of one principle and myriad manifestations of it (*liyi fenshu*)—a proposition shared by practically every neo-Confucian—so Confucian learning might be pursued down a variety of paths. Thus in the way of learning, free choice was better than abiding subscription to some single doctrine. Overemphasis on the intellectual role of doctrinal transmission went against the spirit of seeking the Way through multiple "cases."[56] This idea was elaborated on in the itemized "Organizing Principles" to *Cases of Ming Confucians.*

The first item of the "Organizing Principles" was a criticism of two contemporary works on neo-Confucianism that on the surface seemed quite similar to *Cases of Ming Confucians.* They were Zhou Rudeng's (1547–1629) *Orthodox Transmission of the Learning of the Sages* (*Shengxue zongchuan*) and Sun Qifeng's (1585–1675) *Orthodox Transmission of the Learning of Principle* (*Lixue zongchuan*). Both works were also organized around biographies plus excerpts from the subjects' words and the authors'comments on them.[57] Huang saw in these two works of "orthodox transmission" the common defect of obscurity, confusion, and impurity in the identification and presentation of philosophical doctrines. Zhou was overly subjective, letting his own Chan-laden views blur other Confucian masters' ideas. Sun lacked a sense of discrimination, unable to distinguish adequately the essential points of the Confucian masters. Their documentation was incomplete, their information inadequate. Huang believed that "when a scholar reads my book then he will realize the scantiness, sketchiness, and carelessness of these two authors." These two works would lead the student along a confined path of doctrinal transmission, which was very different from the solid use of evidence in the way of learning that Huang himself advocated.

Huang's own way of presenting the learning of the neo-Confucians is spelled out more explicitly in the sixth entry of the "Organizing Principles." He takes up the criteria for the selection of materials and the intended audience for his book: "In learning, we regard as truth what each person has discovered himself and has made apparent to others. Included in this book are partial opinions as well as opposing. Students should pay attention to the differences. This is the meaning of the same root dividing into myriad branches. To simply add water to water cannot be called learning."[58] It becomes clear, then, that Huang appealed to students who pursued learning for their own moral development, but not to those "vulgar scholars" or "professional students" "who depend upon other schools and copy from other people." It follows that the materials included in his book were not to be used as evidence that would distinguish one subschool from another or evaluate the status of the schools. They were reference for interested scholars, which would be "useful to themselves individually and alone." The cases were irreducibly individual precisely because this book did not aim to teach the lineal transmission of doctrines at all.

The seventh entry of the "Organizing Principles" said that the materials were to help readers attain wisdom by themselves. As Huang emphatically stated,

> [T]he ancients did not lightly transmit their teachings, as they wanted students to make their own discoveries. Even the Buddhists fear that when [the riddle of truth] has been given out, people will play with its externals. This book cannot avoid giving many easy generalizations. If students gather information from it without making genuine effort, I would have done injury to the world for having written it.[59]

This book did not aim at a distinction of the origins and developments of schools of thought in order to establish a hierarchy of philosophical doctrines. Understanding schools of thought was useful for the scholar just entering the gate of learning to help him know the essence of the doctrine(s) he proposed to put into practice. The real intention of the book was to provide the scholar with a set of dossiers on those Ming Confucians whose achievements "were not equaled in former times"[60] for his own guidance. But the student had to reflect on their meaning to arrive at his own understanding as a Chan monk had to contemplate the meaning of "public cases" (*gong'an*) for his own enlightenment. Incidentally, it is in this way that the definition of *xue'an* as a kind of scholarly *gong'an* makes any sense.

Significantly, neither the prefaces nor the "Organizing Principles" to *Cases of Ming Confucians* say anything to indicate the work as a "history" of Confucian learning. Terms like "orthodox transmission" (*daotong*), "orthodox lineage" or "orthodox doctrine" (*zhengzong*), and "doctrinal succession" (*zongtong*) do not appear in the text. Even the fifth entry of the "Organizing Principles," which accounts for the grouping of the cases around regional lineages of learning or schools of thought, explains lineage-based learning as only one learning strategy among others.

> The learning of the Confucians is unlike the learning of the five schools of [Chan] Buddhism, which have to trace back to the Qingyuan and Nanyue schools. Confucius himself did not receive his learning from any particular teacher. Zhou Dunyi arose without any predecessor. What Lu Jiuyuan taught was not what he had learned from anyone else. And yet, from the times of Cheng Yi and Zhu Xi to those of He Ji (1188–1268), Wang Bo (1197–1274), Jin Lüxiang (1232–1303) and Xu Qian (1270–1337)—that is, over an interval of several centuries—the norms of the ancestors' rules were constantly observed. This kind of transmission differs from the Buddhist custom of making only a tenuous association of intellectual lineages. In this book, therefore, divisions into schools of thought are primarily based on their transmissions. [Cases] that arose in isolation and those about less-known later scholars are all collected in the section "Cases of Miscellaneous Scholars."[61]

This, then, argued to the effect that the value of the genuine Confucian learning of the Ming scholars did not depend upon a long-period, larger "lineal transmission" frame of reference, tracing them back to predecessors. Serious scholars need not rule out the viability of acquiring Confucian learning through clearly and continuously transmitted schools of thought, but acquiring it through one's personal realization was more cherished. The main point in preparing cases both for Confucians of defined schools of thought and for independent Confucians was to illustrate the actual practice of learning rather than to argue based on the privileging of some tenuous association of school origins. The word "*an*" as here used has a clear connotation of classification, but it was not the schools that really mattered. To sum up the above analysis, it can be seen according to Huang Zongxi's own words that the *Cases of Ming Confucians* was produced to provide for the student of Confucian learning a wealth of source materials for his further study. The materials themselves were evidence of different models and plans of learning of master Ming Confucians, presented to teach the student how to find his own path in philosophy and practice.

The aim of Huang Zongxi can also be understood from prefaces to the book written before the middle of the Qing dynasty. None of these early readers wrote of it as a historical work, but saw it as a work of philosophy and guide to self-cultivation. This point is especially obvious in the following excerpts from the 1707 preface by Yu Zhun, son of the eminent neo-Confucian minister Yu Chenglong (1617–1684).

> [This book] shows the main course and the tributaries [of the river of learning]. It clarifies the intellectual lineage of each scholar and analyzes the achievements and defects of his learning as well as his difference from other scholars so clearly it is as if one were pointing at his own palm. It furthermore records the scholar's sayings and writings for later scholars to discuss. It is truly the mountain of treasure of this Way and the raft of the scholar [in the course of learning].[62]

The same point is made in different words in the 1691 preface to the first edition by Jia Run, sponsor of the publication of the book, and the 1693 preface by Qiu Zhao'ao (1638–1717), Huang Zongxi's student. These important prefaces, while noting that the schools of thought included in this book were clearly shown in their origins and developments, believed it to be objective and penetrating precisely because the merits and defects of each was shown in an evenhanded way. As said before, the various sayings and writings that this book selected for inclusion were not to be used solely as evidence for establishing lineages of learning in a hierarchy of transmission, but rather, and more important, as individual examples for readers to consider in seeking the foundations for their own learning practice.

Precisely because the *Cases of Ming Confucians* offered narratives of Confucian learning, each of which aimed to teach its own "doctrine" (*zongzhi*), it was viewed by scholars who advocated a unified and authoritative way of learning as some kind of heterodoxy that must be criticized. Tang Jian (1778–1861), who insisted on unreserved respect for and loyalty to the teaching of Zhu Xi, was one such scholar. Tang, in his *Small Records of the Cases of Learning of the Qing Dynasty* (*Guochao xue'an xiaozhi*), charged Huang Zongxi thus.

> Huang Zongxi compiled the *Cases of the Song Confucians, Cases of the Yuan Confucians* and *Cases of the Ming Confucians,* in which doctrines appearing in the last several hundred years, whether pure, flawed, correct, false, just or partial, are all included. Scholars are delighted at the breadth of their coverage and the eloquence of the words in them, and as a result believe that the world's empty and wild talks are all properties of learning. They do not know that instead the core principles of a thousand years' learning have thus been confused and the hearts of posterity have been damaged and submerged. Confucius said, "The study of strange doctrines is injurious indeed."[63] Mencius said, "What arises in the mind will interfere with policy, and what shows itself in policy will interfere with practice."[64] These words do not deceive in the least.... Mr. Huang was a student of the Way himself, why did he never think about this?[65]

This is indeed telling. What Tang Jian attacked was Huang Zongxi's doctrine of learning not from one fixed authority or from one particular school. This nonetheless perfectly reflected the philosophical position of *Cases of Ming Confucians,* a work offering a theoretical argument on the importance of personal choice in the way of Confucian learning.

HUANG ZONGXI'S CONCEPTION OF CONFUCIAN LEARNING

A good way to approach the underlying philosophy behind *Cases of Ming Confucians* is to compare it to the works by Zhou Rudeng and Sun Qifeng that Huang Zongxi criticized. All three were late Ming or early Qing readers in Confucian learning. However, the materials in the books by Zhou and Sun were organized to display the "orthodox transmission" of their titles. From their point of view, genuine Confucian learning was transmitted as orthodoxy the way pure blood was transmitted from an ancestor to a descendant. Only when the transmission was pure could the learning claim to be genuine.[66] This principle of teaching and learning, giving and receiving, began with the recognition of an orthodox founder and depended upon a lineage-like "transmission of mind." In the crowded world of Ming Confucians, the effort to distinguish correct from heterodox lineages of learning resulted in bitter scholarly struggles of a partisan nature.

Huang Zongxi, by contrast, did not use metaphors like the Chan Buddhist "transmission of the mind" and "transmission of the lamp."[67] His metaphor was an integrated traffic network of the rivers and the sea. All rivers, so long as they could lead one to the sea, were useful waterways; conceptually there was no reason to prefer the main watercourse to the tributaries. In this way Huang believed more in the superiority of free choice under the conditions of factual comparison. Even though he personally followed the doctrines of Wang Yangming and Liu Zongzhou, it was precisely because they taught reliance on individual insight over dependence on external authority that he confidently conceived of his book as a *xue'an*—with all the connotations we have found.

A Confucian *xue'an,* then, was an alternative to a work on Confucian learning as *zongchuan,* or "orthodox transmission." Both types led students through a broad history of Confucian learning. But from the student's perspective, where *zongchuan* confined him to following the model of particular masters, *xue'an* writings gave him the possibility of freedom. Because of its evenhanded presentation of independent cases, *Cases of Ming Confucians* allowed the student to find the most appropriate and useful model for his practical emulation in accordance with his own aptitude and circumstances.

A significant change in the conception of the conduct of Confucian learning thus appeared to have taken place in the late Ming. Whereas the emphasis of *zongchuan* writings was on the method of transmission—a demand of direct, lineal give and take—the emphasis of *xue'an* writings was on case study—an advocacy of parallel comparison. It is indeed ironic that the first writer of the *zongchuan* genre, Zhou Rudeng, was presented, mistakenly and intentionally so, as a leading spokesman of the Taizhou school of Wang Yangming thought in the late Ming, which advocated freedom of the self and independent judgment in matters moral and social.[68] *Cases of Ming Confucians* demanded no purity in doctrinal inheritance and conveyed a sense of intellectual independence and openness, which could claim to reflect a deeper understanding of Wang Yangming's principles.

The question remains as to how the *xue'an* writers, in particular Liu Yuanqing and Huang Zongxi, understood both the substance and the method of Confucian learning. Both Liu and Huang turned out to be so absorbed in expounding on epistemological issues that they took ontology for granted in their conception of knowledge. For Liu Yuanqing, the substance of Confucian learning was nature (*xing*)—human nature, to be exact. The issue was how to let this nature work to its fullest capacity. Because he maintained that human nature was substantive but beyond the realm of perceptual knowledge ("not what can be seen" and "not what can be heard"),[69] all the methods of study propounded by the Song masters were only the articulated opinions (*jian*) of worthy Confucians (*ru*) but not the authentic teachings of the sages (*sheng*). Confucians had better learn the way the sages themselves learned, taking their persons as models and their teachings as a standard of learning. Nevertheless, the doctrines of the great Confucians of Song and Ming times were good reference points from which one could better understand the superiority of the sages' teaching. Liu's *xue'an* collection taught by exposing the "problematic" methods of past Confucians for the student to know and to avoid.

Huang Zongxi's ontological premise, as stated in his prefaces to *Cases of Ming Confucians*, was, "That which fills Heaven and Earth is Mind." This "Mind" was understood as referring to the human mind or heart or both, wherein reside the principles of heaven and earth and their unending manifestations, which together constituted knowledge. Again, like Liu Yuanqing, what immediately concerned Huang was the epistemological issue.

> Because man and Heaven and Earth are one body, to exhaust and comprehend the principles of Heaven and Earth is to do it in one's mind. Later scholars misunderstood the idea of the past worthy [Zhu Xi], holding that these principles are hanging within Heaven and Earth and the myriad of things, and are accordingly to be comprehended and exhausted. Does this not almost amount to [Gaozi's idea of] "rightness is external" [to human nature]?[70]

Knowledge was locatable in the mind and therefore was to be sought within the mind. Since the myriad manifestations of the principles found unity in the mind, so "the variations in learning and scholarship are exactly what show the infinity of the body of the Way [*Daoti*]." Huang also likened the body of the Way to the sea, which was the final destination of all rivers large and small. As motion, or change, was the nature of the Way, so variety was the nature of the way of learning. Legitimate methods of learning must be many; what was important was to be knowledgeable about them.

On this methodological issue, Huang asserted that in the "discussion of learning" (*jiangxue*) Ming Confucians surpassed their predecessors of former ages in having completely exposed the fallacies of Buddhist and Daoist doctrines. "Discussion of learning" was almost exclusively understood as the exploration and articulation of methods to arrive at the right knowledge. How did the Ming Confucians achieve this? The key was their flexibility. "The Confucians did not follow a single path in their learning. Some interpreted and elaborated the doctrines of their masters, branching into several schools of thought. Their lifelong learning and scholarship often changed course over time." This process of advancing new methods of learning was the key to the Ming Confucians' success.

Huang's distinction as a thinker lay in his understanding that knowledge is contingent upon a person's individual endowment and preference. The job he assigned to himself was "to distinguish their [the innovative Ming Confucians'] doctrines [*zongzhi*] as well as the origin and development of their learning . . . and let the student choose from them by himself." Since that element of choice was the premise, the presentation of individual cases was the logical outcome. And because of choice, the cases as candidates to be considered in making choices would be meaningless if they were not documented reliably. *Xue'an* writings thus created knowledge by providing evidence based on the facts of each Confucian's progress.

Many of the same ideas and reasoning were also expressed in the variant, earlier preface. On the ontological premise, Huang said, "The Mind has no original substance [*benti*] except what is achieved by its activity [*gongli*]. To exhaust and comprehend principles [*li*] is to exhaust and comprehend Mind's myriad manifestations rather than the myriad manifestations of all things." He was here maintaining that the unity of knowledge and action demand knowledge to be found in action—action of the mind, to be exact—but not vice versa. A person gained knowledge in his own way as his ever-active and individual mind responded to what affected it. Thus Huang could conclude, "[As] the recorded dialogs of the former scholars show that each of them was different, although they all reflected the mind-in-itself [*xinti*], which is always changing and quite without rest, one's insistence upon fixing the situation will turn out to be quite futile and useless."[71] The validity of a single path of action for all truth seekers to get the truth is therefore unpromising.

But Huang's insistence that the outside (perceptual knowledge) was subject to the inside (innate knowledge) also brought him logical difficulty. His premise would dictate that the outside was worth knowing only insomuch as it could confirm the inside. Since no particular scholar or school need be followed specifically in the pursuit of truth, one could seek truth only by depending on the functioning of his own mind. Freedom and uniqueness of the mind was proved when knowledge of the multitude of past dialogues was not necessary. Why, then, the compilation of the *Cases of Ming Confucians*? To get away from this difficulty, Huang predicated the seeking of knowledge upon the cultivation of personal virtues: "Only after cultivating virtue could learning be discussed." This, however, sounds tautological: one has to know how to cultivate virtue in the first place, and the question remains, "by what method?"

To sum up Huang's peculiar argument, he had two propositions to offer: one based on a subjective ontology ("That which fills Heaven and Earth is Mind") and one based on an objective epistemology (the case study). The latter counted as a means to arrive at the former. As conveyed in the preface, he was promoting reliable textual information and independent free choice of method of learning. Huang seemed not to have been worried by the logic that relativism in methodology—freedom to select from a variety of models—might lead to relativism in knowledge. In praising the achievements of the Ming Confucians, he said, "Only where they have given the best of their efforts and exhausted the myriad dimensions of their minds, without working fuzzily or falsely appropriating the chaff of others' learning, have they established schools of thought." For him the universal seriousness of these scholars was one basis for their common ground.

More abstractly, he sought common ground in the ontological proposition that asserted "the myriad manifestations of a single entity [*yiben wanshu*]." Here the metaphor of a water pot for public use that we have discussed is especially telling. To put this metaphor of water philosophically, the whole has no boundary and in terms of quality knowledge is integral, but when one takes a measure of it to get to the whole a boundary is made. Such boundaries, delineating models and methods, are countless, however, and any model might work, contingent upon the person who seeks it. So the case, the *xue'an*, functions by showing an assortment of models that will suffice depending on the situation of the seeker himself.

The crucial thing in the compilation of a *xue'an* book was therefore the correct presentation of the doctrine(s) of a philosophy in the form of each case, which was to focus on exactly "the place where the thinker in question applied his most effective effort [*deli chu*], which is also the student's starting point [*rumen chu*]."[72] As for the problem of boundaries set by the various catchwords and aphorisms that summed up different doctrines, Huang dealt with it by quoting a famous statement by the Tang poet, Du Mu: "A ball may roll around on a game-table: horizontally, diagonally, circularly, or vertically. One does not really know all the directions it may take. All one could know for sure is that it will not leave the table." And Huang added, "This can be applied to the thinkers' doctrines too." It would mean that one needed only to grasp the general principle (the table) to be able to use any method (ball) effectively. Knowledge was to be sought by free play within a defined boundary.

But who or what built the table? Huang had criticized Zhou Rudeng and Sun Qifeng for bias—selectivity in the thinkers they chose to include in their books, exclusivity in defining Confucian learning only in terms of the lineage of *lixue* or *xinxue.* But if their work was tainted with subjective interest, had Huang and other *xue'an* writers achieved objectivity in the selection and presentation of their source materials? Notice this organizing principle from Huang.

> Frequently I find that compilers of the former scholars' recorded dialogues tend to select at random some sayings without knowing why they have made such selections. And yet, if the spirit of a man's entire life has not been revealed, how can his learning be made visible? My own work is compiled [directly] from [careful selection of essentials in] the scholars' collected writings and not copied from the earlier anthologies.[73]

Serious as he was, was he also judicious? Huang can be said to have based his authority as a philosopher on his being socially recognized as a universalist, a serious historian, and a loyal follower of his particular Confucian teachers. Yet for all its broadmindedness, Huang's *Cases of Ming Confucians* selected only certain aspects and versions of the body of learning that is called Confucian.[74] For example, the influential but "heterodox" Li Zhi (1527–1602) was noticeably excluded.

Huang's own preferred path for seeking the truth was revealed in his warning that a mere encyclopedic or referential use of his work missed his intention for the book. He was maintaining that truth was to be arrived at through personal practice. Reading, or even language for that matter, was only the starting point of practice. Knowledge was not knowledge and truth not truth until verified by action. Mere informational reading, however conscientious, was no correct way to acquire truth. In this way, Huang was much in the Wang Yangming tradition of philosophizing, and his presentation of the Confucian way in cases reflected his master's doctrines of the unity of knowledge and action.

CONCLUDING REMARKS

From the foregoing discussion of *xue'an* works produced before the middle of the eighteenth century, it becomes clear that in the two-character term *xue'an* the word "*xue*" means "Confucian learning," which in that historical context was predominantly neo-Confucian learning. The meaning of the word "*an*," however, is manifold. First, it was used in the sense of archival management, meaning to file documents, to set up classified files, to put something into the record, all for future reference. Second, it could be conceived as a Confucian counterpart or version of a Chan Buddhist *gong'an*—a linguistic device for one to reach personal comprehension. Third, it was used in the sense of a legal case, in which statements, judgment, and verdict were embedded in a narrative of particulars concerning an individual person. Fourth, it meant a plan of learning, as could be found in a primer that offered rules and guides to action. All these meanings, however, share the common connotation of "case," so it makes sense for us to translate *xue'an* as a "case of learning."

Xue'an writings by Geng Dingxiang and Liu Yuanqing, who produced the first works bearing that title, have the following characteristics. First, a *xue'an* made its chief content the description of a number of Confucians' ways of learning; it aimed at providing plans and models of learning for the interested student. Second, *xue'an* authors included the Confucians' words to reveal their cases of learning; they did not pass judgment on the cases, out of respect for the reader's own judgment. Third, *xue'an* authors actually made their judgments by means of the materials they selected for inclusion in their books, thereby consciously guiding the course of their readers' paths. Last but no less significant, the basic scholarly attitude of *xue'an* writers was open and egalitarian. These characteristics are also found in the greatest work of the genre, *Cases of Ming Confucians.* Therefore, like these predecessors, it should be recognized as a philosophical work, even though it also has use as history.

Xue'an writings, as best represented by *Cases of Ming Confucians,* use cases to help guide students in a path of Confucian learning (*xue*) where an individual's virtuous practice is the final determinant of the efficacy of his knowledge. An individual *xue'an* case may have the effect of a humanistic narrative, inspiring the reader through empathy with a record of someone's lived experience. A book of *xue'an* cases may roughly produce philosophical knowledge the way a law court may produce legal knowledge. To wit, testimonies are presented in the excerpts of the thinkers' writings and speeches, cross examinations are conducted and references sought from data everywhere in a *xue'an* anthology, verdicts are proposed in the author-compiler's introductions and in the biographies he composed. But the justice of the case is based upon evidence that in the final analysis is presented not by the litigants but by the judge himself. Since the judge—author-compiler—is an interested party in the trial, he is never free from the suspicion that his cases have been subject to manipulation. Can evidence so produced lead to objective knowledge? Isn't the knowledge so generated prescriptive in nature rather than descriptive? For the modern scholar, then, *xue'an* writings can be used to construct a history of thought, but one cannot depend upon them alone faithfully to reconstruct the learning of the Confucians they present. Nonetheless, who is to say that no Ming-Qing student ever found among these cases a satisfactory guide to a virtuous life?

NOTES

1 In *The Records of Ming Scholars,* ed. Julia Ching (hereafter *RM*), a collection of English translations of the prefaces and selected biographies from Huang's work, the term *xue'an* is rendered "records of scholars."

2 Exactly when the *Cases of Ming Confucians* was written is not known. Huang Zongxi merely stated in both his original and revised prefaces that it was completed after the year 1676, the fifteenth year of the Kangxi reign (1662–1722). Modern scholars dispute the date of its actual completion. Chen Zuwu, *Zhongguo xue'an shi,* 122–131, argues for 1684 or 1685, while Wu Guang, *Huang Zongxi zhuzuo,* 17–19, argues for 1678 or 1679.

3 For instance, Yang Xiangkui, ed., *Qingru xue'an xinbian,* 8 vols.; Fang Keli and Li Jinquan, eds., *Xiandai xinrujia xue'an;* and Dai Yi, ed., *Ershi shiji Zhonghua xue'an.* The *Qingru xue'an xinbian,* drawing on the original compilation, is a modern presentation of the biographies and selected writings of major Qing scholars in the fields of neo-Confucian learning, evidentiary studies, and classical studies. The *Xiandai xinrujia xue'an* is the account of eleven scholars who, as the work's "Abstract" states it, "basically belong to the first and second generations of modern neo-Confucians." The *Ershi shiji Zhonghua xue'an* comprises four divisions of learning—learning in a general manner, in history, in philosophy, and in literature—of forty-seven scholars who, according to the work's "Brief Introduction," "have made outstanding or important contributions to the development of twentieth-century Chinese culture." For an earlier, and ambiguously titled, example with no relevance to Confucian learning, see Yanagida Seizan, ed., *Hu Shi chan xue'an.* There are also *xue'an* books for individual scholars, often named after their hometowns or their courtesy appellatives. Well-known works in this category include Rong Zhaozu's *Bu Mingru Dongguan xue'an* for Chen Jian (1497–1567) of the Ming, Hou Wailu's *Chuanshan xue'an* for Wang Fuzhi (1619–1692) of the Qing, and Huang Si'ai's *Nanlei xue'an* for Huang Zongxi, which in actuality covered the "school" of Huang Zongxi.

4 For useful recent introductions to the compilation of *Mingru xue'an,* see Chen Zuwu, *Zhongguo xue'an shi,* 111–159; Wu Guang, *Huang Zongxi zhuzuo,* 11–28; Ching, introduction to *RM;* Cang Xiuliang, "*Mingru xue'an.*" For recent discussions on the book's philosophical relevance, see Liu Shuxian, *Huang Zongxi xinxue de dingwei,* 125–163; Gu Qingmei, "Cong *Mingru xue'an* tan Huang Lizhou"; Hou Wailu, Qiu Hansheng, and Zhang Qizhi, eds., *Song-Ming lixue shi,* 2:781–822.

5 For writings especially bearing on this aspect, see, e.g., Qian Mu, "Huang Lizhou"; Huang Jinxing, "Xue'an ticai"; Chen Jinzhong, "Huang Zongxi *Mingru xue'an.*"

6 The term *xue'an,* apart from appearing in the titles of the works of Geng Dingxiang (1524–1596) and Liu Yuanqing (1544–1609), which will be discussed later, also appears in the 1618 preface that the well-known Confucian scholar Zou Yuanbiao (1551–1624) wrote for Wang Zaijin's (*jinshi* 1592) *Longsha xuelu.* Dr. Lü Miaofen of the Institute of Modern History at the Academia Sinica in Taipei brought my attention to this occurrence. In the context of this book, the term best means "cases of learned expressions of the Confucian masters."

7 See Ching, introduction to *RM*, 8; Chen Zuwu, *Zhongguo xue'an shi*, 132, citing Chen Jinsheng.

8 See Qian Mu, "Huang Lizhou," 288; Chen Zuwu, *Zhongguo xue'an shi*, 135–137.

9 Liang Qichao, *Zhongguo jin sanbai nian*, 46, 48.

10 Liang Qichao [Yinbingshi zhuren], "Liyan," 2–4.

11 On this point, see Struve, "Huang Zongxi in Context," 479.

12 See Chen Zuwu, *Zhongguo xue'an shi*, 6–18.

13 Ibid. Some scholars—Chen Zuwu for one—indeed attribute the origins of the "history of learning and scholarship" genre to the *Shiji* and the *Hanshu*.

14 See ibid., 27–53, for a discussion of the history, content, and value of this book. Chen also notes that the same view has been expressed by Liang Qichao and Chen Yuan (1880–1971).

15 See Zhu Xi, *Yi-Luo yuanyuan lu*. Nivison refers to commemorative writings like epitaphs, memorial tablets, obituaries, etc., as "social biography" in his "Aspects of Traditional Chinese Biography," 457–463. Franke, *An Introduction to the Sources of Ming History*, 74, compares it with "historical biography" found in histories.

16 See Wang Deyi, introduction to *Yi-Luo yuanyuan lu*.

17 Several modern scholars have pointed out the philosophical nature of the *Mingru xue'an*. See, e.g., Chen Jinzhong, "Huang Zongxi *Mingru xue'an*," 129–139; *RM*, 268–269; Struve, "Huang Zongxi in Context," 479–484.

18 For a partial translation of the classification of the *Four Treasuries*, see Wilkinson, *Chinese History: A Manual*, 270.

19 For the imperial cataloguer's "critical abstract" (*tiyao*) of the *Mingru xue'an*, see Yong Rong (1744–1790) et al., eds., *Siku quanshu zongmu*, 1:58.527.

20 For the text of this piece, see Geng Dingxiang, *Geng Tiantai xiansheng wenji*, 13.1a–6a.

21 Geng especially highlighted the last point by saying that Yang Jian in his old age realized the classical teaching of "ascertaining the views of all [with whom one associates], giving up one's own opinion and following that of others." This expression comes from the "Da Yu mo" chapter of the *Book of Documents*. For the translation, see Legge, trans., *The Shoo King*, 53.

22 For a modern account of Geng Dingxiang by Julia Ching, see Goodrich and Chaoying Fang, eds., *Dictionary of Ming Biography, 1368–1644*, 718–772. For a sample of his philosophical writings, see *juan* 35 of the *Mingru xue'an*.

23 Qian Mu, with reference to the *Mingru xue'an*, also reasoned that "what were called '*xue'an*' were the various plans proposed for the learning of the time." See Qian Mu, "Huang Lizhou de *Mingru xue'an*," 292.

24 For the critical abstract of Liu's work, see Yong Rong et al., eds., *Siku quanshu zongmu*, 1:96.815. The date of this work is not certain. Liu Yuanqing's preface to it was undated in the Wanli (1572–1622) edition of the work. In that copy there is a handwritten note by an anonymous author after the preface dated "mid-spring of the year 1596." The name of Geng Dingxiang (d. 1596) also appears in the last line of the book's table of

contents, but Geng's biography and selected words are not found in the text. It appears that the book was finished and block-cut shortly before Geng's death in 1596 and was ready for print soon after that, so only his name was added to the table of contents as some indication of the book's being yet to be expanded.

25 Note that the critical abstract of *Zhuru xue'an* in the *Annotated Bibliography* (96:25a–b) states that it existed in eight *juan,* not twenty-five *juan,* including twenty-seven Confucians. Two of these Confucians, Jin Lüxiang (1232–1303) and Xu Qian (1270–1337), were not included in the edition found in the *Siku quanshu cunmu congshu* collection (SKCM). Also, according to the table of contents, *juan* 14 should be for Hu Juren (1434–1484), *juan* 16 for Luo Qinshun (1465–1547), and *juan* 25 for Geng Dingxiang. All three *juan,* however, are missing.

26 Geng was the original author of the biographies of Xue Xuan (1389–1464), Chen Xianzhang (1428–1500), Wang Yangming, Wang Gen (1483–1541), Zou Shouyi (1491–1562), and Luo Hongxian (1504–1564). In addition, the biography of Hu Zhi (1517–1585) was based on Hu's epitaph, written by Geng. All these biographies are found in *juan* 13 and 14 of the *Geng Tiantai xiansheng wenji;* Hu Zhi's epitaph is found in *juan* 12.

27 Liu is here citing the very first sentence of the *Analects.* I use Legge's translation for the words of Confucius cited here; see Legge, trans., *Confucian Analects,* in *The Four Books,* 1.

28 Liu is here citing Mencius' dictum in Book 7A:1 of *Mencius.* I modify D. C. Lau's translation of Mencius' words here; see Lau, trans., *Mencius,* 182.

29 I follow Lau's translation of "the four germs" for *siduan.* See ibid., 83 (*Mencius* 2A:6).

30 Such were innovations like Zhou Dunyi's doctrine of "regarding tranquility as fundamental" (*zhujing*), Cheng Hao's doctrine of "understanding the nature of humanity" (*shiren*), Zhang Zai's doctrine of "nature in a state of calmness" (*dingxing*), Cheng Yi's doctrine of "self-cultivation" (*hanyang*), Lu Jiuyuan's doctrine of "seeking one's original heart" (*ziqiu benxin*), or Zhu Xi's doctrine of "exhausting principles" (*qiongli*). For English translations and discussions of these doctrines, see Chan, trans., and comp., *A Source Book in Chinese Philosophy,* 463, 523, 525, 562, 574, 610.

31 For the text of this preface, which includes the quotes in the following paragraph, see Liu Yuanqing, *Liu Pinjun quanji,* 4:10b–11b.

32 Liu here was referring to *Mencius* 2A:7; so was Geng Dingxiang as quoted earlier by him in using the expression *zeshu.* Mencius, in the classical text, is citing Confucius' emphasis on the importance of choosing or selecting a place to live, where virtuous manners prevailed, to drive home his own point of making the right choice in the practice of benevolence. See Legge, trans., *The Works of Mencius,* in *The Four Books,* 552–554; Lau, trans., *Mencius,* 83.

33 For the text of this preface, see Liu Yuanqing, *Liu Pinjun quanji,* 4.2a–3b.

34 Yong Rong et al., eds., *Siku quanshu zongmu,* 1:96.815.

35 For this convention of bibliographical classification of the *Four Treasuries,* see ibid., 1:35.289, introduction to the subdivision of the *Four Books.*

36 The *Lunyu xue'an* is included in vol. 1 of the *Liu Zongzhou quanji.* Some of such entries can be seen on 512, 529, 587.

37 Yong Rong et al., eds., *Siku quanshu zongmu,* 1:36.303. Note that the copy of the book reviewed in the abstract was of a ten-*juan* edition.

38 A photographic reprint of this work is included in the *Siku quanshu cunmu congshu* collection (SKCM). The dates of the work and of its author are both unknown. In an extant copy of the book, an undated preface by Fang Bao (1668–1749), written at the request of the author's grandson, Wang Shu (1668–1743), implies that the book was written in the last years of the Ming dynasty or in the early years of the Qing. The critical abstract writer of the *Four Treasuries* actually counted Wang Shen as a Qing figure, which means that he lived into the early Qing period. Wang was from Jintan County but did not have a biography in the county's gazetteer. Wang Shu's biography is found in the 1921 printing of the *Jintan xianzhi* (9–1:14b), compiled by Feng Xu (1843–1927), according to which he was a *jinshi* of 1712. The same gazetteer's "Monograph of Bibliography" (11:3a) erroneously classified Wang's *Xue'an* in the category of "Biography."

39 Yong Rong et al., eds., *Siku quanshu zongmu,* 1:97.822. For a background understanding of these "articles of learning" and the personages mentioned here, see Chan, "Chu Hsi and the Academies," 389–413, esp. 396–399.

40 The text of the extant copy, however, does not include the protocols of the Donglin Academy that Fang Bao mentioned. As for the articles set by Rao and Zhen that Fang mentioned, they probably are the same as those listed in the *Xueze,* whose authorship was attributed to Cheng Duanmeng and Dong Zhu in the *Annotated Bibliography.*

41 This work seems to have been later incorporated into the *Song-Yuan xue'an* itself. No extant copy of it has been found, but its content should in all likelihood be the same as that of the *Mingdao xue'an* of Cheng Hao and the *Yichuan xue'an* of Cheng Yi in the *Song-Yuan xue'an.*

42 Yong Rong et al., eds., *Siku quanshu zongmu,* 1:97.824.

43 *Song-Yuan xue'an,* 13.542, "Mingdao xue'an shang."

44 Ibid., 16.652, "Yichuan xue'an xia."

45 I have no access to Wu Ding's work at issue here. For an earlier review of Chen Jian's work, see Yong Rong et al., eds., *Siku quanshu zongmu,* 1:98.833.

46 Ibid.

47 It is noteworthy that Huang Zongxi had once asked Tang Bin (1627–1687) to write a preface for the *Jishan xue'an,* which is that part of the *Mingru xue'an* for his teacher, Liu Zongzhou. Apparently Huang planned for this independent issue to laud Liu's doctrine. Although this work was obviously never published, its content as found in the *Mingru xue'an* is sufficient evidence that it is a philosophical rather than a historical work. Chen Zuwu, *Zhongguo xue'an shi,* 129–130, maintains that "Jishan xue'an" was Huang Zongxi's original title for the *Mingru xue'an,* and thus the preface that Tang Bin was asked to write was a preface to the latter work. This seems to be unlikely. Tang did respond to Huang's request, although the preface he wrote does not survive. But from Tang's letter to Huang, which mentioned this matter in part, it seems Tang was then dealing with Liu Zongzhou

alone but not with a much larger work such as the *Mingru xue'an*. Tang's letter to Huang, together with an earlier one, is included in *Huang Zongxi quanji*, 11:403–404.

48 See the critical abstract of the *Mingru xue'an* in Yong Rong et al., eds., *Siku quanshu zongmu*, 1:58.527. For a discussion of the imperial compilers' criticism of Huang Zongxi's engagement in school rivalry in the composition of the *Mingru xue'an*, see also Yamanoi Yū, *Min-Shin shisō shi no kenkyū*, 298–319, esp. 315–317.

49 The text of the "Fafan" is identical in all editions of the *Mingru xue'an*. The text of the prefaces, however, differs in the major editions of the book. Huang Zongxi wrote two separate versions of his preface in 1693. He meant for the second to be the final version. It was printed in the earliest, edited edition of 1693 with some change in wording made by the publisher. In the 1735 reprint of the 1693 edition, the first version was also included, again with altered wording. The originals of both versions, however, are preserved in Huang Zongzi's collected works. The publishers changed the wording of the prefaces to enhance their prestige as sponsors of the book, but many later scholars were misinformed as a result. The two corrupted prefaces of the 1735 reprint are included in many later editions, including the once standard Mo Jin (1761–1826) edition of 1821. The preface translated in *RM*, for instance, is based on the first preface in the Mo Jin version. I base my analysis here on the versions included in Huang's collected works, *Huang Zongxi quanji*, 10:73–76.

50 For the source of the term *huangmao baiwei* and its use by the historian Zhang Xuecheng (1738–1801), see Ye Ying, ed., *Wenshi tongyi jiaozhu*, 216, note 127, 524.

51 The translation is modified from *RM*, 42.

52 *RM*, 44, note 16, mistakes Chen Wenhuan for Chen Xigu, whose epitaph Huang Zongxi wrote and is found in *Huang Zongxi quanji*, 10:432–434. Chen Wenhuan was Chen Xigu's father.

53 The *Wanghuitu* was a picture (or a series of pictures) drawn by the Tang painter Yan Liben (d. 673) of an imperial audience with foreigners from all places. The inspiration of this picture was the "Wanghui" chapter of the *Yi Zhoushu*, which, according to an early commentary, was about King Wu of Zhou giving an audience to the dukes and tribute-paying barbarians in the court of the newly founded capital. For these two titles, see Meng Zhufeng, ed., *Hanyu da cidian*, 4:468.

54 See Yong Rong et al., eds., *Siku quanshu zongmu*, 1:96.817, for the critical abstract of the book.

55 Huang Zongxi gave more reasons for declining to contribute the preface in his letter replying to Yun Richu, which is included in *Huang Zongxi quanji*, 10, 215–217.

56 This actually put Huang Zongxi in a position much different from that of his mentor Liu Zongzhou, whose *Transmission of the Orthodox Way in the Ming* (*Huang Ming daotong lu*), now lost, had much impact on Huang's own book. The "Quotations from My Teacher" (Shishuo) entries preceding the main text of the *Mingru xue'an* have been shown to be excerpts from that work of Liu's. For a note on that matter and the entries' relation to Huang's own composition, see Chen Rongjie (Wing-tsit Chan), "Lun *Mingru xue'an* zhi *Shishuo*," 6–8.

57 For a description of these two works and a discussion of their relationship with the *Mingru xue'an* in the context of late Ming–early Qing world of thought, see Chen Zuwu, *Zhongguo xue'an shi*, 55–109.

58 *RM*, 46, translation modified.

59 Ibid., 46–47, translation modified.

60 These are Huang Zongxi's words in the third entry of the "Fafan."

61 *RM*, 46, translation modified.

62 This preface and the next two to be cited are not included in the 1735 edition or the 1821 Mo Jin edition or the 1992 punctuated edition, but they do appear in the 1985 punctuated edition.

63 Book II: 16 of the *Analects*. Translation here follows Legge, trans., *Confucian Analects*, in *The Four Books*, 19.

64 Book 2A:2 of *Mencius*. Translation here follows Lau, *Mencius*, 78.

65 See Tang Jian, *Qing xue'an xiaozhi* (reprint), 401–402.

66 This notion is found in many places in the prefaces and postfaces to these two works.

67 The "transmission of the mind" expression was used in Tao Wangling's preface to the *Shengxue zhongchuan;* the "transmission of the lamp" expression was in Cheng Qizhu's colophon to the *Lixue zhongchuan.*

68 For Zhou Rudeng (Chou Ju-teng), see his biopgrahy by Chaoying Fang and Julia Ching in *Dictionary of Ming Biography, 1368–1644*, 271–274; and by Huang Zongxi in *RM*, 199–201. For Huang Zongxi's misrepresentation of Zhou, see Jie Zhao, "Reassessing the Place of Chou Ju-teng," 1–11.

69 These phrases appeared in Liu Yuanqing's preface to his *Zhuru xue'an.*

70 These lines and those to be quoted in the following, unless otherwise noted, are from Huang's revised preface to the *Mingru xue'an* (not included in *RM*). Huang is here quoting Book 6A:4 of *Mencius*, in which Mencius refutes Gaozi's theory of human nature that "benevolence is internal, not external; rightness is external, not internal." See Lau, trans., *Mencius*, 161.

71 *RM*, 41–43, translation modified.

72 These words, as well as those of Du Mu in the next quotation, come from the second entry of the *Mingru xue'an*'s "Fafan." See ibid., 45.

73 Fourth entry of the *Mingru xue'an*'s "Fafan." Translation here follows *RM*, 46.

74 This easily involves the conditions of truth, which include knowledge and power, among others. For an analysis of this dialectics, which also bears on the discussion of Huang Zongxi's authority as an author, see Foucault, "Truth and Power."

Appendix: Printed Sources Discussed in This Volume

YEAR / FIELD	Law	Religion	Medicine	Philosophy	Forensics
900	疑獄集				
1000					
1100	折獄龜鑑	碧巖錄	小兒藥證直訣		
1200	棠陰比事	禪宗無門關			
	名公書判清明集				
1300		山房夜話			洗冤集錄
1400	大誥				
1500			石山醫案	諸儒學案	
			幼科發揮		
			名醫類案		
			奇效醫述		
			孫文垣醫案		
1600	雲間讞略		程茂先醫案	論語學案	
	莆陽讞牘		寓意草	學案	
	折獄新語		保嬰全書	明儒學案	
	盟水齋存牘			二程學案	
	𥊍辭				
1700	折獄要編		臨證指南醫案	東莞學案	洗冤錄集證
	辦案要略		續名醫類案		
1800	學案初模		古今醫案按		檢驗集證
	刑名雜覽				補註洗冤錄集證
					洗冤錄詳義

Appendix: Printed Sources Discussed *(continued)*

FIELD YEAR	Law	Religion	Medicine	Philosophy	Forensics
900	A Collection of Doubtful Cases				
1000					
1100	The Magic Mirror for Deciding Cases	Blue Cliff Record	Proven Formulae of Medicine for Small Children		
1200	Parallel Cases from under the Pear-tree The Enlightened Judgments by Famous Officials	Gateless Barrier of the Chan Tradition			
1300		Evening Talks in a Mountain Hut			A Collection of Records on the Washing Away of Wrongs
1400	Grand Pronouncements				
1500			Medical Cases of Wang Ji Elaboration on Pediatric Medicine Classified Cases of Famous Doctors Medical Narratives of the Striking and Successful Medical Cases of Sun Yikui	Cases of Learning of the Confucians	
1600	Court Opinions from Songjiang Court Opinions from Puyang New Words on Deciding Cases Court Opinions Drafted at Mengshui Studio Words of Deep Cultivation		Medical Cases of Cheng Chongzhou Notes on My Judgment Complete Text for the Protection of Infants	The Case of Learning from the Analects Cases of Learning Cases of Learning of Ming Confucians Cases of Learning of the Two Cheng Brothers	
1700	Essentials for Judging Cases Important Points for Handling Cases		Medical Cases as a Guide to Clinical Practice More Classified Cases from Famous Doctors	The Case of the Learning of [Chen Jian] from Dongguan	The Washing Away of Wrongs with Collected Evidence
1800	Elementary Models for Studying Cases Miscellaneous Readings for Judicial Administration		Commentary on Medical Cases Old and New		Collected Evidence for Autopsies The Washing Away of Wrongs with Collected Evidence, New Edition with Notes Added Explanation of the Meaning of The Washing Away of Wrongs

Character Glossary

ajiao san 阿膠散
an 安 (well)
an 按 (examine/comment/according to)
an 案 (case/desk)
an wu yiyi 案無疑義
an zhe an ye 案者按也
andu 案牘
Anran 安然
baihuzheng sixian 白虎症似癇
baijia 白痂
Bailudong [xue]gui 白鹿洞學規
baishu san 白朮散
baitong tang 白通湯
Baizhang 百丈
Ban Gu 班固
"Ban'an" 辦案
Bao Zheng 包拯
Baodi xian 寶坻縣
Baxian dang'an 巴縣檔案
Beizhili 北直隸
ben 本
bencao 本草
Bencao gangmu 本草綱目
Bencao leishu 本草類述
benti 本體
benze 本則
bi 筆
bian 變
Bian Que 扁鵲
bian zheng lun zhi 辨證論治
biantong 變通
bianzheng 變蒸
bie 別
bieben 別本
biemen 別門
biji 筆記
bing 病
bingfu 秉拂
bizhao 比照
bo 駁
Bo Juyi 白居易
Bo Yi 伯夷
bo'an 駁案
boxue 博學
boziren san 柏子仁散
bu neng qiong qi bian yi guan qi tong 不能窮其變以觀其通
"Bu zhi fang shuo" 不執方說
bu zhiming 不致命
buji riqi 不記日期
bujin renqing 不近人情
buken qingchuan qishu 不肯輕傳其書
buqi 不起
buxin yuyan 不信予言
"Buyingwei" 不應為
buzhu 補註
can qingfa zhi zhong 參情法之中
canhe 參合
cao 草
Cao Xueqin 曹雪芹
Caodong 曹洞
caogong 草供

cha qi qingxing, kui qi shili, xiangxi yanqiu, xijia kaozheng 察其情形，揆其事理，詳細研求，細加考証
chang 唱
chang an 唱案
Changlu Zongze 長蘆宗賾
chanhou diankuang 產後癲狂
chanhou kuangyan 產後狂言
chanhou xinshen jingji 產後心神驚悸
chanhou xueyun 產後血暈
chanhou zha jian guishen 產後乍見鬼神
Chanmen guishi 禪門規式
chanyi 禪椅
Chanyuan qinggui 禪苑清規
Chao Yuanfang 巢元方
chaoshen 朝審
Chen Jian 陳建
Chen Jue 陳桷
Chen nüke 陳女科
Chen Wenhuan 陳文奐
Chen Xianzhang 陳獻章
Chen Xigu 陳錫嘏
Chen Ziming 陳自明
Chen Zunsu 陳尊宿
Cheng Duanmeng 程端蒙
Cheng Hao 程顥
Cheng Qizhu 程啟朱
Cheng Yi 程頤
cheng yi 誠意
Cheng Zeng 程曾
cheng'an 成案
Cheng'an beikao 成案備考
Cheng'an xinbian 成案新編
Cheng'an xinbian erji 成案新編二集
Chengguan 澄觀
chengjian 成姦
chengshi 程式
chichi 齒遲
Chishui xuan zhu 赤水玄珠
chongkan buzhu 重刊補註
chu lei er tong 觸類而通
chu qi 出奇
chuandenglu 傳燈錄
chuanxiong 川芎
chufen zeli 處份則例
chuishi 垂示
Chūjin 忠尋
Chunyu Yi 淳于意
conglin gongfu zhi zhangshi 叢林公府之長史
Da Ming ling 大明令
Da Ming lü 大明律
Da Qing lüli 大清律例
Da Qing lüli quanzuan jizheng 大清律例全纂集證
"Da Yu mo" 大禹謨
da'an wan 大安丸
Dahui shu 大慧書
Dahui Zonggao 大慧宗杲
Dai Yuanli 戴元禮
dan 膽
"Dan-Xin dang'an" 淡新檔案
dang 黨
dang'an 檔案
Danshui 淡水
dao 刀
Daosheng 道生
Daoti 道體
Daotong 道統
Daoxin 道信
daoxue 道學
Daxue yanyi 大學衍義
deli chu 得力處
Di xue 帝學
dianti guomai 點題過脈
diaofeng 刁風
diaofu 調服
diaojing san 調經散
diaotenggou 釣藤鉤
dibao 地保
Dilun 地論

ding 定
Ding Wenjiang 丁文江
dingshi 定式
dingxing 定性
Dōgen 道元
Dong Xun 董潯
Dong Zhu 董銖
Dongguan xue'an 東莞學案
Dongshan Liangjie 洞山良价
Douzhen chuan xinlu 痘疹傳心錄
du cang xingbu 獨藏刑部
Du Mu 杜牧
duan 斷
dulüzhe 讀律者
Dunwu rudao yaomen 頓悟入道要門
duo 奪
duyushi 都御史
elu 惡露
Enchin 圓珍
er 而
Er-Cheng xue'an 二程學案
erke 兒科
eryu 而癒
fa 法
"Fafan" 發凡
Falin zhaotian zhu 法林照天炷
fan yu she yinan bu neng jin xin yu shu zhe bu zhi fanji 凡獄涉疑難不能盡信於書者不知凡幾
Fan Zuyu 范祖禹
fang 方
Fang Bao 方苞
fang shu 方書
fangbian 方便
fangke elie xiaoce 坊刻惡劣小冊
Fangxingyan jianxianlu 方星巖見閒錄
fangyu 方語
fanjing er xingquan 反經而行權
"Fanli" 凡例
fanzuo 反坐
faxing 法性
feiyu 肺鬱
fen men lei 分門類
fen men xi lei 分門析類
feng 風
fengfo shafo, fengzu shazu 逢佛殺佛，逢祖殺祖
fenzheng 紛爭
fu 伏
fu baiduyao 服敗毒藥
fu hanliangyao 服寒涼藥
fukao 附考
fuke 婦科
Furen daquan liangfang 婦人大全良方
Furen liangfang 婦人良方
futong 腹痛
fuzi 附子
gangchang 綱常
ganying 感應
Gao Panlong 高攀龍
Gaozi 告子
gewu zhizhi 格物致知
gezhi 格致
Gezhi yulun 格致餘論
gong 公
gong'an 公案
gong'an (*koan*) 公案
gong'an xiaoshuo 公案小說
gongdu 公牘
gongfu zhi andu 公府之案牘
gongli 功力
gongzhuang 供狀
Gu Xiancheng 顧憲成
Gu Yanwu 顧炎武
Guan Wudang 關無黨
guanchuan 貫串
guandai ruyi 冠帶儒醫
guanhua 官話
guanyin 官音
guanzhen 官箴

Guanzi 管子
guge 骨格
gui ku xue 鬼哭穴
gun 棍
Guo Yu 郭玉
Guo Ziyi 郭子儀
Guoyu 國語
gusha 故殺
gushi 故事
guwen 古文
Guzunsu yulu 古尊宿語錄
Hakuin Ekaku 白隱慧鶴
Hanshu 漢書
Hanxue 漢學
hanyang 涵養
He Ji 何基
hebao 喝報
hemian 合面
Heze Shenhui 荷澤神會
hihan bukkyō 批判佛教
Honglou meng 紅樓夢
Hongren 弘忍
hu 乎 (literary particle)
hu 狐 (fox)
hu 胡 (barbarian)
Hu Juren 胡居仁
Hu Zhi 胡直
Hua Shou 華壽 (Boren 伯仁)
Hua Tuo 華舵
Hua Xiuyun 華岫雲
Huainanzi 淮南子
Huang Baijia 黃百家
Huang Gutan黃古潭
Huang Lizhou 黃梨洲
Huang Ming daotong lu 皇明道統錄
Huangbo Xiyun 黃檗希運
Huangdi neijing 黃帝內經
huangmao baiwei 黃茅白葦
huangqi 黃芪
Huating 華亭
huatou 話頭
Huayan 華嚴
Huike 慧可
huizuan 彙纂
hunma 混罵
huoluan 霍亂
huosi 火死
hushenfu 護身符
huxiang faming 互相發明
ji 及 (a particle in Classical Chinese)
ji 記 (notes)
"Ji changsuo zhibing ershisan zheng" 記嘗所治病二十三證
Jia Run 賈潤
jiadan 加丹
jiajian 加減
jian 見 (viewpoint)
jian 姦 (illicit sex)
jian 檢 (bone examination)
jiandi 檢地
"Jiangu" 檢骨
jiangu tuge 檢骨圖格
jiangxue 講學
Jianyan shishang bu yi shi 檢驗屍傷不以實
jiaoqi 腳氣
jiaosha 勦殺
jiaxu jiayi 夾敍夾議
jiazuo ziyi 假作自縊
jie 節
jin 斤
Jin Lüxiang 金履祥
jing 經
jing hua bujin 精滑不盡
jingling 精靈
jingqi 精氣
jingyue 經曰
"Jingzhai zhen" 敬齋箴
jinqi zhuo 金漆桌
Jinsi lu 近思錄
jinxinshu ze buru wushu 盡信書則不如無書

Jishan xuean 蕺山學案
jizheng 集證
ju 舉
Ju pu 菊譜
ju shi er lu 據實而錄
ju'an 具案
Jueguan lun 絕觀論
juhua 舉話
Juzhi 俱胝
kaijian 開檢
kaijian ji bu zu ping, quan ping gongzheng dingyan 開檢既不足憑，全憑供証定讞
kande 看得
kanhua chan 看話禪
ke 刻
ke zhi 格致
kesou 咳嗽
kuanyan dezhong 寬嚴得中
kuilan 潰爛
Kūkai 空海
Lan Dingyuan 藍鼎元
lao Zhongyi 老中醫
lei 類
leishu 類書
li 例 (precedent, regulation)
li 理 (principle)
li an 立案
Li Gao 李杲
Li Guanlan 李觀瀾
Li Shizhen 李時珍
Li Xiucheng 李秀成
Li Zhi 李贄
liang 良 (respectable person)
liang 兩 (50 grams)
liangchong gong'an yizhuan lingguo 兩重公案一狀領過
lianguan 聯貫
Liezi 列子
linbi 淋閉
ling 靈
Linji Yixuan 臨濟義玄
lishuo 立說
Liu Meng 劉蒙
Liu Zonghou 劉宗厚
liujunzi tang 六君子湯
Liuzi jieyao 劉子節要
lixue 理學
liyi fenshu 理一分殊
lizhong tang 理中湯
Longjin fengsui pan 龍筋鳳髓判
lü 律
Lu Jiuyuan 陸九淵
Lu-Yang er xiansheng xue'an 陸楊二先生學案
Lu Youzhu 盧友竹
lüli zhi zhong er shenming hu lüli 律例之中而神明乎律例
lun 論
lun bingyuan 論病源
Luo Hongxian 羅洪先
Luo Qinshun 羅欽順
Luzhou gong'an 鹿洲公案
mai 脈
mai'an 脈案
maifu 埋伏
maifu zhaoying 埋伏照應
maijian san 麥煎散
Maijing 脈經
mailuo 脈絡
Mazu Daoyi 馬祖道一
Mazu yulu 馬祖語錄
men 門
meng jiao 夢交
meng yu gui jiao 夢與鬼交
mengyi 夢遺
mianshang zheng 面上証
ming ze wu yuan 明則無冤
mingxing 明刑
Mo Jin 莫晉
mou 某

mozhao chan 默照禪
munei zheng 目內症
muyou 幕友
Muzhou 睦州
Nan jing 難經
Nanjing yuanpan 南京院判
Nanquan 南泉
Nanyang Huizhong 南陽慧忠
Nanyue 南嶽
Nanzhili 南直隸
neibian 內編
neike 內科
neiwai shaoyi 內外少異
nengzhi xing 能知性
ni 擬
"Ni shuihuang bingjie gao" 擬水荒稟揭稿
nian 拈
nianfo 念佛
Nie Shangheng 聶尚恒
Niutou zong 牛頭宗
nue 虐
outu 嘔吐
pan 判
pan an 判案
Pan Jiansuo 潘見所
"Pan Jiansuo lao xiansheng ji" 潘見所老先生寄
panduan 判斷
panjiao 判教
panli 判例
panyu 判語
pi 批
Piaoqi 驃騎
pingchang 評唱
Pingyuan lu 平冤錄
Puzhao 普照
qi shuo sanjian cuochu, jiangqiu fei yi 其說散見錯出講求匪易
Qi xiao yishu 奇效醫述
Qiangu beiyao 錢穀備要
qianhou cengci 前後層次
qianjian shende 前件審得
qiao 巧
qiasi 掐死
qichengzhuanghe 起承轉合
qichuang 漆瘡
qie maili 切脈理
qiji 奇疾
qijian 啟檢
qing 情
qing li fa 情理法
qing shen kehen, fa wu kejia 情甚可恨，法無可加
qingchuan qishu 輕傳其書
qingfa liangping 情法兩平
qinggui 清規
qinghun san 清魂散
qingjie 情節
qingli 情理
Qingpu青浦
qingyi 請益
Qingyuan 青原
qingzi xiangguan 情自相關
qinyi 親誼
qiongli 窮理
Qiu Zhao'ao 仇兆鰲
quan 權
quanzuan 全纂
qufa shenqing 屈法伸情
Rao Lu 饒魯
Ren Hongjun 任鴻雋
renqing 人情
ru 儒
ru yixian chuancheng, yikou tongsheng 如一線串成，異口同聲
"Rui Yun" 瑞雲
Ruli 入理
rumen chu 入門處
ruogan 若干
rushi 入室

ruyi 儒醫
Ryōgen 良源
Saichō 最澄
Sanguo zhi 三國志
Sanlun 三論
Sanwu 三吳
Shaanxi tuyu 陝西土語
"Shang lengshen zuiqiu bingtie" 上冷審罪囚稟揭
shang yi shiren 尚醫士人
shanghan 傷寒
Shanghan lun 傷寒論
shangtang 上堂
she 奢
shen 神
shen suo shengbing 腎所生病
shende 審得
sheng 升 (liter)
sheng 聖 (sage)
shengren sharen suoguan shen zhong 生人殺人所關甚重
Shengsheng zi 生生子
"Shengshengzi yi'an xiaoyin" 生生子醫案小引
shenshu 慎術
Shenxiu 神秀
shenyu 審語
shenzang jianzheng 腎臟兼證
shenzang zhubing 腎臟主病
sheshen chudi 設身處地
Sheyi 歙邑
shi 事
shi an zhi 試案之
Shi Zhongyin 石中隱
"Shibu zhuanji lei zonglu zhi shu" 史部傳記類總錄之屬
shidie shensi 失跌身死
shidao 食刀
shifen cunsu zhi yu 十分村俗之語
shigao tang 石膏湯
shige 屍格
shiren 識仁
"Shishang zashuo" 屍傷雜說
Shishuo 師說
shitu 尸圖
shixue 實學
"Shou zu tawu shang" 手足他物傷
shouwei xiangying 首尾相應
shouxin 獸心
shouxue 受學
Shujing 書經
Shūhō Myōchō 宗峰妙超
shuizhong 水腫
"Shuo fu" 說符
shuozheng 說證
shupan 書判
shuyi 數醫
shuzi 豎子
Shuzui tiaoli 贖罪條例
Sichuansi 四川司
siduan 四端
Siku quanshu 四庫全書
Sima Guang 司馬光
Sima Tan 司馬談
sizhe ji yu zijin 死者急欲自盡
song 頌
Song Jinglian 宋景濂
song'an 訟案
Songjiang 松江
"Songru zhuanlue xu" 宋儒傳略序
songsheng biaowen 頌聖表文
Songshi miben 訟師秘本
Su Shi 蘇軾
Sui'an 遂安
Sun Deng 孫登
Sun Simiao 孫思邈
Sun Ye 孫燁
suozhi xing 所知性
Suwen 素問
tai 胎

Taihuting 太湖廳
taijing 胎驚
"Taishigong zixu" 太史公自序
Taiyiyuan 太醫院
Taiyiyuanshi 太醫院使
Tang Bin 湯斌
Tanglü shuyi 唐律疏義
Tangyin bishi 棠陰比事
Tao Wangling 陶望齡
tian zhi wei 天之緯
"Tiandi" 天地
tiandiao sixian 天釣似癇
Tiantai 天台
tianxing 天性
tianyi wufeng 天衣無縫
tiaojing 調經
tiaoli 條例
tiaoting yu qingfa zhijian 調停於情法之間
Tidu jiumen bujun xunbu wuying tongling yamen 提督九門步軍巡捕五營統領衙門
tiefen yuan 鐵粉圓
titou dao 剃頭刀
tiyao 提要
tong 通
Tong Lian 童廉
tongfeng 痛風
tonghao 同好
tonghua 通話
tongmen 通門
tongshi 同事
tongxing 通行
tongzhi 同志
toumo 透膜
tu 徒
tuge 圖格
tuiguan 推官
tulu xiaoxi 吐露消息
tuxue 吐血
tuyin 土音
tuyu 土語
waike 外科
wang 枉
Wang Anshi 王安石
Wang Bo 王柏
Wang Fuling 王福齡
Wang Fuzhi 王夫之
Wang Gen 王艮
Wang Kentang 王肯堂
Wang Qingren 王清任
Wang Ruyan 王汝言
Wang Shouren 王守仁 (Wang Yangming 王陽明 or Yuyao 餘姚)
Wang Shu 王澍
Wang Shuhe 王叔和
wang xingse 望形色
"Wanghui" 王會
Wanghui tu 王會圖
wanqu 灣曲
wei 衛
wei hebao 未喝報
Wei li zhi dao 為吏之道
Wei Zhongxian 魏忠賢
weixi 委係
wen qingzhuang 問情狀
wen shengyin 聞聲音
wen xilai yi 問西來意
wenbing 溫病
wenji 文集
Wenxing tiaoli 問刑條例
woquan 握拳
wu 巫 (shaman)
wu 物 (thing)
Wu Ding 吳鼎
Wu Xiaofeng 吳小峰
wu yi yu fangmo 無益於仿摹
Wucheng bingmasi 五城兵馬司
wuji guntu 無籍棍徒
wulai 無賴
Wumen Huikai 無門慧開
wuqing foxing 無情佛性

wuse pi 五色批
wuxin 無心
wuxing 五行
wuyuan 無冤
Wuyuan lu 無冤錄
Wuzhou 梧州
wuzuo 仵作
wuzuo zhi chuan yi shi 仵作之傳亦失
xi 係
xi shi 細事
xian 仙
xiancheng gong'an 見(現)成公案
xiangfu 相符
xianggua yuan 香瓜圓
xiangpi 詳批
xiangsha zhuwei gao 香砂助胃膏
Xiangyan 香嚴
xianni 現捉
xiansuo 線索
Xiao-Cao yibi 蕭曹遺筆
xiaobian butong 小便不通
xiaochaigu 小釵骨
xiaodaozi 小刀子
xiaona buwo 消納補斡
xiaqi tang 下氣湯
xijiang weixi 西江未吸
Xin'an 新安
Xindu 新都
xing 刑 (penalties)
xing 形 (physical form, appearance)
xing 性 (human nature, inborn nature)
xing'an 刑案
Xingbu 刑部
Xingbu xianshen 刑部現審
Xinghua 興化
Xingshan Weikuan 興善惟寬
xingshu 刑書
xinmo 新摹
xinti 心體
xintong 心痛
xinzang zheng 心臟症
Xinzhu 新竹
xishi 細事
xiwu 戲誤
xiyuan 洗冤
Xiyuan lu 洗冤錄
Xu Guo 許國
Xu Qian 許謙
Xue 薛
Xue Xuan 薛瑄
xue'an 學案
Xuebu tongbian 學蔀通辨
Xuedou Chongxian 雪竇重顯
Xuedou heshang baize songgu 雪竇和尚百則頌古
xuepai 學派
xueshushi 學術史
Xueze 學則
xuezhong zhi dou 穴中之鬥
"Xugong" 敍供
xuji 續輯
xujian 續姦
xun 巡
xuncao yushi 巡漕御史
xunfu 巡撫
Xunxian 濬縣
Xunzhou 潯州
yan 驗
"Yan funu shi" 驗婦女屍
yan huofen bian shengqian sihou 驗火焚辨生前死後
Yan Jizhong 閻季忠
Yan Liben 閻立本
Yang Jian 楊簡
yangmian 仰面
"Yangu" 驗骨
yanju zhu junzi 讞局諸君子
yankan xunduan zhi changfan 驗勘訊斷之常範
yanxing lu 言行錄

yanyu 讞語
yaoyu 要語
ye 也
yeshi 野史
yi 醫 (doctor, medicine)
yi 意 (intention, judgment)
yi 義 (significance)
"Yi xianzong bingjie" 議縣總稟揭
yi xing lunbian 依形論辨
"Yi youxu beiyun gao" 議優恤北運稿
yi zhe yi ye 醫者意也
Yi Zhoushu 逸周書
yi'an 醫案
"Yi'an xiaoyin" 醫案小引
yiben wanshu 一本萬殊
yicao fumu jingling 依草附木精靈
yichanti 一闡提
yihuang san 益黃散
Yilin gaicuo 醫林改錯
yilü 醫律
yilun 醫論
yi'nan da'an 疑難大案
"Yi'nan zashuo" 疑難雜說
ying 營
yinting zheng 陰挺症
yishi hutu 一時糊涂
yishu kexin 醫書可信
"Yiwai zhudu" 意外諸毒
Yixing 宜興
yiyi 依議
yiyou 議由
Yizhi xuyu 醫旨續餘
Yizong jinjian 醫宗金鑑
Yongming Yanshou 永明延壽
you faming 有發明
you yisheng gongzheng ke ping 有醫生供証可憑
you zi yu kaohe 有資於考核
yu 鬱
Yu Chao'en 魚朝恩
Yu Chenglong 于成龍
Yu menren ding yi bing shi 與門人定議病式
Yu Zhun 于準
yuan 冤
yuanlü dingxing 援律定刑
Yuanmen 緣門
Yuanwu Keqin 圜悟克勤
Yuexi cheng'an sanbian 粵西成案三編
yufu fa 預伏法
yuli yufa juzuo 于理于法俱左
Yulin 榆林
yulu 語錄
yun qi 運氣
Yun Richu 惲日初
yunbi buju 運筆布局
Yunmen Wenyan 雲門文偃
Yuyi 寓意
zafang 雜方
zang 臟
zaoshui 糟水
Zeng Guofang 曾國藩
zengbu zhushi 增補註釋
Zengding zeli tuyao bianlan 增訂則例圖要便覽
zeshu 擇術
zhang an 掌案
Zhang Congzheng 張從正
Zhang Ji 張機
"Zhang, Liu, Li, Zhu, Hua liu mingshi xiaozhuan" 張劉李朱滑六名師小傳
Zhang Yikui 張一桂
Zhang Zai 張載
Zhang Zhongjing 張仲景
Zhang Zhuo 張鷟
Zhangjiashan 張家山
Zhangzhou 漳州
zhaochu 照出
"Zhaodai ruzong jilue xu" 昭代儒宗輯略序
zhaoni 招擬
zhaoyou 招由

Zhaozhou Congshen 趙州從諗
zhaozhuang 招狀
zhe 者
Zhen Dexiu 真德秀
zhenbing 診病
zheng 症/證 (syndromes, clusters of symptoms)
zhenghou 徵候 (diagnostic patterns)
zhengshua zhi can 蒸刷之慘
zhengzong 正宗
zhenji 診籍
zhenru 真如
zhenshi xin 真識心
zhi 之 (literary particle)
zhi 志 (will, primal drive to live)
zhifangshu 治方術
zhiguai 志怪
zhiming 致命
zhiren 知人
zhiri yisheng 直日醫生
Zhiyi 智顗
Zhiyuan yicao 芷園臆草
Zhizheng jiyao 治政集要
zhong 種
zhongfeng 中風
zhongyi 眾醫
Zhou Dunyi 周敦頤
Zhou Shunchang 周順昌
Zhu Huiming 朱惠明
zhu jinshen mingjia 諸縉紳名家
Zhu Xun 朱勛
Zhubing yuanhou lun 諸病源候論
zhufang 諸方
zhujing 居敬
zhuyi 諸醫
zhuyu 著語
Zhuzi wannian dinglun 朱子晚年定論
zi 子
"Zican" 自殘
zige houxia 自割喉下
zili cisong 自理詞訟
ziqiu benxin 自求本心
ziwen 自刎
zixing 自性
zixing zhage 自行扎割
"Zixu" 自序
zixu nianpu 自敍年譜
ziyi 自縊
Zizhi tongjian 資治通鑑
zong 縱
zongchuan 宗傳
Zongjing lu 宗鏡錄
zongtong 宗統
zongzhi 宗旨
Zou Shouyi 鄒守益
Zou yan shu 奏讞書
Zou Yuanbiao 鄒元標
zuanzhu 纂註
zuiming 罪名
Zuo zhuan 左傳
zuo'ou buzhi 作嘔不止
zuotong buzhi 作痛不止
zuowen dai shengxian liyan, xugong dai yongsu dayi 作文代聖賢立言，敍供代庸俗達意
"Zushu Shengsheng zi yi'an xiaoxu" 族叔生生子醫案小序
zuyi 族義

Bibliography

Akizuki Ryūmin 秋月龍珉, trans. *Jōshū roku* 趙州錄 (The record of Zhaozhou). Zen no goroku 禪の語錄, no. 11. Tokyo: Chikuma shobōō, 1972.

Andrews, Bridie. "From Case Records to Case Histories: The Modernization of a Chinese Medical Genre, 1912–49." In *Innovation in Chinese Medicine*, ed. Elisabeth Hsu, 324–336.

App, Urs, trans. *Master Yunmen: From the Record of the Chan Teacher "Gate of the Clouds."* New York: Kodansha, 1994.

Audi, Robert. *Practical Reasoning*. New York: Routledge, 1989.

Avataṃsaka-sūtra. See *Dafangguang fo huayan jing*.

Bai Yuanfeng 白元峰. *Qintang bidu* 琴堂必讀 (Required reading for convening courtrooms). 1841.

Barr, Allan. "The Wanli Context of 'The Courtesan's Jewelbox.'" *Harvard Journal of Asiatic Studies* 57, no. 1 (1997): 107–141.

Barrett, Timothy H. "The Date of the *Leng-chia shih-tzu chi*." *Journal of the Royal Asiatic Society*, 3d series, 1, no. 2 (1991): 255–259.

Benn, Charles David. "Taoism as Ideology in the Reign of Emperor Hsüan-tsung (712–755)." Ph.D. dissertation, University of Michigan, 1977.

Biagioli, Mario, ed. *The Science Studies Reader*. New York: Routledge, 1999.

Bibu zhaoni leichao 比部招擬類鈔 (Record of classified verdicts from the Ministry of Justice). Ming ed.

Black's Law Dictionary: Definitions of the Terms and Phrases of American and English Jurisprudence, Ancient and Modern. 6th ed. St. Paul, Minn.: West, 1990.

Bodde, Derk. "Forensic Medicine in Pre-imperial China." *Journal of the American Oriental Society* 102 (1982): 1–15.

Bourgon, Jérôme. "Chine (culture juridique)." In *Dictionnaire de la culture juridique* (A dictionary of legal culture), ed. Stéphane Rials and Denis Alland. Paris: Presses Universitaires de France, 2003, 188–194.

———. "Uncivil Dialogue: Law and Custom Did Not Merge into Civil Law under the Qing." *Late Imperial China* 23, no. 1 (2002): 50–90.

Brady, Bernard. *The Moral Bond of Community: Justice and Discourse in Christian Morality*. Washington, D.C.: Georgetown University Press, 1998.

Bray, Francesca. "A Deathly Disorder: Understanding Women's Health in Late Imperial China." In *Knowledge and the Scholarly Medical Traditions,* ed. Don Bates. Cambridge: Cambridge University Press, 1995, 235–250.

———. "Science, Technique, Technology: Passages Between Matter and Knowledge in Imperial Chinese Agriculture." Unpublished paper, 2005.

Bulantai 布蘭泰. Preface to *Jianshi kaoyao* 檢屍考要 (A study of essentials for examining corpses), by Zhu Gang 朱綱 [1726]. Undated ed. at the Library of Congress Law Library.

Buoye, Thomas. "Suddenly Murderous Intent Arose: Bureaucratization and Benevolence in Eighteenth-Century Qing Homicide Reports." *Late Imperial China* 16, no. 2 (1995): 62–97.

Buswell, Robert E., Jr. "The 'Short-cut' Approach of *K'an-hua* Meditation: The Evolution of a Practical Subitism in Chinese Ch'an Buddhism." In *Sudden and Gradual: Approaches to Enlightenment in Chinese Thought,* ed. Peter N. Gregory. Kuroda Institute Studies in East Asian Buddhism, no. 5. Honolulu: University of Hawai'i Press, 1987, 321–377.

Cang Xiuliang 倉修良. "*Mingru xue'an*" 明儒學案 (Cases of learning of Ming Confucians). In *Zhongguo xueshu mingzhu pingjie* 中國學術名著評介 (Reviews on famous works in Chinese scholarship), ed. Cang Xiuliang. Ji'nan: Shandong jiaoyu chubanshe, 1990, 2:343–379.

Cao Binzhang 曹炳章, comp. *Zhongguo yixue dacheng* 中國醫學大成 (Collection of Chinese medical learning). Shanghai: Yadong shuju, 1930s. Reprint: 6 vols. Changsha: Yuelu shushe, 1990.

Goodrich, L. Carrington, and Chaoying Fang, eds. *Dictionary of Ming Biography.* New York: Columbia University Press, 1976.

Chace, Charles. *Fleshing Out the Bones: Case Histories in the Practice of Chinese Medicine.* Boulder, Colo.: Blue Poppy Press, 1992.

Chan, Wing-tsit. "Chu Hsi and the Academies." In *Neo-Confucian Education: The Formative Stage,* ed. Wm. Theodore de Bary and John W. Chaffee. Berkeley: University of California Press, 1989, 389–413.

———, trans. *Reflections on Things at Hand,* by Zhu Xi and Lü Zuqian. New York: Columbia University Press, 1967.

———, trans. and comp. *A Source Book in Chinese Philosophy.* Princeton, N.J.: Princeton University Press, 1963.

Chandler, James. *England in 1819: The Politics of Literary Culture and the Case of Romantic Historicism.* Chicago: University of Chicago Press, 1998.

Chang, Kang-i Sun. *The Late Ming Poet Ch'en Tzu-lung: Crises of Love and Loyalism.* New Haven, Conn.: Yale University Press, 1991.

Chen Bangxian 陳邦賢, ed. *Ershiliu shi yixue shiliao huibian* 二十六史醫學史料匯編 (Collected sources of medical history from the Twenty-Six Dynastic Histories). Beijing: Zhongyi yanjiu yuan Zhongguo yishi wenxian yanjiushuo, 1982.

Chen Jinzhong 陳錦忠. "Huang Zongxi *Mingru xue'an* zhucheng yinyuan yuqi tili xingzhi luetan." 黃宗羲明儒學案著成因緣與其體例性質略談 (Brief discussion on the origins and nature of Huang Zongxi's *Cases of Ming Learning*). *Donghai xuebao* 東海學報 25 (1984): 111–139.

Chen Rongjie 陳榮捷 [Wing-tsit Chan]. "Lun *Mingru xue'an* zhi shishuo" 論明儒學案之師說 (On the "Words from my teacher [Liu Zongzhou]" in the *Cases of Ming Learning*). *Youshi yuekan* 幼獅月刊 48, no. 1 (1978): 6–8.

Chen Yuanpeng 陳元朋. *Liang Song de "shang yi shiren" yu "ruyi": Jian lun qi zai Jin-Yuan de liubian* 兩宋的尚醫士人與儒醫—兼論其在金元的流變 (Song "gentleman admirers of medicine" and "literati physicians" with a discussion of their Jin-Yuan evolution). Guoli Taiwan daxue wenshi congkan 國立臺灣大學文史叢刊 104. Taipei: Guoli Taiwan daxue chuban weiyuanhui, 1997.

Chen Zuwu 陳祖武. *Zhongguo xue'an shi* 中國學案史 (History of Chinese cases of learning). Taipei: Wenjin chubanshe, 1994.

Cheng, Chien. *Sun-Face Buddha: The Teachings of Ma-tsu and the Hung-chou School of Ch'an*. Berkeley: Asian Humanities Press, 1993.

Cheng Congzhou 程從周 [Cheng Maoxian 程茂先]. *Cheng Maoxian yi'an* 程茂先醫案 (Medical cases of Cheng Chongzhou) [1633]. Shanghai: Shanghai guji shudian, 1979.

Ching, Julia, ed. *The Records of Ming Scholars*, by Huang Tsung-hsi [Zongxi]. Honolulu: University of Hawai'i Press, 1987.

Chixiu Baizhang qinggui 敕修百丈清規 (Imperial edition of Baizhang's rules of purity), comp. Dongyang Dehui 東陽德輝. 1338. T 2025.

Ch'ü T'ung-tsu. *Law and Society in Traditional China*. Paris: Mouton, 1961.

———. *Local Government in China under the Ch'ing* [1962]. Reprint: Cambridge, Mass.: Harvard University Press, 1988.

Cleary, Thomas, trans. *The Blue Cliff Record*, comp. Ch'ung-hsien [Xuedou Chongxian]; commentated by K'o-ch'in [Yuanwu Keqin]. BDK English Tripitaka 75. Berkeley: Numata Center for Buddhist Translation and Research, 1998.

———. *No Barrier: Unlocking the Zen Kōan*. New York: Bantam Books, 1993.

Cohn, Dorrit. *The Distinction of Fiction*. Baltimore, Md.: Johns Hopkins University Press, 1999.

Collcutt, Martin. *Five Mountains: The Rinzai Zen Monastic Institution in Medieval Japan*. Cambridge, Mass.: Harvard University Press, 1981.

Conglin jiaoding qinggui zongyao 叢林校定清規總要 (Essentials of the revised rules of purity for major monasteries), comp. Jinhua Weimian 金華惟勉. 1274. ZZ 112.

Crombie, A. C. *Styles of Scientific Thinking in European Tradition: The History of Argument and Explanation Especially in the Mathematical and Biomedical Sciences and Arts*. Vol. 1. London: Duckworth, 1994.

Cui Xuegu 崔學古. *Shaoxue* 少學 (Learning for youths). In *Tanji congshu* 檀几叢書, ed. Wang Zhuo 王晫, vol. 2. 17th-century ed.

Cullen, Christopher. "Yi'an (case statements): The Origins of a Genre of Chinese Medical Literature." In *Innovation in Chinese Medicine*, ed. Elisabeth Hsu, 297–323.

Da banniepan jing 大般涅槃經 (Mahāparinirvāṇa-sūtra), trans. Dharmakṣema. T 374.

Da banniyuan jing 大般泥洹經 (Mahāparinirvāṇa-sūtra), trans. Faxian 法顯. T 376.

Dafangguang fo huayan jing 大方廣佛華嚴經 (Avataṃsaka-sūtra), trans. Buddhabhadra. T 278.

Dafangguang fo huayan jing 大方廣佛華嚴經 (Avataṃsaka-sūtra), trans. Śikṣānanda. T 279.

Dagao 大誥 (Grand pronouncements) [1385]. In Yang Yifan, *Ming Dagao yanjiu*, 195–452.

Dagao sanbian 大誥三編 (Further supplement to the *Grand Pronouncements*) [1387]. In Yang Yifan, *Ming Dagao yanjiu*, 339–421.

Dagao wuchen 大誥武臣 (Grand pronouncements to military officials) [1388]. In Yang Yifan, *Ming Dagao yanjiu*, 423–452.

Dagao xubian 大誥續編 (Supplement to the *Grand Pronouncements*) [1386]. In Yang Yifan, *Ming Dagao yanjiu*, 255–338.

Dai Jin 戴金 et al., comp. *Huang Ming tiaofa shilei zuan* 皇明條法事類纂 (Categorized regulations of the august Ming). *Zhongguo zhenxi falü dianji jicheng* 中國珍稀法律典籍集成 (Compilation of rare Chinese legal documents and records), ed. Liu Hainian 劉海年 and Yang Yifan, ser. 2, vols. 4–6. Beijing: Kexue chubanshe, 1994.

Dai Yi 戴逸, ed. *Ershi shiji Zhonghua xue'an* 二十世紀中華學案 (Cases of learning of twentieth-century China). Beijing: Beijing tushuguan chubanshe, 1999.

Danshuiting Xinzhuxian dang'an 淡水廳新竹縣檔案 (Danshui Subprefecture and Xinzhu County archive). Microfilm copy, University of California, Los Angeles. Catalogued by Dai Yanhui 戴炎輝.

Daqing shilu 大清實錄 (Veritable records of the great Qing dynasty). Reprint: Beijing: Zhonghua shuju, 1985.

Dardess, John R. *Confucianism and Autocracy: Professional Elites in the Founding of the Ming Dynasty.* Berkeley: University of California Press, 1983.

de Pee, Christian. "Cases of the New Terrace: Canon and Law in Three Southern Song Verdicts." *Journal of Song Yuan Studies* 27 (1997): 27–61.

Dewoskin, Kenneth J. *Doctors, Diviners, and Magicians of Ancient China: Biographies of Fang-shi.* New York: Columbia University Press, 1983.

Douglas, Robert K. *China.* London: Society for Promoting Christian Knowledge, 1882. Rev. ed.: Chicago: The Werner Company, 1895.

Dworkin, Ronald. *Law's Empire.* Cambridge, Mass.: Harvard University Press, 1986.

———. "The Model of Rules." *University of Chicago Law Review* 35 (1967): 14–46.

Eco, Umberto, and Thomas A. Sebeok, eds. *The Sign of Three: Dupin, Holmes, Peirce.* Bloomington: Indiana University Press, 1983.

Edwards, R. Randle. "The Role of Case Precedent in the Qing Judicial Process as Reflected in Appellate Rulings." In *Understanding China's Legal System: Essays in Honor of*

Jerome A. Cohen, ed. E. Stephen Hsu. New York: New York University Press, 2003, 180–209.

Elman, Benjamin. *A Cultural History of Civil Examinations in Late Imperial China*. Berkeley: University of California Press, 2000.

———. *From Philosophy to Philology: Intellectual and Social Aspects of Change in Late Imperial China*. Harvard East Asian Series 110. Cambridge, Mass.: Council on East Asian Studies, Harvard University, 1984.

———. *On Their Own Terms: Science in China, 1550–1900*. Cambridge, Mass.: Harvard University Press, 2005.

Epstein, Julia. *Altered Conditions: Disease, Medicine, and Storytelling*. New York: Routledge, 1995.

Fulin jinjian 法林金鑑 (The golden mirror of the world of law). Late Ming(?) ed.

Fan Xingzhun 范行准. *Zhongguo yixue shilüe* 中國醫學史略 (Brief history of Chinese medicine). Beijing: Zhongyi guji chubanshe, 1986.

Fang Keli 方克立 and Li Jinquan 李錦全, eds. *Xiandai xinrujia xue'an* 現代新儒家學案 (Cases of learning of modern neo-Confucians). Beijing: Zhongguo shehui kexue chubanshe, 1995.

Fang Ruqian 方汝謙. *Baojian Xiyuan lu* 寶鑒洗冤錄 (The precious mirror of *The Washing Away of Wrongs*). Preface dated 1761. In *Zhouxian xuzhi* 州縣須知, comp. Cheng Yan 程炎, 1794 preface.

Farmer, Edward. *Zhu Yuanzhang and Early Ming Legislation: The Reordering of Chinese Society Following the Era of Mongol Rule*. Leiden: Brill, 1995.

Farquhar, Judith. *Knowing Practice: The Clinical Encounter in Chinese Medicine*. Boulder, Colo.: Westview Press, 1994.

Faure, Bernard. *Chan Insights and Oversights: An Epistemological Critique of the Chan Tradition*. Princeton, N.J.: Princeton University Press, 1993.

———. *The Rhetoric of Immediacy: A Cultural Critique of Chan/Zen Buddhism*. Princeton, N.J.: Princeton University Press, 1991.

———. *The Will to Orthodoxy: A Critical Genealogy of Northern Chan Buddhism*, trans. Phyllis Brooks. Stanford, Calif.: Stanford University Press, 1997.

Fazang 法藏. *Dacheng qixin lun yiji* 大乘起信論義記 (Commentary on the *Treatise on the Awakening of Faith in the Great Vehicle*). T 1846.

———. *Huayan jing tan xuanji* 華嚴經探玄記. (Record of the search for the occult meaning of the *Avataṃsaka-sūtra*). T 1733.

Feng Xu 馮煦, comp. *Jintan xianzhi* 金壇縣志 (Gazetteer of Jintan County). Reprint of 1921 ed. Taipei: Chengwen chubanshe, 1970.

Foguo Yuanwu Chanshi Biyan lu 佛果圜悟禪師碧巖錄 (Blue Cliff record of Chan master Foguo Yuanwu), comp. Puzhao 普照; ed. Guan Wudang 關無黨. 1128. T 1985.

Forrester, John. "If *p*, then what? Thinking in Cases." *History of the Human Sciences* 9, no. 3 (1996): 1–25.

Foucault, Michel. "Truth and Power," trans. C. Gordon et al. In *Critical Theory: A Reader*, ed. Douglas Tallack. New York: Harvester Wheatsheaf, 1995, 66–77. [First published in M. Foucault, *Power/Knowledge: Selected Interviews and Other Writings, 1972–1977*, ed. Colin Gordon (New York: Pantheon Books, 1980).]

Foulk, T. Griffith. "The Form and Function of Kōan Literature: A Historical Overview." In *The Kōan: Texts and Contexts in Zen Buddhism*, ed. Steven Heine and Dale S. Wright. Oxford: Oxford University Press, 2000, 15–45.

———. "Myth, Ritual, and Monastic Practice in Sung Ch'an Buddhism." In *Religion and Society in T'ang and Sung China*, ed. Patricia Buckley Ebrey and Peter N. Gregory. Honolulu: University of Hawai'i Press, 1993, 147–208.

Foulk, T. Griffith, and Robert H. Sharf. "On the Ritual Use of Ch'an Portraiture in Medieval China." *Cahiers d'Extrême-Asie* 7 (1993–1994): 149–219.

Franke, Wolfgang. *An Introduction to the Sources of Ming History*. Kulua Lumpur: University of Malaya Press, 1968.

Fujita Genro 藤田玄路, ed. *Zudokko* 塗毒鼓 (The poison-painted drum). Kyoto: Fujitake zōhan, 1917.

Fukunaga Mitsuji 福永光司. "Issai shujō to sōmoku doseki" 一切眾生と草木土石 (All sentient beings [vis-à-vis] grasses, trees, earth, and stones). *Bukkyō shigaku kenkyū* 佛教史學研究 23, no. 2 (1981): 103–118.

Fuma Susumu 夫馬進. "Shōshi hihon *Xiaocao yibi* no shutsugen" 訟師秘本《蕭曹遺筆》の出現 (The pettifogger's secret handbook, *Xiaocao yibi*, brought to light). *Shirin* 史林 77, no. 2 (1994): 437–483.

Furth, Charlotte. "Body, Blood, and Gender: Medical Images of the Female Condition in China, 1600–1850." *Chinese Science* 7 (1986): 43–66.

———. *A Flourishing Yin: Gender in China's Medical History, 960–1665*. Berkeley: University of California Press, 1999.

Furuta Shōkin 古田紹欽. "Kōan no rekishi-teki hatten keitai ni okeru shinrisei no mondai" 公案の歴史的發展型態における真理性の問題 (The problem of truth in the historical development of the *kōan*). In *Bukkyō no kompon shinri* 佛教の根本真理 (The fundamental truth of Buddhism), ed. Miyamoto Shōson 宮本正尊. Tokyo: Sanseidō, 1956, 807–840.

Gailus, Andreas. "A Case of Individuality: Karl Philipp Moritz and the *Magazine for Empirical Psychology*." *New German Critique* 79 (2000): 67–105.

Gangyi 剛毅. *Shenkan nishi* 審看擬式 (Proposing formulas for investigating cases). Jiangsu shuju, 1889.

Gangyi 剛毅, comp. *Xiyuan lu yizheng* 洗冤錄義證 (Evidence on the meaning of *The Washing Away of Wrongs*). 1891 Jiangsu shuju ed. 2nd ed., Guangdong Governor's office, 1892.

Gao Ju 高舉, ed. *Da Ming lü jijie fuli* 大明律集解附例 (The Ming code with commentaries and attached regulations) [1610]. Reprint: 5 vols. Taipei: Chengwen chubanshe, 1969.

Geng Dingxiang 耿定向. *Geng Tiantai xiansheng wenji* 耿天臺先生文集 (Collected essays of Geng Dingxiang). Reprint of 1598 ed., SKCM, *jibu* 集部, vol. 131.

Giles, Herbert, trans. "The 'Hsi Yüan Lu' or 'Instructions to Coroners.'" *Proceedings of the Royal Society of Medicine* 17 (1924): 59–107. [First published in *China Review* 3, no. 3 (1874): 159–172.]

Gimello, Robert M. "Mārga and Culture: Learning, Letters and Liberation in Northern Sung Ch'an." In *Paths to Liberation: The Mārga and Its Transformations in Buddhist Thought*, ed. Robert Buswell and Robert Gimello. Kuroda Institute Studies in East Asian Buddhism, no. 7. Honolulu: University of Hawai'i Press, 1992, 371–437.

Ginzburg, Carlo. *The Cheese and the Worms: The Cosmos of a Sixteenth-Century Miller*, trans. John Tedeschi and Anne Tedeschi. Baltimore, Md.: Johns Hopkins University Press, 1980.

———. "The Inquisitor as Anthropologist." In *Clues, Myths, and the Historical Method*, trans. John Tedeschi and Anne Tedeschi. Baltimore, Md.: Johns Hopkins University Press, 1989, 156–164.

———. "Morelli, Freud, and Sherlock Holmes: Clues and Scientific Method." In *The Sign of Three*, ed. Umberto Eco and Thomas A. Sebeok, 81–118.

———. *Night Battles: Witchcraft and Agrarian Cults in the Sixteenth and Seventeenth Centuries*, trans. John Tedeschi and Anne Tedeschi. Baltimore, Md.: Johns Hopkins University Press, 1983.

Golding, Martin P. *Legal Reasoning*. New York: Alfred A. Knopf, 1984.

Goodrich, L. Carrington, and Chaoying Fang, eds. *Dictionary of Ming Biography, 1368–1644*. 2 vols. New York: Columbia University Press, 1976.

Goody, Jack. *The Domestication of the Savage Mind*. Cambridge: Cambridge University Press, 1977.

———. *The Interface between the Written and the Oral*. Cambridge: Cambridge University Press, 1987.

———. *The Logic of Writing and the Organization of Society*. Cambridge: Cambridge University Press, 1986.

Goody, Jack, and Ian Watt. "The Consequences of Literacy." In *Literacy in Traditional Societies*, ed. J. Goody. Cambridge: Cambridge University Press, 1968, 27–68.

Graham, A. C. *Chuang-tzu: The Inner Chapters*. London: George Allen and Unwin, 1981.

———. *Disputers of the Tao: Philosophical Argument in Ancient China*. Chicago: Open Court, 1989.

Grant, Joanna. *A Chinese Physician: Wang Ji and the 'Stone Mountain Medical Case Histories.'* London: RoutledgeCurzon, 2003.

Groner, Paul. *Ryōgen and Mount Hiei: Japanese Tendai in the Tenth Century*. Kuroda Institute Studies in East Asian Buddhism, no. 15. Honolulu: University of Hawai'i Press, 2002.

Gu Qingmei 古清美. "Cong *Mingru xue'an* tan Huang Lizhou sixiang shang de jige wenti" 從明儒學案談黃梨洲思想上的幾個問題 (Several questions about Huang Zongxi's thought arising from the *Cases of Ming Learning*). In *Mingdai lixue lunwenji* 明代理學論文集. Taipei: Da'an chubanshe, 1990, 351–394.

Guanding 灌頂. *Da banniepan jing shu* 大般涅槃經疏 (Commentary to the *Mahāparinirvāṇa-sūtra*), comp. Zhanran 湛然. T 1767.

Guy, R. Kent. *The Emperor's Four Treasuries: Scholars and the State in the Late Ch'ien-lung Era.* Cambridge, Mass.: Council on East Asian Studies, Harvard University, 1987.

Hacking, Ian. "Styles of Scientific Reasoning." In *Post-Analytic Philosophy,* ed. John Rajchman and Cornel West. New York: Columbia University Press, 1985, 145–165.

Han Mao 韓懋. *Hanshi yitong* 韓氏醫通 (Master Han's survey of medicine) [1522]. In *Zhongguo yixue dacheng,* comp. Cao Binzhang, 4:389–401.

Han Xuejie 韓學傑 and Zhang Yinsheng 張印生. "Sun Yikui yixue xueshu sixiang yanjiu" 孫一奎醫學學術思想研究 (Research on Sun Yikui's medical thought). In *Sun Yikui yixue quanshu,* by Sun Yikui, 841–866.

Hanan, Patrick. *The Chinese Vernacular Story.* Cambridge, Mass.: Harvard University Press, 1981.

Hanson, Marta. "Robust Northerners and Delicate Southerners: The Nineteenth-Century Invention of a Southern Medical Tradition." In *Innovation in Chinese Medicine,* ed. Elisabeth Hsu, 262–296.

Harbsmeier, Christoph. *Logic and Language.* Vol. 7, pt. 1 of *Science and Civilisation in China,* ed. Joseph Needham. Cambridge: Cambridge University Press, 1998.

Hartwell, Robert. "Historical Analogism, Public Policy and Social Science in Eleventh- and Twelfth-Century China." *American Historical Review* 76, no. 3 (1971): 690–727.

Haruhito Sadate 佐立治人. "Saiban kijun toshite no 'ninjō' no seiritsu ni tsuite" 裁判基準としての「人情」の成立について (On the origin of "human sentiment" as a Chinese judicial norm). *Hoseishi Kenkyū* 法制史研究 45:73–106.

Hawes, Colin. "Reinterpreting Law in the Sung: Zheng Ke's Commentary on the 'Magic Mirror for Deciding Cases.'" *Journal of Asian Legal History* (http://jalh.ukans.edu/article/hawes/pdf) (December 2001): 23–68.

He Ning 和凝 and He Meng 和㠓. *Yiyu ji* 疑獄集 (A Collection of doubtful cases) [10th century]. SKQS, vol. 729.

He Sanwei 何三畏. "Jun sili Ruchu Maogong zhuan" 郡司理孺初毛公傳 (Biography of the prefectual judge Mao Ruchu [Yilu]). In *Yunjian zhilüe* 雲間志略 (Gazetteer of Songjiang Prefecture) [1623]. Reprint: Taipei: Taiwan xuesheng shuju, 1987.

Heine, Steven. *Shifting Shape, Shaping Text: Philosophy and Folklore in the Fox Kōan.* Honolulu: University of Hawai'i Press, 1999.

Heine, Steven, and Dale S. Wright, eds. *The Kōan: Texts and Contexts in Zen Buddhism.* Oxford: Oxford University Press, 2000.

Henderson, John B. *Scripture, Canon and Commentary: A Comparison of Confucian and Western Exegesis.* Princeton, N.J.: Princeton University Press, 1991.

Hirano Sōjō 平野宗淨, trans. *Tongo yōmon* 頓悟要門 (Essentials of sudden enlightenment), by Dazhu Huihai 大珠慧海. Zen no goroku 禪の語錄, no. 6. Tokyo: Chikuma shobō, 1970.

Ho Da-an 何大安. "Lunduan fuhao: Lun an, an de yuci guanxi ji anlei wenti de pianzhang goucheng" 論斷符號：論案、按的語詞關係及案類文體的篇章構成 (Case and commentary: The historical linguistics of *an*/*an*). In *Rang zhengju shuohua: Zhongguo pian,* ed. Ping-chen Hsiung, 320–337.

Hong Mai 洪邁. *Yijian zhi* 夷堅志 (Records of the listener) [12th century]. Modern punctuated edition, ed. He Zhuodian 何卓點. 4 vols. Beijing: Zhonghua shuju, 1981.

Hou Wailu 侯外廬. *Chuanshan xue'an* 船山學案 (Case of learning from Chuanshan [Wang Fuzhi]). Changsha: Yuelu shuyuan, 1982.

Hou Wailu 侯外廬, Qiu Hansheng 邱漢生, and Zhang Qizhi 張豈之, eds. *Song-Ming lixue shi* 宋明理學史 (History of Song and Ming neo-Confucianism). 2 vols. Beijing: Renmin chubanshe, 1987.

Hsieh, Ding-hwa Evelyn. "A Study of the Evolution of K'an-Hua Ch'an in Sung China: Yüan-Wu K'o-Ch'in (1063–1135) and the Function of Kung-an in Ch'an Pedagogy and Praxis." Ph.D. dissertation, University of California, Los Angeles, 1993.

———. "Yuan-Wu K'o-Ch'in's (1063–1135) Teaching of Ch'an *Kung-an* Practice: A Transition from the Literary Study of Ch'an *Kung-an* to the Practical *K'an-Hua* Ch'an." *Journal of the International Association of Buddhist Studies* 17, no. 1 (1994): 66–95.

Hsiung, Ping-chen 熊秉真. "Anju quezao: Yian zhi chuancheng yu chuanqi" 案據確鑿：醫案之傳承與傳奇 (Founded with firm evidence? The history and legend of medical cases). In *Rang zhengju shuohua: Zhongguo pian,* ed. Ping-chen Hsiung, 201–252.

———, ed. *Rang zhengju shuohua: Duihua pian* 讓證據說話：對話篇 (Let the evidence speak: Case records in the West). Taipei: Maitian chuban, 2001.

———, ed. *Rang zhengju shuohua: Zhongguo pian* 讓證據說話：中國篇 (Let the evidence speak: Case records in China). Taipei: Maitian chuban, 2001.

———. *A Tender Voyage: Children and Childhood in Late Imperial China.* Stanford, Calif.: Stanford University Press, 2005.

———. *Youyou: Chuantong Zhongguo de qiangbao zhidao* 幼幼：傳統中國的襁褓之道 (Infant care in traditional China). Taipei: Lianjing chuban shiye gongsi, 1995.

Hsu, Elisabeth, ed. *Innovation in Chinese Medicine.* Needham Research Institute Studies 3. Cambridge: Cambridge University Press, 2001.

———. "Pulse Diagnostics in the Western Han." In *Innovation in Chinese Medicine,* ed. Elisabeth Hsu, 51–91.

Huang Chang-chien 黃彰健. "Da Ming lü gao kao" 大明律誥考 (An investigation on the Great Ming Code with pronouncements). In *Ming Qing shi yanjiu conggao* 明清史

研究叢稿 (Draft studies on the Ming and Qing history), ed. Huang Changjian. Taipei: Taiwan shangwu yinshuguan, 1977, 159–207.

Huang Jinxing 黃進興. "Xue'an ticai chansheng de sixiang beijing: Cong Li Fu de *Luzi xuepu* tanqi" 學案題材產生的思想背景—從李紱的陸子學譜談起 (A discussion on the intellectual background of the "case of learning" genre based on Li Fu's *Genealogy of Learning of Lu Jiuyuan*). *Hanxue yanjiu* 漢學研究 2, no. 1 (1984): 201–221.

Huang Liuhong 黃六鴻. *Fuhui quanshu* 福惠全書 (A complete book concerning happiness and benevolence). Preface dated 1694. 1699 original Zhongshutang 種書堂 ed.

Huang, Philip C. [Huang Zongzhi 黃宗智]. *Civil Justice in China: Representation and Practice in the Qing*. Stanford, Calif.: Stanford University Press, 1996.

———. *Qingdai de falü, shehui yu wenhua: Minfa de biaoda yu shijian* 清代的法律、社會與文化：民法的表達與實踐. 2nd ed. Shanghai: Shanghai shudian chubanshe, 2001.

Huang Si'ai 黃嗣艾. *Nanlei xue'an* 南雷學案 (Case of learning from Nanlei [Huang Zongxi]). Nanjing: Zhongzheng shuju, 1936.

Huang Tiren 黃體仁. *Siranzhai canggao* 四然齋藏稿 (Draft writings held at the Siranzhai studio). Wanli (1572–1620) ed.

Huang Zongxi 黃宗羲. *Huang Zongxi quanji* 黃宗羲全集 (Complete works of Huang Zongxi), ed. Shen Shanhong 沈善洪. 12 vols. Hangzhou: Zhejiang guji chubanshe, 1985–1994.

———. *Mingru xue'an* 明儒學案 (Cases of learning of Ming Confucians) [1693]. Modern punctuated edition ed. Shen Zhiying 沈芝盈. 2 vols. Beijing: Zhonghua shuju, 1985.

———. *Mingru xue'an* 明儒學案 (Cases of learning of Ming Confucians). In *Huang Zongxi quanji*, vols. 7–8.

Huang Zongxi 黃宗羲 and Quan Zuwang 全祖望. *Song-Yuan xue'an* 宋元學案 (Cases of learning from the Song and Yuan) [1837–1838], ed. Chen Jinsheng 陳金生 and Liang Yunhua 梁運華. 4 vols. Beijing: Zhonghua shuju, 1986.

Huangbo Duanji Chanshi Wanling lu 黃檗斷際禪師宛陵錄. (The Wanling record of the Chan master Huangbo Duanji). Attributed to Pei Xiu 裴休. T 2012.

Hucker, Charles. *A Dictionary of Official Terms in Imperial China*. Stanford, Calif.: Stanford University Press, 1985.

Hulsewé, A. F. P. *Remnants of Ch'in Law*. Leiden: Brill, 1985.

Hummel, Arthur, ed. *Eminent Chinese of the Ch'ing Period*. Washington, D.C.: U.S. Government Printing Office, 1943–1944.

Hunter, Kathryn Montgomery. *Doctors' Stories: The Narrative Structure of Medical Knowledge*. Princeton, N.J.: Princeton University Press, 1991.

Hymes, Robert. "Some Thoughts on 'Thinking in Cases' in the Song." Paper presented to the conference on "Thinking With Cases: Specialist Knowledge in Chinese Cultural History," University of Chicago, October 12–14, 2001.

Iriya Yoshitaka 入矢義高, trans. *Baso no goroku* 馬祖の語錄 (Recorded sayings of Mazu). Kyoto: Zenbunka kenkyūjo, 1984.

———, trans. *Rinzai roku* 臨濟錄 (Recorded sayings of Linji). Iwanami bunko. Tokyo: Iwanami, 1989.

Iriya Yoshitaka 入矢義高 and Koga Hideheko 古賀英彥, eds. *Zengo jiten* 禪語辭典 (Dictionary of Zen terms). Tokyo: Shibunkaku, 1991.

Jia Jingtao 賈靜濤. "Zhongguo fayixue shi liushi nian" 中國法醫學史六十年 (Sixty years of history of Chinese forensic medicine). *Zhonghua yishi zazhi* 中華醫史雜誌 26, no. 4 (1996): 231–237.

———. *Zhongguo gudai fayixue shi* 中國古代法醫學史 (A history of forensic medicine in ancient China). Beijing: Qunzhong chubanshe, 1984.

Jiang Guan 江瓘, comp. *Mingyi lei'an* 名醫類案 (Classified cases of famous doctors). Preface dated 1549. First published 1591. Reprint of *Zhibuzu zhai congshu* 知不足齋叢書 ed. Beijing. Renming weisheng chubanshe 1957, 1982.

Jiang Yonglin, trans. *The Great Ming Code*. Seattle: University of Washington Press, 2005.

———. "The *Great Ming Code*: A Cosmological Instrument for Transforming 'All under Heaven.'" Ph.D. dissertation, University of Minnesota, 1997.

Jiangu buyi kaozheng 檢骨補遺考證 (Supplementary evidence for examining bones). Appended to 1881 ed. of *[Chongkan] Buzhu Xiyuan lu jizheng*, comp. Ruan Qixin. Separate ed. with a preface dated 1886.

Jin Shengtan 金聖嘆. "Xu san" 序三 (The third preface [to *The Water Margin*]). In *Jin Shengtan quanji* 金聖嘆全集 (Complete works of Jin Shengtan). Yangzhou: Jiangsu guji chubanshe, 1985, 9–12.

Jingde chuandeng lu 景德傳燈錄 (Jingde-era record of the transmission of the lamp), comp. Taoyuan 道元; ed. Yang Yi 楊億. 1011. T 2076.

Jingjue 淨覺. *Lengqie shizi ji* 楞伽師資記 (Record of the masters and disciples of the *Lankāvatāra*). Written between 713 and 716. T 2837.

Jingying Huiyuan 淨影慧遠. *Dacheng yizhang* 大乘義章 (Essay on the meaning of the great vehicle). T 1851.

Jizang 吉藏. *Dacheng xuanlun* 大乘玄論 (Treatise on the profundities of the great vehicle). T 1853.

Jolles, André. *Formes Simples*, trans. Antoine Marie Buguet [1930]. Paris: Seuil, 1972.

Jonsen, Albert R., and Stephen Toulmin. *The Abuse of Casuistry: A History of Moral Reasoning*. Berkeley: University of California Press, 1988.

Ju Huanwu 巨煥武. "Mingdai panjueshu de geshi jiqi jizai fangfa" 明代判決書的格式及其記載方法 (The form and record-keeping methods of verdicts during the Ming dynasty). *Dalu zazhi* 大陸雜誌 68, no. 3 (1984): 115–140.

Kagamishima Genryū 鏡島元隆, Satō Tatsugen 佐藤達玄, and Kosaka Kiyū 小阪機融, trans. *Yakuchū: Zen'en shingi* 譯註禪苑清規 (Rules of purity for Chan monasteries: An annotated translation). Tokyo: Sōtōshū shūmuchō, 1972.

Kamata Shigeo 鎌田茂雄. *Chūgoku bukkyō shisōshi kenkyū* 中國佛經思想史研究 (Studies in the history of Chinese Buddhist thought). Tokyo: Shunjūsha, 1968.

———. *Chūgoku kegon shisōshi no kenkyū* 中國華嚴思想史の研究 (Studies in the history of Chinese Huayan thought). Tokyo: Tōkyō daigaku shuppankai, 1965.

———. "Chūgoku zen shisōshi ni arawareta mujōbusshō shisō" 中國禪思想史に現われた無情佛性思想 (The theory of the buddha-nature of the insentient in the context of Chinese Chan intellectual history). *[Sōtōshū] Shūgaku kenkyū* 〔曹洞宗〕宗學研究 4 (1962): 51–57.

Karasawa, Yasuhiko 唐澤靖彥. "Hanasukoto to kakukoto no hazamade: Shindai saiban bunsho ni okeru kyōjutsusho no tekusutosei" 話すことと書くことのはざまで：清代裁判文書における供述書のテクスト性 (Between speech and writing: Textuality of the written records of oral testimony in Qing legal cases). *Chūgoku: Shakai to bunka* 中国：社会と文化 10 (1995): 212–250.

Keyworth, George Albert, III. "Transmitting the Lamp of Learning in Classical Chan Buddhism: Juefan Huihong (1071–1128) and Literary Chan." Ph.D. dissertation, University of California, Los Angeles, 2001.

Ko, Dorothy. *Teachers of the Inner Chambers: Women and Culture in Seventeenth-Century China.* Stanford, Calif.: Stanford University Press, 1994.

Kobayashi Shinmei 小林信明, trans. *Resshi* 列子 (Liezi). Shinyaku kanbun taikei 新釈漢文大系 22. Tokyo: Meiji shoin, 1967.

Komazawa Daigaku 駒澤大學, ed. *Zengaku daijiten* 禪學大辭典 (Encyclopedia of Zen studies). 3 vols. [1978]. Reprint (3 vols. in 1): Tokyo: Daishūkan, 1985.

Koseki, Aaron K. "Chi-tsang's '*Ta-ch'eng-hsuan-lun*': The Two Truths and the Buddha-nature." Ph.D. dissertation, University of Wisconsin, 1977.

———. "Prajñāpāramitā and the Buddhahood of the Non-Sentient World: The San-Lun Assimilation of Buddha-Nature and Middle Path Doctrine." *Journal of the International Association of Buddhist Studies* 3, no. 1 (1980): 16–33.

Kuriyama, Shigehisa. *The Expressiveness of the Body and the Divergence of Greek and Chinese Medicine.* New York: Zone Books, 1999.

LaFleur, William R. "Saigyō and the Buddhist Value of Nature." Pts. 1 and 2. *History of Religions* 13, no. 2 (1973): 93–128; 13, no. 3 (1974): 227–248.

Lai, Whalen. "The *Mahāyānaparinirvāṇa Sūtra* and Its Earliest Interpreters in China: Two Prefaces by Tao-lang and Tao-sheng." *Journal of the American Oriental Society* 102, no. 1 (1982): 99–105.

Lang Jinqi 郎錦騏, comp. *Jianyan hecan/Jianyan jizheng* 檢驗合參/檢驗集證 (Collected references for autopsies/Collected evidence for autopsies). Author's preface dated 1829. Earliest extant ed. dated 1835. Reprint: Shaanxi, 1847, with a preface by Jiang Rong 姜榮; Guizhou, 1849, with a preface by Zhou Zuoji 周作楫; Guizhou, 1883.

Langlois, John D., Jr. "'Living Law' in Sung and Yuan Jurisprudence." *Harvard Journal of Asiatic Studies* 41, no. 1 (1981): 165–217.

Lau, D. C., trans. *Mencius.* Harmondsworth, U.K.: Penguin Books Ltd., 1970.

Legge, James, trans. *The Four Books: Confucian Analects, The Great Learning, The Doctrine of the Mean, and The Works of Mencius.* Shanghai, 1923. Reprint: New York: Paragon Book Reprint Corp., 1966.

———, trans. *The Shoo King.* Vol. 3 of *The Chinese Classics.* 2nd ed. Oxford: Clarendon Press, 1895. Reprint: Taipei: Southern Materials Center, 1985.

Lei, Sean Hsiang-lin. "How Did Chinese Medicine Become Experiential? The Political Epistemology of *Jingyan.*" *positions: East Asian Cultures Critique* 10, no. 2 (2002): 333–364.

Leung, Angela Ki Che. "Medical Learning from the Song to the Ming." In *The Song-Yuan-Ming Transition in Chinese History,* ed. Paul Jakov Smith and Richard von Glahn. Cambridge, Mass.: Harvard University Asia Center, 2003, 374–398.

———. "Women Practicing Medicine in Premodern China." In *Chinese Women in the Imperial Past: New Perspectives,* ed. Harriet T. Zurndorfer. Leiden: Brill, 1999, 101–134.

Levenson, Joseph. "The Abortiveness of Empiricism in Early Ch'ing Thought." In *Confucian China and its Modern Fate.* Vol. l. Berkeley: University of California Press, 1968.

Levering, Miriam. "Ch'an Enlightenment for Laymen: Ta-Hui and the New Religious Culture of the Sung." Ph.D. dissertation, Harvard University, 1978.

Li Chan 李梴. *Yixue rumen* 醫學入門 (Introduction to medical learning) [1575]. Beijing: Zhongguo Zhongyiyao chubanshe, 1995.

Li Jianmin 李建民. *Si sheng zhi yu: Zhou Qin Han mai xue zhi yuanliu* 死生之域—周秦漢脈學之源流 (The frontier of life and death: Origins of channel lore in the Zhou, Qin, and Han dynasties). Academia Sinica Institute of History and Philology Monograph 101. Taipei: Academia Sinica Institute of History and Philology, 2000.

Li Qing 李清. *Zheyu xinyu* 折獄新語 (New words on deciding cases) [1630s?]. Modern punctuated edition ed. Lu Youxun 陸有珣 et al. Changchun: Jilin renmin chubanshe, 1987.

Li Tianlin 李天麟. *Shuwen huibian* 淑問彙編 (Collected works on hearing cases). Wanli (1572–1620) ed.

Li Tiaoyuan 李調元. *Danmo lu* 淡墨錄 (Record of skilled civil service examination papers) [1881]. Reprint: *Congshu jicheng* 叢書集成. Shanghai: Shangwu yinshuguan, 1939.

Li, Wai-yee. "The Late Ming Courtesan: Invention of a Cultural Ideal." In *Writing Women in Late Imperial China,* ed. Ellen Widmer and Kang-i Sun Chang. Stanford, Calif.: Stanford University Press, 1997, 46–73.

Li Yu 李漁. *Zizhi xinshu* 資治新書 (A new book to help in government). 1663 original Jieziyuan 芥子園 ed.

Li Yuzhen 李玉珍. "Dangtou banghe: Chanzong wenxue gong'an" 當頭棒喝：禪宗文學公案 (The genuine stick and shout: Literary cases of the Chan school). In *Rang zhengju shuohua,* ed. Ping-chen Hsiung, 107–113.

Liang Qichao 梁啟超 [Yinbingshi zhuren 飲冰室主人]. "Liyan" 例言 (Editorial principles) to *Jieben Mingru xue'an* 節本明儒學案 (Abridged version of *Cases of Learning of Ming Confucians*). Shanghai: Xinmin she, 1905. Reprinted in Liang Qichao, *Yinbingshi congzhu* 飲冰室叢著 (Series from the Studio of Ice Drinks [of Liang Qichao]), vol. 2. Shanghai: Shangwu yinshuguan, 1930?

———. *Zhongguo jin sanbai nian xueshu shi* 中國近三百年學術史 (History of Chinese learning and scholarship in the last three hundred years). Shanghai: Zhonghua shuju, 1936.

Liebenthal, Walter. "The World Conception of Chu Tao-Sheng." Pts. 1 and 2. *Monumenta Nipponica* 12, no. 1 (1956): 65–103; 12, no. 2 (1956): 241–268.

Ling Qiu 凌燽. *Xijiang shinie jishi* 西江視臬紀事 (Records of a provincial judge in Jiangxi). Reprint of 1743 Jianshan shuwu 劍山書屋 ed. XXSK, vol. 882.

Linji lu 臨濟錄 (Record of Linji), comp. Sansheng Huiran 三聖慧然. T 1985.

Link, Arthur. "Tao-sheng: A Biographical Essay." Ph.D. dissertation, University of California, Berkeley, 1957.

Liu Ming-Wood. "The Doctrine of the Buddha-nature in the Mahāyāna *Mahāparinirvāṇa-sūtra.*" *Journal of the International Association of Buddhist Studies* 5, no. 2 (1982): 63–94.

———. *Madhyamaka Thought in China.* Leiden: E. J. Brill, 1994.

———. "The Problem of the *Icchantika* in the Mahāyāna *Mahaparinirvāṇa-sūtra.*" *Journal of the International Association of Buddhist Studies* 7, no. 1 (1984): 57–81.

Liu Shuxian 劉述先. *Huang Zongxi xinxue de dingwei* 黃宗羲心學的定位 (The place of Huang Zongxi in the learning of the mind). Taipei: Yuncheng wenhua shiye gufen youxian gongsi, 1986.

Liu Xizai 劉熙載. "Jingyi gai" 經義概 (Outline of the examination essays). In *Yigai* 藝概 (Outline of the arts). Preface dated 1873. Shanghai: Shanghai guji shudian, 1978.

Liu Yuanqing 劉元卿. *Liu Pinjun quanji* 劉聘君全集 (Complete works of Liu Yuanqing). Reprint of 1852 ed. SKCM, *jibu* 集部, vol. 154.

———. *Zhuru xue'an* 諸儒學案 (Cases of learning of the Confucians) [ca. 1596]. Reprint of Wanli (1572–1622) ed. SKCM, *zibu* 子部, vol. 12.

Liu Zongzhou 劉宗周. *Liu Zongzhou quanji* 劉宗周全集 (Complete works of Liu Zongzhou), ed. Dai Lianzhang 戴璉璋 and Wu Guang 吳光. 5 vols. Taipei: Institute of Chinese Literature and Philosophy, Academia Sinica, 1996.

———. *Lunyu xue'an* 論語學案 (The case of learning from the *Analects*) [1617]. In *Liu Zongzhou quanji,* vol. 1.

Liuzu tanjing 六祖壇經 (Platform scripture of the Sixth Patriarch). Attributed to Fahai 法海. Stein ms. 5475. T 2007.

Liuzu tanjing 六祖壇經 (Platform scripture of the Sixth Patriarch), comp. Zongbao 宗寶. 1291. T 2008.

Lüli guan jiaozheng Xiyuan lu 律例館校正洗冤錄 (*The Washing Away of Wrongs* collated by the Bureau of the Code [of the Board of Punishments]) [1694]. Qianlong (1736–1795) reprint.

Luo Ergang 羅爾綱. *Li Xiucheng zishu yuangao zhu* 李秀成自述原稿注 (Annotation to the drafts written by Li Xiucheng). Beijing: Zhonghua shuju, 1982.

Luo Tianyi 羅天益. *Luo Qianfu zhiyan an* 羅謙甫治驗案 (Efficacious cases of Luo Tianyi) [1281]. 4 vols. Shanghai: Shanghai sanlian shuju, 1990.

Macauley, Melissa. *Social Power and Legal Culture: Litigation Masters in Late Imperial China.* Stanford, Calif.: Stanford University Press, 1998.

Mahāparinirvāna-sūtra. See *Da banniepan jing.*

Mao Yilu 毛一鷺. *Yunjian yanlüe* 雲間讞略 (Court opinions from Songjiang). 1610s–1620s?

Marcus, Steven. "Freud and Dora: Story, History, Case History." In *In Dora's Case,* ed. Charles Bernheimer and Claire Kahane. New York: Columbia University Press, 1985, 56–91.

McKnight, Brian E. "From Statute to Precedent: An Introduction to Song Law and Its Transformation." In *Law and the State in East Asia,* ed. B. McKnight. Honolulu: University of Hawai'i Press, 1987, 110–131.

———. "How Did Cases Become Precedents in the Song?" Paper presented to the symposium on "Looking for Cases in Song & Ming Law: Legal Culture & Legal Reasoning in Premodern China," Southern California China Colloquium, UCLA, May 17, 2003.

McKnight, Brian E., and James T. C. Liu, trans. *The Enlightened Judgments: Ch'ing-ming chi.* Albany: State University of New York Press, 1999.

McRae, John R. "Encounter Dialogue and the Transformation of the Spiritual Path in Chinese Ch'an." In *Paths to Liberation: The Mārga and Its Transformations in Buddhist Thought,* ed. Robert Buswell and Robert Gimello. Kuroda Institute Studies in East Asian Buddhism, no. 7. Honolulu: University of Hawai'i Press, 1992, 339–369.

———. *The Northern School and the Formation of Early Ch'an Buddhism.* Kuroda Institute Studies in East Asian Buddhism, no. 3. Honolulu: University of Hawai'i Press, 1986.

———. "The Ox-Head School of Chinese Ch'an Buddhism: From Early Ch'an to the Golden Age." In *Studies in Ch'an and Hua-yen,* ed. Robert M. Gimello and Peter N. Gregory. Kuroda Institute Studies in East Asian Buddhism, no. 1. Honolulu: University of Hawai'i Press, 1983, 169–252.

Meng Zhufeng 罗竹风, ed. *Hanyu da cidian* 漢語大詞典. 12 vols. Shanghai, 2001.

Metaille, Georges. "The *Bencao gangmu* of Li Shizhen." In *Innovation in Chinese Medicine,* ed. Elisabeth Hsu, 221–261.

Ming Taizu shilu 明太祖實錄 (Veritable records of Ming Taizu), ed. Huang Chang-chien 黃彰健. 8 vols. Taipei: Academia Sinica, 1961.

Ming'an yaolue 命案要略 (Essentials for handling homicide cases). Qing ed.

Minggong shupan qingming ji 名公書判清明集 (The enlightened judgments by famous officials). Original incomplete version with preface dated 1261, held at the Seikadō Bunko, Tokyo. Reconstructed edition in 14 *juan*, 1569 preface.

Minggong shupan qingming ji 名公書判清明集 (The enlightened judgments by famous officials), ed. Zhongguo shehui kexueyuan Lishi yanjiusuo Song Liao Jin Yuan shi yanjiushi 中國社會科學院歷史研究所宋遼金元史研究室. 2 vols. Beijing: Zhonghua shuju, 1987.

Miura Isshū and Ruth Fuller Sasaki. *Zen Dust: The History of the Kōan and Kōan Study in Rinzai (Lin-chi) Zen.* New York: Harcourt, Brace and World, 1966.

Miyamoto Shōson 宮本正尊. "'Sōmoku kokudo shikkai jōbutsu' no busshōronteki igi to sono sakusha" 「草木國土悉皆成佛」の佛性論的意義とその作者 (The significance of the buddha-nature doctrine that "the realm of grasses and trees will all become Buddha" and its authorship). *Indogaku bukkyōgaku kenkyū* 印度學佛教學研究 9, no. 2 (1961): 672–701.

Mu Han 穆翰. *Mingxing guanjianlu* 明刑管見錄 (My limited opinions on how to clarify the law). 1845.

Na Silu 那思陸. *Qingdai zhongyang sifa shenpan zhidu* 清代中央司法審判制度 (System of justice at the highest level in Qing China). Taipei: Wenshizhe chubanshe, 1992.

Nakamura Hajime 中村元, ed. *Bukkyōgo daijiten* 佛教語大辭典 (Dictionary of Buddhist terms). 2 vols. [1975]. Reprint (2 vols. in 1): Tokyo: Tōkyō shoseki, 1981.

Naquin, Susan. "True Confessions: Criminal Interrogations as Sources for Ch'ing History." *National Palace Museum Bulletin* 11, no. 1 (1976): 1–17.

Needham, Joseph, et al. *Science and Civilization in China.* 17 vols. to date. Cambridge: Cambridge University Press, 1954–.

Nivison, David. "Aspects of Traditional Chinese Biography." *The Journal of Asian Studies* 21, no. 4 (1962): 457–463.

Ōta Tatsuo 太田辰夫. "'Kōrōmu' no gengo" 紅楼夢の言語 (The language of *The Dream of the Red Chamber*). In *Chūgokugo shi tsūkō* 中国語史通考 (The study of the history of Chinese language). Tokyo: Hakuteisha, 1988, 289–296.

Penkower, Linda. "Making and Remaking Tradition: Chan-jan's Strategies toward a T'ang T'ien-t'ai Agenda." In *Tendai daishi kenkyū* 天台大師研究 (1998), 1338–1289 [*sic*].

———. "T'ien-t'ai during the T'ang Dynasty: Chan-jan and the Sinification of Buddhism." Ph.D. dissertation, Columbia University, 1993.

Perry, Elizabeth. "When Peasants Speak: Sources for the Study of Chinese Rebellions." *Modern China* 6, no. 1 (1980): 72–85.

Plaks, Andrew. "Terminology and Central Concepts." In *How to Read the Chinese Novel,* ed. D. Rolston, 75–123.

Pu Songling 蒲松齡. *Liaozhai zhiyi [huijiao huizhu huiping ben]* 聊齋志異會校會註會評本 (The complete collated and annotated *Liaozhai's Records of the Strange*), ed. Zhang Youhe 張友鶴. Shanghai: Shanghai guji chubanshe, 1983.

Pulleyblank, Edwin G. *Lexicon of Reconstructed Pronounciation in Early Middle Chinese, Late Middle, and Early Mandarin.* Vancouver: University of British Columbia Press, 1991.

Qi Biaojia 祁彪佳. *An Wu qinshen xigao* 按吳親審檄稿 (Draft court opinions from cases personally tried in the Wu region). Ming ed. National Library of China.

———. *Puyang yandu* 莆陽讞牘 (Court opinions from Puyang). Ming ed. National Library of China.

Qian Mu 錢穆. "Huang Lizhou de *Mingru xue'an,* Quan Xieshan de *Song-Yuan xue'an*" 黃梨洲的明儒學案全謝山的宋元學案 (Huang Zongxi's *Cases of Ming Learning* and Quan Zuwang's *Cases of Learning from the Song and Yuan*). In *Zhongguo shixuemingzhu* 中國史學名著, 2:285–300. Taipei: Sanmin shuju, 1973.

Qian Yi 錢乙. *Xiao'er yaozheng zhijue* 小兒藥證直訣 (Proven formulae of medicine for small children) [1119]. Taipei: Lixing shuju, 1982.

Qinding xuezheng quanshu 欽定學政全書 (Imperially sponsored collection of writings by education commissioners). Ca. 1773 ed.

Qu Zhongrong 瞿中溶. *Xiyuan lu bianzheng* 洗冤錄辨正 (A correction of errors in *The Washing Away of Wrongs*). Preface dated 1827. In *Congzheng xu yulu* 從政緒餘錄, comp. Chen Kun 陳坤, 1881 preface.

Rambelli, Fabio. *Vegetal Buddhas: Ideological Effects of Japanese Buddhist Doctrines on the Salvation of Inanimate Beings.* Italian School of East Asian Studies Occasional Papers series, vol. 9. Kyoto: Italian School of East Asian Studies, 2001.

Rawski, Evelyn. *Education and Popular Literacy in Ch'ing China.* Ann Arbor: University of Michigan Press, 1979.

Reed, Bradly. *Talons and Teeth: County Clerks and Runners in the Qing Dynasty.* Stanford, Calif.: Stanford University Press, 2000.

Rolston, David, ed. *How to Read the Chinese Novel.* Princeton, N.J.: Princeton University Press, 1990.

———. "Sources of Traditional Chinese Fiction Criticism." In *How to Read the Chinese Novel,* ed. D. Rolston, 3–34.

Rong Zhaozu 容肇祖. *Bu Mingru Dongguan xue'an* 補明儒東莞學案 (A supplement to the cases of learning of Ming Confucians from Dongguan). Beiping: National Peking University, 1936.

Rothfield, Lawrence. *Vital Signs: Medical Realism in Nineteenth-Century Fiction.* Princeton, N.J.: Princeton University Press, 1992.

Ruan Qixin 阮其新, comp. *[Chongkan] Buzhu Xiyuan lu jizheng* [重刊] 補註洗冤錄集證 (*The Washing Away of Wrongs* with collected evidence and added notes: New edition). Preface dated 1832. 1864 edition held at Institut des Hautes Études Chinoises, Collège de France, Paris.

Sabean, David. "Peasant Voices and Bureaucratic Texts: Narrative Structure in Early Modern German Protocols." In *Little Tools of Knowledge: Historical Essays on*

Academic and Bureaucratic Practices, ed. Peter Becker and William Clark. Ann Arbor: University of Michigan Press, 2001, 67–93.

———. *Power in the Blood: Popular Culture and Village Discourse in Early Modern Germany.* Cambridge: Cambridge University Press, 1984.

Sakamoto Yukio 阪本幸男. "Hijō ni okeru busshō no umu ni tsuite—toku ni Tannen, Chōkan o chūshin to shite" 非情に於ける佛性の有無について—特に湛然、澄觀を中心として (On the existence of buddha-nature with respect to insentient objects—with special reference to Zhanran and Chengguan). *Indogaku bukkyōgaku kenkyū* 印度學佛教學研究 7, no. 2 (1959): 21–30.

———. "On the 'Attainment of Buddhahood' by Trees and Plants." In *Proceedings of the 9th International Congress for the History of Religions (1958).* Tokyo: Maruzen, 1960, 415–422.

Sasaki, Ruth F. *The Recorded Sayings of Ch'an Master Lin-chi Hui-chao of Chen Prefecture.* Kyoto: The Institute for Zen Studies, Hanazono College, 1975.

Scheid, Volker. "Restructuring the Field of Chinese Medicine: A Study of the Menghe and Ding Scholarly Currents 1600–2000 (Part I)." *East Asian Science, Technology and Medicine* 22 (2004): 10–68.

Schlütter, Morten. "'Before the Empty Eon' Versus 'A Dog Has No Buddha-Nature': Kung-an Use in the Ts'ao-tung Tradition and Ta-hui's Kung-an Introspection Ch'an." In *The Kōan: Texts and Contexts in Zen Buddhism,* ed. Steven Heine and Dale S. Wright. Oxford: Oxford University Press, 2000, 168–199.

———. "Chan Buddhism in Song-Dynasty China (960–1279): The Rise of the Caodong Tradition and the Formation of the Chan School." Ph.D. dissertation, Yale University, 1998.

———. "Silent Illumination, Kung-an Introspection, and the Competition for Lay Patronage in Sung Dynasty Ch'an." In *Buddhism in the Sung,* ed. Peter N. Gregory and Daniel A. Getz, Jr. Kuroda Institute Studies in East Asian Buddhism, no. 13. Honolulu: University of Hawai'i Press, 1999, 109–147.

Scogin, Hugh. "Chinese Interest in Case Law." Paper presented to the symposium on "Looking for Cases in Song & Ming Law: Legal Culture & Legal Reasoning in Premodern China," Southern California China Colloquium, UCLA, May 17, 2003.

Sha Yizun 莎彝尊. *Zhengyin juhua* 正音咀華 (Appreciating the essence of proper pronunciation). 1853.

Shapiro, Hugh. "The Puzzle of Spermatorrhea in Republican China." *positions* 6, no. 3 (1998): 551–596.

Sharf, Robert H. "Experience." In *Critical Terms for Religious Studies,* ed. Mark C. Taylor. Chicago: University of Chicago Press, 1998, 94–116.

———. "The Idolization of Enlightenment: On the Mummification of Ch'an Masters in Medieval China." *History of Religions* 32, no. 1 (1992): 1–31.

———. "Ritual." In *Critical Terms for the Study of Buddhism,* ed. Donald Lopez, Jr. Chicago: University of Chicago Press, 2005, 245–270.

———. "Whose Zen? Zen Nationalism Revisited." In *Rude Awakenings: Zen, the Kyoto School, and the Question of Nationalism,* ed. James W. Heisig and John C. Maraldo. Nanzan Studies in Religion and Culture. Honolulu: University of Hawai'i Press, 1995, 40–51.

———. "The Zen of Japanese Nationalism." In *Curators of the Buddha: The Study of Buddhism under Colonialism,* ed. Donald S. Lopez, Jr. Chicago: University of Chicago Press, 1995, 107–160. [First published in *History of Religions* 33, no. 1 (1993): 1–43.]

She Ziqiang 佘自強. *Zhipu* 治譜 (Manual on governance) [1639]. Reprinted in *Guanzhenshu jicheng* 官箴書集成 (Collected handbooks for government). Anhui: Huangshan shushe, 1997.

Shenhui yulu 神會語錄 (Recorded sayings of Shenhui). In *Shenhui heshang yiji* 神會和尚遺集 (Collected works of Reverend Shenhui), ed. Hu Shi 胡適. Taipei: Hu Shi jinian guan, 1968.

Shi Qi 施杞 and Xiao Mincai 蕭敏材, eds. *Zhongyi bing'an xue* 中醫病案學 (The study of medical cases in Chinese medicine). Bing'an xue quanshu 病案學全書. Shanghai: Zhongguo dabaike quanshu chubanshe, 1994.

Shi Zhongxu 史仲序. *Zhongguo yixue shi* 中國醫學史 (History of medical learning in China). Taipei: Guoli bianyi guan, 1984.

Shiga Shūzō 滋賀秀三. "Chūgoku hō bunka no kōsatsu: Soshō no arikata o tsūjite" 中国法文化の考察—訴訟のあり方を通じて (Inquiry into Chinese legal culture through legal proceedings). *Hōtetsugaku nenpō* 法哲学年報 1986: 37–54.

———. "Criminal Procedure in the Ch'ing Dynasty—With Emphasis on Its Administrative Character and Some Allusion to Its Historical Antecedents." Pts. 1 and 2. *Memoirs of the Research Department of the Toyo Bunko* 32 (1974): 1–45; 33 (1975): 115–138.

———. *Shindai Chūgoku no hō to saiban* 清代中国の法と裁判 (Law and justice in Qing China). Tokyo: Sōbunsha, 1984.

———. "Sindai soshō seido ni okeru minjiteki hōgen no gaikatsuteki kentō" 清代訴訟制度における民事的法源の概括的検討 (A general survey of the sources of law concerning civil cases in the judicial system of Qing China). *Toyoshi-Kenkyū* 東洋史研究 40, no. 1 (1981): 74–102.

Shively, Donald H. "Buddhahood for the Nonsentient: A Theme in *Nō* Plays." *Harvard Journal of Asiatic Studies* 20 (1957): 135–161.

Shoulengyan jing 首楞嚴經 (*Śūraṃgama-sūtra*). T 945.

Sichuan gedi kan'an ji qita shiyi dangce 四川各地勘案及其它事宜檔冊 (Law cases and related archival records from various places in Sichuan). Reprint of Jiajing (1522–1566) manuscript copy, Beijing tushuguan guji zhenben congkan 北京圖書館古籍珍本叢刊, vol. 51. Beijing: Shumu wenxian chubanshe, 1987.

Sima Qian 司馬遷. *Shiji* 史記 (Records of the grand historian). 2nd–1st CBE. 10 vols. Beijing: Zhonghua shuju, 1959.

Sivin, Nathan. *Cosmos and Computation in Early Chinese Mathematical Astronomy.* Leiden: E. J. Brill, 1969.

———. *Medicine, Philosophy, and Religion in Ancient China: Researches and Reflections.* Brookfield, Vt.: Variorum, 1995.

———. *Science in Ancient China: Researches and Reflections.* Aldershot, Eng.: Variorum, 1995.

———. "A Seventh-Century Chinese Medical Case History." *Bulletin of the History of Medicine* 41, no. 2 (1967): 67–73.

———. *Traditional Medicine in Contemporary China.* Ann Arbor: Center for Chinese Studies, University of Michigan, 1972.

Sivin, Nathan, and Geoffrey Lloyd. *The Way and the Word: Science and Medicine in Early China and Greece.* New Haven, Conn.: Yale University Press, 2002.

Sommer, Matthew. *Sex, Law, and Society in Late Imperial China.* Stanford, Calif.: Stanford University Press, 2000.

Song Ci 宋慈. *Xiyuan jilu* 洗冤集錄 (A collection of records on *The Washing Away of Wrongs*). Preface dated 1247. Beijing: Falü chubanshe, 1958.

——— [Sung Tz'u]. *The Washing Away of Wrongs: Forensic Medicine in Thirteenth-Century China,* trans. Brian E. McKnight. Ann Arbor: The University of Michigan Center for Chinese Studies, 1981.

Street, Brian. *Literacy in Theory and Practice.* Cambridge: Cambridge University Press, 1984.

Struve, Lynn A. "Huang Zongxi in Context: A Reappraisal of His Major Writings." *The Journal of Asian Studies* 47, no. 3 (1988): 474–502.

Sueki Fumihiko 末木文美士. "Annen *Shinjō sōmoku jōbutsu shiki* ni tsuite" 安然「斟定草木成佛私記」について (On Annen's private notes on deliberations concerning the realization of buddhahood by grasses and trees). *Tōhōgaku* 東方學 80 (1990).

———. "Annen: The Philosopher Who Japanized Buddhism." *Acta Asiatica: Bulletin of the Institute of Eastern Culture (Tōhōgakkai)* 66 (1994): 69–86.

———, ed. *Gendaigoyaku Hekiganroku* 現代語譯碧巖錄 (Blue Cliff record: A translation into modern Japanese). 3 vols. Tokyo: Iwanami shoten, 2001–2003.

Sun Qifeng 孫奇逢. *Lixue zongchuan* 理學宗傳 (Orthodox transmission of the learning of principle). Reprint of 1667 ed. XXSK, vol. 514.

Sun Xingyan 孫星衍. *Sun shi citang shumu* 孫氏祠堂書目 (Catalogue of the Sun Family Ancestral Hall Library). 1883.

Sun Yikui 孫一奎. *Sun Wenyuan yi'an* 孫文垣醫案 (Medical casebook of Sun Yikui). 1599. Rare Book Library of the Research Institute for Traditional Chinese Medicine, Beijing.

———. *Sun Yikui yixue quanshu* 孫一奎醫學全書 (The complete medical works of Sun Yikui), ed. Han Xuejie 韓學傑 and Zhang Yinsheng 張印生. MQMY.

Sunstein, Cass R. *Legal Reasoning and Political Conflict.* New York: Oxford University Press, 1996.

Tang Biao 唐彪. *Dushu zuowenpu* 讀書作文譜 (A handbook for reading classical essays and writing successful examination essays). N.d. Reprint: Taipei: Weiwen chubanshe, 1976.

———. *Fushi Shanyoufa* 父師善誘法 (A handbook for fathers and teachers to instruct sons to pass the civil service examinations). N.d. In *Wuzhong yigui* 五種遺規 (Five volumes of left regulations), ed. Chen Hongmou 陳宏謀. Taipei: Dezhi chubanshe, 1963.

Tang Jian 唐鑑. *Guochao xue'an xiaoshi* 國朝學案小識 (Small records of the cases of learning of the Qing dynasty) [1884]. Reprint under the title *Qing xue'an xiaozhi* 清學案小志. 2 vols. Shanghai: Shangwu yinshuguan, 1936.

Tang Yan 唐晏. *Liang Han Sanguo xue'an* 兩漢三國學案 (Cases of learning of the two Han dynasties and the Three Kingdoms). Beijing: Zhonghua shuju, 1984.

Tang Yongtong 湯用彤. *Han Wei liang Jin nanbeichao fojiao shi* 漢魏兩晉南北朝佛教史 (History of Buddhism in the Han, Wei, Jin, Southern, and Northern dynasties). 2 vols. Beijing: Zhonghua shuju, 1955. [First published in Changsha, Shangwu yinshuguan, 1938.]

Tokiwa Daijo 常盤大定. *Busshō no kenkyū* 佛性の研究 (Studies on buddha-nature). Tokyo: Kokusho kankōkai, 1973.

Tokiwa Gishin 常盤義伸 and Yanagida Seizan 柳田聖山. *Zekkanron: Eibun yakuchū, gembun kōtei, kokuyaku* 絕觀論：英文譯注、原文校定、國譯 (Treatise on the transcendence of cognition: Annotated English translation, collated text, Japanese translation). Kyoto: Zenbunka kenkyūjo, 1973.

Van Gulik, R. H. *T'ang-Yin-Pi-Shih: Parallel Cases from under the Pear-tree.* Leiden: E. J. Brill, 1956.

Vimalakārtinirdeśa-sūtra. See *Weimojie suoshuo jing.*

Volkmar, Barbara. "The Notch in the River Boat: Sign and Interpretation in Case Histories by Wan Quan (1500–1585?)." Paper presented at the 11th International Conference on the History of Science in East Asia, Munich, Germany, August 15–20, 2005.

Wan Quan 萬全. *Youke fahui* 幼科發揮 (Elaboration on pediatric medicine) [1549]. Beijing: Renmin weisheng chubanshe, 1986.

———. *Yuying jiami* 育嬰家秘 (Family secrets in child care) [1549]. Hubei: Kexue jishu chubanshe, 1984.

Wan Weihan 萬維翰. *Xingqian zhinan* 刑錢指南 (Guidelines for secretary works on law and taxation). 1774.

Wang Daohuan 王道還. "Lun *Yilin gaicuo* de jiepouxue: Jian lun jiepouxue zai Zhong Xi yixue chuantong zhong de diwei" 論《醫林改錯》的解剖學—兼論解剖學在中西醫學

傳統中的地位 (A discussion of anatomy in the *Yilin gaicuo* and of the place of anatomy in the Chinese and Western medical traditions). *Xin shixue* 新史學 6, no. 1 (1995): 95–112.

Wang Deyi 王德毅. Introduction to Zhu Xi, *Yi-Luo yuanyuan lu.*

Wang Huizu 汪輝祖. *Xuezhi yishuo* 學治臆說 (Subjective views on learning governance). Preface dated 1793. In *Rumu xuzhi wuzhong*, ed. Zhang Tingxiang.

Wang Ji 汪機. *Shishan yi'an* 石山醫案 (Medical cases of Wang Ji). Ca. 1531. In *Wang Shishan yixue quanshu* 汪石山醫學全書 (Complete medical works of Wang Ji), ed. Gao Erxin 高爾鑫. MQMY.

Wang Kaifu 王凱符 and Zhang Huien 張會恩, eds. *Zhongguo gudai xiezuoxue* 中國古代寫作學 (Scholarship on writing in traditional China). Beijing: Zhongguo renmin daxue chubanshe, 1992.

Wang Shen 王甡. *Xue'an* 學案 (Cases of learning). Reprint of mid-eighteenth-century ed. SKCM, *zibu* 子部, vol. 20.

Wang Shixiong 王士雄 [Wang Mengying 王孟英] and Yu Zhen 俞震. *Gujin yi'an an xuan* 古今醫案按選 (Selections from "Commentary on Medical Cases Old and New") [1853]. In *Wang Mengying yixue quanshu* 王孟英醫學全書 (Complete medical works of Wang Shixiong), ed. Sheng Zengxiu 盛增秀 et al. Beijing: Zhongguo Zhongyiyiao chubanshe, 1999.

Wang Youhuai 王又槐. *Ban'an yaolue* 辦案要略 (Important points for handling cases) [1793]. In *Rumu xuzhi wuzhong*, ed. Zhang Tingxiang.

———. *Xingqian bilan* 刑錢必覽 (Indispensable readings for legal and financial secretaries). 1793. Reprint in 1814.

———. *Xiyuan lu jizheng* 洗冤錄集證 (*The Washing Away of Wrongs* with collected evidence). Preface dated 1796.

Wang Zaijin 王在晉. *Longsha xuelu* 龍沙學錄 (Record of learning from Longsha [in Nanchang]). Reprint of early seventeenth-century ed. SKCM, *zibu* 子部, vol. 15.

Wansong laoren pingchang Tiantong Jue heshang songgu Congrongan lu 萬松老人評唱天童覺和尚頌古從容庵錄 (Congrong Hermitage record of the commentaries by Old Wansong on the case and verse [collection] by Reverend Jue of Tiantong [Mountain]), comp. Xingxiu 行秀 et al. 1224. T 2004.

Watson, Burton, trans. *The Complete Works of Chuang Tzu.* New York: Columbia University Press, 1968.

———, trans. *Records of the Historian: Chapters from the Shih Chi of Ssu-ma Ch'ien.* New York: Columbia University Press, 1969.

———. *Ss'u-ma Ch'ien: Grand Historian of China.* New York: Columbia University Press, 1958.

———, trans. *The Zen Teachings of Master Lin-chi: A Translation of Lin-chi lu*, by Lin-chi. Boston: Shambhala, 1993.

Wei Zhixiu 魏之琇, comp. *Xu mingyi lei'an* 續名醫類案 (More classified cases from famous doctors) [1770]. Beijing: Renmin weisheng chubanshe, 1957.

Weimojie suoshuo jing 維摩詰所說經 (*Vimalakārtinirdesa-sūtra*), trans. Kumārajāva. T 475.

Widmer, Ellen. "The Huangduzhai of Hangzhou and Suzhou: A Study in Seventeenth-Century Publishing." *Harvard Journal of Asiatic Studies* 56, no. 1 (1996): 77–122.

Wilkinson, Endymion. *Chinese History: A Manual.* Cambridge, Mass: Harvard University Asia Center, 2000.

Will, Pierre-Étienne [Wei Peixin 魏丕信]. "Ming Qing shiqi de guanzhenshu yu Zhongguo xingzheng wenhua" 明清時期的官箴書與中國行政文化 (Official handbooks in the Ming and Qing and China's administrative culture). *Qingshi yanjiu* 清史研究 1999, 1:3–20.

———. "Official Handbooks and Anthologies of Imperial China: A Descriptive and Critical Bibliography." Work in progress.

Wu Guang 吳光. *Huang Zongxi zhuzuo huikao* 黃宗羲著作匯考 (Collected studies on the works of Huang Zongxi). Taipei: Taiwan xuesheng shuju, 1990.

Wu Guanghua 吳光華, comp. *Mouyi beikao* 謀邑備考 (Reference materials for those who make plans in cities). 1758.

Wu Kun 吳崑. "Mai'an geshi" 脈案格式 (A model for pulse cases). In *Mai yu* 脈語 (Words on the pulse). 1584. In *Zhongguo yixue dacheng*, comp. Cao Binzhang, 2:640–652.

Wu Ne 吳訥. *Xiangxing yaolan* 祥刑要覽 (Essentials for the proper use of punishments). Reprint of Jiajing (1520–1566) ed. SKCM, *zibu* 子部, vol. 37.

Wu, Pei-yi. *The Confucian's Progress: Autobiographical Writings in Traditional China.* Princeton, N.J.: Princeton University Press, 1990.

Wu Yanhong 吳艷紅. *Mingdai chongjun yanjiu* 明代充軍研究 (A study of the military exile in the Ming dynasty). Beijing: Zhongguo shehui kexue wenxian chubanshe, 2000.

———. "Mingdai liuxing kao" 明代流刑考 (Life exile in the Ming). *Lishi yanjiu* 歷史研究 6 (2000): 23–43.

Wu, Yi-Li. "Transmitted Secrets: The Doctors of the Lower Yangzi Region and Popular Gynecology in Late Imperial China." Ph.D. dissertation, Yale University, 1998.

Wujia zhengzong zan 五家正宗贊 (In praise of the five houses of the orthodox school), comp. Xisou Shaotan 希叟紹曇. 1254. ZZ 139.

Wumen Huikai 無門慧開. *Chanzong wumen guan* 禪宗無門關 (Gateless barrier of the Chan tradition). 1254. T 2005.

Xijiang zhengyao 西江政要 (A compendium of Jiangxi provincial regulations), comp. Xijiang anchasi 西江按察司. Guangxu (1875–1908) ed.

Xin'an yiji congkan 新安醫籍叢刊 (A collection of medical records from Xin'an). Hefei: Anhui kexue jishu chubanshe, 1993.

Xingbu dang'an 刑部檔案 (Board of Punishments archive). The Number One Historical Archives, Beijing.

Xingming zalan 刑名雜覽. (Miscellaneous readings for judicial administration). Manuscript copy between 1796 and 1860, National Library of China.

Xingmu yaolue 刑幕要略 (Essentials for legal secretaries). Qing edition. In *Rumu xuzhi wuzhong,* ed. Zhang Tingxiang.

Xinmin gong'an 新民公案 (Stories of judgment that reform the people). Preface dated 1605. Reprint: Guben xiaoshuo congkan (Collection of ancient editions of fictions). Beijing: Zhonghua shuju, 1987.

Xu Chunfu 徐春甫, comp. *Gujin yitong daquan* 古今醫統大全 (A comprehensive study of the medical tradition from ancient to modern times). Preface dated 1556. Reprint: 2 vols., ed. Cui Zhongping 崔仲平 and Wang Yaoting 王耀廷. Beijing: Renmin weisheng chubanshe, 1991.

Xu Lian 許槤, comp. *Xingbu bizhao jiajian cheng'an xubian* 刑部比照加減成案續編 (Leading cases with increased or decreased sentences decided by analogy at the ministry of justice). 1843.

———, comp. *Xiyuan lu xiangyi* 洗冤錄詳義 (Explanation of the meaning of *The Washing Away of Wrongs*). 1854. Earliest known edition, 1856. Reprint: Hubei guanshu chu 湖北官書處, 1890.

Xu Shichang 徐世昌. *Qingru xue'an* 清儒學案 (Cases of learning of the Qing Confucians). Taipei: Shijie shuju, 1962.

Xu Shuwei 許叔微. *Shanghan jiushi lun* 傷寒九十論 (Ninety discourses on cold damage). N.d. In *Congshu jicheng xin bian* 叢書集成新編, ed. [Xinwenfeng chuban] gongsi bianjibu〔新文豐出版〕公司編輯部, vol. 45. Taipei: Xinwenfeng chuban gongsi, 1986.

Xue Ji 薛己 et al. *Xueshi yi'an shiliu zhong* 薛氏醫案十六種 (The Xues' medical cases in sixteen sections) [1529]. Beijing: Zhongguo Zhongyiyao chubanshe, 1997.

Xue Kai 薛鎧. *Baoying cuoyao* 保嬰撮要 (Essentials for the care of infants). 1555. Taipei: Institute of Modern History, Academic Sinica Microfilms.

———. *Baoying quanshu* 保嬰全書 (Complete text for the protection of infants). Preface by Wang Ji 王緝 [1660]. Taipei: Xinwenfeng chuban gongsi, 1978.

Xue Qinglu 薛清錄 et al., eds. *Quanguo Zhongyi tushu lianhe mulu* 全國中醫圖書聯合目錄 (Combined catalogue of the nation's library holdings in Chinese medicine). Beijing: Zhongyi guji chubanshe, 1991.

Xue Yunsheng 薛允昇. *Duli cunyi* 讀例存疑 (Concentrating on doubtful matters when reading the substatutes) [1905]. Modern punctuated edition ed. Huang Jingjia 黃靜嘉. Taipei: Chinese Materials Center, 1970.

Yamada Keiji 山田慶兒. "Hakkōpa no keiryō kaibōgaku to jintai keisoku no shisō" 伯高派の計量解剖學と人體計測の思想 (Dissection for measurement in the Bogao school and the thinking about the measures of the human body). In *Chūgoku kodai kagaku shiron* 中國古代科學史論, ed. Yamada Keiji and Tanaka Tan 田中淡. Kyoto: Kyōto daigaku jimbun kagaku kenkyūjo, 1991, 427–491.

Yamada Kōun, trans. *Gateless Gate*. Zen Writings Series, vol. 7. Los Angeles: Center Publications, 1979.

Yamanoi Yū 山井湧. *Min-Shin shisō shi no kenkyū* 明清思想史の研究 (Study of the history of Ming and Qing thought). Tokyo: Tōkyō Daigaku Shuppansha, 1980.

Yampolsky, Philip B. *The Platform Sutra of the Sixth Patriarch: The Text of the Tun-huang Manuscript with Translation, Introduction, and Notes*. New York: Columbia University Press, 1967.

Yan Junyan 顏俊彥. *Mengshuizhai cundu* 盟水齋存牘 (Court opinions drafted at Mengshui studio) [1631]. Beijing: Zhongguo zhengfa daxue chubanshe, 2002.

Yanagida Seizan 柳田聖山, ed. *Hu Shi chan xue'an* 胡適禪學案 (Case study of Hu Shi's study of Chan Buddhism). Taipei: Zhongzheng shuju, 1975.

———. "The 'Recorded Sayings' Texts of Chinese Ch'an Buddhism." In *Early Ch'an in China and Tibet*, ed. Whalen Lai and Lewis R. Lancaster. Berkeley Buddhist Studies Series, no. 5. Berkeley: University of California Press, 1983, 185–205.

———. *Shoki no zenshi* 初期の禪史 (History of early Zen). Vol. 1. Zen no goroku 禪の語錄, no. 2. Kyoto: Chikuma shobō, 1971.

———. *Sodōshū sakuin* 祖堂集索引 (Index to the *Patriarchs Hall Anthology*). 3 vols. Kyoto: Kyōto daigaku jinbunkagaku kenkyūjo, 1984.

Yang Bojun 楊伯俊, ed. *Lunyu yizhu* 論語譯註 (Analects: An translation and annotation). Beijing: Zhonghua shuju, 1980.

Yang Xiangkui 楊向奎, ed. *Qingru xue'an xinbian* 清儒學案新編 (A new compilation of the cases of learning of Qing Confucians). 8 vols. Ji'nan: Qilu shushe, 1985–1994.

Yang Xuefeng 楊雪峰. *Mingdai de shenpan zhidu* 明代的審判制度 (Judicial system in the Ming). Taipei: Liming wenhua shiye gufen youxian gongsi, 1978.

Yang Yifan 楊一凡. *Ming Dagao yanjiu* 明大誥研究 (A study of *The Grand Pronouncements* of the Ming). Nanjing: Jiangsu renmin chubanshe, 1988.

Ye Gui 葉桂 [Ye Tianshi 葉天士]. *Lin zheng zhinan yi'an* 臨證指南醫案 (Medical cases as a guide to clinical practice) [1768]. In *Ye Tianshi yixue quanshu* 葉天士醫學全書 (Complete medical works of Ye Gui), ed. Ke Jia 可嘉 et al. MQMY.

Ye Ying 葉瑛, ed. *Wenshi tongyi jiaozhu* 文史通義校注 (Annotation of *Wenshi tongyi*), by Zhang Xuechang 章學誠. Beijing: Zhonghua shuju, 1985.

Yifa. *The Origins of Buddhist Monastic Codes in China: An Annotated Translation and Study of the Chanyuan Qinggui*. Kuroda Institute Classics in East Asian Buddhism. Honolulu: University of Hawai'i Press, 2002.

Yilibu 伊里布, comp. *Xue'an chumo* 學案初模 (Elementary models for studying cases). First published 1838. 1881 Gansu provincial judge's office edition.

———, comp. *Xue'an chumo xubian* 學案初模續編 (Sequel to *Elementary Models for Studying Cases*). First published 1839. 1881 Gansu provincial judge's office edition.

Yong Rong 永瑢 et al., ed. *Siku quanshu zongmu* 四庫全書總目 (Analytical bibliography of the complete collection of the four treasuries). Beijing: Zhonghua shuju, 1965.

Yoshizu Yoshihide 吉津宜英. "Mujō busshōsetsu no kōsatsu" 無情佛性說の考察 (A study of the doctrine of the buddha-nature of insentient objects). *[Sōtōshū] Shūgaku kenkyū* 〔曹洞宗〕宗學研究 15 (1973): 110–115.

Yu Chang 喻昌 [Yu Jiayan 喻嘉言]. *Yuyi cao* 寓意草 (Notes on my judgment) [1643]. In *Yu Jiayan yixue quanshu* 喻嘉言醫學全書 (Complete medical works of Yu Chang), ed. Chen Yi 陳熠 et al. MQMY.

Yü Chün-fang. "Ch'an Education in the Sung: Ideals and Procedures." In *Neo-Confucian Education: The Formative Stage,* ed. Wm. Theodore de Bary and John W. Chaffee. Berkeley: University of California Press, 1989, 57–104.

———. "Chung-feng Ming-pen and Ch'an Buddhism in the Yüan." In *Yüan Thought: Chinese Thought and Religion under the Mongols,* ed. Hok-lam Chan and William Theodore De Bary. New York: Columbia University Press, 1982, 419–477.

———. "Ta-Hui Tsung-Kao and *Kung-an* Ch'an." *Journal of Chinese Philosophy* 6 (1979): 211–235.

Yu Zhen. 俞震 [Yu Dongfu 俞東扶]. *Gujin yi'an an* 古今醫案按 (Commentary on medical cases old and new) [1778]. In Zhongguo yixue dacheng sanbian 中國醫學大成三編, ed. Qiu Peiren 裘斐然 et al. Changsha: Yuelu shushe, 1994, 12:608–925.

Yuanshu lunyao 爰書論要 (Judicial important points). Qing manuscript.

Yuanwu Foguo Chanshi yulu 圜悟佛果禪師語錄 (Recorded sayings of Chan master Yuanwu Foguo), comp. Huqiu Shaolong 虎丘紹隆. 1134. T 1997.

Yunmen Kuangzhen Chanshi guanglu 雲門匡真禪師廣錄 (Extended records of Chan master Yunmen Kuangzhen), comp. Shoujian 守堅. 1076. T 1988.

Zeitlin, Judith T. *Historian of the Strange: Pu Songling and the Chinese Classical Tale.* Stanford, Calif.: Stanford University Press, 1993.

———. "The Life and Death of the Image: Ghosts and Female Portraits in Sixteenth- and Seventeenth-Century Literature." In *Body and Face in Chinese Visual Culture,* ed. Wu Hung and Katherine R. Tsiang. Cambridge, Mass.: Harvard Asia Center Publications, 2005, 229–256.

Zhang Jiebin 張介賓. *Jingyue quanshu.* 景岳全書 (Complete works of Zhang Jiebin) [early seventeenth century]. Shanghai: Shanghai kexue jishu chubanshe, 1984.

Zhang Jinfan 張晉藩, ed. *Zhongguo fazhi shi* 中國法制史 (Chinese legal history). Beijing: Qunzhong chubanshe, 1982.

Zhang Jiude 張九德. *Zheyu yaobian* 折獄要編 (Essentials for judging cases). Preface dated 1626.

Zhang Kentang 張肯堂. *Xunci* 㽦辭 (Words of deep cultivation) [1634?]. Reprint: Taipei: Taiwan xuesheng shuju, 1970.

Zhang Tingxiang 張廷驤, ed. *Rumu xuzhi wuzhong* 入幕須知五種 (Five volumes of essential knowledge for those entering private secretary work). Zhejiang shuju, 1892.

Zhang Tingyu 張廷玉 et al. *Mingshi* 明史 (Ming history) [1739]. Modern punctuated ed. 28 vols. Beijing: Zhonghua shuju, 1974.

Zhang Wuwei 張五緯. *Jiangqiu gongji lu* 講求共濟錄 (Record of seeking the public benefit). Preface dated 1812.

Zhangjiashan Han mu zhujian [ersiqi hao mu] 張家山漢墓竹簡(二十七號墓)(Bamboo strips from a Han dynasty tomb at Zhangjiashan [tomb 247]), ed. Zhangjiashan ersiqi hao Han mu zhujian zhengli xiaozu 張家山二十四號漢墓竹簡整理小組. Beijing: Wenwu chubanshe, 2001.

Zhangzhou fuzhi 漳州府志 (Gazetteer of Zhangzhou Prefecture) [1877]. Reprint: Taipei: Dengwen yinshuaju, 1965.

Zhanran 湛然. *Jin'gang bei* 金剛錍 (Adamantine scalpel). Ca. 780. T 1932.

———. *Zhiguan fuxing chuanhong jue* 止觀輔行傳弘決 (Delineations for supporting practice and broadly disseminating the *[Great] Calming and Discernment*). T 1912.

Zhao, Jie. "Reassessing the Place of Chou Ju-teng (1547–1629) in Late Ming Thought." *Ming Studies* 33 (1994): 1–11.

Zhaojie shuo 招解說 (On sending a copy of a confession to higher authorities). Jiaqing (1796–1820) manuscript.

Zhaozhou Zhenji Chanshi yulu 趙州真際禪師語錄. (Recorded sayings of Chan master Zhaozhou Zhenji). Late 10th century? ZZ 118.

Zheng Ke 鄭克, comp. *Zheyu guijian* 折獄龜鑑 (The magic mirror for deciding cases). Early twelfth century. SKQS, vol. 729.

Zhiyi 智顗 and Guanding 灌頂. *Mohe zhiguan* 摩訶止觀 (Great calming and discernment). T 1911.

Zhongfeng Mingben 中峰明本. *Shanfang yehua* 山房夜話 (Evening talks in a mountain hut). In *Zhongfeng heshang guanglu* 中峰和尚廣錄 (Extended records of Reverend Zhongfeng), comp. Beiting Ciji 北庭慈寂. *Songban jisha dazang jing* 宋版磧砂大藏經, vol. 37. Shanghai: Songban zangjinghui, 1936. Reprint: Taipei: Xinwenfeng, 1988.

Zhongguo yiji tongkao 中國醫籍通攷. (A comprehensive investigation of Chinese medical books), ed. Yan Shiyun 嚴世芸 et al. 4 vols. Shanghai: Zhongyi xueyuan, 1990–1993.

Zhongyi dacidian: Yishi wenxian. 中醫大辭典：醫史文獻 (Encyclopedic dictionary of Chinese medicine: Written materials of medical history). Beijing: Renmin weisheng chubanshe, 1981.

Zhou Rudeng 周汝登. *Shengxue zongchuan* 聖學宗傳 (Orthodox transmission of the learning of the sages). Reprint of 1605 ed. XXSK, vol. 513. Also included in SKCM, *shibu* 史部, vols. 98–99.

Zhu Qingqi 祝慶祺, comp. *Xuzeng Xing'an huilan* 續增刑案匯覽 (Supplement to Conspectus of judicial cases) [1840]. Shanghai: Shanghai tushu jicheng shuju, preface dated 1886.

Zhu Xi 朱熹. *Sanchao mingchen yanxing lu* 三朝名臣言行錄 (Record of words and deeds of eminent officials of the three reigns). In *Song mingchen yanxing lu wuji* 宋名臣言行錄五集 (Five records of words and deeds of eminent officials of the Song), ed. Zhao Tiehan 趙鐵寒. Reprint of 1868 ed. Taipei: Wenhai chubanshe, 1967.

———. *Wuchao mingchen yanxing lu* 五朝名臣言行錄 (Record of words and deeds of eminent officials of the five reigns). In *Song mingchen yanxing lu wuji* 宋名臣言行錄五集 (Five records of words and deeds of eminent officials of the Song), ed. Zhao Tiehan 趙鐵寒. Reprint of 1868 ed. Taipei: Wenhai chubanshe, 1967.

———. *Yi-Luo yuanyuan lu* 伊洛淵源錄 (Sources of the school of Cheng Hao and Cheng Yi) [1173]. Reprint: Taipei: Wenhai chubanshe, 1968.

Zhu Zhenheng 朱震亨. *Guai'e dan* 怪痾單 (A list of strange diseases) [1448]. Beijing: Zhonghua shuju, 1985.

Zhuangzi jinzhu jinyi 莊子今注今譯 (A modern annotated edition of *Zhuangzi* with vernacular translation), ed. Chen Guying 陳鼓應. Beijing: Zhonghua shuju, 1983.

Zutang ji 祖堂集 (Patriarchs Hall anthology), comp. Shi Jing 釋靜 and Shi Yun 釋筠 [952]. Reprint of Korean ed. in Yanagida, *Sodōshū sakuin.*

Contributors

Hung-lam CHU attended college in Hong Kong and earned his PhD from Princeton University in 1984. He specializes in Ming history and the intellectual history of late imperial China. His major publications include "The Debate over Recognition of Wang Yangming," *Harvard Journal of Asiatic Studies* 48, no. 1 (1988); *Calligraphy and the East Asian Book* (Boston: Shambhala Press, 1989); *Mingru xue'an dianjiao shiwu* (Elucidation of errors in the punctuated editions of Huang Zongxi's *Cases of Learning of Ming Confucians*) (Taipei: Institute of History and Philology, Academia Sinica, 1991); *Zhongguo jinshi ruxue shizhi de sibian yu xixue* (The substance and the practice of Confucian learning in late imperial China) (Beijing: Peking University Press, 2005); and *Mingren zhuzuo yu shengping fawei* (Studies in the lives and works of Ming personalities) (Guilin: Guangxi Normal University Press, 2005). He is currently a professor in the Department of History, The Chinese University of Hong Kong.

Charlotte Furth received her PhD in history from Stanford University in 1966 and is currently a professor of history at the University of Southern California. Her books include *Ting Wen-chiang: Science and China's New Culture* (Harvard East Asia Series 42, 1970) and *A Flourishing Yin: Gender in China's Medical History 960–1665* (Berkeley: University of California Press, 1999). She has written numerous articles on medicine and gender in Ming-Qing China. A previous edited volume is *The Limits of Change: Essays on Conservative Alternatives in Republican China* (Cambridge, Mass.: Harvard University Press, 1976).

Ping-chen HSIUNG received her PhD training at Brown University and since then has produced and edited numerous works devoted to the study of the Ming and Qing dynasties. Her books include *You you: Chuantong Zhongguo de quangbao zhi dao* (Infant care in traditional China) (Taipei: Lianjing chubanshe, 1995) and, most recently, *A Tender Voyage: Children and Childhood in Late Imperial China* (Stanford, Calif.: Stanford University Press, 2005). A fellow at the Institute of Modern History at Academia Sinica, Professor Hsiung is also dean of the College of Liberal Arts at National Central University, Taipei, Taiwan.

JIANG Yonglin, PhD (history), is assistant professor of history at Oklahoma State University and editor of a recent edition of Mao Yilu's *Yunjian yanlüe* (Zhongguo shehui kexue chubanshe, 2006); he is also author of *The Great Ming Code* (Seattle: University of Washington Press, 2005). His articles include "Lun Zhonghua diguo falü de xingshi xing" (Chinese imperial law as criminal law), *Ming Qing luncong* 6 (2005); "Lun Zhonghua diguo falü de zongjiao tezheng—Yi Mingchu falü wenhua weili" (The religious nature of Chinese imperial law—exemplified by Ming legal culture), *Ming Qing luncong* 3 (2002); and "Defending the Dynastic Order in a Local Society: Central-Local Relations as Seen in a Late-Ming Magistrate's Enforcement of Law," *Ming Studies* 43 (2000).

Yasuhiko KARASAWA, a PhD candidate in history at the University of California, Los Angeles, is currently an assistant professor at Ritsumeikan University in Japan. He is working on his dissertation, "Orality, Textuality, and Reality: Legal Case Records in Nineteenth-Century China."

Robert H. Sharf is a D. H. Chen Distinguished Professor of Buddhist Studies in the Department of East Asian Languages and Cultures and chair of the Center for Buddhist Studies at the University of California, Berkeley. He received his BA (religious studies) and MA (Chinese studies) from the University of Toronto and his PhD (Buddhist studies) from the University of Michigan. He is author of *Coming to Terms with Chinese Buddhism: A Reading of the Treasure Store Treatise* (Honolulu: University of Hawai'i Press, 2001) and coeditor (with Elizabeth Horton Sharf) of *Living Images: Japanese Buddhist Icons in Context* (Stanford, Calif.: Stanford University Press, 2001).

Pierre-Étienne Will is a professor at Collège de France and Directeur d'Etudes at Ecole des Hautes Etudes en Sciences Sociales, Paris. He has published *Bureaucracy and Famine in Eighteenth-Century China* (Stanford, Calif.: Stanford University Press, 1990) and, with R. Bin Wong, *Nourish the People: The State Civilian Granary System in China, 1650–1850* (Ann Arbor: University of Michigan Center for Chinese Studies, 1991). He is currently finalizing *Official Handbooks and Anthologies of Imperial China: A Descriptive and Critical Bibliography.*

WU Yanhong, PhD (history), formerly associate researcher at the History Institute of the Chinese Academy of Social Sciences (Beijing) and currently a PhD candidate in the Department of Sociology, Oklahoma State University, is the author of *Mingdai chongjun yanjiu* (Military exile in the Ming) (Beijing: Zhongguo shehui kexue wenxian chubanshe, 2003); "Mingdai beiyouren falü diwei yanjiu" (Legal status of inferior social classes in the Ming), in *Wanming shehui de bianqian*, ed. Wan Ming (Beijing: Shangwu yinshu guan, 2005); and "Mingdai liuxing kao" (Life exile in the Ming), *Lishi yanjiu* 6 (2000).

Judith T. Zeitlin is professor of Chinese literature and chair of the Department of East Asian Languages and Civilizations at the University of Chicago. She is the author of *Historian of the Strange: Pu Songling and the Chinese Classical Tale* (Stanford, Calif.: Stanford University Press, 1993) and *The Phantom Heroine: Ghosts and Gender in Seventeenth-Century Chinese Literature* (forthcoming). She is coeditor (with Lydia Liu) of *Writing and Materiality in China: Essays in Honor of Patrick Hanan* (Cambridge, Mass.: Harvard University Asia Center, 2003). Her current research focuses on the history of Chinese drama, performance, and music.

Index

Production Notes for Furth / THINKING WITH CASES

Cover and interior design by Leslie Fitch, composition by Asco Typesetters

Text in Minion and display type in Gill Sans

Printing and binding by The Maple-Vail Book Manufacturing Group

Printed on 60# Glatfelter Offset B18, 420 ppi

www.ingramcontent.com/pod-product-compliance
Lightning Source LLC
LaVergne TN
LVHW091516200926
848483LV00005B/432/J
* 9 7 8 0 8 2 4 8 3 0 4 9 6 *